MARY, FULL OF GRACE

Mary, Full of Grace

plena sibi, superplena nobis

Édouard Hugon, O.P.

Translated from the 5th Edition and edited by
John G. Brungardt

THOMIST TRADITION
SERIES

CLUNY MEDIA

*"Among all human pursuits, the pursuit of wisdom
is more perfect, more noble, more useful,
and more full of joy."*

~Saint Thomas Aquinas,
Summa contra Gentiles

* * *

THOMIST TRADITION SERIES

While his birth and death and everything in between remain confined to the thirteenth century, the intellectual legacy of St. Thomas Aquinas perdures to the present day. The Catholic Church continues to recognize the sapiential fecundity of this Doctor whom she invokes as "Common" and "Universal." God gave to the world through the wisdom of his Thomas a gift that does not expire.

There was only one Thomas. However, there have been many Thomists—philosophers and theologians who have assimilated the principles of his instruction and found the freedom that only the truth can provide.

The THOMIST TRADITION book series from Cluny Media arises from a dual conviction: (1) the thought of St. Thomas Aquinas contains an incomparable fullness of wisdom, and (2) the writings of the Thomists who followed him play a necessary role in mediating his wisdom to subsequent generations. Admittedly, those figures who constitute the Thomist tradition were by no means equals in regard to talent, influence, and renown. Moreover, their individual and collective contributions to the Thomist tradition elude facile comprehension or easy summary. Nonetheless, this series attempts to make available the key texts of figures—both classic and contemporary, major and minor—who rightly claim membership in the living tradition which bears the intellectual imprint of their master, Thomas.

The THOMIST TRADITION series makes these books available not merely as static works of antiquated value or anachronistic interest. Rather, the series is the fruit of our conviction that each Thomist has participated in a legacy perennially alive and perpetually relevant. Under this inspiration, each carefully selected volume in the series includes a new introduction that explains the book's original historical and speculative context. These introductions also outline their volume's enduring relevance to contemporary questions and disputes. Finally, the texts themselves have undergone extensive editorial review and certain footnotes have been added in order to highlight, explain, and clarify themes and passages of particular significance.

It is our sincere hope that this endeavor from Cluny Media will contribute to the renewed interest in the Thomist tradition among contemporary philosophers and theologians. For 800 years, Thomas and the Thomists have demonstrated unparalleled service in the defense and exposition of the saving truth Christ confided to his bride, the Catholic Church. The THOMIST TRADITION book series is designed both to honor that service and to provide the Thomists of today and tomorrow with resources for their own service to the Truth who sets us free.

Cajetan Cuddy, O.P.
General Editor

THOMIST T✳T TRADITION

THOMIST TRADITION SERIES

TITLES

* * *   * * *

Metaphysics and the Existence of God
by THOMAS C. O'BRIEN, O.P.

What Is Sacred Theology?
by JOSEPH CLIFFORD FENTON

The Natural Law According to Aquinas and Suárez
by WALTER FARRELL, O.P.

Mary, Full of Grace
by ÉDOUARD HUGON, O.P.

Cluny Media edition, 2019

Originally published in 1926 by P. Lethielleux, in Paris,
under the title of *Marie Pleine de Grâce*.

For more information regarding this title
or any other Cluny Media publication,
please write to info@clunymedia.com, or to
Cluny Media, P.O. Box 1664, Providence, RI 02901

VISIT US ONLINE AT WWW.CLUNYMEDIA.COM

ISBN: 978-1950970346

FROM THE 5TH EDITION

*Nous soussignés approuvons la nouvelle édition de l'ouvrage
du T. R. P. Édouard Hugon:* Marie pleine de grâce

FR. CESLAS-M. PABAN-SEGOND, O.P., S. Th. Mag
FR. RÉGINALD GARRIGOU-LAGRANGE, O.P., S. Th. Mag

Imprimatur: F. SERAPIUS TAMAYO, O.P., *Vic. Gen. Ord. Praed.*
Rome, Angelico, le 4 janvier 1926

Permis d'imprimer: V. DUPIN, *v. g.*
Parisiis, die 28ª Augusti 1926

Cover design by Clarke & Clarke
Cover image: Sandro Botticelli, *The Virgin and Child*
(*The Madonna of the Book*), 1480, tempera on wood
Courtesy of Wikimedia Commons

Contents

* * *

APPENDIX

PART I
Texts by and About Hugon

PART II
Translator's Essays

Fr. Édouard Hugon, O.P.
(*Frontispiece from Fr. Henri Hugon's biography,* Le Père Hugon)

* * *

TRANSLATOR'S INTRODUCTION

*For behold from henceforth all generations
shall call me blessed.*

— LUKE 1:48

D ue to its unique character as a theological treatise written by a neo-scholastic Dominican in the early twentieth century, this translation of Fr. Édouard Hugon's book *Mary, Full of Grace* needs some general preliminary remarks for the benefit of the reader. In what follows I consider, first, the life of Fr. Hugon, second, this work. Regarding the work, I treat its historical and theological context so as to set in relief its own theological character and to argue for its enduring relevance. Hugon's "summary Mariology"[1] deserves its proper, treasured place within the tradition of the Church's theological reflection upon Our Lady, who—as Hugon himself argues in this treatise—prophesied such reflections throughout the ages, even until the end of time, as we read in the epigraph above.

THE AUTHOR: A DOMINICAN PRIEST

Fr. Édouard Hugon, O.P., (August 25, 1867–February 7, 1929) was a Dominican priest, philosopher, and theologian.[2] His given baptismal names were Florentin, after his father, and Louis, after his paternal grandfather. Born in the village of Lafarre, France, in the diocese of Puy, he was the oldest of the thirteen children of Florentin and Philomène Hugon. The Hugon family was an ancient one in the region, whose presence there stretched back to at least 1600, when the

i

local parish records begin. One of Hugon's ancestors was also a priest, forced into hiding during the French Revolution; another was a soldier who died during Napoleon's ill-fated Russian campaign; another was awarded the French Legion of Honor by Napoleon III. Yet his father Florentin and his mother Philomène prepared young Florentin Louis for greater things.

His parents had married young in 1866; Florentin was twenty-two, Philomène twenty-one. Together they had seven sons and six daughters: Florentin Louis, Henri, Léonie, Maria, Arthème, Rose, Eugénie, Lucie, Philomène, Célestin, Camille, Albert, and Ferdinand. Two died relatively young. Both parents were devout, but it was above all their mother's influence that confirmed them in the Faith. Her great desire was to see some of her sons become priests (as did Florentin Louis and Henri) and some of her daughters religious (as did Rose).

As a child, Florentin Louis had a lively and inquisitive mind. His mother would fondly recall his ceaseless questions, even at the age of three or four: *Where does this brook come from? Why does water become hot when placed on the fire? Why do flowers bloom in summer and not in winter?* He began lessons in Greek and Latin at the age of fourteen under the tutelage of their parish priest, Fr. Sabathier, and after three months had made such progress that he was able to begin attending the Dominican school in nearby Poitiers. There, he excelled in his studies. His love of Greek continued, and he learned by heart many passages from the *Iliad*. His classmates called him "the little son of Homer," and not only for

---

1. See below, Preface, p. 3.
2. Apart from Garrigou-Lagrange's article and sermon, the central source for biographical material is the book-length biography written by Fr. Hugon's own brother, himself a priest. The biography presented here is its résumé; see Abbé Henri Hugon, *Le Père Hugon*, 3rd ed. (Paris: Pierre Téqui, 1930). The photograph of Fr. Hugon (facing p. i) is the frontispiece of his brother's bibliography. See also Réginald Garrigou-Lagrange, O.P., *In memoriam: un théologien-apôtre, le père maître Édouard Hugon, professeur de dogme à l'Angelico, à Rome, consulteur de la S. Congrégation pour l'Eglise orientale* (Rome: Angelicum, 1929), which is translated below as an appendix; P. Cazes, O.P., "*In Memoriam*: Le très Révérend Père Hugon," *Revue Thomiste*, Vol. 34, No. 12 [nouvelle série] (March–April 1929), pp. 97–99; "Chronique: Décès," *Bulletin Thomiste*, Vol. 6, No. 3 (1929), pp. 529–530; Angelo Walz, "Hugon (Édouard)," *Dictionnaire de Spiritualité*, vol. 7 (Paris: Beauchesne, 1969), col. 858–859.

his recitations but also for his own compositions. His brother Henri soon joined him at the school, where the two developed a close friendship. Indeed, Fr. Henri was later a chaplain in the French Army during the First World War, and the brothers remained close even then, writing to each other during the war and interceding on behalf of refugees and civilians, the one working at the other's behest through the Vatican Secretary of State to appeal to Germany on behalf of those in need.

Upon finishing his studies, Florentin entered the Dominicans in the province of Lyon in 1885, at the age of eighteen. There, he received the name of Édouard. He made his simple profession in 1887 and his solemn profession on January 13, 1890. Religious life was an easy adjustment for the young man, and he dedicated himself assiduously to his studies, especially of St. Thomas Aquinas. Ordained a priest on September 24, 1892, Édouard was promptly sent to teach, first in Rijkolt, Holland, and then in Rosary Hill, New York. Upon his return to France from the United States, he narrowly escaped death when his superior told him to leave on a different day than his confrères, who perished when their transatlantic liner, the SS *Bourgogne*, sank after a collision. He taught in France at Poitiers and Angers before returning to Rijkolt due to the anticlerical persecution in France in the early 1900s, during which thousands of Catholic schools were forcibly closed.

In 1909, he was chosen, along with Fr. Garrigou-Lagrange and Fr. Thomas Pègues, by the Master of the Order, Fr. Hyacinthe-Marie Cormiers, as one of the founding professors of the renewed International Pontifical College Angelicum in Rome. Hugon would teach there for twenty years until his death in 1929. His tenure included service as the university's vice-regent and its regent, during the First World War. His service in Rome extended far beyond his work as a professor. He had numerous theological tasks for cardinals and popes, who relied upon him for theological consultation (Garrigou-Lagrange attests to this in his eulogy). Hugon was instrumental in the elevation of St. Peter Canisius and St. Ephrem the Syrian to the rank of Doctors of the Church.[3] He even offered a theological defense of the validity of the final miracle required for the canonization of St. Joan of Arc

---

3.   Hugon cites St. Peter Canisius near the end of Part I, Chapter 3.

(an argument whose principles the reader will discover in this book).[4] The miracle had been obtained at Lourdes, where Our Lady's intercession was sought through the name of Joan. Some wanted to attribute the miracle to Mary alone, but Hugon argued that the miracle was to be attributed to the saint, just as the favor obtained from a parent due to the mediation of her child is to be attributed to the child. He also played a role in the institution of the Feast of Christ the King, composing not only the Preface of the Mass text but also the draft of Pius XI's encyclical, *Quas Primas*. He exerted considerable efforts in support of the institution of the feast of Mary as Mediatrix.[5] As a theologian and philosopher of the Church, he also contributed to the composition of the famous 24 Thomistic Theses, on which he wrote an extensive commentary.[6] His own philosophical and theological corpus was considerable, consisting in a multi-volume Latin treatises on Thomistic philosophy and theology, as well as numerous books and scholarly articles.[7]

For all his ceaseless work, and from all accounts, his personal life and habits bore the marks of a saint. While a French newspaper once characterized him as "a new Torquemada," full of Dominican wrath, his person and character belied such descriptions. Hugon held himself firm and intransigent only on matters of the principles of faith and reason and his life bore witness to his charity towards the individuals he encountered. During the months of academic vacation, Hugon would travel to visit family and friends and would yearly preach retreats to several religious congregations in France. When in Rome, he had a diligent schedule. He would rise at half-past four in the morning

---

4. See below Part II, Chapter 9, p. 148. See also Gloria Falcão Dodd, *The Virgin Mary, Mediatrix of All Graces: History and Theology of the Movement for a Dogmatic Definition from 1896 to 1964* (New Bedford, MA: Academy of the Immaculate, 2012), p. 136.

5. This is described in Dodd's work, noted above; Cardinal Mercier played a leading role among those seeking to have Mary's mediation defined.

6. See Édouard Hugon, *Principes de philosophie: les vingt-quatre thèses thomistes*, 12th ed. (Paris: P. Tequi, 1946), originally published in 1926.

7. One portion of this *Cursus philosophicus* has recently been translated into English: Édouard Hugon, *Cosmology*, trans. Francisco J. Romero (Heusenstamm: Editiones Scholasticae, 2013).

and celebrate Mass at five. He would teach classes and write before midday and would make the Stations of the Cross every afternoon. He was frequently found walking the streets of Rome saying his rosary. His evenings were filled with other duties, meetings, attending to his voluminous correspondence (he would write at least seven or eight letters a day), confessions, preaching, grading. Yet despite his elevated role and many duties as a son of the Church, he was always humble and attentive to everyone who wished to speak to him. Hugon attended especially to his role as spiritual counselor and confessor (besides his native tongue, he could speak Italian, English, and some Spanish). His students held him very dear in their hearts and frequently wrote to him, from as far away as the United States, Canada, Chile, and even the Middle East. (Hugon's course of Thomistic philosophy was translated into Arabic, and he worked for years with the Eastern Congregation in Rome.) He fondly remembered each and every one of his students and would frequently pray for them.

"The Dominican soul," Hugon once wrote, "is a Christian soul elevated and transformed by three great realities which carry it closer to God: contemplation, apostolate, and sacrifice."[8] He exemplified these Dominican traits. Furthermore, as his brother wrote of him, "One cannot conceive of a truly Dominican life without a special devotion to the Blessed Virgin."[9] Hugon had a great devotion to Our Lady, and through her, to her Son. In a letter giving advice to a friend, he writes:

When you dress in the morning, think already upon your communion.... Assist at Mass in union with Mary and through Mary. Ask of the divine Mother to lend you her heart and her dispositions so as to make your communion.... Throughout the day, remember your morning communion. I exhort you to place each of your days between two Eucharists: the first part will be to give thanks for the communion already made, and the second part will be to prepare for the communion of the following day. How sweet must our day then seem to us, being thus placed

8. Abbé Henri Hugon, *Le Père Hugon*, p. 68.
9. Ibid., p. 82.

between two Eucharists! I would have you receive communion every day. A day without communion is a sky without a sun.[10]

This devotion to Our Lady continued even to his last hour:

A little before he died, the Angelicum's friars came and gathered themselves around his bed, and they intoned the *Salve Regina*. He groaned loudly, says Fr. Garrigou-Lagrange, but as soon as the Marian chant was begun, the rattle stopped, and it did not begin again until the song was over. And meanwhile, he, with a smile on his face, his arms outstretched, looked at a fixed point, as if he saw in front of him, in a sweet vision, the Mother of Heaven who came to fetch him for heaven. No doubt it is a simple hypothesis, and it is known but to God, but he had loved Mary so much. He had glorified her so many times that we would not be surprised that the sweet Virgin came to meet her good servant.[11]

Death came to him swiftly. His visit home to France during the academic holidays of 1928 were his usual rigorous schedule of visits, confessions, writing, and retreats. Yet his friends and family noticed a change in him, a certain thinness and fatigue not present in earlier years. During the visit he even chided his brother priest, "It is I who will be the first of us to die, and it is you who will have to write my biography."[12] His family felt that it would be the last time they would see him alive.

Upon his return to Rome for the opening of the academic term, Hugon resumed his usual routine. Early in 1929, he fell sick for eight days with influenza. It seemed he would make a close recovery, but he succumbed to a complication of double pneumonia, which ran its course in twenty-four hours. After receiving his Eucharistic Lord in viaticum, and having heard his fellow Dominicans sing the *Salve Regina*

---

10. Ibid., p. 79.
11. Ibid., p. 85.
12. Ibid., p. 92.

for the last time, he began to speak in a whisper, as much as his illness would allow. The priest attending his bedside, Fr. Chauvin, attests:

> I came closer to his lips, and I distinctly heard the phrase, "The heart, the heart...of Jesus, nothing more, nothing sweeter," at least ten times, in a smile of true bliss. We were moved to tears, and smiled at him inexpressibly at the thought of his proximate meeting with the heart of his beloved God.[13]

Letters, tributes, and condolences poured into the Angelicum from all over the world upon news of his death. His longtime colleague and confessor, Garrigou-Lagrange, said: "I did not think that I loved him so much; now that he is gone, it seems to me that I am an exile."[14] And Fr. Henri Hugon, at the close of the biography he wrote for his brother, reminds us:

> One day Our Lord told St. Thomas, "Thomas, you have written well of me." Fr. Hugon, also, has written well of Our Lord, has written well of the Blessed Virgin. And we are sure that he has already received the reward promised to the good and faithful servant.[15]

The life of Fr. Hugon, even more than his works that remain, remind us of the role of a true priest and its excellence when lived to the fullest to build up the life of the Church.

THEOLOGY AS A WHOLE AND MARIOLOGY AS A PART

Let us now consider the theological context of Hugon's Mariology in order to gauge its enduring relevance. Indeed, Hugon's little Mariology is a remarkably *complete* one, an exemplar of incorporating all the necessary elements of a theological consideration of Our Lady. This explains its enduring relevance. To see this, let us consider what

---

13. Ibid., p. 100.
14. Ibid., p. 57.
15. Ibid., p. 108.

Catholic theology is, and what part Our Lady has in its considerations, before approaching how Hugon's book fulfills the task of a theology of Mary.[16] We begin with theology as a "whole" and Mariology as one of its "parts."[17]

Hugon's role as professor of theology at the Angelicum included the authorship of *Tractatus Dogmatici*, a treatise of dogmatic theology "by way of commentary on particular questions from the *Summa Theologiae* of the Divine Thomas Aquinas." In it, the Dominican follows St. Thomas in teaching that theology is a true *science*, that is, certain, evident knowledge through causes, yet with various qualifications.[18] Thus, theology is "subalternated to the science [*scientia*] of God and the blessed in heaven, and on that account imperfect for lack of present evidence."[19] This Thomistic position employs the Aristotelian logical doctrine about the nature of the sciences, and in this case, how one science can be "subalternated" to another.[20] For instance, just as mathematics establishes theorems that physics uses (but does not prove), so also God and the saints enjoying the beatific vision know directly that which the theologian can only use indirectly as his starting points, not

---

16. In this task, apart from Hugon's work itself and other sources to be indicated at the proper time, I have found the following works particularly helpful: Aidan Nichols, O.P., *There Is No Rose: The Mariology of the Catholic Church* (Minneapolis: Fortress Press, 2015), hereafter, *There Is No Rose*; Mark I. Miravalle, ed., *Mariology: A Guide for Priests, Deacons, Seminarians, and Consecrated Persons* (Goleta, CA: Seat of Wisdom Books, 2008), hereafter, *Mariology*.

17. How Mariology is a "part" of theology is discussed below, n. 34.

18. Note that by "science" Hugon means a systematic discipline that is broader in its meaning than what is currently meant by the English word "science."

19. Hugon, *Tractatus Dogmatici*, t. 1, *De Deo Uno et Trino Creatore et Gubernatore de Angelis et de Homine*, 5th ed. (Paris: P. Lethielleux, 1927), p. 11.

20. See St. Thomas, *Summa Theologiae* (hereafter, *ST*) I, q. 1, a. 2, c.: "We must bear in mind that there are two kinds of sciences. There are some which proceed from a principle known by the natural light of intelligence, such as arithmetic and geometry and the like. There are some which proceed from principles known by the light of a higher science: thus the science of optics proceeds from principles established by geometry, and music from principles established by arithmetic. So it is that sacred doctrine is a science because it proceeds from principles established by the light of a higher science, namely, the science of God and the blessed. Hence, just as the musician accepts on authority the principles taught him by the mathematician, so sacred science is established on principles revealed by God."

having the intuitive vision of their truth.[21] On this account, theology is a disciplined mode of human inquiry into divine things that relies for its insights, foundations, and explanations upon God's own knowledge of those divine things, providentially imparted to us in revelation and assented to by faith. This dependence upon faith explains theology's limitations, for "faith is the substance of things to be hoped for, the evidence of things that appear not" (Hebrews 11:1), and so must eventually rest upon evidence we cannot intuit in this life.[22] Just as the moon reflects the light of the sun, so too Catholic theology illuminates truths only by participating in a light that is inestimably more luminous in its principle—"We see now through a glass in a dark manner; but then face to face" (1 Corinthians 13:12).

This is the root or origin of theology, but more is required. Fr. Aidan Nichols, O.P., outlines the approach or methodology of theology in three steps: "The first step in classical Catholic theology…consists in exploring the sources of revelation: namely, Scripture and tradition."[23] To use an analogy from the natural sciences, the history of salvation contained in Scripture and tradition is, as it were, the experimental and inductive basis upon which the theologian rests. Second, the "fruits gained in this process" of exploration are interrelated with each other and to the doctrine of the Church, in the light of the "analogy of faith."[24] Finally,

> in a third and final step of the classical method, the outcome of placing the fruits of exploration of the sources of revelation in a position of interrelation not only to each other but also to other key aspects of revelation is systematically reorganized by the selection of an ordering principle which the individual theologian finds especially helpful or illuminating.[25]

---

21. Of course, the analogy limps in no small part because one could study both mathematics and physics. However, the key is to focus on the claim that physics *as such* cannot provide the evidential reasoning for a properly mathematical theorem, but rather that theorem is employed and even contracted to another domain.
22. See St. Thomas, *ST* II-II, q. 4, a. 1.
23. Nichols, *There Is No Rose*, p. 2.
24. Ibid.
25. Ibid.

For example, one thinks here of St. Thomas's ordering principle for his unfinished masterpiece *Summa Theologiae*:

> Because the chief aim of sacred doctrine is to teach the knowl-edge of God, not only as He is in Himself, but also as He is the beginning of things and their last end, and especially of rational creatures…therefore, in our endeavor to expound this science, we shall treat: (1) Of God; (2) Of the rational creature's advance towards God; (3) Of Christ, Who as man is our way to God.[26]

Thus, the Angelic Doctor sets out the rationale for the three parts of the *Summa* by denoting God himself as the principal subject, which is then developed by a consideration of God as efficient and final cause. As John of St. Thomas explains:

> So it is that Saint Thomas, by this threefold consideration of God as cause, namely as effective principle (Part One), as finalizing happiness (Part Two), and as redeeming Savior (Part Three), divides the whole *Summa theologiae*. (This is clear from the second question of the First Part.) Thus from God consid-ered in himself and in his being, we pass to God as efficient and redemptive cause, in order to come back to him as the object of happiness after the glorious resurrection. So it is that the golden circle of theology is closed.[27]

---

26. St. Thomas, *ST* I, q. 2, proem.
27. John of St. Thomas, *Introduction to the Summa Theologiae of Thomas Aquinas*, trans. Ralph M. McInerny (South Bend, IN: St. Augustine's Press, 2003), p. 11. John's division of the *Summa*, more faithfully following St. Thomas's own words, avoids a creature-centric ratio to account for its structure and is thus also more faithful to the formal object of theology itself. The influential and debated suggestion of Marie-Dominique Chenu, that the *Summa* is arranged according to a neo-Platonic *exitus-reditus* schema, could perhaps be folded into John's division by a conciliatory consideration of the notions of God as *principle* and *end*, and Christ as *Alpha* and *Omega*. See Marie-Dominique Chenu, "Le plan de la somme théologique de S. Thomas," *Revue Thomiste*, Vol. 45 (1939), pp. 93–107; Jean-Pierre Torrell, O.P., *Saint Thomas Aquinas, Vol. 1. The Person and His Work*, trans. Robert Royal, rev. ed. (Washington, DC: Catholic University of America Press, 2005), pp. 150–53; and the critical remarks of Rudi Te Velde, *Aquinas on God: The "Divine Science" of the* Summa Theologiae (Aldershot: Ashgate Publishing, Ltd., 2006), pp. 12ff. and 31, n. 2.

To the above, we must hasten to add that the grounding of faith by which we participate in the science of God and the blessed as transcendent principle of theology does not relate to theology *merely* as a science which deduces conclusions, but rather as the intellectual virtue of *understanding* relates to *wisdom*.[28] In this case, sacred wisdom is superior to even itself considered as a mere science, or deductive defense of conclusions from its proper principles, insofar as wisdom is capable of reflecting upon its own principles, ordering and comparing its own considerations to other sciences, and judging the progress or results of those sciences which fall under its purview.

Where, then, does Mariology come in as a part, a "sector or department,"[29] of Catholic theology? One might reply that, just as Christology is the part of theology that studies Christ, so is Mariology the part of theology that studies Mary. So, there are invariant truths within Mariology that are known and taught (e.g., what the Scriptures say about Our Lady, or what the Church has taught about her role in salvation history). These can be included within the first two steps mentioned by Nichols. However, depending upon the third step—the theological ordering principle employed—the shape of specific theological considerations of Mary can differ.

For example, St. Thomas places his most extended treatment of the Blessed Virgin in close relationship to Christ. So, in the third part of his *Summa*, after considering the Incarnation in questions 1–26, questions 27–59 "consider what things the Incarnate Son of God did or suffered in the human nature united to Him."[30] This life of Christ includes four questions on Mary (qq. 27–30), insofar as she features within this order of consideration that structures the *Summa* as a whole and focuses on Jesus the Redeemer within that order.

---

28. On the relationship between science, understanding, and wisdom, see Aristotle, *Nicomachean Ethics*, VI.6, and St. Thomas, *In Ethic.*, lib. 6, lect. 5, in particular nn. 1182–83. See also Francisco Muñiz, O.P., *The Work of Theology*, trans. John Reid, O.P. (Mediatrix Press, 2015), and see Reinhard Hütter, "Theological Faith Enlightening Sacred Theology: Renewing Theology by Recovering Its Unity as Sacra Doctrina," *The Thomist: A Speculative Quarterly Review*, Vol. 74, No. 3 (2010), pp. 369–405, at p. 393.

29. Nichols, *There Is No Rose*, p. 2.

30. St. Thomas, *ST* III, q. 27, proem.

Still, nestling a consideration of Our Lady with a broader treatment of the life of Christ was not the only approach.

> High medieval Scholasticism had dealt with Marian questions incidentally, almost as an aside, in the course of exploring the being and work of the Word incarnate. By contrast, Baroque Scholasticism by a change in literary form treats Mariology as a subject in its own right.[31]

This theological literary genre met with a mixed fate in the era of Thomistic revival initiated by Pope Leo XIII's encyclical *Aeterni Patris.* For instance, Fr. Hugon himself places his "Treatise of the Blessed Virgin, the Mother of God," in the second tome of his *Tractatus Dogmatici,* after the treatise dealing with "The Word Incarnate and Redeemer of Men." Nonetheless, the Incarnation, insofar as God has decreed it, cannot be conceived without Mary's divine maternity, and so it is logical that the consideration of the former be followed immediately by the latter.[32] So, as far as their literary genre goes, they are set "side by side."

Yet one could also consider the entire books written in the neo-scholastic style, devoted only to Mary. A confrère of Hugon's, Fr. Benedict Merkelbach, O.P., ordered his extensive, 400-page *Mariologia* in four parts, considering, respectively, the Blessed Virgin in relation to God and Christ; the Blessed Virgin in her own person and her privileges; the Blessed Virgin in relation to us; and, lastly, our own relationship to Mary.[33] At least in these examples, while their editorial separation from Christological tomes is clear, neo-scholastic Mariologies still retained their logical ordination to a broader theological and Christological whole.

---

31. Nichols, *There Is No Rose,* p. 23.
32. See Hugon, *Tractatus Dogmatici,* t. 2, *De Verbo Incarnato et de B. Virgine M. Deipara,* 5th ed. (Paris: P. Lethielleux, 1927), p. 715.
33. Benedict Henry Merkelbach, O.P., *Mariologia: Tractatus de Beatissima Virgine Maria Matre Dei Atque Deum Inter et Homines Mediatrice* (Paris: Desclée de Brouwer, 1939). We note that Hugon's own division in his *De B. Virgine M. Deipara* has a similar quadripartite division.

We have, then, a first question about Mariology as a "part" of theology. Is it merely a sub-part of Christology, which is itself a part of theology as a whole? Or can Mariology be considered as an independent part?[34] In other words, how exactly do divinely revealed principles shed light upon the singular Virgin from Nazareth? Furthermore, how ought one theologically consider this "part" within itself, regardless or perhaps depending upon its relationships to other areas of theology? That is, if theology is a science, and so must proceed in an orderly way and employ divine illuminating principles and causes, what are the most important principles of Mariology? Is there a "correct" or "true" order to the theology of Mary? Finally, what about the manner in which such theologies are written down? In what theological key or in what style ought they be composed or otherwise expressed by the human tongue?

Such questions were the subject of (at times) acrimonious debate in the twentieth century, both during and after the time of Hugon's writing. Therefore, to understand further the place of his little book, we can turn to consider its place in the broader context of Mariological approaches. On the one end, the late nineteenth and early twentieth centuries saw a resurgence of Thomistic and scholastic philosophy and theology. Hugon was no small player in this revival, as we have seen; however, dying shortly after the end of the long nineteenth century, he was innocent of its later stages. His approach is itself an example of "Neo-Scholastic Mariology, with its robust metaphysics," which

---

34. Following the analysis of Muñiz, *The Work of Theology*, pp. 3–6 and 42–49, we can distinguish between the *integral* parts of theology and its *potestative* parts. (Regarding these parts, see St. Thomas, *De Spiritualibus Creaturis*, a. 3, ad 3.) Integral parts compose the subject as a whole in a more material way; their sum-total composes the whole of theology. The notion of a potestative part—or a part "in power"—is taken from the nature of the soul, whose various powers are its potestative parts. Such a part of a science—in this case, theology—is one that has a function or office which another part does not have, albeit both are fully parts of theology. For instance, systematic theology and moral theology would differ in this way. Mariology is an *integral* part of theology (one among the many material objects theology considers in the formal light of reveal truth), but more importantly its subject is at the same time taken up by various of the *potestative* parts or *functions* of theology (consideration of explicitly or implicitly revealed truths, a dogmatic treatment or moral treatment of the subject, and a consideration of the proper principles from which we draw conclusions). That Mariology as a subject partakes of both sorts of part should be clear from the discussion.

"sought chiefly to describe the unique status of the woman who was the Mother of the Word of God incarnate."[35] This method has been characterized as "a rather abstract, deductive approach which does not sufficiently take into account the concrete facts of revelation proposed to us in Scripture and developed within the living tradition of the Church."[36]

Does this method lean too heavily upon a natural need of the human mind for reasons commensurate to its own capacities, even at the expense of the divinely revealed principles of theology noted by Aquinas? On this "procedural" question, Nichols admits:

> Scholastic Mariologists of the Baroque and modern era sought on these principles to deduce from Mary's divine motherhood all the other elements of Marian doctrine. This overlooks the fact that the mystery of Mary unfolds scripturally as a narrative on which we require to be informed, a story we need to be told for it is itself constructive of Mary's meaning in the divine plan.[37]

As an example, Nichols quotes Charles Journet's comment on Mary's role as the *Theotokos*, that it is a "concept on which the infallible *sensus ecclesiae* has pondered, and from which all of Mary's privileges are deduced, not by frail 'arguments of convenience' but by a genuine unveiling and unfolding."[38] This "'separated Mariology,'" one reads, "in which theologians considered Mary apart from economic or soteriological concerns"—that is, apart from the total "economy" of grace and salvation—"and considered Mariology as a separate branch of theology" has its roots in "Dialectical Scholasticism," that method which "studied things 'not so much in a total synthesis, according to their meaning and relationships, as in themselves, in their nature and their own contours;

---

35. Nichols, *There Is No Rose*, p. ix.
36. George F. Kirwin, O.M.I., "Queenship of Mary: Queen-Mother," *Marian Library Studies*, Vol. 28, No. 1 (2007), p. 165.
37. Nichols, *There Is No Rose*, pp. 43–44.
38. Ibid., citing Charles Journet, *L'Église du Verbe incarné* II (Paris: Desclée de Brouwer, 1953), p. 389.

then [it sought] to analyze the nature and the properties of each thing thus considered in itself and for itself."[39]

On the other extreme, Nichols notes the "biblically orient-ed Mariological writing" that preceded and prepared for the Second Vatican Council, which

> was more concerned with Mary's exemplary status as a woman of faith. This approach, in itself perfectly legitimate (not least, it was a common theme of the ancient Fathers of the church), could morph into something rather more ideological at the hands of some writers for whom the claims for the Mother of God typical of classical Catholic doctrine and traditional devo-tion were thrown into the shade—to put it kindly.[40]

He contrasts this opposition to the neo-scholastics with the middle ground of

> a *ressourcement* theology which, in "returning to sources" not only scriptural but also liturgical and patristic, sought to enrich the inheritance of Latin theology by adding an emphasis that was more cordial—addressing the "existential" dimension proper to persons and prosecuting its task not only in the categories of ontology but in the language of the heart.[41]

This is neither the place nor mine the capacity to adjudicate be-tween the members of this spectrum as Nichols outlines them. Yet, if Hugon's work is to be categorized within the first theological genre, then is it still worth the trouble of reading? To add to this concern, Nichols notes a danger in excessive Mariological fervor:

---

39. Christopher Ruddy, "'A Very Considerable Place in the Mystery of Christ and the Church'? Yves Congar on Mary," in *Mary on the Eve of the Second Vatican Council*, ed. J. C. Cavadini and D. M. Peters (Notre Dame, IN: University of Notre Dame Press, 2017); he is quoting Congar.
40. Nichols, *There Is No Rose*, p. ix.
41. Ibid.

It lies in the maxim, *de Maria nihil satis* (we can never say enough about Mary) when interpreted to mean: Mary's belonging, alone among human persons, to the hypostatic order, gives her in right and actuality all the graces and charisms ever bestowed on any saint, however diverse the roles in salvation the missions of those saints may be.

Of course, this "*de Maria numquam satis*" is a refrain of that Baroque-era missionary priest St. Louis-Marie Grignion de Montfort, and that interpretation of the maxim framing his famous treatise *True Devotion to Mary* would wrongly be confused with a thesis Fr. Hugon defends in this book.[42] Yet is it right to pause over concerns that excess of zeal could lead to a "galloping Mariology" or even a "Mariolatry"?[43]

To answer completely the various difficult questions we have raised is now beyond the scope of an introduction. We can only propose answers that, defensible in themselves and defended at greater length by various theologians, will help to gauge the worth of the contributions of Hugon's book. Thus, we will consider the ordering principles that one ought to employ, the theological "key" in which a theology of Mary might be composed, how such theological contributions should be united to the Mariological contemplation of the Church, and how Hugon's work compares in relation to these questions. It seems likely that, since Mary herself foretold that all generations shall call her blessed, we should expect to find—and we do—a variety of theological genres contemplating and praising Our Lady, and we should hope that the best of these be treasured in the theological memory of the Church.

THE SOULS OF SPEAKERS AND HEARERS OF MARIOLOGY

We should, preliminarily, address a difficulty that arises when reading works about Mary. It comes from the theological temperaments, as it were, of authors and readers, which affect how they present the fruits of their contemplation and how they read the works of others. If you

---

42. See Part II, Chapter 6.
43. Such were the concerns of Yves Cardinal Congar, O.P.; on this, see the analysis of Ruddy, "Yves Congar on Mary," cited above.

loved a person who was central to your life and, indeed, central to all of human history, and knowing her was tied to your very destiny, what measure or what means would you not take to draw closer to her? Yet must such zeal itself be measured, or tempered, or at least set in proportion to a guiding principle? Here, we should take to heart the words of Suárez: "*Est enim sine veritate pietas imbecilla et sine pietate veritas sterilis et jejuna.*—Piety without truth is feeble; truth without piety is dry and sterile."[44] Now piety, in a broad sense, is that part of justice which pays honor to those whom we can never repay adequately; it is the virtue that honors God (specifically called *religion*), one's country, and one's parents.[45] Piety without the truth is an *imbecile*, an "*im-baculus*," someone walking without a needed staff or cane, bound to fall over or wander astray. Truth without piety bears no fruit, for it has no power or ordination towards paying homage to God.

Thus, instead of considering Mariology in a more objective sense and from various historical angles, as we have been so far, let us consider it insofar as it might demand the subjective efforts of a soul seeking out Mary in truth and piety. This is the "theological temperament" of the receiving soul. The desires of the soul to find its completeness both in acts of truthfully knowing God and divine things and piously honoring them form two axes to Mariology insofar as it is received into a heart and mind, which in turn produces theological treatises and writings as so many fruits.

The first axis, truth, is rooted in the knowledge of faith. It can therefore be understood according to a proper ordering of faith and reason. Aristotle argues that every virtue is conceptually flanked by vices; for instance, even the social virtue of "truth" or "veracity" has two opposing vices, that of saying too much (boasting) or saying too little (dissembling).[46] Likewise, a knowledge rooted in faith, insofar as it places

---

44. Francisco Suárez, S.J., *De Mysteriis Vitae Christi*, "Ad Lectorem," quoted by René Laurentin, "Un problème initial de méthodologie Mariale," in *Maria: Etudes sur la Sainte Vierge*, ed. H. Du Manoir, S.J., I, pp. 695–706 (Paris: Editions Beauchesne, 1949), at pp. 701–702.

45. See St. Thomas, *ST* II-II, qq. 81 and 101.

46. Aristotle, *Nicomachian Ethics*, II.8, and see IV.7 regarding "veracity" (in some translations, "the truthful man," as opposed to the "boastful" and "mock-modest").

demands upon human reason, might go too far or not far enough. This axis of Mariological truth has, then, two extremes: a fideistic and rationalistic one. The former diminishes human reasoning and its fallibility to the apparent benefit of faith, while the latter exalts that same human capacity in the name of independence from the demands made upon the mind by the assent of faith.

The second axis is shaped by the virtue of piety crowned or perfected by charity. This we can call devotion. Like the virtue at the mean of the first axis, devotion is also framed by extremes. The first extreme is one that errs by defect; it is a sort of impiety or irreligiosity. It considers Mary as merely the first among many saints or models of holiness. The other extreme errs by excess and can appear almost superstitious. It considers Mary, *per impossibile*, as on a par with the divine, which would truly be a "Mariolatry" and confuse the honor of *hyperdulia* owed to Mary with that of worship or *latria* reserved for God.[47] (Of course, in another sense, one cannot love Mary "too much" insofar as rightly ordered charity can increase without limits in this life—*de Maria numquam satis.*[48])

Now, if the theologian's soul contemplates and teaches while being subjectively moved along both axes, there arise four possibilities. There could be a fideistic bent joined to either the impious or superstitious, or a rationalistic one joined with either of that same pair. Now, the four composites (fideistic impiety, superstitious fideism, irreligious rationalism, or rationalistic devotional excess) are rarely incarnated in pure form. Rather, we see tendencies towards one or the other crop up in various Mariological approaches or reactions. The first could denominatively be called a "protestant" extreme.[49] Much of what the Church teaches about Mary cannot be cited directly from the "plain words" of a *sola Scriptura* fideism without tradition. The second is untutored or foolish pietism; it is found or may appear to some to characterize simple believers, or to be present in what Laurentin calls the "devout"

---

47. See St. Thomas, *ST* II-II, q. 103, and in particular a. 4, obj. and ad 2.

48. Ibid., q. 24, a. 7.

49. For instance, regarding various difficulties which Protestant theologians encounter when discussing the Catholic dogma of the Assumption and the doctrine of Mary's queenship, see Kirwin, "Queenship of Mary," pp. 110–111, fn. 266.

or "mystical" theologians (albeit not as an extreme but rather a tendency).[50] The third extreme is represented in theological reactions against
devotional excesses; Laurentin names the corresponding tendency a
theology of the "critical type,"[51] and Hugon himself sees the Jansenists
in this place.[52] St. Louis-Marie de Montfort would seem to identify this
tendency in what he calls "critical devotees."[53] It seems that this tendency could also characterize the nineteenth-century Dominican resistance—prior to the 1850 definition in *Ineffabilis Deus*—to support for
pronouncing on the Immaculate Conception.[54] Finally, the fourth extreme—rationalism combined with superstition—might appear harder
to find, but some see it in the various excesses of "idiocies: a combination of verbalism, abstract dialectic and sentimentalism" in "maximizing" theologies of Mary.[55] Admittedly, some passages in Hugon's book
might strike the reader as leaning in this direction.

Yet our two axes must be aligned about a third axis, for the knowledge and devotion which characterize the soul receptive of Marian

---

50. Laurentin, "Un problème initial de méthodologie Mariale," p. 698.

51. Ibid.

52. See his Preface. The great reply to what Hugon calls this "Jansenist narrowness" in
regard to Marian devotion is St. Alphonsus Ligouri's *The Glories of Mary*.

53. See *True Devotion to Mary*, n. 93: "Critical devotees are for the most part proud
scholars, people of independent and self-satisfied minds, who deep down in their
hearts have a vague sort of devotion to Mary. However, they criticize nearly all
those forms of devotion to her which simple and pious people use to honor their
good Mother just because such practices do not appeal to them." In St. Louis-Marie Grignion de Montfort, *God Alone: The Collected Writings of St. Louis Marie De
Montfort* (Bay Shore, NY: Montfort Publications, 1995), at p. 318.

54. Nichols, *There Is No Rose*, p. 62: "To accept the *nova opinio* as well-founded was
in effect to say, so the Dominicans objected, that in theological method the *sensus
fidelium* and the liturgical practice of the Church could count as weightier than
the combination of the literal sense of Scripture, the patristic consensus, and the
common doctrine of the high medieval divines. The vulgar crowd, the *novi docto-
res* and the alteration of the calendar could trump these other authorities.... The
Dominicans had failed to develop a positive concept of the *sensus fidelium*.... So
in the wider church, things had progressed beyond the state of affairs when at the
early sixteenth century Fifth Lateran Council, Cardinal Cajetan, the Dominican
Thomas de Vio, was asked by Leo XI to advise him, whether to sanction the
doctrine finally or not. Cajetan replied the pope must choose between, on the one
hand, Scripture and the Fathers, and, on the other, the faithful and the liturgy."

55. See Ruddy, "Yves Congar on Mary," quoting from Congar's personal journal kept
during the September 1963 sessions of Vatican II.

theology can receive more or less intensely the various truths about Our
Lady. These truths could be ranked, as it were, from the most exterior
of historical truths to the most interior, numinous, and hidden ones.
The most exterior truths are those that lie in the shallow realm of purely
human historical studies, those accessible by the dusty light of reason
trained upon contingent matters. These are especially superficial when
compared to what one sees with the eyes of faith. How little could a
historian know directly of her person in such a mode! The best such
an extrinsic vantage point could hope for is seeing in Mary another instance of some maternal "archetype" in the sociology of world religions.
(Yet is she such as to fit the archetypes, or were the archetypes such, in
the most distant or distorted of ways, so as to "fit" or "echo" her, foretold from of old?) The most interior truths are things about Our Lady
known only to the Blessed Trinity. Some of the more interior truths we
hope to know in the light of glory, but for now, Mary is best known
theologically through that light that participates in "the science of God
and the blessed."[56]

How does this analysis assist us? Aristotle observes that the vices
affect evaluations of others and their actions. That is, from the vantage
point of one extreme, even the virtuous mean can appear as if it were
the other extreme. For instance, the brave man's actions appear, to the
coward, to be foolhardy excesses.[57] Thus, the dispositions of our reception of doctrine and theology about Mary can color or distort our
perceptions as much as the theological temperament of an author can
affect his style and approach. Since in various Mariological writings one
might encounter some of the defective or excessive tendencies described
above, we must seek stabilization and temperamental balance through
a deeper share in that participated light of divine wisdom that allows us
to see truths about Mary.[58] That is, only the rectified order of virtue can

---

56. Note that I assume a theological practice not opposed to devotion and even mysticism. Just as "philosophy" names a pursuit broader than a mere academic discipline, so too, "theology."

57. See Aristotle, *Nicomachean Ethics*, II.8, 1108b19–25.

58. For instance, this search for a holistic style of presentation is what Nichols adopts,
There Is No Rose, p. x: "In the spirit of a pope who was both poet and philosopher,
I exclude neither the materials of tradition in its imagistic mode, as with much

be a true judge, and to achieve this right ordering the mode of the receiver must become more proportioned to and measured by that which it receives. This can come about through an intensification of ordered love, *caritas in veritate*, as a norm for theology. This bears fruit in properly theological work that puts "order into what otherwise can appear as the enthusiastic exclamations of holy men about the woman whom they revere devoutly as Queen and Mother."[59] In what does this ordered love of truth consist when it comes to the theologian's objective task of contemplating the theology of the Blessed Virgin Mary?

THE SOURCES, MODE, AND ORDER OF MARIOLOGY

Since theology is carried out by human beings, it is useful to note that human finitude, fallibility, and prejudices can affect not just the literary form of one's presentation but could place undue limitations upon the sources, mode, and order according to which a theological investigation is structured. The twentieth-century debates mentioned above, regarding the proper form of Mariology, have already hinted at this. Let us move, then, from the style of Mariology to its substance.

Nichols helpfully underscores the difference between the Mariology of the neo-scholastics and other theologians as to the sources they employed:

> The theology of *ressourcement* was, in its Marian aspect, a reaction against early modern Mariology. Not only did it seek to bring to the treatment of Mary greater sobriety and conceptual reserve. It sought also the compensating richness of a fuller exposure to the Bible and the Fathers.[60]

---

of the celebration of Mary's role found in the Fathers and the liturgies, nor the deliverances of tradition in its more conceptual manner, as in the great assertions of the councils and the magisterium of the popes, commented and explained as these are by the church's divines, not least via the argumentative strategies of the Scholastics, notably St Thomas and the members of his school."

59. Romanus Cessario, O.P., "*Ego Sapientia*: The Mariology of Laval Thomism," in *Theology Needs Philosophy: Acting against Reason Is Contrary to the Nature of God*, ed. M. L. Lamb, pp. 227–39 (Washington, DC: Catholic University of America Press, 2016), at p. 235.

60. Nichols, *There Is No Rose*, p. 24.

At first, this point might seem to be belied by Hugon's frequent references to Scripture and the Fathers. Yet while in places it is clear that Hugon is reading from the *Patrologiae Latina et Graeca*, at other times he seems to be merely quoting second-hand (for instance, from Contenson or De Vega's references to the Fathers). This does indeed seem to fit Nichols' description: Hugon's is in part a *florelegium* of texts handed down by tradition and even quoted in traditional places or ways. In Hugon's style, all generations call Mary blessed by repeating various theological refrains. It is also true that Hugon does not employ a historical-critical method when appealing to the Scriptures, but they rather enter into his scholastic considerations in an authoritative, if still contemplative, way.

As to the mode of argument employed, we have already indicated that the neo-scholastics favored "rational" or "deductive" methods of argumentation and proofs from "fittingness." (For examples of such arguments, see Chapter 6, below.) Here, the "emphasis is upon concepts which have been clearly defined,"[61] which method can appear *a prioristic*, insensitive to the biblical typologies of Mary one can discover in Scripture and Tradition, and seem innocent of studying Mary's person within the narrative of salvation history.[62] One's mode of proceeding becomes not only intertwined with how one writes but with the sort of substance one's method permits or the principle one considers to be primary.

This interconnection between sources, mode, and substance can be exemplified in the debate over whether Mariology, as to its first or ruling principle, should be done primarily with reference to Christ or the Church.

---

61. Kirwin, "Queenship of Mary," p. 44.
62. Consider the discussion of various methods in Edward Sri, *Queen Mother: A Biblical Theology of Mary's Queenship* (Steubenville, OH: Emmaus Road Publishing, 2005), pp. 2, 5–6, which are employed in Mariological discussions of Mary's queenship: Scripture proof-texting based upon assumptions about what her queenship is, logical deductions from truths revealed in Scripture, the use of extra-biblical typology (interpreting Old Testament figures in the mystical sense as referring to Mary, but without grounding this in the narrative of the New Testament), and "a salvation-historical approach," which attends to Mary "within the narrative contest of the passages being considered."

The movements of biblical and patristic *ressourcement* threw up a new (or was it, rather, very old?) kind of Mariology which soon acquired the nickname of "ecclesio-typical," over against, "christo-typical," Mariology. In other words, this was to be a type of reflection which linked Mary not so much to Christ—which had been the case in all early modern and modern Mariology hitherto—as to the Church, or, to put this more sympathetically, linked Mary to Christ only in, with, and through the Church, the messianic people, prepared in the Old Testament, launched on its great adventure in the New. As we shall see, the tension between christo-typical and ecclesio-typical Mariologies hardened into outright conflict at the time of the Second Vatican Council.[63]

In this regard, Nichols indicates four separate questions to ask: First, does reading Scripture and the Fathers indicate a preference for one or the other approach? Second, does Mariology indeed have one ruling or primary principle? Third, has Mariology gone too far—must it be de-emphasized for ecumenical reasons? Finally, what is "the proper epistemic mode" for Mariology? Should it be more neutral and objective or more engaged in analysis of those persons in salvation history? Nichols then points out:

Once one distinguishes out these four enquiries it becomes obvious, or so it seems to me, that what alarmed the more conservative bishops and theological advisers at Vatican II was not the theme of "our Lady and the Church" as such (how could that be threatening in itself?), but the combining of all four

---

63. Nichols, *There Is No Rose*, p. 132. See also ibid., pp. 24–25: "*Ressourcement* theology was a reaction in the further sense that it wished to uncover a motif neglected by the first systematic Mariologists: namely, Mary's relation to the church, which *ressourcement* theologians thought of in three ways: 1) Mary's relation to the Church as the Church's matrix or origin (this was, we might say, a lesson about the church's past); 2) Mary's relation to the Church as the Church's prototypical member, the Church's most exemplary member (this could be called a lesson about the Church's present); and 3) Mary's relation to the Church as the Church's eschatological icon (a lesson about the church's future)."

issues into a synthetic whole of a distinctive kind. One synthetic combination of the four could run as follows: the ecclesio-typical approach, predominant in Bible and Fathers, is itself the fundamental governing principle of all Mariology, on whose basis Mariology should be practiced minimalizingly, and in a critical epistemic mode. This was the synthesis, or to put it less flatteringly the cocktail of opinions, which produced the low Mariology of the later 1960s and 70s, itself extended through Liberation Theology into the 1980s.[64]

It is therefore advisable, following Nichols, to consider distinctly the way in which Mariology ought to use sources, employ a certain method, and follow from deeper theological principles. Let us consider the last issue first: "What is the primary or fundamental principle of all Mariology?"[65]

Consider this recent answer:

Mariology, by its very nature, cannot be studied in isolation. The concept of "mother" presupposes the concept of "child," and in this case, the reality of a son. Mariology connaturally leads to Christology, as the study of the Mother of Jesus presupposes and calls forth a deeper knowledge and assent to the truths about Jesus Christ, the incarnate Son of God and of Mary. Mariology also organically springs forth into Ecclesiology, since anyone who

---

64. Ibid., pp. 133–34. See also Kirwin, "Queenship of Mary," p. 179: "During the Council debates on Mary it became evident that there were two opposed tendencies which were eventually harmonized through the patient work of theologians. The one sought to bring out the scriptural and patristic bases for Marian doctrine and piety within the life of the Church without proceeding in a polemical or apologetic fashion. The other was more conceptual, more deductive in its approach and sought support for its doctrinal statements rather from the documents of the teaching Church. Scriptural and patristic 'sources' were used for the most part as confirmations of established 'theses.' The first tendency prevailed in the sense that the framework for the doctrinal presentation on Mary which was approved by the assembly of bishops was that of salvation history with its fundamental thrust being supplied by the word of God as it appears and is developed in the writings of the biblical authors and the Fathers of the Church."

65. Nichols, *There Is No Rose*, p. 132.

is spiritually united to Jesus through baptism and filial adoption
has also, in a particular way, received the Mother of Jesus as his
or her own spiritual mother.[66]

That is, the person who is Mary, insofar as she is seen in the participated
light of God's own knowledge permitting theological vision, is in principle one who is irreducibly revealed as "mother." Mary has been revealed
to us as the Mother of God. She has been revealed to us as Mother
of the Church. However, these are known in different ways. Mary's
motherhood of the Church can be inferred from passages in Scripture;
her divine maternity is far more direct. Indeed, Mary as Mother of the
Church is a typological and spiritual assertion—Our Lady as the type
of the Church in her exemplarity of receiving and imitating Christ and
her spiritual maternity of the members of the mystical body seems to be
intelligible in function of the historical and ontological assertion that
Mary is the Mother of God. Indeed, "How can a historical fact (Mary is
the Mother of Jesus) be deduced from a typological assertion?"[67]

     In a conciliatory spirit, Nichols follows the Dominican Albert
Patfoort, who suggests that both Marian principles can, in different
respects, be considered primary:

> There is, wrote Patfoort, no a priori reason why there should not
> be in Mariology two—let us say—primary principles, each of
> them supreme in what he called a given "register" or on a given
> "line." To explain this point he drew a comparison with the situ-
> ation in Christology. In Christology, Christmas (the incarnation)
> and Easter (the redemption) are each primary in a certain respect.
> They generate, then, two coequal primary principles. Could not
> something similar be true in Mariology? The primacy of the
> divine motherhood seen as a primary christo-typical principle
> indicating the functions and perfections Mary would develop

---

66. Miravalle, "Editor's Introduction," in *Mariology*, p. xxi.
67. Nichols, *There Is No Rose*, p. 143. This is the response of a Thomistic reviewer to
    the position of Michael Schmaus, who "went so far as to say that, while Mary's
    status as the type of the Church cannot be deduced from her divine motherhood,
    the divine motherhood can be deduced from her status as type of the Church."

thanks to her unique bond with the Word Incarnate, could coex-
ist with a second primary principle, based on the Mary-Church
idea. For the latter, Mary embodies the Word's reception by a
wider humanity; she is the sign and prototype of the Church, so
this second, ecclesio-typical, primary principle shows how the
functions and perfections of Mary, identified with the help of
the first, christo-typical, primary principle find their expression
in the fullness of influence she possesses in the mystical body
of Christ, the Church. Having two coequal primary principles
might be thought to diminish the unity of Mariology, but in fact
it contributes to the organic quality of that very unity.[68]

While Hugon does not specifically address this debate, we will point
out in what way his reflections, while not anticipating, are at least compatible with Patfoort's suggestions that both principled ways of developing a Marian theology are needed. However, I suspect that Hugon
himself would still prefer to indicate in what way each principle is prior,
and why this is important. Indeed, Nichols, without attending to this
explicitly, places Mary's relationship to the Church after Mary's relationship to Christ, insofar as fully understanding the implications of
the former truth as a principle requires the epistemological and, implicitly, soteriological priority of the latter principle. He does so by noting
that Mary's divine motherhood in a christo-typical light helps identify
her functions as seen in an ecclesio-typical light.[69]

---

68. Ibid., pp. 144–45.

69. Here, we might note that this brings us back to the neo-scholastic mode of "rank-
      ing" Mary's privileges. See, for example, the first problem Reginald Garrigou-La-
      grange raises in *The Mother of the Saviour and Our Interior Life*, trans. B. J. Kelly
      (St. Louis: B. Herder Book Co., 1949), pp. 17–20, as to whether Mary's divine
      maternity or her fulness of grace at her conception is the greater grace. See also
      Hugon, below, Chapters 2 and 4. In the two Translator's Essays, I discuss these
      themes in more detail, relating them to Mary's universal mediation and queen-
      ship. In no small part, we will draw upon the studies by Kirwin and Sri. Kirwin,
      "Queenship of Mary," notes at pp. 168–69: "Every phase of Marian theology has
      been profoundly affected by the new emphasis placed upon her as the personifi-
      cation of the Church, the exalted Daughter of Sion. Mary remains an individual
      but she is more than that. In a real but mysterious way the whole Church is found
      in her. Our understanding of Mary and of her role in redemption must come

If we take as a starting principle Mary as Mother of Christ, which leads naturally, in the economy of grace, to Mary as Mother of the Church, and recognize the due limitations of proceeding from this principle entirely in a "deductive" mode without reliance of upon Scripture or Tradition, then is there still a place in Mariology's way of proceeding for conceptual analysis, arguments, or philosophical doctrine? (For these characterize much of Hugon's work both as to theological substance and its style.) For instance, can we apply, *mutatis mutandis*, the following defense of philosophical reasoning in Christology to the pursuit of theology about Mary?

> In speaking of ontological *Christology*, I am referring not to a subject of philosophy as such, or to philosophical reflection on Christ (for example, Aristotelian-inspired analysis of the person of Christ). Rather, I am referring specifically to a biblical mystery: Christ is revealed in scripture as a person who truly exists. The *personal being* of Christ is subject to theological investigation. The mystery of God made man has an inward 'form' or ontological determination. On the one hand, this subject eludes explanation by recourse merely to the ordinary categories of human experience and philosophical forms of ontological analysis. On the other hand, this mystery is luminous and has a certain internal intelligibility. It can be studied for its own sake and considered in itself in a properly theological manner. Such a study has always had a distinctively ontological character to it. What does it mean to say, for instance, that Christ is a divine person, or to speak of the union of his divine and human natures in one hypostasis? How can we understand the relation between his human and divine natures, in their real distinction and necessary inseparability? How ought we to understand the fact that Christ possesses an individual human nature, and consequently both an organic body and a spiritual soul? How are all these

---

from our understanding of her relationship to Christ and to the Church. Her mediation, her so-called co-redemptive activity, her intercession, and her queenly role must be explained according to this ecclesial emphasis."

truths at play when we consider the human knowledge of Christ, or his human action? What are the knowledge and action of Christ that are present in the redemption and in his experience of the crucifixion?[70]

In a similar way, the *personal being* of the Mother of Christ can be the subject of speculative theological investigation, for her essential relatedness to the luminous mystery of the Word Incarnate, which "has a certain internal intelligibility," thereby participates in the intelligibility of that truth and allows us to contemplate and understand Mary. What does it mean to say that Mary is full of grace? Is it a grace by which she is the Mother of God, and if so, what does this *add* to her person beyond a mere title? What does it mean that she was *conceived*—that is, came into being as a human person—immaculately? If Mary cooperates with Christ in his acts of redemption, what does this mean in regard to her actions at the foot of the cross and her continuing actions in our regard now in heaven? Indeed, if we are to avoid metaphors, what does her assumption and glorified bodily existence in heaven say about her personal mediation and influence over the Church? We therefore adopt White's striking assertion: "In some real sense it is true to say: ignorance of ontology is ignorance of Christ."[71] In some real sense, although not without qualification, ignorance of ontology is ignorance of Mary.

Mariology, then, obtains its theological order from a primary principle, namely, Mary as that human person uniquely related as Mother to Christ and also to His Church. It is not unfitting that its mode include conceptual, deductive arguments, even ones employing philosophy, the handmaiden of theology.[72] However, this method of ordering

---

70. Thomas Joseph White, O.P., *The Incarnate Lord: A Thomistic Study in Christology* (Washington, DC: Catholic University of America Press, 2015), p. 6.

71. Ibid., p. 8.

72. See St. Thomas, *ST* I, q. 1, a. 5, s.c., and see his *Super Boetium de Trinitate*, q. 2, a. 3. Here, the words of Jacques Maritain are helpful, from *An Essay on Christian Philosophy*, trans. E. H. Flannery (New York: Philosophical Library, 1955), n. 15: "A word about the adage *philosophia ancilla theologiae*. Its origin, of course, is to be sought in St. Peter Damiani, who intended to silence philosophy with it. The Scholastic position is something entirely different. Therein philosophy is placed in the service of theology when, and only when, in its own workings theology

and developing theology cannot be to the detriment of other modes.[73] Finally, the sources of Catholic theology—revealed truths in Scripture and Tradition, and the teachings of the Church Fathers—are, as it were, the inductive and experiential basis through which the participated light of theology is able to illumine its object, in this case, Our Lady. A complete Mariology, therefore, must attend to such sources, mode, and principles. It theologically contemplates Mary in light of her Motherhood (of Christ and Church) as fundamental principle, drawing from the sources of Catholic revelation and methodically ordering its reflections, which should not abandon the full range of the modes of theological argumentation, which must include philosophy in its ancillary mode.

FR. HUGON'S TREATISE IN REVIEW

With this characterization of Mariology in mind, let us turn to consider Hugon's treatise itself. The subject of the book as a whole is captured by its very name: "Mary, full of grace." He calls the book "a complete study of this title" of Our Lady.[74] It is divided into two parts according to a simple rule, a saying that Hugon takes from St. Bernard: *Plena sibi, superplena nobis*—For herself full, for us overflowing.[75] That is, the first part of the book considers Mary's fullness of grace in her own person, and the second part of the book considers this fullness of grace insofar as it relates to us: "Mary is called 'full of grace' because she has received the plenitude of graces for herself and because she is the dispensatrix of graces for all the saints."[76] Hugon also comments as to the methodology operating in the background of his considerations,

---

    employs philosophy as an *instrument* of truth in order to establish conclusions which are not philosophic but theological. *Ancilla*, then, it may be, but not *serva*, for theology handles philosophy in accordance with its own proper laws; a Minister of state yes, but a slave it can never be."

73. Consider the contrast between "conceptual" and "imagistic" modes mentioned by Nichols (n. 57, above), or the various approaches mentioned by Sri (n. 61, above).

74. See below, Preface, p. 3.

75. St. Bernard, Sermon II on the Assumption, n. 2; see St. Bernard of Clairvaux, *St. Bernard of Clairvaux: Sermons for the Autumn Season*, trans. I. Edmonds, O.C.S.O., with revisions by M. Scott, O.C.S.O., Cistercian Fathers Series No. 54 (Collegeville, MN: Liturgical Press, 2016) 19.

76. See below, Preface, p. 4.

namely, that "the method to understand Mary is to compare her with her divine Son."[77] A question we should have, then, is why Hugon thinks that this division, with this method, can offer a *complete* study of Mary's title "full of grace."

In the first part of the book, about Mary's fullness of grace in itself, Hugon begins in Chapter 1 by considering grace in general, as well as in both the natural and supernatural senses, and how Mary is full of grace in both ways. The more important of these, of course, is the supernatural. Nonetheless, Hugon includes several moving paragraphs describing the natural graces of Mary (that is, her gifts of nature). He then turns to consider the traditional divisions of grace, which leads him to distinguish between different *plenitudes* of grace: those of excellence (proper to Jesus Christ), of superabundance (the special privilege of Mary), of sufficiency (which belongs to any saint), and of universality. This last Hugon indicates as belonging to the Church, a plenitude "in which one finds united the ensemble of good deeds and celestial gifts."[78] Yet he notes that he will "consider whether some such plenitude belongs to the Blessed Virgin."[79]

This distinction between the plenitude of superabundance and universality permits Hugon to divide Part I into two thematic parts: Chapters 2–5 consider Mary's superabundance of grace, and Chapter 6 considers the universality of her grace. Here Hugon again says that these topics must be considered so that his study of Mary, full of grace, might be *complete*. The plenitude of superabundance is itself subdivided into three aspects: the plenitude of Mary's first sanctification, or her Immaculate Conception (Chapter 2), the plenitude of Mary's second sanctification and the grace of her divine maternity (Chapters 3–4), and Mary's final plenitude of grace, taking into consideration her life, meritorious actions, her presence at Calvary and at Pentecost, and the moment of her final moment on earth (Chapter 5). In this way, Hugon arranges his consideration of the fullness of Mary's graces in accordance with the narrative of Our Lady's life in relation to Christ and thus to

---

77. Ibid., p. 3.
78. Chapter 1, p. 14.
79. Ibid.

key moments of salvation history. Indeed, since he omits no key moment of that history, his treatment can be called complete.

The treatment of the universality of Mary's plenitude of grace in Chapter 6 argues that Mary's universality is analogous to the universality of grace accorded to the Church. Hugon hints at this idea earlier on:

> Just as all the worlds of nature, both the corporeal and the angelic world, are united in man who thus becomes a sort of résumé of creation, *microcosmus naturae*, so also all the marvels of the supernatural are condensed in Mary, who is the masterpiece and the résumé of grace, *microcosmus Ecclesiae*.[80]

In Chapter 6, Hugon develops an extensive defense of two principles, namely, "Every favor or grace which one of the saints enjoyed was more nobly and more perfectly imparted to the Mother of God,"[81] and, "It is fitting that such graces were accorded to the Mother of God, therefore they were accorded to her."[82] He then uses these two principles to discuss the universality of Mary's privileges of body, the gifts of her intellect and will, her psychological integrity, and the gratuitous graces which she received. In this way, Chapter 6 adds to the narrative and historical completeness of Chapters 2–5 a certain qualitative completeness by arguing for the plenitude of the kinds of graces Mary received.

One might suspect that in this chapter the "maximizing" Marian theology of Hugon is revealed, a "galloping Mariology" of the sort that would be resisted by some theologians. Is this an abuse of the maxim *de Maria numquam satis*, as Nichols explained it above? It does not seem so. Indeed, Hugon recognizes the theological modesty that must attend his considerations in this chapter, for he ends it with the following remarks:

> We willingly recognize that some of our conclusions could be controversial and that they oblige no one where the Catholic

---

80. Chapter 4, p. 58.
81. Chapter 6, p. 99.
82. Ibid., p. 103.

faith is concerned. We have indicated the main authorities upon which we rest our teaching: St. Ambrose, St. Thomas Aquinas, St. Anthony, St. Thomas de Villeneuve, Cajetan, Medina, Suárez, Contenson, St. Alphonsus. We have advanced here deductions or inductions which do not always give rise to absolute certitude, but which deserve to be taken into consideration by the theologian.[83]

This self-reflective epistemic modesty is matched by Hugon's qualification of his own arguments in "The Instrumental Causality of the Most Holy Virgin," which is included as an appendix to the main text. He states there: "For our part, we would hold back from concluding fully and be content to have explained the arguments from fittingness which seem attractive, worthy of God, worthy of Mary, and capable of producing probable certainty."[84]

If Hugon's consideration of the plenitude of the superabundance of Mary's graces is complete both as to her person, life, and qualitative variety, it is also complete insofar as Hugon attends diligently to Mary's role in salvation history, her relationship to Christ, and her relationship to the nascent Church. This is particularly clear in his consideration of the gratuitous graces, which "have external and social roles: to obtain what is useful for the Church, the spiritual good of one's neighbor during the return to God."[85] This consideration of Mary's relationship to the Church militant, suffering, and triumphant is only strengthened in the second part of the book.

Following his method of understanding Mary always in relation to Jesus, Part II considers Mary's role in the acquisition and distribution of graces for all other persons. This approach alone proves the completeness of Hugon's consideration. In Chapter 7, which serves as introduction to the second part, he reflects on Mary, inseparable from Christ, as key to understanding her role as Mother of grace for us all:

83. Ibid., p. 127, n. 39.
84. See below, p. 209.
85. Chapter 6, p. 121.

If one wishes to express this relation precisely, one must say that the Mother of grace is the secondary cause wherever Christ is the principal cause. We happily contemplate in Jesus first of all our immaculate ideal; Mary is after him the model of predestination. Jesus is the meritorious cause who obtains grace for us by rights; Mary is a meritorious cause by way of fittingness and by right of friendship. Jesus offered satisfaction equal to and even superior to all the crimes of humanity; Mary, without paying such adequate ransom, made satisfaction in her own way for our faults. Jesus, in glory, remains our recognized intercessor; his wounds, those marks he retains, still act to intercede for us, and every heavenly gift reaches us through him, just as every prayer of the Church is made in his name. Mary is, after him, the all-powerful one who pleads our cause, the one through whom every prayer must rise and every grace descend. To understand the universal action of Mary, one must study her exemplary causality, her meritorious power, her role in satisfaction, and her power of intercession.[86]

Thus, Mary as joined to Christ is, in a secondary way, a cause of grace in all the modes that Christ is a cause of grace for us. She is an exemplar cause of the predestined (Chapter 7), a cause of merit and satisfaction (Chapter 8), and a universal mediatory or intercessory cause (Chapters 9–11). However, Hugon extends this consideration of Mary's universal mediation beyond those graces granted to fallen humanity. He continues and considers how Mary is Mother of grace even to the angels (Chapter 12) as well as a cause of glory to the saints in Heaven and a cause of satisfaction for the suffering souls in Purgatory (Chapter 13). In his concluding peroration (Chapter 14), Hugon asserts:

> It is therefore established that the influence of Mary, more universal than that of the sun, extends as far as the supernatural realm: *Nec est qui se abscondat a calore eius.* No soul can entirely avoid her light and her warmth.[87]

---

86. Chapter 7, p. 132.
87. Chapter 14, p. 195.

In this way, then, Hugon's consideration of Mary's overflowing plenitude of grace is also complete, having considered all the ways in which
she is a cause, and all of the possible objects of her effects (that is, the
Church militant, suffering, and triumphant).

From this overview of Hugon's treatise, his "summary Mariology,"
it should be clear that he employs the primary principle of Mariology
highlighted in the previous section, that is, Mary's divine maternity
seen in relationship to Christ. However, Hugon does not ignore Mary's
relationship to the Church. This is clear from several places in his
text. As just indicated, the entire second part of the book should be
read as a meditation upon how Mary is the Mother of the Church.
Furthermore, by arguing that Mary possesses a universality of grace
in Chapter 6, Hugon can be read as showing how she is a type of the
Church which also possesses a universality of graces. Indeed, he argues
that her universality of intercession can be likened to her being the
heart of the Church, a principal member second only to Christ, the
head.[88] Furthermore, Hugon devotes extensive argument to show how
Mary's intercessory power is complete, both as to any individual member of the Church and to the Church as a whole.

Concerning the first, he argues:

> Let us now consider theological proofs. The first is drawn from
> the Gospel. In every solemn circumstance when Christ distributed
> grace during his earthly life, he willed that it would be through
> the intercession of Mary. It is through her that he sanctifies the
> Forerunner, through her and at her behest that he reaffirms the
> faith of the Apostles in the miracle of Cana, through her that he
> confirms in grace the Apostle John at Calvary, where from his lips
> came that marvelous phrase: *Woman, behold thy son; Behold thy
> mother.* These three scenes summarize the entire supernatural econ-
> omy. The principal operations of salvation flow from three orders of
> grace: the call to faith (which is the first step), justification (which
> causes our progress), and perseverance (at the end of our journey).[89]

---

88. See Chapter 10, p. 165.
89. Chapter 10, p. 161.

And concerning the second, Hugon proposes the following:

> After the Ascension, Our Lord wills that the effusion of the
> Holy Spirit take place through the intermediation of the august
> Virgin. He teaches us by this mystery what the economy of grace
> will be for all subsequent time. Pentecost was the image of all
> that God had to perform in souls until the end of time. Christ
> will maintain the order that he established for the distribution
> of his gifts from the beginning of his Church, for all other graces
> are the consequences and as it were the particular application
> of that great and holy even which sanctified and confirmed the
> nascent Church. Now, this first effusion of grace in the Upper
> Room was accomplished through Mary; therefore, until the end
> of time, the gifts of God will be transmitted through her.[90]

Hugon encapsulates this reasoning in an even shorter space: "The virginal fecundity of Mary works its effects upon the Mystical Body just as
much as upon the physical body of Christ. This spiritual childbirth is
but the complement of her divine maternity."[91] In conclusion, Hugon's
Mariology in miniature makes excellent use of the twofold guiding
principle of the discipline: Mary as that human person uniquely related
as Mother to Christ and also to His Church.

This overview should also make clear that Hugon's mode of proceeding does not shy away from deductive arguments which include
appeals to the principle of fittingness, nor does his prose omit references
to substantial philosophical and ontological principles, following St.
Thomas's example. While his theological temperament has or might
appear in parts to have tendencies towards the fourth extreme discussed
above, the type that leans towards rationalism combined with excess of
devotion, an attentive reading shows his "conceptual sobriety." Hugon's
is a Mariological mode where Scriptures and the Fathers enter in as
echoed antiphons in the Church's age-old contemplation and praise
of Mary. Indeed, the mode is very much in the style of the scholastics

---

90. Ibid., p. 162.
91. Ibid., p. 164.

who cite without ceasing the Fathers, doctors, saints, and great theologians so as to present their words again and recall their meaning to our theological memories. If all generations will call Mary blessed, a part of this includes recalling her praises from generations past. While no *ressourcement* theologian, Hugon, with his meditative focus upon Mary's causal role in the Church's origin, as its exemplary member qua exemplar cause, and her maternal role even in the Church's glory, offers more points for comparison than contrast.[92]

One might object to Hugon's choice of subject matter itself. Even if he appropriately uses the various theological principles and modes of theological argument to develop his Mariology, his focus seems to be excessively upon grace itself. At times, the various comparisons or analogies to the existence, intensity, extent, and increase of Mary's graces could strike the reader more like theological "scorekeeping" than reflections on the economy of salvation. However, Hugon's subject matter should rather be considered from the point of view of its ontological foundation, the participation in the life of God and God's universal causality, which operates in primacy without derogation of secondary causes. Hugon's almost anatomical focus upon the ontological reality of grace is both cosmological and concrete; that is, it shows the universal and ordered extent of grace's action in Mary's very person and in her life. His talk of grace is not by way of woozy, wooly, or hand-wavy comparisons; grace is a reality, and like other realities created by God, it is marked by His wisdom and providence, and therefore possesses its own *logos* or inner logic and order that surpasses every human order, but without itself being a source of disorder or chaos to the order of nature. Finally, the principles Hugon employs to help us understand Mary's graces are never taken to be ones that provide us with their totalizing conceptualization, as is evident when, in moving terms, the "little son of Homer" gives descriptions yielding to poetry and metaphor.

We concluded in the previous section that the necessary parts of a complete Mariology are as follows: It must theologically contemplate Mary in light of her Motherhood (of Christ and Church) as fundamental principle, draw from the sources of Catholic revelation and thus

---

92. See Nichols, *There Is No Rose*, pp. 24–25, cited above, n. 63.

methodically order its reflections without abandoning the full range theological argumentation, including that of philosophy in an ancillary mode. Hugon has indeed done so, and provided us with even more. His summary or abridged Mariology is complete by focusing for subject matter upon Mary's fullness of grace, a focus which leaves no aspect of the mystery of Mary untouched, at least in some way.

THE ENDURING RELEVANCE OF *MARY, FULL OF GRACE*

The enduring relevance of this book is now clear. While it is not, as Hugon himself notes, an extensive theological treatise of the length of other books, it attains to a universality of consideration by employing the essential principle of Mariology together with a focused subject matter that touches upon every aspect of Mary's life and her life in the Church, that is, her fullness of grace. As stated already, Hugon's work is one among many that fulfills Mary's prophecy about herself in the Gospel of Luke. While it is itself, as it were, a brief verse or a few vibrant chords in the repeated antiphons of Mary's praise when compared to longer books, it is also a work that contains by reflections and echoes all that could be said in praise of Mary as in a miniature, all thanks to Hugon's specific scope. We can now understand the following judgment: "This book I consider one of the best written on the Blessed Virgin."[93] With these words, Reginald Garrigou-Lagrange recommends *Mary, Full of Grace*, written by his confrère, colleague, and friend.

Its Dominican character and discipleship to the Angelic Doctor also make clear its place in the Thomistic tradition of theology. In scope and style, it is unlike the ponderous academic treatises of dogmatic theology which Hugon wrote. It also does not read as do other shorter neo-scholastic Mariologies; for instance, compare it to Garrigou-Lagrange's *Mother of the Savior*, which is more academic in tone, for all its other excellences. Hugon's book is a joyous Thomism, drawing from traditional principles and arguments to train them upon his beloved object of speculation and contemplation, Our Lady. His poetic and literary talent also shapes his prose in an elegantly simple and straightforward way. He cuts no theological corners, and yet presents a Thomistic

---

93. Garrigou-Lagrange, *The Mother of the Saviour and Our Interior Life*, p. 33, fn. 22.

Mariology that is approachable to the generally educated lay reader. His tendencies towards a "maximizing Mariology" are never without the ordered power of exposition befitting a student of Thomas.

Other arguments in Hugon's book are relevant also for their historical worth for the Church as such. Here consider Chapter 11 in particular, where Hugon offers a few "final doctrinal precisions" regarding Mary's titles as *Mediatrix* and *Coredemptrix*. Hugon was himself a partner in the efforts of Cardinal Mercier to advance the cause of defining as dogma that Mary is mediatrix of all graces.[94] As we now know, these efforts did not come to fruition. The Second Vatican Council did not define any new dogma in regard to Our Lady; nor did Hugon live to see the definition regarding Mary's Assumption, promulgated by Pope Pius XII in *Munificentissimus Deus* in 1950. However, there are yet theological hopes in this regard. Nichols draws attention to the words of the American Mariologist Mark Miravalle:

> "The corpus of Marian dogma will not be complete until the Church presents a dogma directly defining the nature of Mary's co-redemptive mission with the Redeemer and her corresponding ecclesial relation to us in the order of grace," a reference to the further mysteries of Mary's mediation of graces and motherhood of the Church.... Such a dogma, arguably, is needed to fill a gap between what the Catholic Church defined in 1854 about Mary's beginnings and what she defined in 1950 about Mary's end.[95]

---

94. See Dodd, *The Virgin Mary, Mediatrix of All Graces*, pp. 133ff. Indeed, Hugon's Chapters 9–11 can be read as an extended defense of their case, for Hugon concludes Chapter 11 with these words (p. 176): "That is why we join our voice with that of Cardinal Mercier, and those of so many other prelates, priests, and faithful throughout the whole world, to hasten this proclamation, one that is so glorious for Mary and of such benefit for Christians." Indeed, the original publication of Hugon's book in 1904 does not include Chapter 11, which mentions Mercier's efforts (unlike the fifth French edition, used for this translation).

95. Nichols, *There Is No Rose*, pp. 87–88, incorporating text from the footnote. We should note that Mary's role as co-redemptrix and mediatrix are distinct, if related, notions. See also Arthur Buton Calkins, "Mary Co-redemptrix: The Beloved Associate of Christ," pp. 349–410, and Alessandro M. Apollonio, F.I., "Mary Mediatrix of All Graces," pp. 411–66, in *Mariology* (ed. M. Miravalle).

As long as and even after the infallible *sensus ecclesiae* ponders these privileges or unique roles of Our Lady, therefore, Hugon's arguments in favor of Mary's co-redemption and mediation will serve valuable theological purposes.

ON THE TRANSLATION

The translation has been made from the fifth edition of the book, published in 1926; it was originally published as *La Mère de grâce* in 1904.[96] On occasion, the first edition has been consulted to fill in small details, by way of footnotes, that the last edition leaves out.[97] I have attended to clarity and accuracy in rendering Hugon's style, and have done my best to capture the prose of the one who at a young age was called "the little son of Homer." I have rendered some expressions into a more contemporary English idiom (e.g., "Holy Spirit" for "Holy Ghost" or similar locutions for Mary). Some exceptions have been made to be more faithful to Hugon's theological vocabulary, for instance, the use of the expression "the just (*les justes*)" as a substantival adjective and synonym for "the saints," where he uses the former and not the latter. The table of contents of the French edition listed topical summaries under each chapter heading. These have been incorporated within the text itself as section headings in italics in addition to any section headings originally included.

There are two sets of notes to the text. The first set is Hugon's own footnotes. On occasion, I have expanded Hugon's references with more complete information and, as frequently as seemed helpful without becoming a distraction, I have also supplemented them with brief quotations of the relevant text that Hugon either indicated directly or seems to have had clearly in mind. These supplementations have been done without notice. I have reproduced Hugon's Latin when convenient, correcting any errors without notice unless these interfere with the meaning of the text or the argument. Since his style of citation is much more abbreviated than is the fashion today, and since many of

---

96. Some selections from its pages also appeared in the *Revue Thomiste*.

97. Although, as noted above, Chapter 11 of the 5th edition (1926) is not included in the original 1904 arrangement.

these older texts are more difficult to find, unless they are online, I have included these in the "References." When available, I have quoted English translations, even if Hugon cites a French edition. Translations or editions which were not available to Hugon at the time of the last edition are cited in the second set of notes. The second set of notes are translator's notes, which supply clarifications, suggestions for further consideration, and expanded quotations from the sources Hugon cites. Generally, in this second set of notes, for texts originally in Latin that I cite, I provide translations but not the original text. There are also other translations frequently employed, particularly the Douay-Rheims Bible, translations of the Fathers from New Advent, and translations of Aquinas from the websites of The Aquinas Institute or the Immaculate Conception Priory.

The main text is followed by an appendix in two parts. Part I contains essays by or about Hugon. The first is a chapter from a book written by Hugon on the nature of instrumental causality.[98] In it, Hugon defends his view on the instrumental causality possessed by Our Lady, addressing the question as to whether or not she is not only a *moral* cause of grace but a *physical* one as well. It thus complements material in the second part of the main text. The second is a short essay of Hugon's, "The Role of Meekness in the Spiritual Life," which discusses meekness and tranquility.[99] Its more practical tone serves to complement the speculative character of the main treatise. Then, I have included the eulogy for Hugon given by Garrigou-Lagrange, on May 9, 1929, at the office for the dead "*Quarantième*," or the fortieth day after his death.

Part II contains two essays of my own. These treat of various aspects of Mariology, both philosophical and theological, in order to follow and expand upon some indications that Hugon gives in the course of his book. The first, "*Ancilla Domini et Ancilla Theologiae*: Mary and Philosophy," reflects upon the relationship between philosophical speculation and Marian theology, in particular as it relates to some of

---

98.   Édouard Hugon, *La causalite instrumentale dans l'ordre surnaturel*, 2nd ed. (Paris: Pierre Téqui, 1924), pp. 194–204.

99.   This text is also an appendix in the brief biography written by Abbé Henri Hugon, *Le Père Hugon*, pp. 128–36.

the topics of Hugon's book. Its author is not only famous for the 24 Thomistic Theses, but he also frequently wrote on and taught philosophy a great deal. The essay meditates upon the axiom that faith perfects reason while reason also serves the faith. The second appendix, "Mary, Queen of the Universe," defends the fact of Mary's queenship, proposes the principal reasons for it, and discusses certain of its characteristics. I hope that Fr. Hugon—whose writings include, besides Marian theology, extensive treatments of scholastic philosophical cosmology—would have smiled approvingly upon these two additions, had he read them.

At the end of the book, I have included a list of the older texts which Hugon cites along the way. Many of these works are now available for free online. Also included are some of the various online texts I have consulted to complete the translation and notes.

There are many people who deserve gratitude for their help in preparing this book. I would like to thank Fr. John Martin Ruiz, O.P., head librarian at the Pontifical Faculty of the Immaculate Conception at the Dominican House of Studies (Washington, DC), for providing me with a digital copy of Garrigou-Lagrange's *in memoriam* to Fr. Hugon. I also thank my wife Marina, for reading through drafts of the translation and the appendices. All remaining errors are my own. Last but certainly not least, Fr. Cajetan Cuddy, O.P., and John Emmet Clarke receive my thanks for all their help during the process of publication.

Hugon considered his work one of gratitude and love for Our Lady, and so also does this lay Dominican. This translation is dedicated to my brother, Fr. Michael G. Brungardt. May Our Lady, St. Dominic, and St. Thomas Aquinas intercede for us!

John G. Brungardt
The Assumption of Mary
August 15, 2019

MARY, FULL OF GRACE

plena sibi, superplena nobis

* * *

PREFACE

Marian theology has seen both consoling and fruitfully pious developments in our days, which our great chapters have brought fully to light.[1] The immortal encyclicals of Pope Leo XIII on the rosary comprise a doctrinal monument unto themselves, a veritable dogmatic treatise on the Blessed Virgin, further supplemented by the declarations of his successors.[2] It is to do present-day Thomistic work that we enter this movement, especially at a time when the Church is preparing to exalt Mary, Mediatrix of all grace.[3]

Our end here is modest. After the magisterial work of Fr. Terrien we do not have to treat the magnificent subject of the glories of Mary in its totality.[4] An invocation of the Church suffices for our plan: *Mary, full of grace!* She scandalized Jansenist narrowness and yet she contains such sweet mysteries, she hides such profound theology, she is a summary of such fundamental Christian truths![5] The complete study of this title permits us to touch on important questions which come down to the theology of the Blessed Virgin, and, since the method to understand Mary is to compare her with her divine Son, we will have to keep in mind the great principles of the treatise of the Incarnation.

This summary Mariology cannot, of course, replace longer works, but we think that it has its use and interest, and we dare to offer this little book to the Immaculate Virgin as a token of gratitude and a tribute of love.

Mary is called "full of grace" because she has received the plenitude of graces for herself and because she is the dispensatrix of graces for all the saints: *Plena sibi, superplena nobis*—For herself full, for us overflowing.[6] Hence, there are two fundamental divisions of our work:

* PART I: *The Plenitude of Graces in Mary*

* PART II: *The Role of Mary in the Acquisition and Distribution of Graces*

---

1.   TRANSLATOR'S NOTE: Hugon refers to the first and second International Marian Congresses held at Lyon (1900) and Fribourg, Swizterland (1902). The first edition of the text names these congresses, but the fifth omits them.

2.   We have drawn out some of the consequences of this teaching of the Sovereign Pontiff in a little work titled *The Rosary and Sanctity* [*Le Rosaire et la Sainteté*] (Paris: P. Lethielleux, 1900).

3.   TRANSLATOR'S NOTE: This refers to an anticipated dogmatic declaration on the subject, a movement which Hugon mentions in Chapter 11. His hopes were not realized. Mary's role as Mediatrix is linked to her role of participatory co-redemption.

4.   TRANSLATOR'S NOTE: The treatise referred to is Jean-Baptiste Terrien, S.J., *La Mère de Dieu et la mère des hommes, d'après les Pères et la théologie*, 3rd ed. (Paris: P. Lethielleux, 1900).

5.   TRANSLATOR'S NOTE: The spectrum of Marian devotion and theology, and the Jansenists' place in it, is outlined in the introduction.

6.   TRANSLATOR'S NOTE: This phrase is from St. Bernard, Sermon II on the Assumption, n. 2; see St. Bernard of Clairvaux, *St. Bernard of Clairvaux: Sermons for the Autumn Season*, p. 19.

* * *

PART I

THE PLENTITUDE OF GRACES IN MARY

$$* * *$$

CHAPTER I

The Diverse Plenitudes of Grace

Grace in the most general sense

The word "grace" denotes, in general, all that which is given gratuitously. The goods of nature, as such, are graces, for we possess them due to the liberal generosity of God. Creation, existence, conservation, all that there is to being and life in us, are an alms that Providence willingly makes to us. There is not one bit of being in all our nature which is due to ourselves: the Almighty gives all and sustains all by a continual and immediate influence. Precarious and dependent, we have unceasing need of being supported by him. Such is the good almsdeed of every moment, the benefaction which is not owed, the gratuitous gift. There is in this way a sort of grace in the natural order which attends each creature to make it exist, live, and prosper. Such grace is the nurse-maid of the universe, as the Book of Wisdom states: "*Omnium nutrici gratiae tuae*—Thy grace that nourisheth all" (Wisdom 16:25). It is particularly remarkable in man since it fulfills in him all the perfections of the soul and all the beauty of the body.[1]

Mary's natural graces: perfection of soul and body

Mary has received these natural graces in their plenitude. Her soul has exhausted, in a way, the riches of both the ideal and the real. Jesus Christ, the perfect man, is the most complete representative of humanity. His body was formed by the supernatural power of the Holy Spirit. God works such miracles only to bring forth masterpieces: he is thus the model of all that is pure and beautiful in the material world. His soul, which is the prototype of the spiritual world, which touches the Divine Person and source of all beauty, gathers together in itself all that which is great, generous, and exquisite in the souls of artists, of poets, of orators. It infinitely surpasses genius. It is, so to speak, the realization of an ideal specimen. But, as Jesus and Mary are united in the same eternal plan, and since God contemplated them in advance as part of the same design, they are as the mold or mirror of one another. There has never been a creature that so closely imitates and reproduces the beauty of Jesus as does the soul of Mary. She is indeed the faithful mirror in which the soul of Jesus contemplates and recognizes itself. She is therefore incomparably beautiful, and it was necessary indeed that the soul destined to bear all the marvels of grace herself already be the marvel of nature.

The dignity of the soul is reflected in its powers, just as the brightness of an essence is reflected in its properties. We conclude, then, that there is complete perfection in all the faculties of the noble Virgin: deep insight and surety of intelligence, strength of will, and harmony of the lower powers.

In all other men, the body is usually recalcitrant to the soul's action. The indispositions of matter interfere with the superior clarity of the mind, and the sun inside the soul, prisoner of the flesh, must hold back within itself the overflow of its light. The body lacks brightness. It is base and vulgar.

Yet, in Mary, can we conceive of similar indispositions? Should Providence, which turned aside from her the stream of original corruption, which at no point permitted that her body be soiled for an instant, suffer that it be rebellious to the action of the mind? This flesh and this

---

1.   TRANSLATOR'S NOTE: St. Thomas teaches that mercy is at the root of creation. Since in every act of God truth is found, so also justice will be found; however, mercy is prior to and more powerful than justice. See *ST* I, q. 21, a. 4. In this way, grace is "the nurse-maid of the universe." This was of speaking about the goods of nature as a *grace* is ancient—the Second Council of Arles defines the natural law as "the first grace of God." See Russell F. Hittinger, *The First Grace: Rediscovering the Natural Law in a Post-Christian World*, 2nd ed. (Wilmington, DE: Intercollegiate Studies Institute, 2007), p. 66.

soul had to be wedded together and live in perfect harmony, so as to prepare the tabernacle where the Word would make his home and take his delights. The soul thus communicated to the body those perfections and that superior brightness which constitute its beauty.

The beauty of Mary

Furthermore, due to his Son's dignity, God had to give beauty to Mary. When he molded the primordial slime, he thought of the body that the Word would one day don: "For whatever expression the clay took upon it, the thought was of Christ who was to become man."[2] Have we not more than enough reason to say with Bossuet that God, in forming the body of Mary, had Jesus Christ in mind and was laboring for him?[3] It was an obligation, as it were, to place in that flesh whatsoever

---

2. Tertullian, *De resurrectione carnis*, ch. 6; *Patrologia Latina (PL)* 2:848.

    Translator's Note: See Tertullian, *Treatise on the Resurrection: The Text Edited with an Introduction, Translation, and Commentary*, ed. and trans. E. Evans (Eugene, OR: Wipf and Stock Publishers, 2016), p. 19: "For whatever expression the clay took upon it, the thought was of Christ who was to become man (which the clay was) and of the Word who was to become flesh (which at that time the earth was). For the Father had already spoken to the Son in these words, *Let us make man unto our own image and likeness. and God made man* (the same thing of course as 'formed'): *unto the image of God* ('of Christ,' it means) *made he him.…* Thus that clay, already putting on the image of Christ who was to be in the flesh, was not only a work of God but also a token of him. What is the use now, with intent to sully the origin of the flesh, of flinging about the name of earth, as of a dirty ignoble element, when even though some other material had been to hand for the sculpturing of man, it were needful to bear in mind the dignity of the Artificer who both by choosing judged it worthy and by handling made it so?"]

3. Jacques-Bénigne Bossuet, *Devotion to the Blessed Virgin*, "First Sermon on the Birth of the Blessed Virgin," pp. 39–40.

    Translator's Note: Jacques-Bénigne Bossuet was a seventeenth-century French bishop whose oratorical prowess was likened to St. John Chrysostom and St. Augustine. See Jacques-Bénigne Bossuet, *Devotion to the Blessed Virgin: Being the Substance of All the Sermons for Mary's Feasts throughout the Year*, trans. F. M. Capes (New York: Longmans, Green, and Co., 1899), pp. 39–40: "Art and nature alike produce their works gradually, and God himself does the same. The pencil precedes the brush; the architect's design maps out the building to come. There is no *chef d'oeuvre* accomplished in the world but goes through its preliminary stages; whilst nature, in the development of her designs, often tries her 'prentice hand in ways that seem almost like play. The work in which our Maker most remarkably follows the same plan is that of the Incarnation, for the sake of which He declared that He would 'move the heaven and the earth'—this being His One Work above all others.

exquisite thing that rendered it capable of becoming the mold from which the most perfect body of the Word Incarnate would come. As we have said concerning the soul, the body of Mary is the faithful mirror where God contemplates and recognizes the beauty of his Son. Cajetan states: "We must believe that the Blessed Virgin has been, as far as possible, like unto Christ in all things."[4] Just as spiritual beauty is realized in the soul of Christ and of his Mother, sensible beauty has found its complete expression in the body of Jesus and the body of Mary.

The Blessed Virgin has collected to herself the perfections of the exalted women of the Old Testament: the grace of Rebecca, the charm of Rachel, the beauty of Judith, the majestic sweetness of Esther. Her mere presence is an apparition of immaculate beauty. From St. Gregory Nazianzen, St. John Damascene, Richard of St. Victor, Denis the Carthusian, Gerson, and all the way up to the most recent authors writing of Mary, the Fathers and churchmen are unanimous in affirming that the Blessed Virgin is perfectly beautiful: beautiful in mind, beautiful in body, beautiful in appearance.[5]

Although its fullfilment was not to be till 'the middle of years,' He nevertheless began it from the beginning of the world. The natural and the written Law—ceremonies and sacrifices—priesthood and prophets—were all, speaking reverently, merely sketches or outlines of the 'perfect Man, Christ Jesus.' They are called by an ancient writer *Christi rudimenta*, and the grand work itself was reached only through a succession of images and figures that served as preparatory designs. But when the time comes close for the Mystery, God plans something yet more excellent than these: He forms the blessed Mary, that He may represent Jesus Christ to us more naturally than before. He is about to send Him on earth, and so combines all His most beautiful characteristics in the person of her who is to be His mother."

4.   Thomas de Vio Cajetan, *De Spasmo Virginis.*

TRANSLATOR'S NOTE: This work appears not to have any modern edition. See Garrigou-Lagrange, *The Mother of the Savior*, p. 152: "Cajetan wrote a special tract, *De spasmo virginis*, refuting the idea that Mary fainted on the road to Calvary. In this he was at one with Medina, Toletus, Suárez and with theologians generally, who all agree that Mary did not collapse under her grief. By her courageous bearing of trials Mary merited to be called Queen of Martyrs."

5.   See St. Gregory Nazianzen, *Tragoedia de Passione Christi, Patrologia Graeca (PG)* 38:134ff.; St. John Damascene, Serm. 1, *De Nativitate Virginis, PG* 96:670; Richard of St. Victor, *Comm. in Cantic.*, ch. 26; Denis the Carthusian, *Opera Omnia*, t. 36, *De Laudibus Virginis*, lib. 1, a. 7, 25–27, and a. 17, 37–38; Jean Gerson, *Serm. de Concept. B.V., Opera Omnia*, t. 3, 1319.

TRANSLATOR'S NOTE: These works are not available in any modern English translations, and Hugon does not quote any specific lines or pages; I point to

Both miracle and grace were added to nature so as to form in Mary an array of beauty never before seen and never seen since: the charm of the virgin, the majesty of the mother, perfect integrity and fecundity without equal. She possesses at once both the grace of spring and the riches of summer; she gives her fruit while remaining in flower.

She is beautiful in the temple of Jerusalem where the Divine Spirit prepares her for her mysterious destiny. She is beautiful in her maiden chambers where she lives in meditation and prayer. She is beautiful when she cradles the Infant-God or when she caresses him on her breast. She is beautiful in the home at Nazareth, next to the gracious youth who is her son and her God. She is beautiful on the roads of Judah and Galilee, accompanying the heavenly preacher and meditating upon his parables. She is beautiful on the mount of Calvary, when she assists the dying divine one and where she becomes the mother of humanity. She is beautiful in the upper room, where she instructs the apostles and protects the infant Church. Finally, she is beautiful on the throne of glory where she reigns at the side of Jesus, above all the choirs of angels.

She is assuredly the living apparition of beauty, and I understand that the poet has represented the archangel in ecstasy in contemplating Mary's eyes.[6] What shall be the rapture of such a sight as she, with the exquisite charms of her body and the incomparable graces of her soul! She is one part of the happiness which awaits us in eternity.

---

indicative passages. The *Tragoedia* of St. Gregory is likely to be spurious. In the mentioned sermon, St. John Damascene exclaims in one place, *PG* 96:670: "O most beautiful [*ôraiotaton, speciosissima*] and sweet girl! O lily among thorns!" Richard of St. Victor writes, *PL* 196:483: "Therefore you deserve to be called beautiful, because you were beautiful in appearance, beautiful in both mind and body." Denis the Carthusian, in a. 7, discusses Mary's true nobility, and in a. 17 her physical beauty, concluding, 38: "Certainly, O most beloved Virgin, so worth is you most illustrious flesh, that the body of no pure creature, nor of the heavens, nor the planets or the stars, can vie with it for nobility or be equal in dignity." Gerson, too, after literary comparisons to the royal beauty of Priam and Hector, exclaims: "Thus, that Virgin was most beautiful," and proceeds to discuss her moral and spiritual beauty.]

6. Translator's Note: The poet here is, of course, Dante; see *The Divine Comedy: Paradise*, trans. A. Esolen (New York: Modern Library, 2004), Canto XXXII, 103–105: "Who is that angel of such joyous gaze looking into the eyes of our sweet Queen—so deeply in love, he seems to be ablaze?"

And this immaculate beauty, even on earth, was never the occasion of sin for anyone.[7] Chaste beauty transfigures the heart that it enraptures just as the brightness of a soft light gladdens without disturbing. God is primal beauty, primal virginity, primal love, and this beauty renders pure all those who approach it. One becomes a virgin by loving it. So also with Mary. Her beauty bears souls to the God that she reflects, the flower of her virginity is a perfume such that one can taste heaven. To love purity is to love Mary. Happy are those holy souls who, in their meditations, realize this. Happy are the artists, such as Fra Angelico, who catch a glimpse of this in one of their ecstatic conceptions. Indeed, happy are we all, when we are so given to see such purity in heaven, where we will live by her life and love by her love.

Supernatural grace

Such is the first plenitude of grace and beauty that belong to Mary. We only touch upon these considerations so as to arrive at our subject properly speaking: supernatural grace.

Graces which confer pleasing gifts and gratuitous graces

The gratuitous good *par excellence* is that which surpasses all the forces, energies, properties, and demands of nature and places us at

---

7. See St. Thomas, *In III Sent.*, d. 3, q. 1, a. 2, sol. 1, ad 4: "But in the Blessed Virgin the inclination of the *fomes* was wholly taken away, both as to venial sin and as to mortal sin. And what is greater, as it is said, sanctifying grace not only repressed illicit desires in her but also had efficacy in others, such that, although she was physically beautiful, she was never coveted by anyone."
    TRANSLATOR'S NOTE: The "*fomes pecatti*," or what the Catechism of the Catholic Church calls "the tinder for sin," (n. 1264) is also called concupiscence, the disordered, pre-volitional inclination towards sin that is a result of the Fall, which "is left for us to wrestle with, it cannot harm those who do not consent but manfully resist it by the grace of Jesus Christ." (ibid.) Perhaps the physical beauty, and not just her perfect moral and spiritual purity, can be drawn from "Thou art all fair, O my love, and there is not a spot in thee," (Song of Songs 4:7) as Richard of St. Victor and Gerson do (see above). See also St. Alphonsus Ligouri, *The Glories of Mary*, Discourse IV, and St. Louis-Marie Grignion de Montfort, *True Devotion to Mary*, n. 49, in *God Alone: The Collected Writings of St. Louis Marie De Montfort*, p. 303. Both saints refer to the account of St. Denis the Areopagite, who says of his meeting Our Lady, ibid., "that when he saw her he would have taken her for a goddess, because of her incomparable beauty, had not his well-grounded faith taught him otherwise."

the level of God. The Church has defined the necessity of this grace, contrary to Pelagius and his disciples, and we have no need to establish this fundamental dogma here.

Certain graces have for their object our sanctification and to unite us to God and, due to the fact that they effect this adhesion to the sovereign Good, they embellish our souls and render us the friends of the Lord. Many persons search without ever finding such a gift of being pleasing. We are more blessed in the supernatural order, we who have received *gratia gratum faciens*, grace that makes one pleasing to the only King whose favor it matters to possess.

Other graces, be they ever so excellent and precious, by themselves do not suffice at all for sanctification. Their purpose is external and social: to procure the good of our neighbor, the conversion of sinners, or for the benefit of the Church. These are graces such as prophecy, the gift of tongues, the power of healing, the virtue of miracles, etc. These are called by the name gratuitous graces—*gratiae gratis datae*—since their presence does not necessarily render us the friends of God.

Actual grace and habitual grace

The grace which confers the gift of being pleasing, *gratum faciens*, is divided into actual graces and habitual graces. The first are temporary aids, supernatural flashes that seize the intellect, swift impulses which take hold of the will. They prepare and dispose to salvation (as do pious movements which precede the state of grace), or they complete the work of salvation by developing the strengths already present in the soul (as does the aid which follows upon justification). Habitual grace is continually attentive to our soul to preserve its warmth and life, it brings the soul new and permanent being, a second nature, which is a birth to divine life. Habitual grace confers the character of children of God and actual grace the activity of the children of God. Habitual grace unites us to the Lord and sanctifies us by this contact; actual grace makes us feel the touch of the Holy Spirit. With actual grace, God passes by; with habitual grace, God remains.

The plenitudes of excellence, of superabundance, of sufficiency, of universality

The plenitude of grace can be understood in several ways. The first *absolute plenitude* is when grace extends to all effects and is given with all excellence and possible intensity. This is what belongs to Jesus Christ. He is the universal, efficacious origin who attains each and every supernatural effect: all operations of salvation derive from him. He encapsulates all the capacities of grace, like an abyss without an edge which could contain all the waters and the seas. In the hypostatic union he touches upon the infinite source of graces, the divinity, and, as it is impossible to be closer to God than he, one could not conceive a grace more profound and more extensive than his. This is absolute plenitude, without limit, to the ultimate possible degree, at least to the ordinary power of God.[8]

One can then distinguish *the plenitude of sufficiency*, which renders the just capable of accomplishing meritorious and excellent actions and of arriving at the end of eternal salvation. This grace is common to all the saints. Lastly, there is *the plenitude of superabundance*, which is poured out upon men like an overflowing reservoir. Such a grace is the special privilege of Mary.

The source, the river, and the streams each have their fullness, but each in a different manner. So also do Christ, Mary, and the saints. Jesus has the plenitude of the source, since he is the ocean without limit and without bottom, from which one can draw without ceasing and yet which always remains full. The saints have the plenitude of streams, currents that vary in length and in depth but which are always limited. Mary has the plenitude of the river, a river majestic and overflowing which carries us to the tides of the vast ocean, Jesus Christ.

---

8.   TRANSLATOR'S NOTE: The "ordinary" power of God is His *ordered* power, that is, his power considered together with his wisdom. See St. Thomas, *De Potentia*, q. 1, a. 5, ad 5: "The absolute and the regulated are not attributed to the divine power except based upon our consideration. To the power of God considered in itself, which is called *absolute*, something is attributed which is not attributed to it insofar as when it is compared to his wisdom, which is called *ordered*." (My translation and emphases.) Thus, Hugon is claiming that abstractly or "absolutely" considered in itself the grace of Christ is not some "maximum limit" on the power of God. However, when taken together with the wisdom of God's plan of salvation, the grace of Christ is the greatest possible plenitude of grace.

Furthermore, we make mention of the *plenitude of universality*, which is what pertains to the Church, and in which one finds united the ensemble of good deeds and celestial gifts. There is no grace which the Church, taken in all her totality and with all the duration of her existence, does not possess and ought not possess. We will consider whether some such plenitude belongs to the Blessed Virgin.

Which plenitudes will we study in Mary?

Since there exists a progression in these diverse graces—the plenitude of the first instant is not that of the second sanctification when Mary conceived Christ, nor that of the final plenitude—our study, in order to be complete, must therefore review the following important points:

* The plenitude of the first sanctification (Chapter 2)

* The plenitude of the second sanctification and the grace of Divine Maternity (Chapters 3–4)

* The final plenitude (Chapter 5)

* The plenitude of universality (Chapter 6)

* * *

CHAPTER 2

The Plenitude of Mary's First Sanctification

Christ and Mary have this privilege, that their stories begin before their birth and never end. Both of them, although in different ways, have received from the first instant a singular sanctity which implies at one and the same time the exclusion of original sin and the infusion of all graces.

Our Lord is immaculate in his conception for two reasons

Our Lord, for his part, is exempt from the debt of original sin for two reasons. The first is in virtue of his conception. Formed from a virgin by only the operation of the Holy Spirit, outside of the ordinary course of things, he escaped from the stain that human generation carried along with it. Not having followed the common course by which men enter into life when he came into this world, he is necessarily shielded from the primal corruption carried by those impure waters. Pierre de Celle makes another comparison: "He arrived, the Son of God, born of the Virgin, without the leaven of fault, and he chose from the mass of human nature the most pure flour of flesh immaculate, without taking the ferment of original sin."[1] This is the first and fundamental reason.

There is another reason: the fact of the hypostatic union. Just as all the actions and all the properties are attributes of the person, and since there is only a single supposit in Our Lord, original sin would be imputed to the very person of God! The grace of substantial union is therefore an insurmountable barrier against all sin, original and actual.

The reasons for the Immaculate Conception of Mary

The same reasons do not obtain in Mary's case. Born in the ordinary course of human generation, she had to come into contact with its stain, and she did not have, furthermore, a substantial grace which could preserve her from it. But an exemption was urgently required due to other reasons. Was it possible that the temple where the Word would dwell be profaned for a single instant? Should not the Virgin receive, from the first moment, a preparation worthy of the future Mother of a God? The original disgrace would forever be reflected upon the Son. With what insolence could the Demon then say to Christ Jesus: "I defeated you once, for she from whom you received flesh was for an instant under my power."

Furthermore, Mary was to be the reparatrix of the human race. How would she be able to crush the head of the serpent, if the serpent had first already made her feel his cruel and disgraceful bite? Ah! Humanity is not deceived! It has always proclaimed aloud its faith in a privilege which is a glory to us all. The saints preached publicly what the faithful believed. On this subject, here is the precious testimony of St. Vincent Ferrer:

> Mary did not wait until the time of her birth in order to be sanctified, nor the last week or the last day. From the first instant, when her body was formed and her soul created, she was sanctified, for she was already rational and capable of sanctification.[2]

---

1. Petrus Cellensis, *De panibus*, ch. 4, *PL* 202:943: "Venit igitur Dei Filius natus ex Virginae, absque fermento culpae, et tulit de massa humanae naturae, solummodo farinam incorruptae carnis, non fermentum seu fomentum originalis peccati."

2. "Sextus gradus est super omnes alios; est sanctificatio beate Marie, quia ista sanctificatio non fuit cum debuit nasci, nec in ultimo die seu ebdomada, sed in eodem die et hora, ymo in momento formato corpore et creata anima fuit sanctificata, quia tunc fuit rationalis et capax santificationis." I *Sermo de Conceptione beate Marie*, Toulouse Manuscript, p. 346. Fr. Fages, O.P., historian and editor of St. Vincent Ferrer, shared with us the text of the manuscript. For a more complete study, see our *Tractatus Dogmatici, t. 2, De Verbo Incarnato et de B. Virgine M. Deipara*, 5th ed. (Paris: P. Lethielleux, 1927).

It does not enter into our plan here to explore the theology of the Immaculate Conception. The reasons for that dogma are known to all, the theologians have developed them at length, preaching has caused them to penetrate deeply into the hearts of the faithful, and so it would be useless to rewrite such a glorious page contained in all hearts.

The positive side of the first sanctification

This privilege, magnificent though it be, is but the negative side of the first sanctification. It is the abundance of graces, above all else, that makes this first sanctification beautiful.

I. THE FIRST GRACE

The initial grace in Jesus Christ was also the final grace

In Christ Jesus the first plenitude of grace was also the last. His dignity demands that there was never the least succession in his graces and his virtues: in a single act he attained the summit. Moreover, to utilize another image to help us, he could never be closer to the source than he was then, for he touched God himself already by that personal union which does not admit of degrees, which could never be closer than at the first instant. From the outset, therefore, the divine ocean was emptied into the soul of Jesus with such abundance that nothing could be added. His grace being perfect, his virtues are found to be of the highest degree, that of heroism: the natural or infused virtues, the gifts and fruits of the Holy Spirit, gratuitous graces, all that which belongs to the economy of the supernatural already adorns the soul of he who is, from the first instant, the head of all humanity and the source of our sanctification. The consummate graces of the angels and of men would form an abyss, were they all united together, but it would be possible to sound their depths and even to add to them further. They cannot be thus compared with the grace of Our Lord: nothing can be added to it. It has a type of infinity.[3]

---

3. See our work already cited, *Tractatus Dogmatici*, t. 2, *De Verbo Incarnato*, q. 5, a. 5, n. 6, 454: "In Christ, the grace of union is simply speaking infinite; however,

Grace progressed in the case of Mary

The perfection of the Blessed Virgin is not of the same character. Mary, at her conception, attains God less than she does later when she conceives the Word of life. Thus, her initial grace is not a consummate grace. However, it is ever the preparation and foundation of the divine maternity. Now, does it not seem that the basis of a dignity in some manner infinite ought to surpass the height of all the graces accorded to creatures?

A twofold question is raised on this subject: (1) Is the grace of the first sanctification in Mary superior to the consummate grace of the angels and of the great saints taken separately?[4] (2) Is it superior to the consummate grace of all the angels and saints taken collectively? The Fathers and theologians of old have not discussed all the details, but they provide the principles that will permit us to resolve this difficulty.

The first grace in Mary was superior to the consummate grace of the angels and of the saints taken separately

The answer to the first question does not seem in doubt: It is now-adays a common doctrine that the initial grace of Mary surpasses the consummate grace of the greatest saints. Moreover, for ages illustrious doctors have declared the same opinion. St. John Damascene has already said, regarding the subject of the birth of the Virgin, that she is holier than the seraphim and that she surpasses the most sublime

---

habitual grace, in its moral being, is infinite, yet in its physical being it is finite, according to the notion of being; yet it is in a way infinite according to the notion of grace [*secundum rationem gratiae*]."

TRANSLATOR'S NOTE: Here, Hugon follows and expands upon St. Thomas, *ST* III, q. 7, a. 11, c. He also refers us to St. Thomas's *De Veritate*, q. 29, a. 3, which asks whether or not the grace of Christ is infinite, and concludes that "the grace of Christ was finite according to its essence, but it was infinite according to the perfection of the notion of grace [*secundum perfectionem rationis gratiae*]." See also White, *The Incarnate Lord*, pp. 99–100, for implications of this doctrine to our understanding of the Incarnation.

4.   TRANSLATOR'S NOTE: By "consummate grace" of the saints or angels, Hugon means the graces that the saints possess upon entry into beatitude, after which their graces cannot increase through merit. Thus, Hugon argues, *Tractatus Dogmatici*, t. 2, p. 256, that the first condition of merit is that one be *in statu viae*, still "on the way." The other condition is that one be *in statu gratiae*, in a state of grace.

heights of angels and of men.[5] What is said of her birth can, of course, be applied to her conception. Suárez regards it as a pious and probable opinion which accords to Mary, from her first instant, a grace superior to the consummate grace of the angels and of men.[6] The Dominican Justin of Miéchow wrote in the seventeenth century in his theological lectures on the litanies: "From her conception, the Blessed Virgin had an abundance and a plenitude of graces such as neither man nor angel has ever possessed or even could have possessed."[7] Olier has elegantly explained this teaching.[8] Contenson and St. Alphonsus Ligouri go even further, as we will say below. As to the authors of our era, it would be useless to cite particular testimonies since all the current works of Mariology are unanimous on this point.

Two reasons: The disposition for the divine maternity and the love of God for the Virgin

Without discussing all the proofs that are customarily brought to bear, we will content ourselves to two reasons which appear to us to be particularly clear and decisive.

From the first instant, Mary was marked as the Mother of God, and it was necessary that grace already dispose her in view of this destiny,

---

5. St. John Damascene, *Orat. de Nativ. Virg.*, PG 96:648ff.

6. Suárez, *Opera Omnia*, t. 19, *Commentaria ac Disputationes in Tertiam Partem D. Thomae, Mysteria Vitae Christi*, d. 4, s. 1, n. 4, 57: "Fourth, I add that it is a pious belief and a verisimilitude that the grace of the Virgin in her first sanctification was more intense than the highest grace achieved by angels or men. Typically, in support of this truth, is adapted Psalm 86:1, 'The foundations thereof are in the holy mountains,' because the foundations of the sanctity of the Virgin were begun where the other saints were finished."

7. Justin Miéchow, O.P., *Conférences sur les litanies de la Très Sainte Vierge*, 134th Conference.
   TRANSLATOR'S NOTE: It is clear from a mere perusal of the headings of Miéchow's conferences how much they have influenced Hugon. See also the 137th Conference, pp. 443–44.

8. TRANSLATOR'S NOTE: From his later citation, Hugon appears to mean a quotation from the *Manuel Biblique*. The later quotation is from Jean-Jacques Olier's 30th Letter. A critical edition of these letters of the Sulpician founder has recently been published: Jean-Jacques Olier, *Correspondance : Nouvelle édition des lettres suivies de textes spirituels donnés comme lettres dans les éditions antérieures*, 2 vols., ed. G. Chaillot, I. Noye, and B. Pitaud (Paris: Honoré Champion, 2014).

that she receive the perfection of a future Mother of God. She did not yet have her supreme dignity, but she required a fitting preparation. In a word, her first sanctification had to be the foundation of the divine maternity.

Now a dignity of this genus, which has a type of infinity, surpasses all the mountains of sanctity, and all the highest regions of grace do not seem to be a foundation capable of supporting it. This is explained in Psalm 87:1, "*Fundamenta ejus in montibus sanctis*—The foundations thereof are in the holy mountains." The start of Mary's graces lies at the summit of the other saints. And they only arrive there at the term of consummate grace, while in the case of the Virgin it is part of her first sanctification. The summit of all sanctity is but the lowest level of her own. One interprets in the same sense the passage where the prophet Isaiah looks upon all the other mountains: "... *praeparatus mons domus Domini in vertice montium*—the mountain of the house of the Lord shall be prepared on the top of mountains" (Isaiah 2:2).

There could be some discussion about the exegetical value of these two interpretations, but in pious usage they have an incontestable authority, based on the daily application that the Church makes of these texts to the Blessed Virgin in the liturgy. The holy Doctors and ecclesiastical writers, Gregory the Great, John Damascene whose testimony we have cited, Contenson, Poirier, Olier, Terrien, all unanimously rehearse this opinion. St. Gregory the Great states: "That mountain naturally stands upon the summit of the other mountains, for Mary's height is resplendent above all the other saints."[9] The words of Olier merit recognition:

> *The foundations*, that is to say, the first stirrings and the beginnings of the life of the Most Holy Virgin are elevated far above *the highest mountains* of the Church, that is to say, far above the apostles, who are the most perfect and most eminent souls of the Church.... How does it happen that God loves more the

---

9. See St. Gregory the Great, *In Librum I Regum*, *PL* 79:25, lib. 1, cap. 1, n. 5: "Mons quippe in vertice montium fuit, quia altitudo Mariae supra omnes sanctos refulsit."

entryways or the gates than *"all the tabernacles of Jacob"*? The entryways of the Most Holy Virgin are two: the one hidden and unknown, which is her holy Conception, the other is obvious, namely her Nativity.[10]

A second proof which is commonly given and which we find to be excellent is that Mary was loved by God above the angels and the saints—even those of the most consummate sanctity—for the Word looked upon her and loved her as his future mother. Now, the divine love is creation: for God, to love is to make good; love in the supernatural order is to give grace. If he loves Mary more than the great saints, then he wills to her more of the good, he accords to her more grace.[11]

This first grace is superior to all the graces of angels and men even when taken collectively

Let us now tackle the second question: Is this initial grace superior to the consummate graces of all angels and men taken collectively? The testimonies on this point are less explicit. A good number of the authors that we have cited on the first question do not weigh in on this one. Suárez does not address it, although he maintains that the *final* grace of Mary is more perfect than the ultimate grace of the angels and of the saints even taken collectively. We must recognize that this opinion is opposed by certain theologians. Terrien is not among this number, but he shows himself to be very hesitant and even seems to regard the opinion as less probable.[12]

---

10. Jean-Jacques Olier, cited in *Manuel Biblique*, t. II, n. 756, 1st ed.
    TRANSLATOR'S NOTE: Olier alludes to Psalm 87:2, "The Lord loveth the gates of Sion above all the tabernacles of Jacob." I have also inserted a few phrases at the beginning of the quote that are evidently missing from the edition cited by Hugon's text. This correction does not alter the sense or purpose of the quote in Hugon's text; see Jean-Jacques Olier, *Oeuvres completes de M. Olier: réunies pour la première fois en collection, classées selon l'ordre logique* (Paris: Migne, 1856), p. 772.

11. See St. Thomas, *ST* I, q. 20, a. 4, c: "God's loving one thing more than another is nothing else than his willing for that thing a greater good: because God's will is the cause of goodness in things."

12. Jean-Baptiste Terrien, S.J., *La Mère de Dieu et la Mère des hommes*, t. 1, p. 391.

Those who maintain this view

This doctrine has, however, illustrious champions. St. John Damascene seems to teach it since he says that Mary, from her birth, surpassed all the heights of angels and men. We think that it is also the opinion of St. Vincent Ferrer: "Mary, at her conception, receives in their plenitude graces which are given to the other saints only partially." Which is to say: All the other graces are parts which, united together, do not equal the complete plenitude with which Mary was favored from the first moment.[13] This opinion is also expressly held by Véga; Contenson explains it in beautiful language; St. Alphonsus is also a recognized defender of the view.[14] One may cite Billuart also, from his sermon *Panegyric for the Virgin*. After having distinguished with St. Thomas a double plenitude of grace, he concludes that "Mary has received a plenitude of grace *above that of all other creatures*, since she has been elevated to the most sublime state, namely the dignity of the Mother of God." Further on he adds:

> Ordinarily, other creatures receive grace after their birth by the salutary waters of baptism, or in proportion to the need they

---

13. St. Vincent Ferrer, II *Sermo de conceptione Beate Maria*, Ms. 346: "Caeteris per partes datur gratia Dei, Mariae autem *tota se diffundit gratiae plenitudo*.... In virgine Maria formato corpore et creata anima statim fuit sanctificata. Laetificat civitatem, scilicet Angelos, qui gratiae divine revelatione viderunt gratiam sanctitatis Virginis et fecerunt festum in caelo de eius conceptione."

    TRANSLATOR'S NOTE: The text of the quote reads: "The others are given the grace of God in parts, however, he himself poured out whole the plenitude of grace to Mary.... In the virgin Mary, the body formed and soul created, she was immediately sanctified. She gladdens the city, namely the Angels, who, thanks to divine revelation, saw the grace of sanctification of the Virgin and made merry in heaven over her conception."

14. De Véga, *Theologia Mariana,* t. 2, n. 1157, 8: "Mary's grace not only at the end of her life, but at the moment of her conception [*puncto conceptionis*], surpassed the grace of angels and men collected into one." Vincent Contenson, O.P., *Theologia Mentis et Cordis,* t. 3, lib. X, diss. 6, ch. 1, 263: "Surely, the first grace was such that one may believe that the first grace of Mary begins where the graces of all others end, such that the primal grace of Mary was of a greater, more perfect, and more intense degree than the grace of all angels and men whatsoever that have existed from the beginning to the end of the world." St. Alphonsus Ligouri, *The Glories of Mary,* Part II, Discourse 2, p. 373: "The grace of the blessed Virgin surpassed the grace not only of each saint in particular, but of all the saints and angels together."

have so as to practice the virtues having reached the age of reason. But Mary, beyond the scope of these laws, was sanctified in the womb of her mother and from then on graces flowed abundantly in her heart. Mary receives a plenitude of grace and she receives it in an extraordinary manner beginning in her mother's womb.[15]

In our own day Monsabré, in his conferences at Notre-Dame Cathedral, has repeated the opinion of Contenson and of St. Alphonsus Ligouri.[16] Tanquerey also adopts the view in his theological work.[17]

The two preceding reasons apply here as well

On our own modest part, we do not hesitate to adopt this position. It is enough for us to review the two previous decisive proofs which allowed us to resolve the first question. Well understood and followed out to their consequences, they make our thesis quite substantially probable. The initial grace, being the basis and the preparation for the divine maternity, must be proportioned to that dignity, since it is an axiom that every disposition is measured to the ultimate character for which it initiates and prepares.[18] Here, the ultimate character, namely the divine maternity, is an incommensurable dignity that exceeds as

---

15. Charles René Billuart, O.P., *Sermons*, p. 117.

16. Jacques-Marie-Louis Monsabré, O.P., *Exposition du dogme Catholique: préparation de l'Incarnation, Carême 1877*, Conf. 30, "Le paradis de l'Incarnation," pp. 289ff.

17. Adolphe Tanquerey, *Synopsis Theologiae Dogmaticae*, t. 2, n. 1252: "In the first instant of her conception, the Blessed Virgin received a greater grace in her first sanctification than each individual man or Angel.... In addition, it is very probable that the Blessed Virgin received from the beginning a greater degree of grace than all pure creatures have received taken all at once. For from the beginning, she was loved more than all creatures together, because she was already loved as the Mother of God, and the degree of grace is proportioned to the love which God has towards a certain creature." See also François Xavier Godts, C.SS.R., *La sainteté initiale de l'Immaculée, exposée et défendue selon la doctrine de Saint Alphonse* (Bruxelles: De Wit, 1904).

18. TRANSLATOR'S NOTE: This axiom is a specification of the relationship between potency and act. For instance, it is of the nature of matter to be ordered to the various forms to which it stands in potency; this order can be called a disposition. Again, for example, such a disposition is present in the relationship between body and soul in a living thing. Without the proper disposition of its organic matter, the soul can no longer enform the living thing, and it dies.

does the infinite all the perfections and every dignity of creatures taken together. Therefore, the first sanctification, so as to have some bearing upon this dignity, even from afar, must surpass the gifts and graces of all creatures at once.

Such is Contenson's reasoning.[19] One could object that it is in vain since he does not consider the proximate preparation for divine maternity.[20] We reply: This shows that the first grace was not as perfect as that of the second sanctification, when Mary became Mother of the Word, but it does not show that this initial grace is less than all the graces of the angels and the saints. It is nothing but a distant disposition, well enough. This does not hinder the conclusion that it was a suitable disposition, since it already was preparation for the Virgin to become the worthy mother of God: "The first [perfection] was a kind of disposition, by which she was made worthy to be the mother of Christ: and this was the perfection of her sanctification."[21] It was, we say, a worthy foundation of, or at least one suitable for, the divine maternity. Very well! Heap up all the perfections and sanctity of all creatures: Would you have a worthy foundation, or only a suitable one, for this noble maternity? All graces added to one another would without doubt make a high and gigantic mountain, but from its peak to the sublimity of mother of God is an insurmountable distance. Its summit would reach only the base of the mountain of divine maternity. Thus, they would not attain the height of that initial grace which laid in Mary the suitable foundation for her future dignity. This mountain, formed of all accumulated sanctity, would elevate one quite close to God, but higher still stands the mountain upon which the house of the Lord rests, the divine maternity. Thus, reaching so closely to God, Mary had to receive more grace that all the saints taken together.

We arrive at the same conclusion if we, for a moment, gauge the love with which God cherished Mary from the first moment when she

---

19. Translator's Note: See Vincent Contenson, O.P., *Theologia Mentis et Cordis*, t. 3, lib. X, diss. 6, ch. 1, sp. 2, pp. 263–64.

20. Translator's Note: That is, Contenson's reasoning touches on only Mary's first sanctification as a remote preparation for her divine maternity, and not a proximate preparation later during her life.

21. St. Thomas, *ST* III, q. 27, a. 5, ad 2.

left his hands. He loved her more than all the saints taken together, since he already willed for her a good that the perfections of all creatures could never attain, the infinite good of her sublime maternity. He regarded her and loved her already as his future mother.[22] His mother being more precious to him than all else, he loves her more than all else. Furthermore, recall what the ancient and pious exegetes teach us when speaking about Psalm 86, that God loves all the gates of Sion, that is to say the beginning of Mary, more than all the tents of Jacob taken together, that is to say more than all the saints at once. Now it is a theological principle that grace corresponds to love: for God, as we have remarked, to love is to produce grace. If, therefore, he loves the Blessed Virgin more than all the saints combined, he confers upon her more grace than all the saints as a whole. The conclusion is unavoidable. "He has always loved Mary as mother," says Bossuet, "He has considered her as such from the first moment that she was conceived."[23] Therefore, from that moment, we can add, he has conferred upon her more grace than to all the saints.

We know the objection that will be made: On the pretext of exalting the noble Virgin, you look to exclude the progression which the nature of sanctity requires! Oh? How, pray tell, do we exclude this state of progression? A grace superior to that of all creatures combined is far from being infinite, and, compared with the dignity of the mother of God, it is but an incomplete disposition and distant preparation. She can be made yet more perfect, and nothing we have said prevents us from conceiving her as more abundant in grace at the time of her motherhood, or more perfect at the hour of her death.

---

22. St. Lawrence Giustiniani, *Serm. de Nativ. Virg.*, 365: "Illam profecto adhuc in matris utero decubantem adamavit Verbum, sibique in genetricem elegit, utpote superabundanti iam benedictione praeventam, iamque Sancti Spiritus magisterio deputatam."
    Translator's Note: The quote reads: "She was so perfected in her mother's womb to draw down the adoring Word, he having chosen her as generatrix for himself, inasmuch as she already superabounded in blessings beforehand, the Holy Spirit already having esteemed her officially."

23. Bousset, *Oeuvres*, t. 4, 264.

II. The Consequences of the First Grace

Virtues and gifts

The excellence of the first sanctification calls forth attendant virtues, gifts, and other supernatural ornaments. These divine riches are not only the fineries of grace, they follow it always and everywhere just as properties accompany an essence and heat the light of the sun. Mary, who from the first instant was prepared for her destiny as the Mother of God, ought not be less perfect than Eve at her creation. Now, it is common teaching that our first parents, at the outset of their existence, were adorned with infused riches which completed the state of justice. Since grace in the Blessed Virgin is extraordinary, it demands all there is to be had of the extraordinary, the consummate, and the perfect among the virtues and gifts. The gratuitous graces themselves, if they are not as yet exercised, are still there in germ, all prepared to blossom. The virtues must be present to the same degree as their principle, namely, the first grace. Since that exceeds the summit of all the saints, the virtues of the first instant already attain the supreme pinnacle where the consummate virtues of the just reach, that is to say, heroism.[24] We believe, therefore, that this blessed infant to have possessed all the virtues to a heroic degree.

Knowledge in Jesus Christ

The first plenitude exercised its influence on the vast domain of the spirit. Our Lord had, from the first moment of his conception, the full use of free will. In him, reason knew no slumber. His glance, open from the first instant, was fixed forever on the divine essence and contemplated the light from light which is the ineffable vision of the blessed. Principle and head of the supernatural order, cause of all beatitude, Christ must enjoy the first of that glory which he will give to others and which, furthermore, pertains to him by right as an inseparable privilege in virtue of the grace of union. Since the master of creatures must not lack any of the perfections which embellish his subjects, we must

---

24. **Translator's Note:** This coheres with Hugon's argument regarding heroism and Christ, and the principle that Mary is the perfect mirror of Christ.

find in the soul of Jesus, from the first moment, an infused knowledge after the manner of the angels, that is, powerful ideas impressed directly by God and permitting him to see and read all truth. These two knowledges were perfect in their origin, since the state of progression does not belong to Our Lord. They extend to all that is real: present, past, and future. It is necessary, indeed, that the judge and king of the universe know all that must be submitted to his tribunal and all that will fall under his empire.[25] This twofold supernatural knowledge does not extinguish the native capacity of his intelligence. Endowed with an activity far superior to all the forces of genius, he received, quickly and easily, that experiential knowledge that we must gather by a difficult labor throughout the fields of creation. It is clear that this latter mode

---

25. The Holy Office, in its decree of 6 June 1918, recognized as *certain* the doctrine which attributes to the soul of the Savior beatific universal knowledge, that is to say it extended to all that which God knows by his science of vision: *Acta Apostolicae Sedis*, vol. X (1918), p. 282.

TRANSLATOR'S NOTE: This decree is discussed by Simon Francis Gaine, O.P., in the opening chapter of his book-length defense of this traditional doctrine: *Did the Saviour See the Father? Christ, Salvation, and the Vision of God* (London/New York: Bloomsbury Publishing, 2015), pp. 6–7: "The [third question] put to the Holy Office was whether it could be 'safely taught' that the opinion of certain more recent theologians on the limited knowledge of Christ's soul was to be received *no less than* the teaching of older theologians on Christ's 'universal knowledge'. The answer was that this could not be safely taught: the older and more established teaching, which was linked in scholastic theology to Christ's beatific vision, must have a higher level of acceptance in the teaching of Catholic theology. The first two questions were more explicitly linked to the beatific vision. The first was whether it might be 'safely taught' that Christ did *not* possess the knowledge had by the blessed (that is, the inhabitants of heaven) while on earth. In other words, could it be safely taught that Christ did not during his earthly lifetime possess the beatific vision? The Holy Office replied that such a proposition could *not* be safely taught. To the contrary, then, the safe teaching endorsed by the Holy Office was that Christ *did* so possess the beatific vision. The second question was whether the opinion could be safely taught that *denied* the possibility of being certain of the teaching that Christ knew all that God knows, past, present or future, in the Word, that is, all that God knows by the 'knowledge of vision,' and was ignorant of nothing. In other words, could it be safely taught that the thesis that Christ had knowledge of all that God had actually caused to be by the knowledge of the beatific vision was in fact an uncertain thesis? The answer was again negative. The safe teaching was rather that Christ's possession of the 'knowledge of vision' could be dubbed certain." See also White, *The Incarnate Lord*, pp. 236–74, for a chapter-length defense of the teaching that Christ possessed the beatific vision while on earth.

of his knowledge is not perfect in its origin. Our Lord could progress in this knowledge day to day while his mind rested in the plenitude of wisdom.[26]

Mary had the use of free will from her first instant

For Mary, nothing allows us to affirm or to suppose that she enjoys the beatific vision from the first moment. Yet must we attribute to her infused knowledge, the use of free will, or rather believe that her reason lay dormant like that of other infants and was not awakened until later? St. Francis de Sales and St. Alphonsus Ligouri do not even want to permit doubt on this point: "There is no doubt," says the first, "that she was all pure and had the use of reason as soon as her soul was placed in the tiny body formed from in the womb of St. Anne."[27] St. Alphonsus adds, citing Fr. Colombière:

> It is not now an individual opinion of some few divines, it is the opinion of the whole world that the holy infant, when she received sanctifying grace in the womb of St. Anne, received at the same time the perfect use of reason, with a great divine light corresponding to the grace with which she was enriched. Hence we may believe, that from the first moment when her pure soul was united to her most pure body, she was enlightened with divine wisdom to comprehend eternal truths.[28]

St. Thomas is not opposed to this opinion. The habitual and permanent use of free will from the maternal womb seems to him, it is true, the exclusive privilege of Christ who possessed it by a *proper* right, but he does not deny that the Blessed Virgin could have at certain moments and above all from the first instant enjoyed the use of her reason and liberty by a gratuitous and *communicated* favor. It is in this way, for that matter, that Cajetan and Contenson explain the text of the Angelic Doctor.

---

26. **TRANSLATOR'S NOTE:** Hugon most likely has in mind and is expanding upon St. Thomas's conclusion in *ST* III, q. 12, a. 2.

27. St. Francis de Sales, *Sermons*, 9 "The Presentation of Our Lady in the Temple."

28. St. Alphonsus Ligouri, *Glories of Mary*, p. 384.

Christopher of Véga, who strongly defends this doctrine, cites in support St. Bernardine of Siena, Salmeron, Azor, Vasquez, Salazar, etc.[29] One is not in doubt of Suárez's opinion.[30] Three illustrious Dominicans, Cajetan, Contenson, and Justin of Miéchow, are of the same view.[31] St. Vincent Ferrer had already taught that Mary enjoyed the use of reason from the first moment and was capable of sanctification: "She was sanctified, because she was at that time rational and capable of sanctification."[32] Terrien declares that he has only found two decided adversaries of the privilege of Mary: Jean Gerson and Muratori.[33]

Three Proofs

Therefore, this privilege is not seriously contested, although it does not involve the faith. We have three fundamental reasons to prove it.

(1) Mary was owed the reception of justification in the manner of an adult

The first proof is furnished us by St. Thomas.

---

29. Véga, S.J., *Theologia Mariana*, t. 1, n. 956, 387.

30. Suárez, *Opera Omnia*, t. 19, *Mysteria Vitae Christi*, d. 4, s. 7, 70–72.

31. See Cajetan, *In IIIam ST* q. 27, a. 3; Contenson, *Theologiae Mentis et Cordis*, lib. X, d. 6, c. 1, 256–66; Miéchow, *Conférences sur les litanies de la Très Sainte Vierge*, 93rd Conference, 163–64.
    TRANSLATOR'S NOTE: The Dominican agreement is not as unanimous as it is made to sound. See Cajetan's commentary (Leon.11:295), n. 7, where he distinguishes two ways in which the use of free will could be had in the womb, namely, along with the infusion of the soul, or by a special grace. He does not go so far as to positively affirm the second of Mary. Indeed, Suárez (in the place just cited by Hugon) reads Cajetan as being *against* such an extension. Contenson interprets St. Thomas as arguing against the habitual and permanent use of free will, but proposes that a weaker mode of exercise could be present, in a more transient mode. Miéchow holds back from going any further than Contenson's view out of respect for St. Thomas. Likewise, Hugon appears to have a generous interpretation of St. Vincent Ferrer's short remark quoted next.

32. Ms. 346, cited above: "Fuit sanctificata, quia tunc fuit rationalis et capax sanctificationis."

33. Terrien, *La mère de Dieu*, t. II, p. 27.
    TRANSLATOR'S NOTE: Terrien's discussion of Gerson attacks the grounds upon which the latter asserts that the thesis under discussion is merely a pious belief, being founded neither on Scripture nor probable reasons. Hugon incorporates the spirit of Terrien's reply in what follows.

Christ was sanctified by grace in the first instant of his conception. Now, sanctification is twofold: that of adults who are sanctified in consideration of their own act; and that of infants who are sanctified in consideration of, not their own act of faith, but that of their parents or of the Church. The former sanctification is more perfect than the latter: just as act is more perfect than habit; and that which is by itself, than that which is by another. Since, therefore, the sanctification of Christ was most perfect, because he was so sanctified that he might sanctify others; consequently he was sanctified by reason of his own movement of the free-will towards God. Which movement, indeed, of the free-will is meritorious. Consequently, Christ did merit in the first instant of his conception.[34]

Let us establish an analogous argument for Mary. Her first sanctification is superior to the consummate sanctity of adults. A grace of this excellence demands to be received in the soul following a manner at least as perfect as that by which adults are justified, otherwise this would result in an inferiority in Mary, a veritable imperfection. Now, this mode requires the cooperation of free will. One must conclude that, if our first parents possessed, from the moment of their justification, the use of reason and freedom, Mary had these in a superior degree and, consequently, that she merited from the first instant. We cannot conceive that it is otherwise. Mary is already the one preferred, the unique one of the Lord, loved more than all creatures put together. God gave himself to her by an unprecedented grace; it was necessary that she give herself to God by a supreme love that presupposes awareness and freedom.

(2) *Her extraordinary graces had need of free will in order to bear fruit*

The second reason is no less plausible. The grace of the first moment is too extraordinary for her to be able to remain inert and unproductive. It is not in the sweet governance of Providence to deposit such riches in a soul which would never have means of bearing fruit. But, if

---

34. St. Thomas, *ST* III, q. 34, a. 3, c.

Mary is deprived of the use of her reason, all these eminent perfections are condemned to a type of sterility. You say: They are not entirely useless, since they serve to ornament that beautiful soul. But is this not truly too little for these gifts, so extraordinary, to remain purely decorative? There are seeds which expect to bloom, powers which wait to be used, activities which need to be exercised. If all these supernatural faculties are deprived of their regular development, they suffer violence. This usage is extraordinary, without doubt, but the graces and virtue of the first moment are much more so. Thus, why admit their existence and deny what is necessary for their blossoming? Given the condition and the excellence of the initial grace, the use of reason would seem natural, for it is necessary such that all the gifts are preserved from sterility and avoid a fatal inertia that is repugnant to their tendencies and their powers.

Since this privilege is needed due to the excellence of the initial grace, then, it must be accorded to Mary, if such an act is possible from the beginning. Now, the use of free will, which consists in the operation of the intellect and will, can be done in an instant. It is not a drawn-out act, imperfect and successive as motion is, but a sudden act, faster than a glance. We conclude, therefore, that Mary, just like Christ, had the use of free will from the first moment of her conception.[35]

In order to understand the possibility of knowledge from the first instant, one must note that infused ideas are able to be caused without the exercise of the senses or the cooperation of the imagination.

What is essential to intellectual knowledge is that it attain an immaterial object. There are diverse manners to attain it. Ordinarily we attain such by multiple acts and as it were by successive steps: The external senses begin the series, the imagination then forms a representation

---

35. We apply to Mary, the analogy being so manifest, what St. Thomas says of Our Lord, in *ST* III, q. 34, a. 2, c: "We must, therefore, say that in the first instant of his conception Christ had that operation of the soul which can be had in an instant. And such is the operation of the will and intellect, in which the use of free-will consists. For the operation of the intellect and will is sudden and instantaneous, much more, indeed, than corporeal vision; inasmuch as to understand, to will, and to feel, are not movements that may be described as acts of an imperfect being, which attains perfection successively, but are the acts of an already perfect being, as is said, *De Anima* III. We must therefore say that Christ had the use of free-will in the first instant of his conception."

which is the mirror and vicar of the object, the mind exerts its power upon this image, the mysterious work of abstraction, and produces a new image of a completely different order, infinitely superior, which represents the object in its spiritual state. Such is the natural and ordinary mode. This is not the only way that is possible. If our mind could be given its ideas without its own effort, why would God not communicate to it directly, without the mediation of the external world? This would be infused knowledge, akin to that which belongs to the angels or the separated souls, and which is not an unprecedented event in the history of the saints. The ideas come from on high, knowledge is effected in the higher regions of the soul, and the support of the sense faculties is no longer indispensable. It is a miraculous mode, I grant, but it is not impossible. Do not the scholastics teach us that our intellect, after the resurrection of the blessed, could make use of or dispense with, as it will, the cooperation of the imagination and the senses?[36]

(3) *She could not have been less favored than St. John the Baptist; the possibility of knowledge by means of infused ideas*

Here is a final proof that we have found in all the authors favorable to this Marian privilege. Every grace, every gift, every favor which some one of the saints was able to enjoy has been granted to Mary.[37] Now, John the Baptist had the use of reason from his mother's womb. This is enough for us to conclude that Mary received this privilege from the moment of her conception. The principle invoked here is incontestable, above all since it deals with a favor which is related to the sanctification of the soul. This is the case because the use of free will was necessary in order to prepare the august infant for the infusion of grace, to prevent the sterility of such supernatural riches. As to the facts relevant to John the Baptist, the Evangelist seems to affirm it clearly.

The stirring of the infant is indicated by St. Luke as an extraordinary event (Luke 1:41), and St. Elizabeth adds under divine influence

---

36. TRANSLATOR'S NOTE: We discuss further this second argument, as well as Hugon's general position regarding Our Lady's use of reason and free will from conception, in the Appendix, Part II, "*Ancilla Domini et Ancilla Theologiae*: Mary and Philosophy."

37. TRANSLATOR'S NOTE: Hugon defends this principle at greater length below, in Chapter 6.

that the infant leapt for joy (Luke 1:44). Joy follows upon knowledge, and spiritual joy is a response to rational knowledge. That of John the Baptist was of this sort, for it was not provoked by a sensible object but by a supernatural one, the presence of Jesus Christ. Thus Cajetan observes: "It is evident, however, that John's joy was not over some sensible thing, but over Christ having arrived."[38] His joy and his knowledge were therefore rational, and this implies the use of free will. He received this with the grace of justification, so the Holy Fathers say unanimously; St. Irenaeus remarks: "John, when he was in the womb of his mother, upon knowing Jesus in the womb of Mary, exulted and hailed the Lord."[39] St. Ambrose: "He had the use of his intellect, who testified to it in the very act of his stirring."[40] And we cite once more the celebrated phrase of St. Leo the Great: "The Precursor received in the maternal womb the spirit of prophecy and, before his birth, hailed the Mother of God by signs of joy."[41]

The Church clearly professes this belief in her liturgy. She affirms that John sensed the king of glory hidden in his wedding chamber, the womb of Mary—"You sensed the King residing in the wedding chamber."[42] Further, thanks to John, the Church of God knew the author of her spiritual generation: "*Per quem suae regenerationis cognovit auctorem.*"[43]

---

38. Cajetan, *In IIIam ST* q. 27, a. 3, n. 7: "Constat autem Ioannis gaudium non de re sensibili, sed de Christi adventu fuisse."

39. St. Irenaeus, *Adversus Haereses*, lib. III, c. 16, *PG* 7:923: "Joannes, cum adhuc in ventre matris suae esset, et ille in vulva Mariae, Dominum cognoscens, exsultans salutabat."

40. St. Ambrose, *Expositio Evangelii sec. Lucam*, lib. II, n. 34, *PL* 15:1561: "Habebat intelligendi usum qui exultandi habebat effectum."
    TRANSLATOR'S NOTE: The quote from St. Ambrose reads slightly differently: "Habebat intelligendi sensum, qui exultandi habebat affectum." The meaning is not too much altered, if "sensum" is rendered as "thought."

41. St. Leo the Great, *Sermo in Nativ. Domini* 10, c. 4, *PL* 54:232: "Praecursor Christi futurus Joannes, spiritum propheticum intra viscera matris accepit, et nondum editus puer, genitricem Domini signo clausae exultationis ostendit."
    TRANSLATOR'S NOTE: The quote from Pope St. Gregory the Great reads slightly differently in Latin, but the sense is not altered.

42. Hymn for Vespers, for June 24 (*In Nativitate S. Iohannis Baptistae*): "Senseras regem thalamo manentem."

43. Postcommunion, for June 24 (*In Nativitate S. Iohannis Baptistae*).

The privilege to persevere: God does not withdraw his gifts, the graces of the first sanctification require the permanent use of free will

It is therefore to be believed that the august Virgin performed acts of intellect from the first moment. But was this privilege preserved? The authors upon which we have relied are not as unanimous on this latter point. They even seem at several places to think that such a favor would not have been accorded to anyone but Christ. And yet a good number maintain that Mary enjoyed the use of her reason continuously: among others, St. Francis de Sales, St. Alphonsus Ligouri, Suavé, and Terrien.[44] There are even those who attribute this privilege to John the Baptist: Origen, Francisco of Toledo, and Juan de Maldonado.[45]

Whatever is the case with the Precursor, we think that Mary always kept the use of her free will. One of the reasons that we have used to support this from the moment of conception seems to us to keep the same demonstrative force for the following time. The primordial graces of the Virgin are too abundant and too extraordinary to remain sterile in her soul. A fleeting instant does not suffice to develop them with the amplitude the befits them; such fecund powers demand a continuous exercise to satisfy the vehement aspiration which carries them ceaselessly towards perfection. It would do them violence to arrest their development. And why would God withdraw this privilege? It is not too difficult for him to habitually maintain what he granted for a moment; the infused knowledge that was possible at the origin is equally possible subsequently. He who gives without repentance does not withdraw his

---

44. Charles Suavé, S.S., *Jesus, intime: élévations dogmatiques*, t. III, p. 262; Terrien, *La mère de Dieu*, t. II, ch. 1, 3ff.

45. Origen, *In Luc.*, lib. II; Francisco de Toledo, *Comm. in Luc.*, c. I, annot. 118, 107; Juan de Maldonado *Comm. in Quatuor Evangelistas, Lucam*, c. I, 235–38.

    Translator's Note: In addition to Origen, Hugon cites the commentaries of two famous Jesuit theologians. For the comments of Origen, see *Homilies on Luke*, trans. J. T. Leinhard, S.J. (Washington, DC: The Catholic University of America Press, 1996), Homily 7, 30: "The soul of the blessed John was holy. While he was still enclosed in his mother's womb and still to come into the world, he recognized the one whom Israel did not know. Hence 'he leapt'—and he did not simply leap, but he leapt 'for joy.' For he had perceived that his Lord had come to sanctify his servant before he went forth from his mother's womb."

benefits, above all since such withdrawal would impose a real restriction of activity which they make possible and which have a need of free will in order to be developed.

In any event, if the privilege is removed as soon as it is received, Mary wanes from the outset, she is less perfect in later moments than in her first moment. Is it fitting that such a holy creature could be so deprived without her fault, when her dignity demands that she progress without ceasing from height to height, from perfection to perfection? This very question suffices to convince us that she kept the use of her free will.

In Our Lord this permanent exercise of intellect and will is a natural right, and one can say in this sense, along with St. Thomas, that it is his prerogative and exclusive privilege. For Mary it is not held under the same title, but propriety and the very dignity of the future Mother of God claim it and require it.

We have not said all there is to be said, but we must restrain ourselves, and, furthermore, there are profundities and mysteries here that would always escape us. The little that we have explained suffices to prove that Mary, in her first sanctification, was full of grace in her soul, in her faculties, and even in her immaculate flesh.

* * *

CHAPTER 3

The Plenitude of Mary's Second Sanctification

The perfections of the first moment impressed upon the soul of the Virgin such a vigorous energy that she continued to scale peak after peak. Graces were accumulated without ceasing in virtue of that admirable traffic of merit which we will have space to discuss in what follows. At the time of her birth, this supernatural growth had already reached proportions that are impossible for our human intelligence to measure. This sacred commerce always continued with a fruitfulness that knew no restriction. Grace was yet added to grace. The years lived in the temple stimulated this marvelous development: the soul of Mary, directed by the Holy Spirit himself, nourished and enriched on the purer sap of the supernatural, *per Spiritu saginata*, as St. John Damascene says, arrived early on at that state which is the age of perfection in grace.[1]

The soul of Mary at the moment of the Annunciation

At the moment when the angel came to greet her, Mary already had the fullness of her maturity, even though she was quite young. She is ready to bear fruit. The Word, drawn by her charity, her virginity, her humility, seeks refuge in her womb. Consent is given him, and, in an instant, the most sublime of miracles is accomplished: The Word is made flesh. Thereupon in the soul of the Virgin a marvelous change, worthy of so great a mystery, comes about. Her grace is transformed and reaches an order so much the more superior that one can already call it a consummate grace, not because it marks the final terminus of merit but because it fixes and confirms her immutably in her already impeccable good will.[2]

Three reasons which demand the plenitude of graces

The conception of the Son of God, more efficacious than all our sacraments, conferred on the Blessed Mother all supernatural riches. Three reasons demand on her part from that moment onwards a plenitude of superabundance.

I. First Reason

The state of proximate preparation for the divine maternity

The grace of the second sanctification is a proximate and immediate preparation for the divine maternity. There must, therefore, be a proportion, if not equality, between the last perfection and the disposition which it is charged to begin. Furthermore, it is a law of providence that, when a creature is called upon for a special ministry, God prepares it in a manner which is worth of the role to be filled. If the grace of the first instant, though a distant and unfinished preparation, were so full and so fecund, what is there to say about this present grace, which is the immediate, final, and complete preparation? It must be that this second sanctification is measured by the maternity itself, that it be at its level, surpassing all human and angelic heights, and attain to the confines of divinity. We would use up in vain all comparisons in order to convey the idea. Supposing that a creature must receive fitting preparation so as to become the mother of thousands of worlds, each more perfect than

---

1. Translator's Note: This is quoted by St. Alphonsus Ligouri, *The Glories of Mary*, p. 401, n., who cites St. John Damascene's *An Exposition of the Orthodox Faith*, Bk. 4, ch. 15: "Deinde in domo Dei plantata, atque per spiritum saginata, instar olivae frugiferae virtutum omnium domicilium efficitur.—Then planted in the House of God and increased by the Spirit, like a fruitful olive tree, she became the home of every virtue."

2. St. Thomas, *ST* III, q. 27, a. 5, ad 2: "In conceptione autem filii Dei *consummata* est ei gratia confirmans eam in bono."

the next, or so as to be more accomplished than the first among all the saints, more elevated than the cherubim and seraphim—and so forth— would need, to be sure, a dignity which would defy our conceptions. Yet all that could not compare, even from afar, with the divine maternity.

Mary, worthy of God!

The grace of preparation which disposes Mary to this high office is therefore ineffable. All that we can say about this is that she is worthy of God. It is certain, indeed, that the Word made his mother worthy of himself. If the stars are not pure in her presence, Mary is pure before them; if the seraphim themselves do not merit to approach substantial Sanctity, Mary merits it, and she is holy enough so that Sanctity draws near to her, lives with her, and enters into an indissoluble union with her, as strong as eternity. We could fully appreciate the plenitude of this grace if we could comprehend this phrase: Worthy of God! Yes—if she is worthy of God, she has divine proportions and we can only compare them with the grace of Jesus Christ.

She reflects this from her soul to her body so that from this flesh thus sanctified could be formed the flesh of a God: "From there to the body, so that from her own flesh she could beget God."[3] What results, for her entire person, is a fresh beauty. Just as the dwelling of the Trinity

---

3. TRANSLATOR'S NOTE: Hugon refers us to St. Thomas, *ST* III, q. 27, a. 4, and quotes the following Latin text: "Deinde in corpus, ut ex carne sua posset generare Deum." This quote appears in the original *Revue Thomiste* article that is the source of this chapter, and it bears the same erroneous reference. However, it is found verbatim in Contenson's *Theologiae Mentis et Cordis*, t. 3, lib. X, diss. 6, ch. 1, 264: "Tertio gratia Mariana triplicem habuit refusionem, nimirum in animam ad vitandum omne peccatum, et operandum omne bonum: deinde in corpus, ut ex carne sua posset generare Deum: demum in omnes homines, talem enim ei Deus contulit gratiam, qua Maria esset «plena sibi, et superplena nobis» ut ait S. Bernardus.—The third Marian grace had a threefold refulgence: without doubt, in her soul to avoid all sin and accomplish every good; from there to the body, so that from her own flesh she could beget God; finally, to all men, so greatly did God bestow grace upon her, that Mary might be «for herself full, for us overflowing» as St. Bernard says." Besides being a *locus* for that perfect epigraph framing Hugon's entire book, it seems reasonable that one Dominican reading another Dominican might mistake the ultimate origin of the quote as the cited text of the Angelic Doctor, insofar as that Dominican's article asks whether Mary's sanctification in her womb preserved her from all actual sin, which is similar to the first "refulgence" mentioned by Contenson.

leaves in the just a hidden majesty which is sometimes revealed at the hour of death, just as the Hypostatic Union imparts to the Humanity of the Word a perfection and a beauty which reveals Jesus to be above all infants and men, so also the grace of the divine maternity adds to the entire being of Mary an excellence and appeal which makes the Virgin like the very revelation and charm of God.

II. Second Reason

The union with the author of grace

The second cause of this plenitude is the union with the author of grace. The more that a being is united to its principle, the better does it receive its influence. The closer one is to a source, the more one participates in the abundance of its currents. The more one draws near to a hearth, the better one feels the effects of its heat and light. Now, the source of grace is Jesus Christ, a principal cause by its divinity, an instrumental cause by his humanity. The Blessed Virgin Mary was of all creatures the one who drew nearest to Christ as to his humanity, since Christ received his human nature from Mary. Thus, Mary had to receive from Christ a plenitude of grace greater than all other creatures.[4]

The contact of Mary with the humanity and divinity of Jesus

Let us attempt to to explain the reasoning of St. Thomas. What determines the measure of graces is the union, more or less near, with the humanity and divinity of Jesus Christ. Now, is it possible to be closer than Mary to his captivating humanity? One can say that this nature is something Marian, since it was taken from Mary, and that,

---

4. St. Thomas, *ST* III, q. 27, a. 5, c.: "In every genus, the nearer a thing is to the principle, the greater the part which it has in the effect of that principle, whence Dionysius says (*Coel. Hier.* IV) that angels, being nearer to God, have a greater share than men, in the effects of the Divine goodness. Now Christ is the principle of grace, authoritatively as to His Godhead, instrumentally as to His humanity: whence (John 1:17) it is written: *Grace and truth came by Jesus Christ.* But the Blessed Virgin Mary was nearest to Christ in His humanity: because He received His human nature from her. Therefore it was due to her to receive a greater fullness of grace than others."

for nine months, it was nourished by her and breathed through her. If it is enough to seize hold of the fringe of the divine mantle in order to be saved—"for virtue went out from him, and healed all" (Luke 6:19)—and if Jesus could sanctify John the Precursor while in the maternal womb, ought he not do as much in his own august Mother, who touched more than his mantle, who touched his humanity by such a singular union? Since this contact is the most intimate of all, since there is no limit in this union, there must be no limit to the grace that flows from it. It seems that the ocean must empty itself entire.

It is also difficult to be closer than Mary to the divine nature, for the Mother of God, as we will explain in the following chapter, belongs to the hypostatic order and this elevates her to the very confines of divinity. And, furthermore, since the two natures are inseparable in Our Lord, since the unction of the Word embalmed the whole being of Christ, since there is no part in him which is not entirely penetrated by the oil of divinity, to touch the visible Christ is to reach the God-Christ. The one follows infallibly upon the other: *Per Christum hominem ad Christum Deum*; by Christ the man, to Christ God.[5] Mary, being of all creatures the one who is closest to the visible Christ, also draws nearest to Christ divine. Attached more closely than the rest of humanity to the reservoir of the Godhead, source of graces, she thereby receives the plenitude of the conception of the Word.

This contact amounts to a law for conferring grace

It will not be difficult to understand that such a contact must have produced grace, if one considers that Our Lord seeks above all the

---

5.   TRANSLATOR'S NOTE: Fr. Hugon alludes to St. Augustine, in his *Tractates on the Gospel of John*, Tract. 13, n. 4: "Let us hear Himself: *I am the way, the truth, and the life*. If you seek truth, keep the way, for the way and the truth are the same. The way that you are going is the same as the whither you are going: you are not going by a way as one thing, to an object as another thing; not coming to Christ by something else as a way, you come to Christ by Christ. How by Christ to Christ? By Christ the man, to Christ God; by the Word made flesh, to the Word which in the beginning was God with God; from that which man ate, to that which angels daily eat. For so it is written, *He gave them bread of heaven: man ate the bread of angels*. What is the bread of angels? *In the beginning was the Word, and the Word was with God, and the Word was God*. How has man eaten the bread of angels? *And the Word was made flesh, and dwelt among us*."

union which is made by charity. Just as, conceiving Jesus in the flesh, the Virgin conceives him in spirit (as the saintly Fathers are wont to repeat), even so, by being united to him by physical human contact, she was necessarily joined to him, and more intimately so, by the spiritual contact of grace. And, for his part, Our Lord longed to live above all in her spirit and heart. He would suffer veritable violence if there were none but this material, bodily union: he cannot will the physical tie without the moral embrace of charity also, the union of nature without the union of grace. A maternity so supernatural cannot be conceived without supernatural love. The mere fact of being born from Mary and being in perpetual contact with her amounts, therefore, to a law, a sacred obligation for him to give grace.

The Incarnation and the sacraments

The true notion of the Incarnation suffices for us to conclude that there was, on God's part, a type of institution to confer grace by the physical human contact of the Word with Mary, just as there was later a divine institution to confer supernatural life by the physical contact of the sacraments with our souls. Weak secondary causes, the sacraments, however, produce their effect in an ever-infallible manner in the subjects which place no obstacle. The contact of the endearing humanity, conjoined instrument of the divinity, must act with a very great efficacy. Not only does the Virgin not put any obstacles in the way, but she bears the most perfect dispositions of heroic virtue. On Mary's part, nothing hinders grace; it is necessary, on Jesus's part, to give to her without limit, in swift, unstoppable streams.

The Incarnation and the Eucharist

The excellence of the sacraments, as well as their efficacy, grow in the measure in which they unite us more to God, and the most perfect of them all is the one which contains the divine power and very person of Jesus Christ. The conception of the Word, which bring to Mary the power and the person of God, must achieve all that which communion produces, and even more so. In the Eucharist, Our Lord is given in his entirety, but under foreign appearances. In the Incarnation, he delivers himself wholly to Mary under his true form and by an immediate contact. Through the Eucharist he causes us to live by him, but without living by us, for he does not receive anything from the communicant. In the Incarnation he is formed from the substance of his mother, he lives in Mary as the fruit on the tree upon its sap, he draws from her nourishment and breath. Must he not, in his turn, nourish her from his divinity? To each stream of life which the Virgin shares with him, he answers with new fonts of grace, and each movement which comes to him from Mary provokes the expansion of his supernatural gifts. If he lives by his mother, his mother lives by him all the more.

All the effects of the Eucharist, all the ardor of communion, are surpassed here and bear no comparison. And yet, what marvels the banquet of the Eucharist produces each day! Saint Thomas tries to give us some idea of this:

> This sacrament confers grace spiritually together with the virtue of charity. Hence Damascene (*De Fide Orth.* IV) compares this sacrament to the burning coal which Isaias saw (Isa. 6:6): *For a live ember is not simply wood, but wood united to fire; so also the bread of communion is not simple bread but bread united with the Godhead.* But as Gregory observes in a Homily for Pentecost, *God's love is never idle; for, wherever it is it does great works.* And consequently through this sacrament, as far as its power is concerned, not only is the habit of grace and of virtue bestowed, but it is furthermore aroused to act, according to 2 Cor. 5:14: *The charity of Christ presseth us.* Hence it is that the soul is spiritually nourished through the power of this sacrament, by being spiritually gladdened, and as it were inebriated with the sweetness of the Divine goodness, according to Song of Songs 5:1: *Eat, O friends, and drink, and be inebriated, my dearly beloved.*[6]

All these effects of the great sacrament taken together—since the institution of the Eucharist, and the most fervent communions of the saints throughout the ages, and the final communion of the last saint in that supreme sacrifice which will mark the end of time—all these do not

---

6.   St. Thomas, *ST* III, q. 79, a. 1, ad 2.

suffice so as to make us understand what the Conception of the Word worked in Mary. The presence of Jesus alone, by itself and by its proper power, conferred the habits of grace and charity; it brought forth and multiplied their acts. It inundated the Virgin with all the torrents of celestial pleasures. Jesus said to his Mother: "Drink and be inebriated, my beloved, on all my love and all my graces!" And she answered: "Drink and be inebriated, my beloved, on all my tenderness and all my gratitude!" It is necessary to stop here and to recollect oneself before these secrets which it is not permitted to man to express.[7]

III. THIRD REASON

Mutual love

This suggests to us a third reason for this plenitude: the reciprocal love of the Son for the Mother and the Mother for the Son. A principle often invoked here is that grace answers to love and is measured by it. Already at the moment of her conception Mary is the favorite, the most cherished of all creatures taken together. But what to say when she becomes the Mother of God! Certainly, Christ loved his apostles, and above all his vicar; they were the chosen and intimate few to whom he revealed all his secrets and confided to them what was dearest to him here below, his immortal spouse, the Church. He loves his saints, who he sustains through his heart. He now joins them to his beatitude in raptures and ecstasies, to his kingship by the empire which he accords to them above creatures, to his omnipotence by the power of miracles,

---

7. TRANSLATOR'S NOTE: This language of inebriation is not foreign to considerations of Marian graces in theological tradition. For instance, St. Louis Marie Grignion de Montfort considers five ways in which Mary is the source of special graces; see *True Devotion*, n. 45. The first states that Mary possesses the key to the cellar of the Bridegroom, as it says in Song of Songs 2:4: "*Introduxit me in cellam vinariam; ordinavit in me caritatem.*—He brought me into the cellar of wine, he set in order charity in me." Our Lady, spouse of the Holy Spirit, returns with joy from the wine cellar, as we read in St. Bernard of Clairvaux's sermon on this verse; see *Cantica Canticorum: Eighty-Six Sermons on the Song of Solomon*, trans. S. J. Eales (London: E. Stock, 1895), Sermon 49, pp. 297–98: "She appears so refreshed and excited in word and gesture, that it is *as if* she were inebriate." My emphasis. She is "not drunk, as you suppose" (Acts 2:15), but filled with the Holy Spirit.

to his divine knowledge by the gift of prophecy. He loves us all infinitely since he has given us his sweat, his tears, all his heart, his blood, all
his humanity and all his divinity. The Eucharist is the memorial of this
love taken to excess.

The love of God for us

If God created a new heavens and a new earth each day so as to
prove his affection we would be astounded at this. Well! In order to
come to us in the Eucharist, he must work a more difficult and greater
miracle than the creation of the heaven and the earth. The changing of
bread to the Body of Jesus and the wine to his Blood causes a tremor
through all of nature. The Red Sea held back its waves at the voice
of Moses. At the voice of the priest nature suspends its laws, miracles
follow the one upon the other, the world is shaken, as it were, by the
incredible feat of the consecration and, so as to maintain order in the
midst of this great disturbance, one must have a power greater, in a
sense, than the power to create: "In this conversion there are many
things more difficult than in creation."[8] And this mystery of charity
continues without interruption in all times and in all places. For as long
as there is a priest to celebrate and a faithful to communicate, Jesus will
renew such marvels, more astonishing than the creation of the universe.
This can allow us to comprehend the goodness of God for each and
every one of us, but still not his affection for Mary.

Mary, the most loved of all creatures

God is called love: "God is love" (1 John 4:16). His goodness is
the sun that reaches all creatures, which illuminates and warms all the
shores and summits of the angelic royalty and the most humble frontiers of being. All these rays, which spread throughout the ensemble of
creation, constitute a gigantic array of irresistible force.

For the Virgin, it is more than an array. It appears as if the sun con-
centrates itself entirely upon her with all its light and heat. One must
attempt to sound the powers of this infinite star of love, and only then
will one understand the plenitude of the graces in Mary.

---

8.   St. Thomas, *ST* III, q. 75, a. 8, ad 3.

It is clear that she must be more loved than all creatures, for to be the Mother of God is incomparably greater than to be the mother of any other being now existing or of those in any possible world. The love of Christ for his Mother contains all that there is that is exquisite in nature, for it comes from a heart where every human feeling is carried to the sublime. It contains all that there is of the sublime in the supernatural, for it comes from a soul to which grace and charity have communicated aspirations and longings which resonate even into eternity. But above all it is the love of God.

Love of the heart, love of the soul, love of the divinity

Indeed, there are in Our Lord three sources of affection which are three abysses: his heart, his soul, and his divinity. His beloved soul enjoys all that which delights his heart, and his divinity loves all that which causes his soul and heart to tremble. Yes, Jesus Christ loves in God because, God and man together, he wills by his divine will all that which his human will could cherish. He loves in God because he wills in his Mother a Mother of God. He could not look upon her without perceiving this substantial tie which unites him to her, that tie of the hypostatic order in virtue of which Mary touches the confines of the divinity. If he loves his Mother in God, he must realize in her that love of which a Creator is capable, infinite, which has at its service an infinite power, abysses of grace which our minds could neither measure nor understand nor fathom.

While the divine love has no need of being aroused like ours, it nonetheless acts with greater efficacy where it is better received. One conceives, indeed, that grace is distributed with greater abundance when love, grateful and cooperative, knows better to respond to considerate and gratuitous love. So as to appreciate the graces of Mary, we are obliged to say a few words about her love for Jesus.

Love of Mary for Jesus—maternal love: what causes maternal heroism

It is first of all a maternal love. One knows of what heroism mothers are capable and how their hearts rise quickly to the sublime. This love has something of ecstasy about it that throws one out of oneself and prevents one from thinking of oneself so as to be entirely focused on the beloved child. A woman was dying of the cruel malady which had taken her son some years before. Her pains were dreadful, intolerable; she did not complain, she did not think or speak of them because they reminded her of the agony of her son. Instead of saying "How I suffer!" she repeated: "Oh! How my pour child had to suffer!" Such is maternal affection, yet it is not yet that of Mary for Jesus.

The Holy Virgin Mary, perfect from all points of view, excelled in all sensitivity of the maternal heart, but she had feelings and transports that other mothers will never know, for she is more a mother than all other mothers. Her Son belongs to her completely, since no other creature contributed to this virginal childbirth, and she belongs completely to her Son, for she has none but him. For Mary, Jesus is unique, the only child; for Jesus, Mary is unique, the sole author of his days here below. This is a singular fact, those are affections of such a separate kind, about which it is impossible to grasp its nuances and refinements.

Love of a virgin mother: the exquisite tenderness of a virginal heart

At any rate, it is a love of a virgin mother. The heart becomes more generous and more loving in the measure that it is more pure. Among other mothers, affection is more or less divided; the heart being no more a virgin, it is not entirely for the infant. In the heart of Mary, who became more virginal still by maternity, there is not a single bit which is not filled with love for Jesus. Divine charity penetrated her being in all its profundity: not a part of her heart, her soul, or her powers—nothing was empty of love. She loves with all her will, with all her spirit, with all her strength, and she is entirely mother and entirely mother of love for him whose Father is also love: "So that it left no part of that virgin heart empty of this love, but she loved with all her heart, all her soul, and all her strength, and was full of grace…that she might be the mother of charity, of which God, who is Love, is the Father."[9]

This affection of mother and virgin, which already unites all the excellences of the natural order, was transformed by the highest powers

---

9.   St. Bernard of Clairvaux, *Cantica Canticorum*, Sermon 29, n. 8, 191.

of grace. We have said that all the virtues of Mary were carried to a perfect degree, namely, heroism. This is even truer of her charity. Among
other mothers, love is not necessarily the charity which sanctifies, nature is not always elevated by grace, and the mother could be afraid of
clinging too much, in her infant, to what is created. For Mary, all that
which arises from nature is embellished by grace, all love is charity, all
that is given to the child is directed to the Lord. She has no need to fear
human excesses, for, in loving her Son, she loves her God. If nature all
alone works such marvels in the maternal heart and gives birth so often
to the sublime, what would happen when all its forces were associated
with the powers of grace! The sensitivities of nature and the perfections
of the supernatural produced in Mary a nuance of love, of maternal love
which was not formed in other hearts.

Tenderness of nature, tenderness of grace, tenderness of a divine sort

Yet this is not enough. There is more than the tenderness of nature, more than the tenderness of ordinary grace; it seems that hers are
tendernesses quite set apart. This august maternity being of a superior
order to that of grace, it is necessary that its love be of the same sort. It
is quite evident that this affection is still created and finite, but it flows
forth from the love of the Father for the Son, in the same way that the
maternity is a participation in the fecundity of the Father. Thus Mary
loved Christ with the heart of a virgin mother, with the heart of a saint,
with a heart which had something of the divine, for to a divine maternity belongs unique affections. The love of the Son for the Mother, the
love of the Mother for the Son, the two are unfathomable, and from
these two result that ocean of graces which is one of the depths belonging to the Incarnation.

Ceaseless progress

A progress without cessation had to occur during those nine
months, so to speak *ex opere operato,* by the permanent contact with
the author of sanctity. Of what manner of continuity? Was it at each
instant or rather at certain determinate moments? We do not have to
settle the matter. It suffices for us to know that the presence of the Word

in the womb of Mary was a permanent cause of grace and that, since she knew no hindrance, it must have habitually produced its effects. If the plenitude was already incomprehensible at the first instant when the Word was made flesh, what a level it must have attained at the birth of the God-Child!

Mary, always in contact with her Son, had with her a permanent cause of grace

And we should not think that the source of graces dried up after Jesus had left the maternal womb, for Mary remained always in contact with her Son. Each time she gives him to drink of her virginal milk, she receives in exchange the nourishment of grace; when she wraps him in swaddling clothes, she is clothed by him in the finery of immortality; when she lays him with love in the crib, he invites her to the table of heavenly delights.[10] When she soothes him sweetly, when she holds him in her arms or near her heart, and when she gives him her kisses of virgin and mother, she received from him the kiss of the divinity. Now, a ceaseless connection with a human saint suffices, says St. Canisius, to make one more pure, more saintly, more divine: "Through her constant caressing of the divine flesh, she was thereupon made more pure, more holy, and more divine."[11]

We are reminded, more than once, that even for strangers the touch the fringe of Our Lord's mantle sufficed so as to restore health.

---

10. St. Augustine, Appendix *PL* 39:2104: "Creatori succum porriges lactis, et cibis coelestibus satiaberis. Pannis involves puerum, qui tibi immortale condonabit indumentum. In praesepio pones infantilia membra, qui coelestem tibi praeparabit mensam."
   TRANSLATOR'S NOTE: Fr. Hugon paraphrases this spurious sermon of St. Augustine.

11. St. Peter Canisius, *De Maria Virgine Incomparabili, Et Dei Genitrice Sacrosancta*, lib. 4, cap. 24, 494: "...per crebram divinae carnis contrectationem ipsa subinde mundior, sanctior atque (ut sic dicam) divinior effecta fit?"
   TRANSLATOR'S NOTE: Fr. Hugon appears to have taken this citation directly from Véga's *Theologia Mariana*, t. 2, n. 1164, 11, without double checking the reference, for Véga's citation misleads to ch. 26. St. Peter's text, at least in the 1572 Ingolstadt edition, is in ch. 24. This text's Latin differs slightly from Véga's text, only omitting the "ut sic dicam" (as I will assert). Still, the sense is captured well by Hugon's translation, since St. Peter's rhetorical question ends by indicating his own position, and the sentence begins, "Who then, except the foolish, would question..." and ends with the quoted text.

Is it not the case that the immediate relationship with his sacred flesh invites the Word Incarnate to confer grace upon her who is his Mother, his Sister, and his Spouse?

And, even if this physical contact no longer existed, the bonds of maternity become no more distant or less strong, love is just as passionate and still has the same effects. That is, from the Incarnation, Mary always had with her a permanent cause of grace, such that it is impossible to establish the degree of continuity according to which the grace was conferred, and that her sanctity progressed in an extraordinary manner, until she arrived at that consummate plenitude about which we will try to discuss in depth later.

Although all the privileges of the Virgin are a consequence of her maternity, the second sanctification meanwhile reminds us in a more direct way of her title and her dignity as Mother of God. In order to fully understand this grace of the second sanctification, we must also study the grace of the divine maternity.

CHAPTER 4

The Grace of Divine Maternity

It is not our purpose here to establish the dogma of the divine maternity, its multiple harmonies, its incomprehensible dignity, or its innumerable consequences. Yet there is in this maternity a twofold aspect that relates to our subject and which it is useful to illuminate: the divine maternity considered as a grace of sanctification, and the divine maternity compared with habitual grace.

I. THE DIVINE MATERNITY AS A GRACE OF SANCTIFICATION

Substantial grace in Jesus Christ

Two types of grace filled Our Lord Jesus Christ: the one created and accidental, the other substantial and infinite. Sanctifying grace inundated all the depths of his soul, fulfilled all his powers, and it became an abyss so full that God himself, in His ordinary power, could not add to it.[1] Yet, anterior to this accidental grace, we must conceive in Christ the uncreated grace of the hypostatic union: this is the consecration *par excellence* of the Messiah, it sufficed all by itself to sanctify him.

What is it, indeed, to sanctify a soul? It is to elevate it, to fasten it to God, to confer upon it by a participation in the divine nature the adoption of children. The hypostatic union did all this and more than this.

It binds humanity to God in a grip so strong and so close that a single person results. This is the divine being that Christ receives, and not a created participation. In virtue of this eternal bond, Jesus merits the title of child of God far more than those justified by habitual grace: He is God's own Son. Grace does not accomplish this for adoptive sons. Lastly, the hypostatic union excludes both sin and the very power to sin, for it requires that all the actions belong to the person of the Word, according to the principle *actiones sunt suppositorum*—actions belong to supposits.[2]

Sin, therefore, would be imputable to a divine supposit. It is absolutely repugnant that the shadow of evil touch the glorious and immaculate humanity that the Word comes to govern. Thus, the grace of union alone is an eminent power of sanctification, it embalms Christ entirely, it reaches all the depths of his human nature, it penetrates them with the joyous and divine unction that makes Jesus the most beautiful of all human children.

This thesis of the substantial sanctity of Jesus Christ, while it is contested by Durandus and the Scotist school, is taught by the majority of theologians. To it, the Thomists have dedicated long and beautiful pages.[3]

Is the divine maternity a sanctifying grace?

An analogous question can be posed on the subject of the Blessed Virgin. In addition to habitual grace (about which we have already

---

1. TRANSLATOR'S NOTE: See the Translator's Note to Chapter 1, p. 14, above.

2. TRANSLATOR'S NOTE: Or: actions belong to individuals. That is, there cannot be a "doing" or "acting" without a some thing doing or acting, or some who doing or acting or undergoing. This axiom is the basis for imputing something done to its agent cause, in both an ontological and moral sense. Although clear to common sense, it is a principle challenged by any view that denies the reality of substance.

3. See the superb discussion of Jean-Baptiste Gonet, *Clypeus Theologiae Thomisticae*, v. 5, *De Incarnatione Verbi Divini*, disp. 11, 608–18, and disp. 20, 757–83; see also our *Tractatus Dogmatici, De Verbo Incarnato*, q. 2, 323ff.
    TRANSLATOR'S NOTE: The opening question asked by Gonet in his treatment of the grace of union in *Clypeus*, 608, is: "Whether the humanity of Christ was sanctified through some substantial gift distinct from habitual grace?" Gonet cites Durandus as holding to the negative answer. For a contemporary consideration, see Thomas Joseph White, *The Incarnate Lord*, pp. 84–91, for a discussion on the grace of union in Christ and how Aquinas refines his thinking on this question.

spoken), was there in Mary a kind of substantial grace? In other words, had the divine maternity already on its own the power to sanctify? This topic was debated by the scholastics under the heading: *Utrum maternitas Dei seipsa sit forma sanctificans?*—Whether the maternity of God itself is a sanctifying form?

The school of Salamanca and a good number of theologians answer in the negative, but eminent writers, such as Ripalda and Cristóbal de Véga, uphold the affirmative.[4] The reasons on both sides are expounded with great force and subtlety. We cannot discuss them here. They at least prove, we say with Contenson, that the divine maternity demands sanctity for Mary as an irresistible requirement that God would never have violated:

> The arguments at least evince that the divine maternity, if not immediately and formally sanctifying, is nonetheless radically and remotely so, and it is even, if one permits the expression, *exigentive* that Mary be sanctified.[5]

The divine maternity at least requires sanctity, and so calls for all its effects

Without claiming that she is a saint substantially, as with the grace of union in Jesus Christ, nor that it sufficed entirely of itself to justify her, being nothing but a relation in itself, we think that the divine maternity could be called a grace of sanctification because it would not have been granted to a creature without immediately calling for sanctity with all its privileges and all its effects: participation in the divine nature, friendship with God, the indwelling of the Trinity, exclusion of sin, and claim to the eternal inheritance. These we are going to expound in broad strokes.

---

4. See Juan Martínez de Ripalda, *De Ente Supernaturali*, disp. 79, 49ff.; Véga, *Theologia Mariana*, t. 2, n. 1602, 324ff.

5. Contenson, *Theologia Mentis et Cordis*, t. 3, lib. X, diss. 6, ch. 2, 285.
   TRANSLATOR'S NOTE: Contenson coins a Latin word "*exigitive*" to describe adverbially the exigency or demand of Mary's sanctification.

The divine maternity demands a participation in the divine being

First of all, the maternity of Mary calls for a share in the divine being. She imitates and recreates within time the generation by which the
Father engenders the Son in eternity: "The temporal generation of Christ
is an image of eternal generation."[6] United to her Son by a bond at least
as close as that of other mothers, Mary has a true consanguinity with
him and she contracts through it a marvelous and unprecedented affinity
with the divinity itself. Indeed, an *affinity*, because, related by blood to
Christ, she by that very fact had to enter into a real relationship with the
family of her child, that is to say with the entire Trinity. This is the stron-
gest affinity that could be conceived, for he who is by nature the Son of
God is also by nature, although in another manner, son of Mary. She
alone, by the operation that she exercised towards God when she gave
birth to and nourished him, reaches the very confines of the divinity.[7]

---

6.   Pseudo-Albert, *Mariale*, ch. 38.

     TRANSLATOR'S NOTE: Although Fr. Hugon cites St. Albert the Great, this work is
     no longer attributed to him. T. R. Heath, O.P., proposes, in notes to St. Thom-
     as Aquinas, *Summa Theologiae: Volume 51, Our Lady: 3a. 27-30* (Cambridge
     University Press, 2006), p. 86: "Its author probably was a German Dominican
     belonging to St. Albert's circle, but not St. Albert himself, since its doctrine differs
     clearly and significantly from Albert's teaching in other works." In what follows,
     we will cite it as Pseudo-Albert, *Mariale*.

7.   This celebrated expression, *to attain the very borders or the confines of the divinity*,
     is commonly attributed to St. Thomas and it conveys the thought of the Angelic
     Master well, who speaks of affinity with God, but we must state that it is Cajetan's
     expression. Here is the entire text of the illustrious commentator, *In IIam-IIae ST*
     q. 103, a. 4, n. 4: "Note that union according to bodily consanguinity with the
     assumed humanity of the Word of God is called 'affinity' to God in the text. Such
     that those consanguineous to Christ, insofar as he is man, are akin to [*affines*]
     God for the reason that God is the name of the divine nature, to which no one
     is consanguineous. Yet human nature attains to the borders of the deity from
     without, just as a wife with virginal womb coming from without in marriage.
     Thus, therefore, His mother is said to be placed akin to [*affinis*] God. Now, not
     all those of such affinity deserve hyperdulia…but only the Blessed Virgin, who
     alone attained to the borders of the deity by her own natural operation when she
     conceived, bore, gave birth to, and gave to drink of her own milk."
     TRANSLATOR'S NOTE: The Latin *affinis* derives from "ad" (using the accusative with
     a sense of direction) and "finis," giving a root sense of "to or at the very border of,"
     and thus can name neighboring things or places and consequently (given family
     life), the neighboring homes of family members and those kin related by marriage.

This proximity and this contact demands a community of nature and of life between her and God. It is above all the Virgin who has to say: "God is my life. His being moves in me, as my flesh has become his; he has elevated me to his level: it is no longer I who lives, it is he who lives in me."

The divine maternity merits divine friendship

Further, she merits divine friendship. Without any doubt, the mother has a right to a love which is not refused by adoptive children. A natural duty is imposed on children to love their mothers, as well as for the mother to love her children. Neither God nor Mary could escape from an obligation as pleasant as it is natural and sacred. This love is all the stronger as the union is the closer. In this case the union is sovereign, the most intimate of all, a sort of substantial union, as St. Albert says, for something of the substance of Mary became that of Jesus Christ, as St. Augustine also remarks: "The flesh of Christ is the flesh of Mary."[8] The divine maternity is thus not conceived without a mutual and sovereign love between God and Mary. It becomes an impetuous and penetrating force which binds them to each other. It makes the one enter into the other, so to speak, by the most efficacious and the most marvelous of unions.

Mary is wholly mother. Her Son belongs completely to her. No other creature shares with her the honor of having brought him into the world; no other will share this choice love which comes from his birth. Jesus is entirely for his Mother as his Mother is entirely for him. Indeed, there must be an absolute gift of the one to the other. We note that this divine maternity is supernatural. It therefore leads to a love of the same order, that is to say that supernatural and ineffable charity which produces sanctity.

Indeed, the love of God is creative. Our affections always suppose a good to which they are drawn, but this is not the case with divine love. For us, it is the object which captivates love; for God, it is love

---

8.   St. Augustine, *Sermon on the Assumption*, ch. 5, *PL* 40:1145.

TRANSLATOR'S NOTE: In the *Patrologia*, this sermon is said to be written by "an unknown and pious author." This line, nonetheless, is frequently quoted, e.g., by Suárez, *Mysteria Vitae Christi*, disp. 1, s. 2, n. 1, 7.

which produces its object.[9] God loves in his creatures that which he himself produces, and in this way by crowning our merits he crowns his own gifts. If he has for Mary a supernatural and sovereign love, he must make her sovereignly agreeable to his eyes and realize in her all that there is of what is excellent and exquisite in the kingdom of the supernatural. Just as all the worlds of nature, both the corporeal and the angelic world, are united in man who thus becomes a sort of résumé of creation, *microcosmus naturae*, so also all the marvels of the supernatural are condensed in Mary, who is the masterpiece and the résumé of grace, *microcosmus Ecclesiae*. Creative love has placed in her all that is perfect in each of the saints: the purity of virgins, the strength of martyrs, the devotion of confessors, the wisdom of doctors, the detachment of hermits.[10] Indeed, she is sovereignly a saint because she is sovereignly loved.

The divine maternity presupposes a special indwelling of the Holy Trinity

Yet charity and sanctity cannot be understood without a special intimacy with the adored Trinity: this is the sweet mystery that theology calls the indwelling of the three Persons in the souls of the just. Grace consecrates our soul with its invisible unction and in so doing makes it a temple which designates the divine host: it establishes by means of charity a perfect friendship with God. Now, friendship wants to enjoy, and there is not complete joy wherever there is separation. This is why friendship tends with all its strength towards connection. If it does not obtain it, this is due to a helplessness which causes it distress. At the very least, friendship looks to realize this reunion in thought and more than once it orders the mind to voyage to the place of the imprisoned heart. If human

---

9. See St. Thomas, *ST* I-II, q. 110, a. 1, c.: "A difference must be noted between the grace of God and the grace of man; for since the creature's good springs from the Divine will, some good in the creature flows from God's love, whereby He wishes the good of the creature. On the other hand, the will of man is moved by the good pre-existing in things; and hence man's love does not wholly cause the good of the thing, but presupposes it either in part or wholly."

10. See the beautiful sermon of St. Thomas de Villanova, *In festo Nativ. B. V. M.*, Serm. 3, in *Canciones*, t. 2, 396ff.

    TRANSLATOR'S NOTE: In Chapter 6, Hugon returns to this theme of the universality of Our Lady's grace, that she is a "microcosm of the Church."

friendship must groan at its infirmity, the divine friendship itself has at its command an infinite power. The union is accomplished as soon as it is desired. God is present to the soul—the soul is present to God. By grace, the Trinity is more truly present to the just one than he is to himself.

The divine maternity demands this special indwelling for Mary, by reason of the relationship that it established with each of the three Persons.

As has been stated so many times, Mary is the associate of the Father in the generation of the Son, and she could speak the same words: "You are my son, this day I have begotten you" (Psalm 2:7). Doubtlessly, one must guard oneself against an exaggeration that could become a grave error. In giving birth to Jesus, Mary did not cause him to be God, nor communicate to him the divine being. The Father, by begetting him from eternity, did not cause him to be man. However, since the same Christ is at the same time God and man, Mary is truly the mother of he who is the Son of the Eternal Father, and the Eternal Father is truly the father of the son of Mary, and he begets him in a new way in the womb of the Virgin. The words of Bossuet are apropos here:

> To establish with you an eternal society, he willed that you be the mother of his only Son, and that he be the Father of yours. O prodigy! O abyss of charity! What mind does not lose itself in the consideration of these incomprehensible kindnesses that he had for you, since you touch him so closely by this common Son, the inviolable knot of your holy union, the surety of your mutual affection, that you be given in love the one to the other?[11]

Is it possible, consequently, that the Father not dwell with Mary? Must he not live with her by a presence entirely unique who was called her *comparentalis,* his associate in the generation of the same Son who belongs to both of them albeit in different ways?[12]

---

11. Bossuet, *Oeuvres,* t. 7, pp. 135–36.
12. This is an expression of Denis the Carthusian.
    Translator's Note: It seems there are various instances of this expression in Denis' corpus. For instance, see *Opera Omnia,* t. 36, *De Laudibus Virginis,* lib.

And what about her relation with the Second Person? The Son willed to dwell in the womb of Mary and subsequently in close proximity to her. But is one to believe that this material proximity was enough for him? It is above all in the soul of Mary that he entered by a wholly remarkable presence of his divinity. He was mystically united to this beloved soul in a kiss softer and stronger than the one whose lips pressed Mary's lips.

Finally, the Holy Spirit overshadowed Mary, arose in her as in His temple and preferred sanctuary. He made her his collaborator in the Incarnation, that work of mercy and love which is appropriated to the Third Person. The Spirit of grace must take his delights in her and make for himself in her heart a home more beautiful and more beloved than the most perfect among those that he chooses to make in the hearts of the just.

We can truly say to the Blessed Virgin: *Dominus tecum*. The Lord is with you, not only by the presence of his humanity, but also and above all by the indwelling of the Three Persons in your soul full of grace.

The divine maternity gives a sovereign power of intercession

Another privilege of holiness is the power of intercession by which the just know how to act so efficaciously on the goodness of God. This irresistible power belongs to Mary in virtue of her maternity. Loved infinitely by her Son, she is incomparably pleasing to him, and it is not possible that she is denied by the One who owes her obedience. The pious Arnold of Chartres writes:

> Man can approach God with assurance: the Son is there to plead his cause before the Father, and before the Son, the Mother. The Son shows to the Father his wounds and his open side, Mary shows to Christ the heart upon which he rested and the womb that nourished him. There can be no refusal where prayers are more eloquent than any tongue, these memories of kindness, these emblems of love.[13]

1, a. 4, 22: "[Maria], quae comparentalis est Patri aeterno"; t. 40, *De Remediis Tentationum*, a. 25, 162: "Deo Patri comparentalis"; t. 41, *De Quatuor Hominis Novissimis*, a. 61, 582: "comparentalis Deo Patri".

13. Arnold of Chartres, *Libellus de Laudibus B. Mariae Virginis*, PL 189:1726: "Securum accessum jam habet homo ad Deum, ubi mediatorem causae suae

The divine maternity ensures impeccability

It is not conceivable that a creature have the right to divine friendship and that it remain in sin. That is to say, this august maternity excludes evil and the very power of evil. To be the mother of God is an imperishable, eternal privilege. It demands between Mary and her Son an imperishable, eternal love which does not permit sin to show itself even a single time. Thus the beatific glory and the divine maternity have this common privilege of excluding the possibility of sinning. The state of glory has this because it fixes the will in perfection, chaining it irrevocably to its last end, to the sovereign good which fills up all desires and completes all its powers. The divine maternity enjoys this because it entails the rights, graces, and privileges such that all the flaws of free will are removed.[14] This teaching of St. Thomas is also taught by St. Bonaventure, St. Albert the Great,[15] and before them by the Fathers of the Church.[16] The tradition can be summed up in this phrase of

---

Filium habet ante Patrem, et ante Filium matrem. Christus, nudato latere, Patri ostendit latus et vulnera: Maria Christo pectus et ubera: nec potest ullo modo esse repulsa, ubi concurrunt et orant omni lingua disertius haec elementiae monumenta et charitatis insignia."

TRANSLATOR'S NOTE: I have translated Hugon's French paraphrase here. For more on Arnold, who is commonly thought to be "the first Latin author to articulate the doctrine of Mary's cooperation in the salvation of the human race," (says Gambero), see Luigi Gambero, *Mary in the Middle Ages: The Blessed Virgin Mary in the Thought of Medieval Latin Theologians*, trans. T. Buffer (San Francisco: Ignatius Press, 2005), pp. 148-154, as well as Aidan Nichols, *There Is No Rose*), pp. 75–76.

14. St. Thomas, *In III Sent.*, d. 13, q. 1, a. 2, qa. 3, s. 3, ad 2: "The power of sinning is taken away in two ways. Either in this manner, that free will is joined to the last end which fulfills it such that no defect remains in it, and this comes about through glory .... In another way, it is taken away in this manner, that so much grace is poured into it that every defect is removed, and thus in the case of the Blessed Virgin, when she conceived the Son of God the power of sinning was taken away, although the Virgin remained a pilgrim on life's journey [*in statu viae*]."

15. Pseudo-Albert, *Mariale*, ch. 153.

16. See St. Bonaventure, *In III Sent.*, d. 3, p. 1, a. 2, q. 3, ad 4: "Regarding the objection about the impossibility of sin, it should be said that it is correct as to what regards the common rule. But nothing prevents it such that a special grace be given to someone during this life [*in via*], which is commonly given to the rest in heaven [*in patria*], and to that person especially who, when still upon earth, was the queen of those rejoicing in heaven."

Richard of Saint-Laurent: "Mary had the privilege of impeccability from the moment that she conceived the Son of God."[17] If some more recent theologians have seemed not to be of this opinion, the divergence is more in words than in the matter itself.[18]

The divine maternity confers an inalienable right to the eternal inheritance, and even to the dominion over all things

Finally, this maternity conferred certain rights to the eternal heritage. If the adopted child is called to enjoy the goods of strangers, cannot the natural mother lay claim to the prerogative of her son? Now, eternal beatitude is due to Christ as a natural good which accrues to him by right, by reason of the hypostatic union. It is also necessary that Mary, his necessary and principal heiress, possess that kingdom which she had so deservedly merited by her heroic correspondence with all grace. Pious authors go further, and pushing the argument into its utmost consequences, maintain that the Holy Virgin is, by her motherhood, queen of the whole universe.[19] For, if she is a mother, she is naturally heiress of the entire patrimony of the Son: *si mater, et haeres.* The Son of Mary received dominion over all things, both by right of birth in virtue of the Hypostatic Union and also by right of conquest in virtue of his works and their merits. Mary will be by right queen with him. This is why we call our Sovereign by the antonomasia *Our Lady.*[20]

This is the teaching of the Fathers as well: "He who is born of the Virgin being king and lord," says St. Athanasius, "His mother is truly queen and sovereign."[21] And St. John Damascene states: "Assuredly she

---

17. Richard de Saint-Laurent, *De Laudibus B. Mariae Virginis*, lib. 3, 188 (7th Privilege): "Quod peccare non potuit ex quo filium Dei concepit."
18. See Terrien, *La Mère de Dieu*, t. 2, 77. We revisit this question of impeccability in Chapter Six, below, p. 116.
19. TRANSLATOR'S NOTE: Concerning this claim, see the Appendix, Part II, "Mary, Queen of the Universe."
20. Contenson, *Theologiae Mentis et Cordis*, t. 3, lib. X, diss. 6, ch. 2, 281: "The Mother of God is queen and lady over all creatures, whether in heaven or under heaven. Whence she is simply and by antonomasia called 'Our Lady'."
21. St. Athanasius, *Sermo de Deipara*: "Quando quidem ipse rex est qui natus est ex Virgine idemque Dominus est Deus, eapropter et Mater quae eum genuit et regina et domina proprie et vere censetur." [CONT. NEXT PAGE]

who played the part of the Creator's servant and mother is, in all strict-
ness and truth, in reality God's Mother and Lady and Queen over all
created things."[22] The Mother must possess all the riches of the Son.[23]
St. Bernardine of Siena celebrated with much eloquence and piety the
royal power of Mary. Here are a few words of that beautiful sermon
which must be read in its entirety:

> All creatures serve the glorious Virgin insofar as they serve the
> Trinity. For all creatures, of whatsoever rank, be they spiritual,
> as the angels, or rational, as human beings, or corporeal, as
> are the heavenly bodies and the elements…all of which are
> subject to the divine command are subject to the same glorious
> Virgin.[24]

We have no further need to prolong this demonstration. It is clear
enough that the divine maternity cannot but be attended by the state of
justice and that, if it is not the very form of sanctity, then it is its root
and foundation, it calls for its effects and privileges. There are some of
these superior properties, these moral requirements which oblige God

---

TRANSLATOR'S NOTE: Hugon cites St. Athanasius here, and seems to be quoting
the Latin of Véga's reference in *Theologia Mariana*, v. 2, 350. I have not been able
to find this passage in the *PG*.

22. St. John Damascene, *An Exposition of the Orthodox Faith*, Bk. 4, ch. 14.

23. St. John Damascene, *Homilia II in Dormitione B. V. Mariae, PG* 96:742: "Oporte-
bat Dei Matrem ea quae sunt Filii possidere."
TRANSLATOR'S NOTE: The translation into Latin is Hugon's own.

24. St. Bernardine of Siena, Serm. 61, art. 3: "Tot enim creaturae serviunt gloriosae
Virgini Mariae, quot seviunt Trinitati. Omnes, nempe, creaturae, quaecunque
gradum teneant in creatis, sive spirituales, ut Angeli: sive rationales, ut homines: sive corporales, ut corpora coelestia, vel elementa…; quae omnia sunt divino
imperio subjugata, gloriosae Virgini sunt subjecta."
TRANSLATOR'S NOTE: The citation appears to follow that found in St. Alphonsus
Ligouri's *The Glories of Mary*, p. 26, as well as Véga, *Theologia Mariana*, v. 2, 353;
I have been unable to find the edition to which Hugon refers, and this reference,
even though frequently repeated in his sources, either refers to a text not available
or is perhaps erroneous. The quoted text appears in St. Bernardine of Siena, *Sancti
Bernardini Senensis Ordinis Seraphici Minorum Sermones*, t. 4 (Venice: Andreae
Poletti, 1745), p. 92, as part of Sermon 5, *De Nativitate B. V. Mariae*, ch. 6; this
edition is cited hereafter.

and commit his honor. The maternity of Mary is thus a grace of sanctification. It remains for us to compare it with habitual grace.

II. The Divine Maternity as Habitual Grace

Two aspects of the divine maternity

We could first see in the maternity of the Blessed Virgin only the simple fact of having given flesh and blood to Christ, of having carried him in her womb and nourished him with her milk. This consideration of the purely physical order, although it is not to be disdained, does not constitute the true dignity of Mary.

In this respect, grace is to her the preferable good, and this explains the testimonies of the Fathers that Mary was happier to conceive God by faith that in the flesh, and to carry him in her heart by grace than in her womb by motherhood. Our Lord speaks in the same sense when he answers the pious woman who praised this material privilege too much: "Yea rather, blessed are they who hear the word of God, and keep it" (Luke 11:28).

The divine maternity belongs to a superior order of relationship with the divine

But let us consider this maternity in its true colors, insofar as it terminates in the production of the God-Man, establishes with God those parental bonds and affinity which cause Mary to touch the boundaries of the infinite, and bring her ineffable privileges. Thus understood, she is incomparably superior in grace in numerous respects.

The order of nature, the order of grace, the hypostatic order

In the first place, she belongs to a more refined order of divine communication. The Lord communicates himself according to three degrees or three hierarchies of perfections. There is first the order of nature, in which he is revealed as creator with his essential attributes (his infinite power, his wisdom, his goodness, his beauty). Such is the unfathomable sentence, the immense book which teaches us to read, better than all the works of genius, the name and the ideas of the supreme artist.[25] So also, according to St. Thomas, it is preferable to acquire knowledge in nature than by the mediation of a teacher.[26] Books or words are but signs of human thought, while nature is the direct sign of the divine thought.

Next is the order of grace, which is a most perfect participation in the intimate life of God, an outpouring of his fruitful being, which makes our soul into a faithful mirror wherein Heaven contemplates and recognizes itself. It places us, so to speak, at the level of the Trinity, renders the Three Persons present in our hearts and begins here below that felicity which is completed in the vision and raptures of glory.

Finally, above all the created hierarchies, there lies the hypostatic order. This does not contain a mere accidental participation in God, but it attains to God himself and touches his sacred person in such a way that a human nature subsists in this person and by this person. As far as the heavens are from the earth as the east from the west, as Scripture says, so far and even further is the order of grace superior to that of nature, and the hypostatic order to that of grace.[27] Properly speaking, it is Jesus Christ who belongs to the hypostatic order, but the divine maternity belongs to it in some way. The Incarnation produced

---

25. Victor Hugo, *The Songs of Twilight*, XX, addressing the world:

N'êtes-vous qu'un livre,	Are you not but a book,
Sans fin ni milieu,	Without middle or end,
Où chacun pour vivre	Where each, so to live,
Cherche à lire un peu!	Seeks to read but a little!
Phrase si profonde	A sentence profound
Qu'en vain on la sonde!	And in vain do we sound you!
L'oeil y voit un monde,	*The eye sees a world there,*
L'âme y trouve un Dieu!	*Yet the soul, in you, finds a God!*

26. St. Thomas, *ST* III, q. 12, a. 3, ad 2: "Whoever learns from man does not receive knowledge immediately from the intelligible species which are in his mind, but through sensible words, which are signs of intelligible concepts. Now as words formed by a man are signs of his intellectual knowledge; so are creatures, formed by God, signs of His wisdom. Hence it is written (Sirach 1:10) that *God poured wisdom out upon all His works.* Hence, just as it is better to be taught by God than by man, so it is better to receive our knowledge from sensible creatures and not by man's teaching."

27. TRANSLATOR'S NOTE: See St. Thomas, *ST* I-II, q. 113, a. 9, ad 2: "The good of the universe is greater than the particular good of a single thing [*bonum particulare unius*], if we consider both in the same genus. But the good of grace in someone [*bonum gratiae unius*] is greater than the good of nature of the whole universe."

an ineffable relation of which Jesus and Mary are the two terms. Since one of the terms, Jesus, belongs to this order, the other term which corresponds to him, Mary, must be related to it at some point. The maternity of the Virgin will therefore touch some aspects of the hypostatic order and, for that very reason, infinitely surpasses the order of grace in dignity.

The union of grace is not as close as that of the divine maternity

From this flows another difference: the union which grace establishes between God and the soul is far less close than that of the divine maternity. For the latter is nearly a substantial unity, as we have remarked with St. Albert the Great. Mary and Christ are, so to speak, one single flesh: a part of the mother's substance has been seized, elevated, transformed by the Word; she has received the seal, the imprint of divinity. God and she have kissed in this sweet and powerful embrace which resulted in a single person. The august Virgin, who gave that portion of her own substance, therefore preserves with Christ a bond indissoluble and strong as eternity. From thence comes such rights, privileges, and intimate ties which render her dearer to God than does ordinary grace for the other saints.

Habitual grace can be lost, the divine maternity cannot be lost

Grace sends forth deep and durable roots in the soul; it establishes itself with a force that embraces all the powers of a being, and it takes a violent shock to uproot it. But it can be undermined and, as sad experience shows so frequently, there are storms which break its resistance. As strong as grace might be, it is not unable to be lost. The divine maternity has nothing to fear; there is no attacking or killing it. It is inconceivable that Mary could lose her titles, her Jesus, who is her eternal estate. She will eternally be entitled to the reverence and love of her Son, which excludes, as we have said previously, the very power of sinning.[28]

---

28. See above, p. 61.

Adoptive filiation and the divine maternity

One prerogative of grace is to confer divine adoption upon us. The heroes of pagan antiquity had to have recourse to sacrilegious fables so as to call themselves the sons of a god. For us, it is a reality. We are brought by grace into the celestial family and become children and heirs. We can repeat with pride the words of St. Paul: "*Genus sumus Dei*—We are the offspring of God" (see Acts 17:28–29).

The divine maternity includes this privilege, it already supposes that Mary is an adoptive daughter of God, for we have shown that this dignity leads to all the effects of grace. We will see that natural maternity is superior to adoptive sonship.[29] The latter only results in a spiritual and mystical parentage, the maternity of the Blessed Virgin establishes a natural parentage, a consanguineous relation with Jesus Christ, and an affinity with the entire Holy Trinity. Adoptive sonship does not as strictly engage God in our regard. The divine maternity imposes upon Jesus the duties of justice that children owe by natural obligation to their parents, and it confers upon Mary rule and power over Jesus, for such is the natural right which accompanies maternal dignity.

Jesus, the most affectionate and the most obedient of all sons, most certainly does not take away that privilege from his noble mother whose love and ward he is.

Even the highest adopted children in glory merit but the cult of *dulia*. The Mother of God has the right to the cult of *hyperdulia*, which is of a superior kind and order because it honors that unique perfection in virtue of which Mary touches upon the borders of the divinity.[30] Thus, with numerous theologians, we believe that the divine maternity surpasses almost infinitely all the prerogatives of adopted children.

The other graces in Mary are only properties of her maternity

The fourth difference is that the other graces in Mary are nothing but a property of her divine maternity. What sets the measure of the

---

29. Pseudo-Albert, *Mariale*, ch. 141, ad 4: "What contains something further within it is more choiceworthy than that which contain nothing else within it. But to be the mother of God by nature contains within itself to be the adoptive child of God."
30. See St. Thomas, *ST* II-II, q. 103, a. 4, and Cajetan's commentary. TRANSLATOR'S NOTE: See n. 7, above.

graces allotted to a creature is the dignity or the function to which God has destined them.[31] The super-eminent role of the mother of Christ calls for proportionate graces, and, in divine knowledge the election of that maternity must precede the election of these sorts of graces. This entire ensemble of incomparable gifts must be a means, a preparation to the office and the glory of that maternity. God, who decrees the end before the means, willed the maternity of Mary before the other gifts. They are nothing but an overflowing from this first source. We conclude, with Suárez, that the dignity of the mother of God has above that of grace, the excellence of nature above properties, of the source above the brook, of the cause above the effect, of the final term over the dispositions which prepare for it.[32]

The divine maternity, by contrast, cannot flow from grace in any way. It could only be by way of merit; but merit will never reach that point. It is an axiom (as famous as it is incontestable) that a being cannot act outside of its own order.[33] That it realizes the ideal of this species and exhausts all the beauty of this order is all that is permitted to its efforts. An essential, ineluctable law is there to stop it and say: You will go no further. The divine maternity is beyond the sphere of merit. What is in the range and scope of merit is the increase of grace and glory, which is the term and crowning of grace. But the privilege of being mother of God goes beyond all the hierarchies of creation, since it belongs to the hypostatic and divine order. In the same way that nature will never cross beyond the bounds of grace, never will grace cross beyond the

---

31. See St. Thomas, *ST* III, q. 27, a. 4, c.: "God so prepares and endows those, whom He chooses for some particular office, that they are rendered capable of fulfilling it, according to 2 Corinthians 3:6: (*Who*) *hath made us fit ministers of the New Testament*."

32. Suárez, *Opera Omnia*, t. 19, *Mysteria Vitae Christi*, d. 2, s. 2, n. 4, 9: "This dignity of the mother of God compares to the other created graces as the first form to its properties, and conversely the other graces compare to it as dispositions to the form. Therefore, this dignity of maternity is more excellent just as form is more perfect than the properties and dispositions."

33. TRANSLATOR'S NOTE: On the axiom itself, see Signoriello's *Lexicon Peripateticum*, 234: "Nulla res habet potestatem supra suum esse.—No thing has power beyond its own being." See St. Thomas, *De potentia*, q. 6, a. 7, ad 4: "Nothing has a power that surpasses its being, since everything's power rises from its essence or presupposes it."

frontier of the hypostatic order. We observe, moreover, that this dignity and the Incarnation are two correlative terms: to merit one would be to merit the other. Now we know that the Incarnation is the infinite good that no one could or would be able to merit. It is also clear that the Blessed Virgin did not merit her election to divine maternity. The principle of merit, says the theological axiom, does not fall under merit. This election is the principle of all the graces, of all the merits, of all the glories of Mary. It is therefore entirely gratuitous, it is the distinguished, unique grace, the source and measure of all the others.

It must be recognized, however, that Mary merited the favor of this title by fittingness, by that right of friendship which has so much power over the heart of God. If the saints of the Old Testament were able to hasten the epoch of the Incarnation by their ardent desires, their fervent requests, and their endless prayers, Mary must have contributed more than all together. Moreover, by virtue of the graces already received, she merited the degree of purity and holiness which disposed her to become the worthy mother of God: "*Meruit, ex gratia sibi data, illum puritatis et sanctitatis gradum ut congrue posset esse mater Dei.*"[34]

But this is only a secondary point of view. It remains established that the graces derive from the motherhood and not vice-versa, and that is enough to raise the divine maternity above all graces.

Habitual grace is always limited, the divine maternity is a type of infinity

Another consideration will make us see this difference even better. As excellent as the highest of graces is, it is not the last word of the Almighty, there could be something better. Grace reproduces God only in a limited way, and, as divine perfection can be participated infinitely, an insurmountable distance will always remain. After perfect grace, one can conceive a grace still more perfect, higher, ever higher, and so on, without ever attaining to the summit. This is, moreover, the application of this general theory—maintained by St. Thomas, Suárez, and the majority of theologians against Durandus, Henry of Ghent, Arriaga— that God could always produce something more excellent than all that

---

34. St. Thomas, *ST* III, q. 2, a. 11, ad 3.

which we conceive of perfection, be it in the order of nature or in the order of grace.[35] But the divine maternity is an infinite dignity and, in a sense, God could not make anything better than it. And indeed, every relation draws its nature and its dignity from its term. Here the term, the Son of Mary, is infinite. The maternity must exist in such fashion. Furthermore, one cannot imagine a greater marvel, in the same way that it is impossible to go further than the infinite. The Blessed Virgin is clothed with the sun, that is to say with the dignity of her Son. All the stars of created greatness crown her and her last adornment is made from the infinite. St. Thomas says that the Blessed Virgin, by the very fact that she is the mother of God, possesses a certain infinity from the infinite good which is God, and, in this respect, He could have done nothing better, just as nothing could be better than God.[36] And Albert adds: "The Son gives to the perfection of his Mother a veritable infinity, for one knows the tree by the worth of its fruits."[37]

Thus, God can go beyond time and space but he cannot go further than the feat of the motherhood of Mary. He can give us a new earth and new heavens, he cannot make a mother more perfect than the mother of a God.[38]

Mary, in virtue of her maternity, is the eldest of creation

This suggests to us a new preeminence of the divine maternity over

---

35. TRANSLATOR'S NOTE: This is a claim that St. Thomas defends in various places. See *ST* I, q. 25, a. 6, ad 3 and 4. See also *In I Sent.*, d. 44, q. 1, a. 2,*ST* I, q. 56, a. 2, ad 4; and *De potentia*, q. 3, a. 16, ad 17.

36. St. Thomas, *ST* I, q. 25, a. 6, ad 4: "The humanity of Christ, from the fact that it is united to the Godhead; and created happiness from the fact that it is the fruition of God; and the Blessed Virgin from the fact that she is the mother of God; have all a certain infinite dignity from the infinite good, which is God. And on this account there cannot be anything better than these; just as there cannot be anything better than God."

37. Pseudo-Albert, *Mariale*, ch. 230.

38. St. Bonaventure, *Speculum*.

     TRANSLATOR'S NOTE: This work is properly to be attributed to Conrad of Saxony, a fact known at the time of Hugon's writing. The 1904 Latin text reads slightly differently; see Conrad of Saxony, *Speculum Beatae Mariae Virginis*, lect. 10, 134: "God can make a greater world, and a greater heaven he can make, but a greater mother than the mother of God he cannot make."

grace. Mary, in virtue of her maternity, is first in the divine laws and becomes the eldest of creation. Grace does not accomplish that. No doubt
grace places us above all the frontiers of nature, higher than the world,
higher than the angelic substance considered by itself. It raises the soul
to the highest summits of creation, and establishes it, in some way, the
eldest of creatures, since all the things of the universe are for the elect.
But this is only a secondary meaning and an accidental point of view,
while maternity truly constitutes the Blessed Virgin as the beloved of
creation both in the order of nature and that of grace.

It is not the case, however, that the will to create Mary preceded,
in divine thought, the decree to produce the world. Without the fall of
the man, there would be no Incarnation, and consequently no divine
maternity.[39]

We know that the contrary opinion has illustrious representatives.
In our day, it has seduced ardent souls, mystics focused on an ideal in
which the whole world would be empty if they did not find Jesus there.
Yet, have they considered carefully that the very name which is so sweet
to them, "Jesus," given by God as the proper name, the characteristic name expressing the true nature of the Word Incarnate, signifies
"Savior"? Thus, if there were no sinners to save, Jesus would not be.

This is not the place to treat this famous subject completely; a simple remark will be sufficient for us.[40] We defy those authors to bring to
us from the Scriptures, the Fathers, or the Councils, a single clear testimony which assigns another cause to the Incarnation than the salvation
of the human race. The promises of the Old Testament announce, in
the Messiah, the role of a Savior who must crush the head of the serpent
(Genesis 3:15), cleanse the numerous nations in his own blood (Isaiah
52:15), blot out the iniquity of the world (Daniel 9:24). The New
Testament calls him Jesus, affirming that his mission is to save men
from their sins (Matthew 1:21), to make himself the physician of human sickness (Luke 5:31–32), to give life to those who believe in him,
to cure the world (John 3:16–17), to redeem sinners (1 Timothy 1:15).
The Fathers express themselves with yet further clarity. St. Athanasius:

---

39. TRANSLATOR'S NOTE: See "Mary, Queen of the Universe" in the Appendix, Part II.
40. TRANSLATOR'S NOTE: See St. Thomas, *ST* III, q. 1, a. 3.

"That the Son of God was made man would not had occurred, unless the need of men had been its cause."[41] St. Cyril of Alexandria: "If we had not sinned, neither would the Son of God have been made like unto us."[42] And the incisive formula of St. Augustine is well known: "If man had not sinned, the Son of Man would not have come."[43]

As is easily noted, the Fathers not only do not invoke other motives for the Incarnation, but they expressly exclude it in virtue of their formulations: *Except.... If...not.* Furthermore, in the present matter, not to assign other reasons is to positively exclude them. It is a supernatural fact that depends uniquely upon the divine will and which revelation alone would permit us to affirm. Now, a revelation which is not mentioned in the Catholic tradition is of itself null. Silence, in this case, is a true denial. Indeed, not to indicate other motives is to ban them. Although the divine power is not limited to the present order (it could have acted otherwise), we must conclude that, in fact, the Incarnation would not have taken place without the sin of man: "So that, had sin not existed, the Incarnation would not have been."[44] The other opinion, in our view, is more seductive than sound.

In what sense, then, is Mary, after Jesus, the eldest of creatures? Although God has decreed the Incarnation as a means of saving man, He has willed that all things be directed towards Christ as towards their center and directed towards him as to their end and their ideal. In the order of intention and of final causality, Christ was the first in sight, then creation, glory, justification, and the permission of sin,

---

41. St. Athanasius, *Orationes contra Arianos*, lib. III, *PG* 26:268: "Quod autem Filius Dei homo factus est, nunquam accidisset, nisi hominum necessitas causam praebuisset."

TRANSLATOR'S NOTE: This is Hugon's Latin translation of the Greek text.

42. St. Cyril of Alexandria, *Dialogus de Sanctissima Trinitate*, Dialogue V, *PG* 75:968: "Si non peccassemus, neque factus esset nobis similis Filius Dei."

TRANSLATOR'S NOTE: This is Hugon's Latin translation of the Greek text.

43. St. Augustine, *Sermo VIII, De verbo Domini*, *PL* 28:940.

TRANSLATOR'S NOTE: Hugon quotes St. Augustine's Latin as follows: "Si homo non peccasset, Filius hominis non venisset." However, the *PL* 28:940 has "perisset" for "peccasset". This is, instead, St. Thomas's Latin quote of St. Augustine's phrase, from *ST* III, q. 1, a. 3, s.c. The sense is not greatly changed.

44. St. Thomas, *ST* III, q. 1, a. 3, c.: "Ita quod, peccato non existente, Incarnatio non fuisset."

even though it is the opposite in the order of execution and material causality.[45] Thus, without the Fall of man, Jesus would not have been. But, in decreeing the Incarnation to right this Fall, God saw further; he regarded his Christ before all things and ordained that all things which would exist be for his sake and that he would be the end of all. In this way, Jesus was the first in the eternal thought, the first in the sight of the Almighty, the foremost of the divine works.

It is in an analogous sense that Mary, inseparable from Christ in the plan of mercy, is the eldest of creation, the first in the thought and the works of God. The Eternal One decreed at one and the same time the existence of Mary and the fact of the Incarnation, and he contemplated in advance, in the same scene, the radiant figure of his Christ and the immaculate figure of Mary. The Blessed Virgin thus takes a place at the side of Jesus in the prophecies and to her apply the magnificent praises of the Wisdom Books.

She is therefore the eldest of all creatures, even in the supernatural order, because she is the ideal of all perfection and of all purity, the model of our predestination. St. Augustine calls her *formam Dei*—the mold of God. Just as the Lord used Mary to form the first of his elect, so also does he will that all his saints be cast from this same virginal mold, such that when they emerge they are like Christ, predestined.[46]

Although the Incarnation presupposes the Fall, Jesus and Mary are yet the first in the thought and the work of God

Finally, she is the eldest of creation because she is the sovereign masterpiece, the first and last work of God. The sublime divine work,

---

45. Gonet, *Clypeus Theologiae Thomisticae*, v. 5, *De Incarnatione Verbi Divini*, disp. 2, 485: "Thus, among the divine decrees there is an order of constitution, namely, such that in the genus of final causality the decree of the Incarnation was prior to the decree of creation, of glorification, of justification, and of the permission of sin, while the reverse is true in the order of material causality as already explained. Nonetheless, in the order of execution the decree of creation was prior, then the decree of justification, then the decree of reparation from that, and finally the decree of glorification."
TRANSLATOR'S NOTE: I discuss this theme in "Mary, Queen of the Universe," in Appendix, Part II

46. TRANSLATOR'S NOTE: Note that this image is also employed by St. Louis-Marie de Montfort in *True Devotion*, see nn. 218–21.

which made Isaiah shudder, is the Incarnation of Jesus and the maternity of Mary.[47] God emptied, so to speak, all his treasures of nature and grace into this work. Somehow, eternity is shaken, the ages were as if in travail to give birth to this marvel which is called *negotium saeculorum*, the great affair of the ages. And, when the Almighty had realized it, when he had made his Christ and the Mother of his Christ, the ages were able to rest, for it was the fulness of time, and God himself rested so as to admire and contemplate his masterpiece, to see that it was beautiful, for it was the occasion of saying: "God saw that it was good" (Genesis 1).

In such a manner, then, the divine maternity surpasses all the effects and all the privileges of habitual grace. She is above all grace, she is the grace of graces. Yes, it is of a divine and infinite grace that Mary must be the mother: *Mater divinae gratiae*.

---

47. "And you shall say in that day: Praise ye the Lord, and call upon his name: make his works known among the people: remember that his name is high" (Isaiah 12:4).

* * *

CHAPTER 5

The Final Plenitude

The grace of Mary increased up until the conception of her Son

The ancient authors considered that the presence of Jesus Christ, from the moment of the Incarnation, was enough to fulfill the capacities of the soul of Mary, and that grace having become perfect could not further increase. What can one add to the abyss when the abyss is full? From then on, all progress in sanctity was impossible. This is the thesis of Peter the Venerable.[1] It is also attributed to Alexander of Hales (but without foundation, we believe) and to Almain.[2] Some have even quoted the words of St. Thomas in this sense: "The grace of the Virgin was consummated at the conception of her Son, confirming her in the good."[3]

The defenders of this opinion have not considered that there are diverse degrees of plenitude. The Mother of God has always possessed the measure which was fitting to her condition at the time, and her present capacities were always fulfilled, but these abysses were themselves successively expanded. They were more vast at her birth than at her first sanctification, more profound from the moment of the Incarnation, unfathomable and immense on the day of His blessed death. Grace was increased in the same proportions, and she never acquired her definitive plenitude except at the instant when she took her place in glory.

Say what one will, the doctrine of St. Thomas is very clear on this point. If he calls the second sanctification a *consummate* grace, it is not that it must mark the term of merit and exclude all further progress, but because, being a new cause of impeccability, it confirms the will anew and immutably in the good—*confirmans eam in bono*. He distinguishes, as we have done in following him, three plenitudes or three degrees of perfection in the holiness of Mary: the grace of the first sanctification, which disposed her to become the worthy Mother of God; the grace of the second sanctification by the presence of the Son of God incarnate in her womb and by virtue of which her will ever fixed in what is perfect; lastly, the final grace, which was consummated at the moment of glorification and perfected in the enjoyment of the sovereign good. Progress did not stop with the Incarnation, but, beginning with her glorious existence, it only ended with mortal life, for the second fullness—adds the great Doctor—is superior to the first, and the final fullness prevails over the second sanctification: "That the second perfection excels the first, and the third the second, is clear."[4] Can one declare in more explicit terms that there has been growth until the day of celestial glorification?

The causes of this increase

From whence arises, then, the impossibility? Either on the part of grace, which would have attained the highest degree, or on the part of Mary, who would have arrived at the end. But, first of all, grace has capacities that expand it indefinitely. Its measure, like that of love, is to be without measure, *modus sine modo diligere*, as Saint Bernard says.[5] Jesus

---

1.   Peter the Venerable, lib. III, Letter VII, *PL* 189:285–287; at 286d.

2.   See Alexander of Hales, *Summa Universae Theologiae*, III, q. 8, mem. 3, a. 2, ad 1. See also Jacques Almain, III, Dis. 3, q. 3.

     TRANSLATOR'S NOTE: Hugon maintains the same qualification regarding Alexander of Hales in his *Tractatus Dogmatici*, t. 2, *Tractatus De B. Virgine Deipara*, q. 2, a. 3, n. 5, fn. 2.

3.   St. Thomas, *ST* III, q. 27, a. 5, ad 2: "There was a threefold perfection of grace in the Blessed Virgin. For at first in her sanctification she received grace inclining her to good: in the conception of the Son of God she received consummate grace confirming her in good; and in her glorification her grace was further consummated so as to perfect her in the enjoyment of all good."

4.   Ibid.

5.   St. Bernard of Clairvaux, *De diligendo Deo*, cap. 1, n. 1.

Christ alone, the universal principle of salvation, was able to realize in his soul all the powers of grace. No creature, not even Mary, is capable of exhausting that which expands without end. Therefore, on the part of grace, there is no obstacle to growth. On the other hand, the Mother of God, even after the conception and birth of her Son, remains in the ordinary conditions of one on the way. The end, for her as for the saints, only arrives when grace is succeeded by glory. And then, should riches so extraordinary be condemned to remain unproductive? Should her many services to Christ be deprived of merit? Should all her works and sufferings endured for him not contribute to making her more agreeable to God and thereby the more full of grace?

We must therefore consider it indubitable that there was progress up until the moment of death. Three causes contributed to this increase: merit, the use of the sacraments, and the supernatural mysteries in which the Mother of the human race has taken such a large part. These are the various points which remain to be studied in order to form an adequate idea of the final plenitude.

I. Continuous Merit

The notion and scope of merit

Merit requires free, morally good acts, made in a state of grace, in the sight of God, by a person who is still a wayfarer. All the actions of the Blessed Virgin combine these qualities. As for freedom, Mary has enjoyed it from the moment of her conception and, after Christ, no one has been free as much as she, for no one has been exempt as she from original sin, from ignorance, error, and from concupiscence, which are the enemies of liberty. All her works are good and excellent. The initial plenitude already sufficed to exclude sin, and subsequently the conception of the Word completed the confirmation of her will in the good. The state of grace and divine maternity are inseparable notions. But this grace does not remain inert. It excites charity, which, itself endowed with an activity ever awake, inspires and stimulates the other virtues, directs all actions, and impresses upon all of them a generous impulse to carry them towards God and eternity. Finally, we know that Mary remained until death in the state of a wayfarer, progressing. Thus, she has all the conditions for merit.

Merit extends as far as the supernatural motion God uses to direct us to our end. Now, this delicate and powerful touch is communicated to us not only for the sake of the supreme term, but for the entire course and progress of the motion. The term is glory; the course and all progress is the increase of grace. That is to say that the merit attains to glory as well as the increase of grace and charity.[6] So, for each of her actions the Mother of God merited a new degree of glory for eternity and a new grace for her soul here below.

It remains for us to show that this merit was continuous. Let us recall first of all the famous doctrine that, in practice, no truly deliberate act can be indifferent: as long as a work is reasonable, it is imputable to man, it is good or bad, and it demands a sanction. We know that for Mary all acts are good. Now, in the righteous, all good deeds are meritorious: *habentibus charitatem omnis actus est meritorius vel demeritorius.*[7] The state of justice, in fact, calls for charity, and charity is active, it cannot fail to provoke, to excite our powers, to incline them towards God. It directs from the beginning our intention towards the last end, and by this primal movement it communicates its influence to all the virtues, just as the will imposes its command on all the powers of the soul. This impulse continues even after the will's command has ceased; it still remains in the virtues and their acts, such that all our works are vivified by charity and become meritorious. Stimulated by its native forces to enter into activity, charity often renews its effective impulse so that our intention is sufficiently directed towards God, so that all good acts are seized by this general momentum and taken to eternity.

In the just all good acts are meritorious

This is how all the actions of the just are drawn into the stream that sanctifies, how, in virtue of the impress received they remain oriented towards the end of charity and related to God, even without the

---

6.   See St. Thomas, *ST* I-II, q. 114, a. 8.
7.   St. Thomas, *De Malo*, q. 2, a. 5, ad 7: "In those having charity every act is either to one's merit or demerit."

need of active consideration of that end. Eating and drinking according to the measure of temperance, they recreate decently according to the norms of *eutrapelia*, apart from all vulgarity, and trifling nothings have no place there.[8] All are grand, all are noble, for these actions have for their measure the eternity which is at stake.

In Mary all acts are deliberate, good, and meritorious

Let us review in a single argument that beautiful and consoling teaching: every good act is rooted to the end of a virtue, and every virtue converges to the end of charity (for she is the queen who commands all the virtues, as the will commands all the powers). The actions which escape this universal imperium are necessarily apart from the last end, disorderly, stained with demerit.[9] In the Mother of God, there is nothing disordered: All her deliberate acts are good, all those good acts are crowned with merit. What then will be the sum of her spiritual treasures at the end of her glorious career?

But, if even the least fault never severed the thread of her merits, was there not at least an interruption due to unintentional acts? St. Ambrose, Suárez, Contenson, and many other theologians, regard it as

8. *Eutrapelia*, in the vocabulary of Aristotle and St. Thomas, is the particular virtue which governs decent recreation and presides over allowed relaxations.
    Translator's Note: See Aristotle, *Nicomachean Ethics*, IV.8, and St. Thomas's commentary on Book IV, Lecture 16. The virtue of *eutrapelia* is the mean with regard to amusement, and the one who has it is called a ready wit: "The man who jokes well by his saying what is not unbecoming to a well-bred man, or by his not giving pain, or even giving delight, to the hearer." (1128a25) The man who goes too far is the buffoon, and the humorless man is the boor; these are the two vices opposed to this social virtue of amusement, or, perhaps, being of good cheer.

9. St. Thomas, *In II Sent.*, d. 40, q. 1, a. 5, c.: "In the one who has grace, an act must be either meritorious or demeritorious, because, just as what is evil will be demeritorious, thus also will what is good be meritorious. For, as charity commands all the virtues just as the will all the powers of the soul, it is necessary that what act soever that is ordered to the end of some virtue be ordered to the end of charity. And, since every good act is ordered to the end of some virtue, it will remain ordered to the end of charity and thus it will be meritorious. And thus, to eat and to drink while keeping to the measure of temperance, and to play and recreate while keep to the measure of *eutrapelia* (which holds the mean in play, as is said in the *Ethics*, Book II), will be meritorious in the one who has charity, which establishes God as the last end of his life." See our *Tractatus Dogmatici*, t. 2, *Tractatus De Gratia*, q. 7, "On Merit, the Other Effect of Grace," 253ff.

certain that there was never an unintentional act in her, at least during her waking hours.[10] Why, therefore, is it such that our acts prevent the intellect and the will from exercising control? It is due to ignorance, concupiscence, and the passions. Nothing of the sort was true of Mary. Her infused knowledge guarded her against all improvidence and her Immaculate Conception, along with the privilege of absolute integrity, assured her immunity from concupiscence and the storms of the senses. As her soul was submissive to God, so also was her body submissive to the soul and the inferior faculties to reason. There was in her nothing of the imperfect or unintentional. Such is the harmonious order in a creature who is an abridged world of nature and grace: *microcosmus gratiae*.

An intelligence so lively, incapable of idleness, always bore upon some object, and the will followed upon such knowledge: from this follows the continuous exercise of free choice, the absolute continuity of good and meritorious acts.

This ceaseless waking activity did not prevent repose

This ever watchful activity did not absorb the Mother of God to the point of paralyzing her exterior life. The regular exercise of her faculties was not harmed in the least, just as in Jesus Christ the beatific vision and infused knowledge did not at all impede the normal course of human life.[11] This miraculous knowledge of which we are speaking exerts itself solely in the spiritual sphere of the soul, without the concurrence of the imagination and sensation. The inferior faculties preserve all of their autonomy and their particular pursuits remain no less natural or easy.

One should also understand that the uninterrupted working of infused knowledge should not prevent either the periodic repose of the faculties nor even sleep. That this repose was very limited due to that perfect and harmonious constitution and that even during that time

---

10. Translator's Note: Hugon briefly discusses and cites some of these opinions in his *Tractatus Dogmatici*, t. 2, *Tractatus De B. Virgine Deipara*, q. 2, a. 3, n. 8, 764.

11. Translator's Note: See the Appendix, Part II, "*Ancilla Domini et Ancilla Theologiae*: Mary and Philosophy." for a consideration of this theme.

love frequently provoked awakening, we will believe willingly, but we will not admit, as certain old mystics, that the Virgin never enjoyed true sleep or repose. Nature demands it, and the supernatural state would not set up obstacles to it. As St. Francis de Sales says, it is

> a sleep of love, so that even her spouse wishes that she should sleep as long as she pleases.—Ah! take heed, "I adjure you,' says he, 'that you stir not up nor make the beloved to awake till she please." No, Theotimus, this heavenly Queen never slept but with love, since she never gave repose to her precious body, but to reinvigorate it, the better afterwards to serve her God, which is certainly a most excellent act of charity.[12]

Sleep did not check the continuity of merit: infused knowledge

"While the body slept, the mind was awake," says St. Ambrose.[13] "Even during her sleep," adds St. Bernardine of Siena, "the Virgin enjoyed a more elevated contemplation than any other mortal did when awake."[14] If Solomon had had the use of reason in that beautiful dream, the holy bishop of Geneva concludes, "how much more probability is there then that the mother of the true Solomon had the use of reason in her sleep?"[15]

---

12. St. Francis de Sales, *Treatise on the Love of God*, Book III, ch. 8, p. 148; see Song of Songs 2:7.

13. St. Ambrose, *De Virginibus*, lib. II, c. 2, n. 8, *PL* 16:209: "Cum quiesceret corpus, vigilaret animus."

14. St. Bernardine of Siena, t. 3, Sermon VII, *In Festo Purificationis*, 342: "Quia dormiendo contemplabatur plus in Deo, quam quisquam alius vigilans."

15. St. Francis de Sales, *Treatise on the Love of God*, Book III, ch. 8, p. 150.

TRANSLATOR'S NOTE: The context in full, pp. 149–50: "But mark, I pray you, that I neither say nor mean to say that this privileged soul of the Mother of God was deprived of the use of reason in her sleep. Many are of opinion that Solomon in that beautiful dream, though really a dream, in which he demanded and received the gift of his incomparable wisdom, had the true use of his free-will, on account of the judicious eloquence of the discourse he made, of his choice full of discretion, and of the most excellent prayer which he used, the whole without any mixture of inconsistency or distraction of mind. But how much more probability is there then that the mother of the true Solomon had the use of reason in her sleep, that is to say, as Solomon herself makes her say, that her heart watched while she slept?" St. Francis de Sales references 1 Kings 3:5–15, and then Song of Songs 5:2: "I sleep, and my heart watcheth."

We cite favorably the same opinion of Suárez, Contenson, and Terrien.[16]

This doctrine will be admitted by all those who understand well the nature of infused knowledge. This is an operation entirely independent of sensible conditions, receiving no support from the inferior faculties nor having to ask service of the imagination. It is not hampered when the senses are, it does not sleep when they do, it remains alert while they are drowsy. It is an imitation of angelic knowledge: completely clear, a day without end and without night, without fatigue or slumber. If Mary enjoyed this privilege from her conception, it is still possible during her repose, for in that state her mind is no less free nor the will less perfect than in the first instant. Thus, since the blessed moment which began her existence up until that which marked her death, Mary did not know the least interruption either in her acts of free will or in her growth in merit, since all her free acts were meritorious.

Mary, heart of the Church

According to a beautiful image, Mary is the heart of the Church, the supernatural and perfect organ which never ceases in its activity, as in a man the heart always keeps working day and night without ceasing, even while the other members suspend their own work. If our body could say: "I sleep, but my heart is awake; I rest, but my heart labors," the Church would say this more truly still: "I sleep," that is, my other members sometimes cease in their meritorious acts. Sleep, fatigue, distractions, and negligence prevent all their acts from being deliberate, and it is all too often that deliberate acts are not even completely good or meritorious. "But my heart, Mary, is always awake, nothing happens that suspends her work of sanctity, whether day or night." Thanks to Mary, there was at least one creature in the Church to practice to the letter the counsel of the Apostle, "May all that you do be for the glory of God."

---

16. See Suárez, *Opera Omnia*, t. 19, *Mysteria Vitae Christi*, d. 18, s. 2, 283–87; Contenson, *Theologia Mentis et Cordis*, t. 3, lib. X, diss. 6, ch. 1, 264; Terrien, *La Mère de Dieu*, t. 2, 205.

How grace is increased by actions

Now we must recall that grace always increases by the meritorious acts produced in virtue of a preexisting habit. If the act surpasses the habit itself in intensity, the soul acquires each time a new and double merit equal to the sum of all the preceding merits. We have established that the graces of the Virgin Mary from the first instant are superior to all those of the angels and of men taken even collectively. The intensity of the initial movement in a creature so well disposed surely equals the intensity of the grace itself, and the impulse is transmitted with a force that multiplies itself each time. In this way, the prodigious sum of the origin is doubled in the second act, and so forth, indefinitely without limit or ceasing. This is the supernatural trade that Mary practiced with such industry.

The sum total: Miéchow's table

How, then, to appraise the definitive total in such a long and saintly life? Our ancient authors have attempted this subject with ingenious theories, naïve without doubt but very faithful, based upon theological reality. We cite here, as an example and as a curiosity, the multiplication of Justin de Miéchow, of our order:

> Let the first action be one hundred. The following would be two hundred, four hundred…sixty-four thousand, one hundred and twenty-eight thousand, etc. In proceeding this way, you arrive at the thirtieth step at merely a total of twenty six billion four hundred forty-two million seven hundred forty-seven thousand six hundred.[17] And what would it be if we would calculate it out to the hundredth, or the millionth step? Thus, at the end of her life, this increase would be inexplicable and incomprehensible.[18]

Now, for such a calculation we begin the summation from a rather low

---

17. TRANSLATOR'S NOTE: If the series' first member is 100, and it increases each iteration by a factor of two, then the thirtieth member (the result of multiplying 100 by 2 a total of 29 times) would be a bit higher: $100 \times 2^{29} = 53,687,091,200$.

18. Miéchow, *Conférences sur les litanies de la Très Sainte Vierge*, 137th Conference, p. 445.

starting point, so as not to baffle the intelligence too much. But the intensity of her first act is already prodigious, more than a thousand, more than a billion, since she already surpasses the merits of the angels and of men taken together.

II. THE EXCELLENCE OF HER PERSON

The continuity of acts does not express all the value of merit. One must consider yet again the nobility of the person and the excellence of her works. It is to the person which the operations, properties, rights, and privileges are attributed. It is also to the supernatural dignity of the person that merit owes its excellence. Merit somehow takes on the proportions of the person, her scope, her profundity—it has no other measure than that, and it attains infinity when personhood itself is infinite. Thus, in Jesus Christ all acts have an infinite value by reason of the person whose properties they are. Mary is, after her Son, the highest and most sublime manifestation of God.

The dignity of the Mother of God

The excellences of the grace of that indefinable perfection which arises in her due to her divine maternity form in her a type of dignity entirely apart, which raises her above all the saints and gives to her actions a value which the works of other creatures could not have. We would not claim, with some authors,[19] that she has graces and actions of a species and order entirely new, but it should be conceded that her grace is wholly singular.[20]

Mary holds primacy of place in regard to filial adoption

Fr. Chardon, O.P., has written many interesting pages in this

---

19. For example, see De Véga, *Theologia Mariana*, t. 2, n. 1179, 20.
20. TRANSLATOR'S NOTE: By this Hugon evidently does not mean to deny that Our Lady's graces belong to the hypostatic order, something he had defended in the previous chapter. Rather, he seems to have in mind a position that is distinct from that of De Véga's, who (at the place cited) claims that at least after the Incarnation, Mary had a new type of infused grace that was incompatible with the presence of faith due to the excellence of its new sort of infused knowledge.

regard, the most theological and original of which we know concerning this subject:

> Common grace gives adoptive children to God, but the singular grace of Mary places her in a relationship of affinity with God. Common grace can flow forth upon an infinity of subjects. The grace proper to the Mother of God cannot belong to any person but Mary. And, as in the divine nature there is but one God, and in the hypostatic union there is but one Person of God, thus in the order of affinity with God there is none but Mary .... This exceptional condition into which Mary is placed does not remove her divine adoption; on the contrary, it perfects it and gives it a greater radiance. One cannot deny that she is the adoptive daughter of God, and we must also proclaim at the same time that she is the Mother of God. As an adopted daughter, she is thereby predestined to grace and glory, and as possessing a relationship of affinity with God, she is predestined to be the Mother of God.[21]

After having explained how in Jesus Christ filial adoption is precluded by natural filiation, and how the two filiations, natural and adoptive, are incompatible in the same subject (although the grace of union which makes for natural filiation is not contrary to the habitual grace which makes for adoptive filiation in any other person than that of Jesus), Chardon concludes:

> Since Mary is, after her Son, the first subject of sanctifying grace, and since this grace does not find in the mother the obstacle or, if you will, the incompatibility which it finds in the Son so as to produce adoption, it is easy to see that Mary is, by grace, *the first adoptive daughter of God.* Assuredly, she is not the first in the filiation of grace. That primacy belongs to her Son, as St. John says: "We have seen the only Son of the Father, full of grace."

---

21. See Chardon, O.P., *La croix de Jésus*, ed. Bourgeois (Paris: Lethielleux, 1895), pp. 294ff.

Nor is she the first in regard to the original source of the grace of adoption. That is why she not only receives from her Son the denomination of adopted child, as do others, but she also participates, in a certain way, in the primacy of filiation which distinguishes her Son by nature from other children. To be sure, she is not, as He is, the natural offspring of God. But just as He is the first and only Son of God by nature, she is by analogy the first adopted daughter in the order of grace, that grace of which He is the original and uncreated source.

It remains to be said, regarding this incompatibility between adoptive and natural filiation in the sacred soul of Jesus, that Jesus conceived of the design of giving to his Mother this adoptive filiation, so that she would become the first adopted daughter by grace. It was reserved to Him to be the primordial and abundant source, he willed such to her as an effect.... Mary is the first subject of the effect of the grace of adoption, just as Jesus is the unique subject who possesses personal grace. Just as he is the unique Son by nature, she is the first adoptive daughter. She bore on earth and now bears in heaven the character of an adopted child of God, as Jesus bears the character of the child of God by nature.... One clearly sees, then, that the primacy of adoptive filiation must have for its foundation a grace which would be superior to those of all the other adopted children and inferior to that which is proportioned to the excellence of the Son of God by nature. Mary being the Mother of Him who is the fulness of all grace and being joined to him so closely in that holy humanity which she gave to him, she had to be, without any doubt, endued with a grace that would have some resemblance to the divine likeness who had established her august maternity.[22]

This excellence adds to the worth of her merits. Heaven sees in her the first adoptive daughter of of God. All that comes from her is so divine, so delightful to the Lord, and thus more meritorious.

---

22. See ibid., ch. 25, "On the Primacy in Adoptive Filiation."

She possesses more excellently than all others the conditions of merit: liberty and charity

Furthermore, she possesses more excellently than all others the conditions of merit. Let it suffice to examine the two principal conditions: liberty and charity. Liberty, that which makes an act human, also powerfully confers meritorious dignity upon it. When a soul chooses the good with complete spontaneity and its whole volition, this is more than just generosity. Nothing meaning more to us than our liberty, it honors God in the most exquisite way to give the most of ourselves, and consequently to obtain that lofty reward bearing us towards him with even more liberty. Who did this better than Mary? Free choice in her reaches its height, free of ignorance and shackling passions. Its domain is so thoroughly universal and absolute that it does not suffer a single indeliberate act. All this perfection is for God. Mary, in each one of her actions, gives to him with all the ardor of her will and with all the impetus of a perfect liberty possessed of all the powers of nature and grace. Such intensity of liberty is necessarily answered by an intensity of merit.

Yet, it is above all charity which gives to actions their prize. Charity has the first and last word in everything; it is the basis of the commandments and the end of the law. It must be the principle, term, and measure of merit. Indeed, actions have the more worth the more that they bear upon God, and it is by charity that they are aimed right at heaven. The degree of charity is therefore also the degree of merit. Furthermore, perfection here below is a resemblance of that found *in patria*. There above, charity is the cause of perfection and joy, while here below it gives worth to our works. The other virtues have need of the sweet warmth of charity in order to bloom with the fruit and perfume of merit. Without it, their acts could indeed have savor, but only that belonging to imperfect fruits, the ones born late which never ripen. All that is sustained by its influence lies within the sphere of merit, which is of such size and weight that it measures and weighs the eternal reward. Small actions, common actions done with more charity are greater and weightier before God in the scales of heavenly justice than incredible feats done with little charity. Likewise, recompense due to acts is by reason of charity, which is incomparable next to the recompense owed them by reason of their object: "The reward corresponding to merit by reason of charity, however little it be, is greater than any reward corresponding to the act by reason of its genus."[23] The whole existence of Mary is a tapestry of charity: the Mother of beautiful love lived with love as she died with love.

We have shown that, from the first instant, her charity had already attained to a heroic degree, since she was already at the height of grace. The first act began with such impetus possessed of a prodigious intensity that it doubled each time (according to the inventive calculation reported above). It did so without ceasing, for there was never an interruption of free actions. Her charity, therefore, seized all the virtues, all their acts, and made them its own, truly weaving her glorious life out of love itself. Recall what we said previously about the virginal and maternal love of Mary.[24] Finally, in numerous circumstances—the Incarnation, the sorrowful Passion, the scenes of Pentecost, her ardent communions, and so many other events of her life—this abyss of tenderness grew infinitely. Her body could not resist such vehemence and the happy victim at last died of love.

III. The Excellence of Her Works

To appreciate all the import of this merit, one must consider once more the excellence of Mary's works.

The hierarchy of virtues

Just as there is a hierarchy among the virtues, so also is there an order among actions. While charity alike belongs to each of them, preeminence belongs without doubt to the work whose object is the most noble, just as virginity surpasses conjugal continence and the act of contemplation outweighs the simple active life. The Mother full of grace undertook the most noble works—she had the perfect form of all the virtues. In her, one can say, all is purity and simplicity, grace and truth, justice and mercy. She is truly the garden of delights where one can admire an entire variety of flowers and enjoy the perfume of all the

---

23. St. Thomas, *In IV Sent.*, d. 49, q. 5, a. 1, ad 5.
24. **Translator's Note:** See above, Chapter 3, p.49.

virtues.[25] Her faith is beyond all praise, for it was prepared to conceive the Eternal One. Her humility drew God to her bosom. Prudence is one among her titles: *Virgo prudentissima*—Virgin most prudent. Her justice reigns as queen of all the saints, her temperance queen over virgins, her strength queen of martyrs. The natural virtues and the infused virtues are arrayed in her with all the energy and extent that they could have, with the diverse forms and in the various states in which they can be exercised: virgin, spouse, mother, active, or contemplative. They all find in Mary their ideal.

The four periods in the life of Mary: her ministry on behalf of the God-Man was more meritorious than the perfect actions of the saints; her heroism during the passion; her progress after the Ascension

Her life is divided into four periods. The first she spends in the Shadow of the Lord, in the temple of Jerusalem, entirely consecrated to prayer and the study of both the divine law and the Scriptures. It is like a prolonged and continuous act of contemplation, the way of union, the life of the perfect.

The second period begins with the Incarnation and corresponds to the joyful mysteries of the Rosary. The single act of consent given to the message of Gabriel: *Fiat mihi secundum verbum tuum*, possessed such an excellence that, at that moment, says St. Bernardine of Siena, the Virgin merited more than all creatures—angels or men—in all their deeds, acts, and thoughts.[26] From that day, and above all after the birth of Jesus, contemplation became for the Mother of God the food by

---

25. See the beautiful homily of St. Sophrone on the Blessed Virgin, *PG* 87/3:3217ff.

26. St. Bernardine of Siena, t. 2, serm. 51, ch. 1.

TRANSLATOR'S NOTE: I have not been able to locate Hugon's reference; however, see St. Bernardine of Siena, *Sancti Bernardini Senensis Ordinis Seraphici Minorum Sermones*, t. 4 (Venice: Andreae Poletti, 1745), 91, as part of Sermon V, *De Nativitate B. V. Mariae*, ch. 3. See also Fr. James Mercer, "St. Bernardine of Siena and Marian Mediation," in *Mary at the Foot of the Cross, VII: Coredemptrix, Therefore Mediatrix of All Graces*, ed. P. D. Fehlner (New Bedford, MA: Academy of the Immaculate, 2008), pp. 251–71, who translates this passage as follows, at p. 253: "The glorious Virgin merited more in her single act of consent, namely of the conception of the Son of God, than all creatures, whether angels or men, in all their acts, movements and thoughts."

which she was nourished, the sphere in which she moved. Who will describe her conversations with the Word Incarnate, where, face to face and heart to heart with him, she learns the secrets of eternity, penetrates into the holy profundity of that adorable love, and from there plunges into the abyss of the Godhead? Oh! One must stop here a few moments with Mary in this most exquisite of tabernacles: the heart, soul, and divinity of Jesus, the very source of holiness and bliss.

The devotion of the active life unites with the ecstasy of contemplation, as the visit to Elizabeth and John the Baptist shows, and in the care that she lavishes upon her Son, carrying him, nursing him, caring for him, clothing him, rocking him, and later accompanying him and assisting him during his preaching. Likewise, one may consider, along with other pious authors, that the sole fact of nursing the Word of Life was more meritorious than the supplications of the martyrs, not only because of the principle of the act (heroic charity), but also because of its terminus, the sweet person of her child. Her ministry to Christ himself surpasses that of all other ministries, just as the virtues that attain to God himself exceed in their nobility those whose object is not divine worship. Blessed, indeed, is the bosom that bore Jesus, the breasts that nursed him, the lips that kissed him, the hands that tended to him. Joyful the creature that filled this role for so many years. Who else was able to offer to her God the service and devotion of both virgin and mother?

The Passion was an especially heroic and fruitful time. That exceedingly heroic act was the one by which this mother offered her only Son for the salvation of the human race. Knowing from its origins the eternal plan of redemption, she had long since made that sacrifice which cost her all the sufferings of nature and grace, and, as she was without ceasing concerned to obey the divine will and save poor souls, she frequently renewed this offering of sorrow and love. She accompanied the God-Man in all his agony and martyrdom, and her mystical immolation upon Calvary is the utmost of sorrow here below. It even seems that hers was the utmost of human suffering. Her heart had to break, for her grace and divine maternity added to her nature such exalted tenderness and sensitivity. Yes, she could say that there is no other sorrow like that of her own. Why, if such sufferings and bitterness are as the ocean, her love and her merits are all the more profound.

In the fourth period, which begins with the first of the glorious mysteries, she becomes the transfigured ideal of contemplation. She follows her Son to heaven in her mind and heart, and she still enjoys him here below thanks to the union and the embraces of the Eucharist. She is, as it were, caught between heaven and earth, imitating the life of the blessed, thinking of God and loving him. Her face shines already with the first rays of glory. She lives in its splendor and she could say, with the Psalmist, that night itself becomes her light in the bosom of her delight.[27] At the same time, she practices the perfect works of the active life, for she instructs the apostles, encourages the faithful, directing the newborn Church. In such a way she ends her days, in the exercise of the heights of activity and contemplation, up until the moment when a last moment of ecstasy delivers her from the earth and leads to her definitive union with God—as one flame is joined to flame, as love is joined to love.

The worth of her acts elevated by the special motion of the Holy Spirit

The already extraordinary worth of her actions is again elevated and transformed by the special motion of the Holy Spirit. The Paraclete dwells in each just soul, but the degree of this union is proportioned to grace. When this reaches its apogee, his indwelling is perfect. It is thus in Mary where the Trinity has dwelt completely. Such must be the most sublime of unions after that which eternally binds the humanity of Jesus to the divine person. The Holy Spirit, who is the principle of every action, perfectly deployed his divine powers in such a perfect soul and, so that she might be more apt to receive such influence from on high and be led with more docility, he adds to her virtues his seven gifts, which becomes the seeds of heroism. The gifts are the measure of grace to the utmost degree. They take possession of one's acts, elevate them, and communicate to them a new excellence. In this way, Mary's works are as flowers whose fruit is sublimity, or like a lyre whose song is heroism itself. That is to say, the sublime was natural to her, and heroism was like the warp and woof of her life.

---

27. TRANSLATOR'S NOTE: See Psalm 138:11: "And I said: Perhaps darkness shall cover me: and night shall be my light in my pleasures."

Such is, then, the perfection of merit in the august Mother of God: continuous actions, dignity of person, excellence of works made greater still by the influence of the gifts and divine touch of the Holy Spirit.

IV. The Sacraments and Mysteries

Along with merit there was a second cause of the increase of grace in Mary: the sacraments. They are the conveyances of celestial virtue; grace flows through these signs, and at the moment when they reach the body, grace touches the soul. One can be certain that Mary, so faithful to the prescriptions of the Old Law, gave to the first Christians the example of true devotion and respect towards the sacraments.

What sacraments could Mary have received?

It is clear, on the other hand, that she could not have received all of them. During the time when she lived with St. Joseph, marriage had not yet been elevated to the dignity of a sacrament. Penance, which exists to repair our shame and our ruin, would never have been possible for a soul that is purity itself and the sanctuary of the Holy of Holies. Queen of apostles and patriarchs, Mother of the clergy, the Blessed Virgin possessed in a superior manner all the graces that the priesthood can confer upon us, and it goes without saying that her sex did not permit her to receive holy orders.

St. Albert, St. Antoninus, and St. Bernardine of Siena, among others, have thought that she received extreme unction.[28] We think, along with numerous theologians, that she could not have been the recipient of this sacrament. First of all, extreme unction of the dying is a remedy against the consequences and remnants of sin, and it counters in the soul weaknesses and torpor that could not be conceived in her case. Second, the Mother of the Almighty had no need to dread the temptations or assaults of hell and its legions. Finally, the recipients of this

---

28. Pseudo-Albert, *Mariale*, chs. 72 and 64; St. Antoninus of Florence, *Summa Theologica Moralis*, III, tit. 14, c. 8; St. Bernardine of Siena, *Mariale*, IVa, serm. 9.
    Translator's Note: The latter two references to St. Antoninus of Florence, O.P., and to St. Bernardine I have been unable to locate.

sacrament are the faithful who are gravely ill. In her case, there is no infirmity. Even age did not affect her body, and love alone was capable of drawing the soul from its beautiful temple where nothing had announced or prepared for its ruin. If a final grace was necessary to crown her sanctity upon her death, God could provide it himself without the intermediary of a sensible sign that presupposes the imperfection and infirmity of soul and body.

There is an analogous controversy as regards confirmation. We think that the mystery of Pentecost was her official investiture with the Holy Spirit, the official coronation that produced all the effects of confirmation, and that there was no further need of the exterior sacramental form.

No doubt concerning baptism and the eucharist

As to baptism, it was not necessary for Mary. She had no need of rebirth by water since, preserved from the original loss, she was not dead in Adam. Her maternity, which is title enough for the entire inheritance of Christ, constituted her by rights as a member of the Church. There was no need of a sensible rite to so incorporate her. Still, this in no way left her without the character and grace of that sacrament. On the other hand, it is fitting that she received baptism so as to have, as do all the faithful, the eternal seal of its character and acquiring by it a particular resemblance with Christ and other Christians, to impress her once more with the mark of the Passion (of which baptism is the reminder and symbol), and to give to all an example of obedience and humility.[29] Theologians also are more or less unanimous on this subject, as can be seen from the evidence reported in the work of St. Canisius.[30] Received with such extraordinary

---

29. See St. Thomas, *In IV Sent.*, d. 6, q. 1, a. 1, qa. 3, ad 3: "It should be said that those sanctified in the womb should be baptized for three reasons. First, in order to acquire the character, by which they will be numbered among the people of God and entitled in a certain way to receive the divine sacraments. Second, so that by receiving baptism they may be conformed to the Passion of Christ bodily as well. Third, on account of the good of obedience, for the command about baptism was given to all and should be fulfilled by all, unless an emergency should exclude the sacrament."

30. St. Peter Canisius, *Mariale*, lib. 1, ch. 2.

dispositions, the sacrament had to produce graces that led to the over-flowing of an already-filled abyss.

There is no doubt as regards the Eucharist. It is certain that to Mary, among the faithful, belongs the honor of being the first to put into practice daily communion. All authors are pleased to see her among those who persevered in prayer and in communion and the breaking of bread (Acts 2:42). This sacramental presence of her Beloved reminded her of all her raptures in the first moment of the Incarnation; it renewed the joys of her maternity and the delights of their first embrace. Once again, Jesus flooded the soul of his Mother with all his love and graces, and the Virgin responded with urges of tenderness and gratitude. The torrents of the supernatural fell down without ceasing upon her soul, and each day its capacities for grace were enlarged and filled once more. We will not try to gauge this daily increase. It is enough for us to say that once God had filled one abyss, he was hollowing out another so as to be always giving.

Contact with Jesus, cause of grace

A last title to the augmentation of grace—and this again *ex opere operato*—was the principal mysteries of the Incarnation and the Redemption. Contenson, summarizing the traditional teaching, points to a number of these causes: the conception of the Word; the presence of the Lord in the womb of Mary, in her arms, upon her heart; the death of Jesus, and the descent of the Holy Spirit.[31] We have already shown, in our examination of the second sanctification, how the union of Mary with the humanity and divinity of the World had sanctified her. Such physical contact required the spiritual contact of grace, such that progress without ceasing occurred during those nine months, that afterwards her maternal role of nourishing Jesus, carrying him, caring for him, were titles enough to the production of grace.

---

31. Contenson, *Theologia Mentis et Cordis*, t. 3, lib. X, diss. 6, ch. 1, sp. 2, 264–65: "The grace of Mary was enlarged in many ways *ex opera operato*: in her conception of the Word, in her reception of the Eucharist, in the presence of the Savior born in her womb, in her arms, suckling at her breasts, dying on the cross, and in the coming of the Holy Spirit, by which one may easily gather the summit and abyss of grace that Mary had at the end of her life."

However, we must repeat the remark made previously on this subject. It is difficult, even impossible, to determine to what degree of continuity God worked in the soul of his Mother. We do not claim that it was at each instant, but we think that this presence of the Word, whether it be in her maternal womb, or later on in the ordinary affairs of life, was a permanent cause of sanctity. Such a supremely effective principle, it seems, must often work its effects, and all the more infallibly that it encounters no obstacle on the part of the subject. Yes, this ceaseless contact with the sweet Humanity of Christ, we join with Canisius in saying, sufficed to render the Virgin more pure, holy, and divine.

The drama of Calvary, the martyrdom of Mary, her spiritual maternity gives her the right to new graces

The drama of Calvary was for her a mystery of sanctity. The crucifixion of Jesus is the central point of Redemption, the principal source of salvation—the solemn moment where the Passion was completed, where the veil that separated man from God is torn, where heaven opens—which must be the moment of grace *par excellence*. Naturally, such waves poured forth most of all upon Mary, who shared first and foremost, before all others, in the mystery of the cross.

She assuredly merited it, for she also suffered her own dolorous passion, she was immolated for the human race, she is a martyr. Supreme witness of love, a martyr is a cause of grace for the saints. Should not the holocaust of Mary realize in an eminent way all that found in the martyrdom of the sword? Hers is superior to it in love, and so must surpass it in grace.[32]

Moreover, at that moment Jesus created in Mary a new maternal heart. By saying those great words, *Behold, your son*, he had to pour into her heart a love vast enough to embrace humanity entire, strong enough to come to the aid of all the unfortunate, tender enough to soften the bitterness of all crushed hopes. But this charity must have some cause,

---

32. The Fathers and Doctors of the Church are unanimous in giving Mary the title of martyr. See Véga, *Theologia Mariana*, t.2, n. 1252, 54–55, who cites St. Jerome, St. Ambrose, St. Ephrem, St. John Damascene, St. Anselm, St. Bernard, St. Laurent Justin, St. Albert, St. Bernard, St. Anthony, etc. This concerns "martyr" in a superior and broader sense.

and the word of Christ, efficacious and creative as his own love, produced this new grace which gave a mother to the human race.

This spiritual birth is but a complement to Mary's divine maternity. The blessed creature who gave to Christ human life must also engender him in souls. She is the mother of the natural body and the mystical body. Her maternity in the two cases is entirely supernatural. Thus, the Holy Spirit had to intervene here as at the first instant of the Incarnation so that the power of the Most High confer upon Mary this new virginal fecundity. The first maternity was accomplished in the spirit and by divine power, the second was equally perfected in the spirit and in grace.

Pentecost, supreme confirmation

The testament of Calvary instituted Mary as mother of humanity, the mystery of Pentecost would give supreme confirmation to her. The Apostles received on that day, along with the investiture of the Holy Spirit, the fullness of gifts and graces such that they would be strengthened in sanctity and acquire the complete revelation of all the truths of salvation.[33] The Queen of the Apostles received this plenitude first and to a superior degree. This was the definitive consecration of her mystical maternity and the consummation of her sanctity.

The grace of her last moment

As Pentecost supplied her with confirmation, so also can one believe that there was an exquisite grace at her last instant so as to replace extreme unction, which she could not receive, to put the seal upon her predestination and prepare her immediately for the perfection of beatific life. Whatever this was, all the profundities of soul are here combined: grace grew without ceasing after her first instant, by the communication of merit, by the efficacy of the sacraments, by the power of mysteries,

---

33. This is the traditional opinion, which Bañez explains in these terms: "The Apostles immediately received the fullness of the gifts of the Holy Spirit upon the arrival of that Spirit on the day of Pentecost, and in such abundance that they became cognizant of every truth concerning those things that belonged to the necessity of salvation." See his *Scholastica Commentaria in Secundam Secundae Partem Angelici Doctoris S. Thomae*, q. 1, a. 7, 39.

it achieved its highest degree. She had to stop there and be transported into glory.

Is there any need to repeat that she is superior to the grace of the angels and men taken all together? This proposition, which is debatable when it concerns the original plenitude, becomes certain, according to St. Alphonsus, once the issue becomes her final sanctity. Cornelius à Lapide has already explained this opinion,[34] which is also that of Suárez, Miéchow, Contenson, and of all present-day theologians. We do not wish to tarry here over this thesis. What we have said about the initial grace acquires here the force of peremptory proof. We confine ourselves to this reflection. Mary is loved more than all other creatures; thus, she has more grace than all creatures together, since grace is measured by love.

Yet that is to say too little. For us who admit to this plenitude at the first instant, this is but the foundation of high sanctity, since this grace at its origin surpasses the summit of all the saints combined. We have seen how it is transformed in the moment of the Incarnation, how it increases indefinitely by the communication of merit and the power of the sacraments or mysteries. The original plenitude is already unfathomable, its growth is yet more prodigious. How, then, to estimate her final plenitude? It is better to take refuge in a mute admiration, as do the saints: "The grace of that woman is ineffable, her merit the astonishment of all the ages, of the cherubim and seraphim."[35]—"O Virgin incomparable... Oh, saint more saintly than the saints, thrice holy treasure of all sanctity."[36] "Of all things even the greatest is lesser than the Virgin; the Creator alone surpasses this creature."[37]—"Our human fragility is incapable of praising her worthily."[38]

---

34. TRANSLATOR'S NOTE: Hugon cites "Corneílle de la Pierre, In Prov., XXI, 29," which I take to be Cornelius à Lapide, Comentaria in Scripturam Sacram, t. 6, Commentaria In Proverbia Salomonis, XXI:29. This passage, however, does not discuss the opinion mentioned.

35. See the homily attributed to St. Epiphanius, Homily V (dubious works), PG 43:487ff.

36. TRANSLATOR'S NOTE: No citation is given by Hugon.

37. St. Andrew of Crete, On the Dormition of Mary, III, PG 97:1100.

38. St. Peter Damian, Sermon 46, On the Birth of Mary, PL 144:761.

Conclusion

We conclude that, if this plenitude is not infinite—given that every quality, even the supernatural ones, are necessarily limited—it attained the highest degree that a mere creature could reach. It is, in fact, the last consequence of the divine maternity, proportional to it, and it is by this maternity that it must be measured. Therefore, just as one does not conceive of a creaturely dignity greater than being the Mother of God, likewise there could not be in fact—although the contrary is an absolute possibility—a grace more elevated than her final grace, the last and supreme consequence of the divine maternity. Yes, that does merit the astonishment of the ages, and it is sweeter still to think that knowing a sanctity so wonderful will be one among our joys in eternal beatitude.

* * *

CHAPTER 6

The Plenitude of Universality

I. THE TWO RULES

We have just sounded out, insofar as our strength allows, the sublimity and profundity, that is, the intensity of Mary's heavenly benefits. In this respect, there is no limit, since hers is the fullest grace which could, in fact, be received in a simple creature. Let us now try to explore their extent. In this other respect, is there some limit, or must it be admitted that the Mother of God possessed the plenitude of universality?

All the graces accorded to the Church are found in Mary

Let us appeal to the ensemble of privileges and gifts which have been or will be accorded to the Church in the entire duration of her existence. The answer is found in this rule that is accepted as an axiom among the Fathers and theologians. Every favor or grace which one of the saints enjoyed was more nobly and more perfectly imparted to the Mother of God.

The meaning of this principle

Let us clearly understand our principle. It does not concern the specific gifts which fill the annals of the saints. Our task is not to examine whether the Virgin received these favors in particular, especially as science cannot consider singular and contingent instances. Because the servants of God have walked on water, have received supernatural nourishment, or have been granted the miracle of bilocation, we do not thereby conclude that all these happened to Mary as many times and in the same way. It suffices that such gifts be contained in the graces of a superior order. We are concerned only with the privileges the absence of which would constitute a sort of inferiority, like the sanctification of her soul and the use of free will from her mother's womb.

Our rule also has nothing to do with anything judged incompatible either with the state of progression and the needs of life (such as there being a final plenitude from her first moment, or the beatific vision communicated to Mary in a permanent way during her life), or with the perfection of her soul and body (for which reason we have declared her incapable of receiving penance or extreme unction), or, lastly, with her condition as a woman (thus too we exclude her from receiving the character of orders and the particular powers of that vocation). However, we claim that she possessed all such in a more excellent manner. The queen of the clergy, who exercises eminently the role of priest in giving Jesus to the world, received to a higher order and degree all the graces of the priesthood, just as she had, in her final moment, a superior grace to replace extreme unction, which she could not receive.

Proofs by the testimony of the saints and rational arguments

Our principle thus understood is but a simple echo of tradition. St. Ambrose, commenting on the Song of Songs, imagines Our Lord addressing himself to Mary in these words:

> My Father has decreed that other souls are to be redeemed by my blood, but in contemplating you alone, I see such a summit of perfections, such an abyss of graces and celestial gifts, such that you alone are to me everyone, and you alone so far from insufficient wealth that I would leave behind everyone else and return to heaven with you.[1]

---

1. St. Ambrose, *In Cantica Cantorum*, ch. 6, *PL* 15: "Patrem alias animas meo sanguine redimendas statuisse, at te unam contemplans tantum perfectionum

Such is the oratorical explanation of our principle. All the privileges of the saints are so condensed in Mary, that it suffices to look at her, her alone, so as to contemplate all the perfections and all the riches of other souls. St. Thomas has summarized this teaching of the Fathers in a few words both profound and luminous: "Everything belonging to perfection ought to have been displayed in the Blessed Virgin."[2] Elsewhere, he recounts the same principle to show that the Blessed Virgin had been sanctified before her birth. We must believe, he says, that she of whom is born the only Son of the Father, he who is full of grace and truth, received for herself alone greater privileges than all the other saints. Now, Jeremiah and John the Baptist were sanctified in their mother's wombs; therefore, even more must this be said of the Blessed Virgin.[3]

St. Antoninus, following St. Albert, enunciated a similar rule that both regard as a first principle in this matter: Just as whenever it is a question of sin the Mother of God must be excluded, so too when it is a matter of some good, it is clear that every privilege conceded to a creature is found in Mary.[4] The pious and wise Idiot says in the same sense: "O Virgin, you have every privilege within; no one is equal to you, no one your superior, except God."[5] St. Vincent Ferrer encapsulates this doctrine in an axiom borrowed from the Fathers: "To others, the grace of God is given in part; in Mary, it is pour out in all its fullness."[6]

Furthermore, we have very decisive reasons in favor of our rule. The other saints, as elevated as they may be, always remain servants. Mary has the title and rights of mother, and does not the mother merit

---

cumulum, tantum intueor, ut tu sola sis mihi pro omnibus, teque sola dives parum absit ut reliquas omnes pro derelictis habeam coelumque repetam."

TRANSLATOR'S NOTE: Although Hugon quotes St. Ambrose's commentary on the Song of Songs, he does not provide a precise citation. I have not been able to locate the quote.

2. St. Thomas, *In IV Sent.*, d. 30, q. 2, a. 1, sol. 1: "In Beata Virgine debuit apparere omne illud quod perfectionis fuit."

3. See St. Thomas, *ST* III, q. 27, a. 1.

4. St. Antoninus, *Summa Theologica Moralis*, IVa, tit. 15, ch. 10.

5. *Contempl.*, ch. 2.

TRANSLATOR'S NOTE: The quotation is to be attributed to Raymond Jourdain, Abbot of Celles, in his sermon on the nativity of Mary. He who took the pen name of "Idiot" out of humility, says St. Alphonsus Ligouri, see *The Glories of Mary*, p. 57.

6. "Caeteris per partes datur gratia Dei; Mariae autem tota se deffundit gratiae plenitudo." Toulouse Manuscript, p. 346.

more honors and privileges than all the servants combined? In virtue of her maternity, she is the heiress of Christ, just as he himself, through the Hypostatic Union, is the heir of the Father. All the goods of his Son are passed down to him by right; can one imagine that upon others are bestowed something from which she, the natural heiress, is excluded? What is more, she is the queen of all creatures. It is inadmissible that she might be deprived of the least perfection which enriches her subjects. She is the unique, the favored, the one more beloved than all worlds, real or possible. Since the divine love is efficacious, since for God to love is to give, he pours into her more graces and goods that all other beings together.

During her life, did Mary at times enjoy the beatific vision?

A number of writers have inferred from this rule that, during her life, the Blessed Virgin must have enjoyed at some times and transiently the beatific vision. Here is their argument. St. Augustine admits that Moses was elevated to the contemplation of the divine essence.[7] St. Thomas concludes that St. Paul received the same privilege. It is inadmissible, he says, that the dispensator of the Old Law saw God face to face while the preacher of the New Testament, the apostle and doctor of the Gentiles, was deprived of this favor.[8] How much more true is it to say that it is inconceivable that the mother, the spouse, the unique and beloved one, was honored less than these servants! Yes, if it is admitted in the case of Moses and St. Paul, the conclusion is out of the question for Mary. We recognize that the subject raises quite the problem. Still, it would be wrong to condemn with a mere smile the opinion that two great geniuses of Catholic theology, St. Augustine and St. Thomas, have found so reasonable: "Therefore it is more becoming to hold that he saw God in His essence."[9]

---

7. St. Augustine, *De Genesi ad Litteram*, lib. 12, chs. 26–27, *PL* 34:476–77.

8. St. Thomas, *Commentary on 2 Corinthians*, ch. 12, lect. 1, n. 452: "Furthermore, it is not probable that Moses, the minister of the Old Testament to the Jews, saw God, and the minister of the New Testament to the Gentiles, the teacher of the Gentiles, was deprived of this gift."

9. St. Thomas, *ST* II-II, q. 175, a. 3, c.: "Et ideo convenientius dicitur quod Deum per essentiam vidit."

The rule of fittingness

Even so, without adopting their opinion on this particular point, it could perhaps be permitted to resolve the debate in a way that is favorable to Mary. The holy Doctors, indeed, are not satisfied with this rule. It is not enough, they declare, that the privileges of creatures are found in the Mother of God, one must admit every perfection that is due to or which is in keeping with her dignity. If you can say: "It would be fitting were she enriched with such a favor," then conclude: "This gift has been given to her." Well then, is it not fitting—add the pious theologians— that the heiress of the treasures and beatitude of Christ enjoy, at least at times and in a transitory way, something of that blessed vision to which her title of mother already gave her a right for all eternity?

Whatever the conclusion might be, the principle itself—"It is fitting that such graces were accorded to the Mother of God, therefore they were accorded to her"—is beyond question, if it is understood with the restrictions already indicated (that is, as long as it concerns perfections which are not incompatible with Mary's condition, her sex, and her state and progression along the way).

Proofs by testimony of the saints and rational arguments

Behold in what passionate terms St. Thomas of Villanova, archbishop of Valencia, explains this: "It suffices that you are the Mother of God. What beauty, what virtue, what perfection, what grace, or what glory is there that is not fitting for a Mother of God?"[10] Then, afterwards addressing himself to the pious faithful, the eloquent bishop exclaims:

Let loose your imagination, widen all the powers of your mind, to try to represent to yourself a Virgin the most pure, most wise, and most beautiful as one could possibly conceive, full of all graces, radiant with every glory, bedecked with every virtue, favored with every gift, in which God has placed all His indulgences. Endeavor to perfect this portrait, increase the perfections

---

10. St. Thomas of Villanova, *Conciones, In Festo Nativitatis B. V. M.*, Serm. 2, 391: "Sufficit tibi quot mater Dei est. Quaenam, obsecro, pulchritudo, quaenam virtus, quae perfectio, quae gratia, quae gloria Matri Dei non congruit?"

as much as you are able, add to them according to what strength you have: *Quantum potes, tantum auge, quantum vales, tantum adde.*[11] Mary is more beautiful than such beauty, greater than such grandeur, more excellent than such perfection. The Holy Spirit does not describe all that she is, he has left that to you to portray within your soul, thereby allowing you to understand that she lacked no grace, no excellence, no glory with which our understanding could adorn such a creature. Or better yet, it surpasses all conception.[12]

St. Alphonsus Ligouri is no less explicit: "[I would rather be] of the number of those who fully and firmly believe all that can be believed, without error, concerning the greatness of Mary."[13] And this agrees with the language of Fr. Rupert, who counts among the best homages to this august Mother that of firmly believing in all that can enhance her glory.[14] So too thinks the Church, who has us read these words in the Mass for the glorious Virgin: "You are favored and worthy of all praise, because of you is born the Sun of Justice, Christ Our Lord."[15]

This rule of fittingness is clear enough in itself. The maternity of Mary, reaching to the confines of the divinity, demands (we have repeated it many times) privileges which are of the same height, and consequently nothing seems too good for such dignity.

Thus, Jesus Christ has all the tenderness of a filial heart. Alas, in us gratitude and love, too often bound and helpless, soon find the limits of their benefits. For Jesus, love is efficacious, his heart has at its disposal an infinite power. What is fitting for his Mother he wills, and what he

---

11. TRANSLATOR'S NOTE: "Increase it as much as is within your ability, add to it as much as is within your power."

12. Ibid.

13. St. Alphonsus, *The Glories of Mary*, p. 175.
    TRANSLATOR'S NOTE: Hugon's paragraph is a paraphrase of the succeeding lines of St. Alphonsus' text.

14. Abbot Rupert of Deutz, *De Laud. Virg.*: "Eius magnalia firmiter credere."
    TRANSLATOR'S NOTE: St. Alphonsus attributes this to Abbot Rupert (*PL* 167–170); this phrase is also used by Richard de Saint-Laurent, *De Laudibus B. Mariae Virginis*, lib. 7, 475.

15. St. Alphonsus, *The Glories of Mary*, p. 175.

wills is done. This is enough to demonstrate the truth of our twofold principle that summarizes the plenitude of universality: Every privilege conceded to the saints belongs first of all to the Mother of God; every prerogative which the highest mode of fittingness claims on her behalf and which, furthermore, is not incompatible with her state, has surely been accorded to her. It is in such a way that the holy Doctors have reasoned: It was fitting that the Virgin was preserved from the original stain, therefore she was Immaculate in her Conception; it was fitting that Christ, upon his triumphant resurrection, showed himself first of all to Mary, therefore she enjoyed the first apparition; it was fitting that her most holy body, which evil had never touched, where the Word had dwelt, was preserved from the corruption of the tomb, therefore one must admit her glorious Assumption. We must already regard these conclusions as certain in virtue of our principle even though, on the other hand, they are proven demonstrably by tradition.

What we have said of her initial plenitude, second sanctification, and consummated grace was already an application of these two rules. Our intention here is not to follow out all their other consequences, but rather, in order to obtain in summary an idea of her plenitude of universality, we will examine her privileges of body, intellect, will, lower powers, and lastly gratuitous graces.

II. PRIVILEGES OF BODY

We have noted the beauty of the Blessed Virgin. The same arguments demonstrate that her body had to be perfect, immune from every malady and capable of defying the injuries of time. In taking our flesh upon himself, Christ did not also assume all of its weaknesses. If he condescended to undergo those which were able to contribute to our salvation, his perfection necessarily excluded any which would have seemed to be a natural flaw, even physically. His miraculously formed body could not but be a masterpiece. The highest instance of humanity, the human ideal, he is entirely healthy in body as he is in the powers of his soul. He could very well suffer at the hands of his executioners or submit to exterior fatigue, but he did not have in his bodily constitution any interior cause of decay—no physical ailment, nothing able to cause disorder or deterioration, even the slightest indisposition. Such is perfect integrity, a wholesome nature, which is not subject to decline.

Mary's physical well-being: no deformity or illness

Now, we know that Mary must resemble her Son in all things. Neither flaw, nor disorder—even physical—is to be found in the immaculate clay from which the Word willed to mold his body. They are both virginal, the body of Christ and the body of Mary, each full of health. In them nature deploys all its powers, and their organs, also the instruments of the supernatural, enjoy a harmonious interplay with a fulness of strength that excludes every morbid ailment. As the Blessed Virgin bore fruit when in full bloom, she also advanced in age without losing that perfect youth which is ally to maturity.

If ever a soul was mistress of the body it animated, it was assuredly Mary's soul. Here, there are no material indispositions to interfere with the superior clarity of her spirit, which is why her body was so beautiful. Nothing can stop the superabundant energies of her wholesome soul or paralyze its influence upon the supple instrument to which it is united, which is why her body was exempt from every disease. It obeyed its spirit, and this submission even excluded every cause of decay. The closer it was joined to the soul, the more it had to be perfect and strong; complying with all of its orders, her body drew ever closer to the source of life and thereby received its influence more fully. It partook in the force of an immortal principle, and it was partnered, in some way, to its youth and incorruptibility. Her soul, without doubt, could not on its own render her body immortal, but it shared with it more fully its power than is the case in other human beings.

The conception of the Word another cause of her physical well-being

Another cause of Mary's physical well-being was the conception of the Word and her continuing contact with his blessed Humanity. Theologians say that the fruit of the mysterious tree in the Garden of Eden was the virtue of preserving the body in strength and granting it immortality. Is this not an analogy of the divine maternity? From the moment that the Word of Life was incarnate in a created body, a sort of unction was conferred upon him, an indelible seal against malady, as it were the anticipation of glorification. The tabernacle where God dwelt became like the ark which could not be dented by those seeking to harm it. Indeed, through her contact with the flesh of the Lord, the virginal body of Mary draws an abundance of life, capable of withstanding many assaults: age will not succeed in bending her body, inflicting painful suffering upon it from without, not will it be subjected to humiliating weakness. Her body remains mortal, of course, but it is sound.

Refutation of the legend of the "spasm"

This suffices to refute the opinion, which has been given more than its due, on the subject of the spasm or swooning of the Virgin on the road to Calvary. The illustrious Cajetan wrote a special treatise so that justice might be done regarding this legend so injurious to the dignity of the Mother of God.[16] Medina, Toledo, Suárez, and the ensemble of theologians have also condemned this opinion. The Gospel has done so before them. It represents the Mother of God in a heroic attitude at the foot of the cross: *Stabat*. If the ordeal of Calvary and the most horrific circumstances of the Passion did not succeed in subduing her, if her courage remained strong throughout, can one admit that she would have fainted before the most terrible part of that *via dolorosa*? The spasm—to use the traditional term—implies some nervous breakdown, a turmoil in her senses, a physical and moral failure, a veritable humiliation of her nature. All that could not have occurred while her soul was mistress of her body. Since in her case the lower faculties were obedient without resistance to the will's orders, and the body heeded to influences of the soul, we strenuously refuse to believe in such a failure. Furthermore, at that moment, unique in the history of the world and the history of the supernatural, the abundance of her graces, the power of her virtues, and her sublime gifts all joined together to result in heroism. Our piety cannot imagine otherwise for the Mother of God, and the Gospel does not tell us otherwise. Her body, soul, mind, courage, will, were standing: *Stabat*. She must share in the sufferings of Jesus, but in her spirit and not by the weakness of her body. Her affliction

---

16. Cajetan, *De spasmo Virginis*.

is unfathomable. This gentle Mother is, as it were, submersed under waves of pain, but she does not break. She is wholly resigned to the divine will, and constantly renews her offering of her Son for the salvation of the human race. She is no less generous or obedient, no less strong and courageous than Abraham: "For neither was she less obedient, indeed less courageous, than Abraham."[17]

It was, then, not without reason that the Spanish Inquisition thought it had to forbid images depicting this apocryphal and rash legend. Medina tells us that preachers of this ill-considered devotion, who would entertain the faithful with this fable and its intemperate language, had to submit to a formal retraction.[18]

As to the expressions of pious theological writers, they should not be taken seriously. They are instances of hyperbole, aimed at making us more sensitive to the affliction of Mary by comparing her to other mothers succumbing to their pain. Just as anthropomorphisms serve to reveal the invisible divinity to us, so too such expressions contain a portion of the truth, as long as one keeps in mind they are only comparisons.

III. Privileges of Intellect

We have considered previously that Mary was decorated with infused knowledge from the first moment of her Immaculate Conception, which was not a fleeting favor but a knowledge that was retained and developed without interruption, even during sleep, and due to which privilege all the actions of the Blessed Virgin were deliberate and meritorious.[19] At present, we should make the notion of this gift more precise.

Mary's knowledge is proportional to her accompanying graces

Mary's knowledge must be proportional to the graces belonging to her, necessary as it is to allow her supernatural gifts to be cultivated,

---

17. St. Antoninus, *Summa Theologica Moralis*, IVa, tit. 15, ch. 41: "Neque enim minoris fuit obedientiae, addo et fortitudinis quam Abraham."
18. Bartolomé de Medina, *Expositio in IIIa P.*, q. 27, a. 4, 518: "… iussu inquisitorum revocatuntur eiusmodi dicta ab concionatoribus."
19. Translator's Note: See above, Chapters 3 and 5.

such as prudence, counsel, and the other virtues, and for these to fully flourish. Her knowledge is supernatural as are the acts which they direct. This corollary of grace must be just as marvelous and extraordinary. As a condition of love, the two go hand in hand. But if there is a proportion between knowledge and charity, who could measure the extent of such knowledge? Since all the favors of the saints are found in the Mother of God, we must attribute to her a knowledge comparable to that of the angels and our first parents. Even on earth she is, by right of her maternity, queen of the cherubim and seraphim. As we have said, it is not fitting that she lack a perfection which adorns her subjects and which is compatible with her state of life and condition. Adam received sufficient natural and supernatural light so as to become a master in intellect just as he had to be the father of men. The Mother of God and the Mother of the human race deserves much more. Her double maternity, belonging to a superior order and cooperating with a more perfect economy, gives her the right to a more noble type of knowledge.

Her ceaseless relationship with her Son brought about new insights

Her ceaseless relationship with her Son did bring about new insights. Since she united her soul to the soul of the Word, she penetrated into those serene depths wherein are hidden all the treasures of truth and wisdom. The light from Christ's intelligence shone upon her own and revealed new secrets to her with each encounter. If the apostle John, who was only His friend, knew such mysteries by resting for a few moments upon the Lord's chest, what must be said of joyful Mary, who had lean upon and taking shelter next to her virginal and maternal heart the Master of all divine and human knowledge—and not just once, but every day for so many long years!

Knowledge of supernatural things

It is therefore without hesitation that we attribute a knowledge conformable to her dignity in relation to all that concerns the supernatural order: that which in the Scriptures is related to the Messiah; those things touching upon the great mysteries of the Trinity, the Incarnation, the Redemption; that which comes under the realm of grace and virtue, that which the prophets, apostles, and evangelists have announced. These she knew, for she possessed more fully than them all the economy of salvation.

A profound knowledge of the natural order

As to the knowledge of the natural order, we will not claim that she must have amused herself with the logicians' subtleties or tarried over all the details of the physical and mathematical sciences, but we maintain that she had a very clear and profound knowledge of created things. This is not the satisfaction of some vain curiosity, but a necessary adornment of her intelligence. The desire to know is one of the most noble of the human passions, it instigates progress and inspires great works which stand as a conquest and permanent victory of genius. An aspiration so legitimate must be satisfied, and God would not refuse his Mother a perfection without which the mind is restless, incomplete, and unsatisfied.

Furthermore, this knowledge had to be employed for contemplating heavenly mysteries. The world is the first revelation of God, the first book where his eternal ideas are printed, the first vestige of his attributes, the first image of his beauty, the first echo of his voice. Should not Mary know every page of that book, whose beauty rouses her to greatly praise the Creator, that echo in which she hears the voice of the beloved? The visible universe is a rough sketch of the invisible world, nature supporting grace, just as the life of reason supports the mystical life. Analogies taken from the sensible order are the ordinary way by which we attain to the notion of the First Being, and material creatures are the place from whence our soul sets forth to the spiritual and the infinite. A perfect understanding of the natural order was therefore necessary to Mary so as to comprehend well the economy of salvation, to appreciate the relationship between nature and grace.[20] Such demands Heaven feels obliged to satisfy.

---

20. TRANSLATOR'S NOTE: See the Appendix, Part II, "*Ancilla Domini et Ancilla Theologiae*: Mary and Philosophy," for a consideration of this and related passages about Mary in this chapter.

This knowledge was restricted, especially in its origins, but these were limits, not lacunae

We are not afraid to confess that such knowledge was limited, especially at the outset. God did not judge it fitting to manifest immediately certain truths the knowledge of which were not necessary for the Blessed Virgin's present condition. Thus we see in the Gospel that Mary asks questions of the Angel (Luke 1:35), that she wondered (Luke 2:33), that she does not understand all that is contained in the words of Jesus regarding the affairs of his heavenly Father (Luke 2:48ff.). There is no need of recalling the various explanations that these texts have been given. It is enough to observe that even the most perfect knowledge, even prophetic vision, even the intuition of the angels, is always limited. But these are limits rather than lacunae. An angel is not ignorant even when he does not see everything, so too with Mary, even while all the details of the Incarnation and Redemption were not yet revealed to her. Such is not a true ignorance for the one who knows all which is useful to her condition. The Mother of God, in the diverse epochs of her life, knew all that interested her in the present moment, just as she always had the fulness of grace that corresponded to her current capacities.

Mary, free from error

It is more evident still that she was never subject to error. Error is born of ignorance and adds a deformity which produces intellectual ugliness. Man in the state of innocence had a perfect virginity of mind; by the Fall his understanding was wounded and violated. Mary, who is exempt from original sin, is entirely whole in body, soul, and mind. The virginity of her intelligence is as inviolable as that of her body. Her title as Mother of God is a guarantee for her against error, which is not just an imperfection and is more than a fault. It is the disorder and shame of the mind.

Response to a difficulty

The Gospel seems to raise a difficulty. Mary thought that her Son would be found among the group of their relatives and friends when they were returning from the Temple. The answer is no less well known than the objection. The Blessed Virgin does not affirm that the Child Jesus was in truth in the group, but she regards (*existimantes*, Luke 2:44)[21] that such a supposition is plausible. In that, she is not mistaken, since such was truly possible given the circumstances. The perfection of the Mother of God demanded that she was never led into error, not that she possessed absolute certitude regarding every event. Divine inspiration surely preserves the sacred writers from every false assertion, but it does not grant them evidence and certitude as to all the details, which is why the Bible reports certain facts as probable or in a dubious manner. Likewise, Mary was in every circumstance preserved from error, but as to the particulars of a given case she did not have all the aspects of certitude, and thus had to employ conjectures or opinions, which, however, always enjoyed a real and solid probability.

Progress in knowledge and its contributing causes

This knowledge grew right alongside the proportional increase of grace, from the first sanctification all the way until the final consummation, as one radiant day that lasted from a brilliant dawn to the noonday zenith. The particularly fruitful periods of grace were also fruitful times of new insights. One must think that the sublime moment in the history of humanity, that moment when the Word was made flesh, marked an extraordinary progress: a fullness of supernatural life in her soul, a revelation to her mind, while the greatest of miracles was worked in her body. The time she spent at Nazareth, the frequent one-on-one discussions with the God of all knowledge, the contact with his soul, are all titles to further knowledge. When Mary became the mother of the human race at Golgotha, she received light in relation with this new destiny. The descent of the Paraclete brought to her a wealth of his gifts of knowledge, wisdom, and understanding. Her life of contemplation after the Ascension of her Son transformed her spirit: she lived in a light bordering upon that of heaven.

---

21. TRANSLATOR's NOTE: Fr. Hugon refers to the Latin text of the verse: "Existimantes autem illum esse in comitatu, venerunt iter diei, et requirebant eum inter cognatos et notos.—And thinking that he was in the company, they came a day's journey, and sought him among their kinsfolks and acquaintance."

Diverse causes contributed to this progress. There was the direct infusion of new ideas, according as God judged them useful for her and as the condition of the Blessed Virgin required. The immediate illumination of the Holy Spirit caused her to discover in the old ideas new aspects. There were revelations received by the ministry of angels, for it is just that these faithful messengers would above all give to their queen those same services they had lavished upon so many saints. Finally, there was the action of her own understanding. Just as the supernatural knowledge of Our Lord did not proceed from the native resources of his mind, but he was permitted the rapid acquisition of perfect experiential knowledge, so too the infused knowledge of Mary did not stymie the regular development of her faculties. These already possessed, on a merely human level, an extraordinary activity, for they flowed forth from a soul which was nature's masterpiece. Mary knew how to read easily from the book of the world, the Scriptures, from the entire breadth of revelation, into the mysteries which surrounded her, and to which her thoughts and reflections would ceaselessly return: *conferens in corde suo*. Guided by infused light, her natural knowledge had a penetration that genius itself is not granted, and from the two resulted a treasure of knowledge which would baffle our timid and meager ideas. Next to the beatific vision, there is no knowledge as clear, as profound, and as sure as that which Mary enjoyed during her mortal life, just as, next to glory, there is nothing which could compare with the grace of the Mother of God.

IV. PRIVILEGES OF WILL

The virtues raised to the highest degree

The privileges of her will entail an absolute exemption from sin along with an abundance of the virtues. The virtues, the property and inseparable adornment of grace, are at their height. Grace is here found at its apogee, and the virtues at the supreme degree of heroism. We will not stress this point, given what we have said about her three plenitudes. As to the exemption from all fault, this is an important point of Catholic teaching. The Christians of old were wont to repeat the axiom set down by St. Augustine: whenever it is a question of sin, one must exclude Mary.[22] The Council of Trent proclaimed with even more authority and in a decisive manner the belief of the Church in the most special privilege of the Blessed Virgin (*speciali privilegio*), of having been preserved from all fault, even from the slightest venial sin.[23]

Exemption from all sin: St. Thomas and Contenson

If such declarations were lacking, the two rules explained above would provide us a sure guarantee of her absolute innocence. All manner of praise a creature could receive has been given to Mary. An innumerable multitude of angels have never sinned; we must therefore say the same of Mary. It belongs to the dignity of the Mother of God; we conclude she had this privilege.

St. Thomas explains in plain and measured terms this rule of fittingness God never fails to follow:

> God so prepares and endows those whom He chooses for some particular office that they are rendered capable of fulfilling it, according to 2 Cor. 3:6: (*Who*) *hath made us fit ministers of the New Testament.* Now the Blessed Virgin was chosen by God to be His Mother. Therefore there can be no doubt that God, by His grace, made her worthy of that office, according to the words spoken to her by the angel (Luke 1:30, 31): *Thou hast found grace with God: behold thou shalt conceive,* etc. But she would not have been worthy to be the Mother of God, if she had ever sinned. First, because the honor of the parents reflects on the child, according to Prov. 17:6: *The glory of children are their fathers:* and consequently, on the other hand, the Mother's shame would

---

22. St. Augustine, *De Natura et Gratia*, lib. 1, ch. 26; *PL* 44:267: "Excepta itaque sancta virgine Maria, de qua propter honorem Domini nullam prorsus cum de peccatis agitur."

23. Council of Trent, Session 6, Can. 23: "If anyone says that a man once justified cannot sin again and cannot lose grace and that therefore the man who falls and sins was never truly justified; or, on the contrary, says that a man once justified can avoid all sins, even venial ones, throughout his entire life, unless it be by a special privilege of God as the Church holds of the Blessed Virgin, let him be anathema" (Denzinger, n. 1573).

have reflected on her Son. Second, because of the singular affinity between her and Christ, who took flesh from her: and it is written (2 Cor. 6:15): *What concord hath Christ with Belial?* Third, because of the singular manner in which the Son of God, who is the *Divine Wisdom* (1 Cor. 1:24) dwelt in her, not only in her soul but in her womb. And it is written (Wis. 1:4): *Wisdom will not enter into a malicious soul, nor dwell in a body subject to sins.* We must therefore confess simply that the Blessed Virgin committed no actual sin, neither mortal nor venial; so that what is written (Song 4:7) is fulfilled: *Thou art all fair, O my love, and there is not a spot in thee*, etc.[24]

Contenson completes the Master's thought as follows:

> The grace of Mary excluded not only every actual fault but the moral capacity to sin. We note first of all, as an interior preservation, a particular providence which kept watch over the Blessed Virgin and kept from her all occasions of evil. Next, as an interior cause, there was an uninterrupted series of efficacious graces that informed her mind, so that she would know the good, as also her will, that she might do it. There was a continual focus of mind upon God, an ardor of her will, the guard of her senses, and the privilege that bound or even extinguished the source of concupiscence. In this way, the Mother of Christ never had any part in earthly afflictions: never the slightest lust, never did she feel the bite of sensuality, never did an unwanted thought distract her.[25]

One can readily understand that Mary was impeccable from the moment that she conceived the Word of Life. It suffices to recall the three reasons that we have applied when considering her second sanctification: the proximate disposition of the divine maternity entailing enough grace to suppress all defects of free choice; the indissoluble

---

24. St. Thomas, *ST* III, q. 27, a. 4, c.
25. Contenson, *Theologia Mentis et Cordis*, t. 3, lib. X, diss. 6, ch. 1, spec. 2, 266.

union with the author of sanctity; the reciprocal love between the Blessed Virgin and her Son removing the possibility of evil. The role of mother gives her the right to friendship with her child, and so just as human motherhood does not cease, it established between God and Mary an imperishable, eternal friendship which permits no sin to arise, not even once.

Impeccable or impeccant? The diverse opinions among the theologians

It is also certain that, even before the Incarnation, the Immaculate was guarded against all fault, whether by an interior grace in her soul or by the exterior protection and assistance of the Holy Spirit. The difficulty lies in determining whether this privilege suppressed the very power of sinning, or whether it was only an efficacious preservation, not permitting the exercise yet without excluding the power of evil. Some, for instance Suárez, have thought that hers was a state of impeccance rather than impeccability, whether before or after the Incarnation. Others, above all in the Middle Ages, held that she was impeccant before but impeccable for all time after the conception of the Word.

We admit her impeccability from the first moment

For our part, we conclude that she truly was impeccable from the first instant. Indeed, the Word, from that moment when he infused the initial grace in her, already looked upon and loved Mary as his future mother. He had to already realize in her all that the demands of his divine sonship require. These require that his love be indissoluble and that the grace produced be imperishable. Is not the indissolubility of love and the imperishability of grace impeccability?

Proof taken from St. Thomas

A passage of the *Disputed Questions on Truth* will let us understand the fundamental principle of this doctrine.[26] To render someone

---

26. St. Thomas, *De Veritate*, q. 24, a. 9.

    TRANSLATOR'S NOTE: This article asks whether in this life a man can be confirmed in the good (*confirmari in bono*). The text of Hugon is a paraphrase of a portion of the article's *corpus*, and then a utilization of the two conditions discussed by

impeccable is to empty him of every source of evil. Now, the fatal origin of sin belongs either to an error of reason, when it is led astray by the particular nature of the last end and the means to it, or it is due to an obstruction which the lower passions bring to the continuous, right exercise of reason. Thus, two conditions must be met by absolute impeccability: first, a continuous, right contemplation of divine things, such that God is the measure and end of every action; second, an interior grace so powerful that it maintains all the impulses of the inferior powers under the empire of reason. Our Lord Jesus Christ, elevated from his first instant to the Beatific Vision, ever enjoyed this perfect state. It was his by right.

No mortal could have met these two conditions without a gratuitous and absolutely extraordinary privilege. Yet such were according to Mary from the beginning. The first condition is assured her by her infused knowledge, the gifts of wisdom and counsel. As we have shown when explaining her merit, as the divine Mother had the continuous use of reason and free will, so was God the constant rule of her life and works. The second condition was guaranteed her by the gift of integrity, by which all her inferior faculties submitted in obedience to her mind. These two conditions being realized in the instant of her Immaculate Conception, we conclude that from that moment she enjoyed a true and perfect impeccability.

St. Thomas: "A person cannot be made altogether impeccable unless every source of sin is removed. Now the source of sin is found either in an error of reason, which is led astray in a particular case concerning the end (good) and the means to it, which he naturally desires in general; or in the obstruction of the judgment of reason by some passion of the lower powers. Although it could be granted to someone in this life through the gift of wisdom and of counsel that his reason should in no way err regarding the end (good) and regarding the means in particular, yet to have the judgment of reason unobstructable surpasses the state of this present life for two reasons: primarily and principally because it is impossible for reason in this life here below to be always in the act of correct contemplation so that the reason for everything we do is God; secondly, because the lower powers do not happen to be so subject to reason in this life that the act of reason is in no wise obstructed by them, except in the case of Our Lord, Jesus Christ, who was at the same time on the way to God and in possession of Him."

V. INTEGRITY

It remains for us to explain the privilege of integrity, which particularly concerns the lower order of powers.

What "integrated nature" means

A nature is integrated when there does not exist in it any division between the parts which compose it, when the lower realm is entirely subordinate to the higher realm: the body to the soul, the senses to reason, the sensible appetite to the will. In order that every division might be cast aside, it is necessary that nothing be able to separate the soul from the body and that there never be any trouble or disaccord between the mind and the lower faculties. Perfect integrity thus includes preservation from death, error, and concupiscence. Such was the privilege with which our first parents were favored, and all this arose from the fact that the soul was entirely submitted to God. Original sin destroyed that harmony. Thenceforth: perpetual conflict between soul and body, a lamentable division arose which opened the door to sickness and was finished by a catastrophe, the separation of the two elements in death. Between the faculties arose a ruinous discord, which prevented the senses from faithfully serving reason, and appetite from being the supple minister of the will. Thus arises the disorder, that interior combat which has made the saints groan. This is not a morbid quality added to our nature, but once the supernatural bond that maintains the powers is removed, the inferior faculties follow their blind drives, like a spirited charger when the reins are lost.

Concupiscence

While the will remains free to consent or to resist these tumultuous movements, it is not within its power to suppress every revolt, for concupiscence is not a slave that the master orders about at pleasure, but rather like a citizen governed by laws against which he can rebel.[27]

---

27. See Aristotle, *Politics*, I.5, and St. Thomas, *ST* I, q. 81, a. 3, ad 2.
    TRANSLATOR'S NOTE: This difference is also drawn out by St. Thomas in *ST* I-II, q. 56, a. 4, ad 3: "The body is ruled by the soul, and the irascible and concupiscible powers by the reason, but in different ways. For the body obeys the soul blindly without any contradiction, in those things in which it has a natural aptitude to be

Such is the explanation of the frequent rebellions which deprive reason of control and dominion of the will, which are not of themselves faults, but which nonetheless remain a disorder and source of shame, and which can even incite one to sin. Concupiscence is not itself evil, but it is the doorway to it. It arises from sin and inclines one to sin; the fatal result of original sin, it possesses attractions and sources of surprise which could become actual sin.[28]

The grace of baptism, while it confers enough strength to vanquish temptations, does not suppress the cursed root. Although the just are well-equipped enough so as to avoid yielding to temptation, they are not protected from every sudden thing, and so they cannot prevent every disordered movement. Hence the moral impossibility of preserving oneself from venial sin throughout one's entire life, much less from involuntary faults.[29]

One sees that the loss of integrity implies a twofold punishment. The first is purely physical: suffering and death. The other harms moral perfection: ignorance, error, lust, passions. The first, far from being a disgrace, can ennoble us. One is made greater by a great pain, especially when it is not deserved and borne with dignity. And the death of the innocent suffered for a worthy cause is the ultimate triumph of heroism. The second is a profound shame, which never transpires without a

---

moved by the soul: whence the Philosopher says (*Polit.* I, 3) that the soul rules the body with a despotic command as the master rules his slave: wherefore the entire movement of the body is referred to the soul. For this reason virtue is not in the body, but in the soul. But the irascible and concupiscible powers do not obey the reason blindly; on the contrary, they have their own proper movements, by which, at times, they go against reason, whence the Philosopher says (*Polit.* I, 3) that the reason rules the irascible and concupiscible powers by a political command such as that by which free men are ruled, who have in some respects a will of their own. And for this reason also must there be some virtues in the irascible and concupiscible powers, by which these powers are well disposed to act." Note that the reference to the *Politics* incorrectly indicates I.3; it should indicate I.5.

28. Council of Trent, Session 5, Decree on Original Sin, Can. 5: "Of this concupiscence, which the Apostle occasionally calls 'sin' [see Romans 6:12–15; 7:7, 14–20], the holy council declares: The Catholic Church has never understood that it is called sin because it would be sin in the true and proper sense in those who have been reborn, but *because it comes from sin and inclines to sin.*" Our emphasis; see also our *Tractatus Dogmatici*, t. 2, *De Peccato Originali et De Gratia.*

29. Council of Trent, Session 6, Can. 23 (quoted above, p. 114).

certain disorder or disgrace. The first could be useful for our salvation, and God willed to use the suffering and death of his Son to redeem the human race; but the second, which comes from sin and which drives one towards sin, is a sort of blemish of which God avoids even the slightest bit. Jesus and Mary thus accepted the first punishment, which they never would have contracted seeing as they were wholly immaculate in their conceptions. But they could never submit to the second in any way, that is, to error and concupiscence, which are truly moral privations and the shameful result of the original loss.

Never could a disordered movement occur in Mary

It is not enough to confess that the glorious Virgin Mary never consented to a disordered movement. These internal revolts could never even have arisen. The effect had been eradicated in the most complete manner, seeing as it had been suppressed along with its cause. Just as in the case of Christ, Mary was taken as the dough of human nature made from the purest of flours, hers was a flesh immaculate into which neither the leaven of sin nor the ferment of concupiscence entered.

The fomes peccati never existed in her

Today, the theology of the Immaculate Conception has become clear and very precise. There is no longer need to distinguish between two states of the privilege of integrity, as did the old scholastics. According to them, before the Incarnation the font of concupiscence was only bound or dormant, of the sort such that it could never have provoked the least rebellion. After the conception of the Word, it was completely and forever extinguished. When speaking this way, these theologians never intended to derogate from the dignity of the Mother of God. On the contrary, they instead proclaimed that never the least shadow of evil could have passed over this virgin nature. Yet they wished to highlight above all the efficacy of the presence of the Word in the womb of Mary.

As for us, we make the second sanctification into a yet greater abundance of graces, and we have explained how it is superior to the initial plenitude.[30] As to the exclusion of evil, we do not consider there

---

30. See Chapter 3.

to be a difference between the two periods. The Incarnation need not have destroyed what had never existed. The Immaculate Conception, taking away the cause—that is, original sin—suppressed the effect—namely, concupiscence. The cursed font, therefore, was closed from the first moment, or, better yet, it never existed.

Thus, in virtue of a primordial grace so abundant that it turned aside all the faults of free will, within the Blessed Virgin all must be in harmony, without conflict or division. Her soul is submissive to God, body to soul, senses to reason, appetite to will. Far from the possibility of fault, there is only room for merit. One sees that her Immaculate Conception, impeccability, integrity, and continuous merit are as multiple, yet inseparable, elements of the same privilege.

VI. Gratuitous Graces

We arrive at last at the gratuitous graces. They have external and social roles: to obtain what is useful for the Church, the spiritual good of one's neighbor during the return to God.[31]

The nine kinds described by St. Paul

St. Paul enumerated nine main types (1 Corinthians 12:8–11).[32] In the first place are those having to do with knowledge and instruction

---

31. Translator's Note: See St. Thomas, *Commentary on 1 Corinthians*, ch. 12, lect. 2, n. 726–27: "And lest such a manifestation seems futile, he adds: *unto profit*, namely, for the common good. In this is designated the end of these gifts, and this either when the true doctrine of the Church is proved or when someone's holiness is proposed as an example. Hence he says below: *seek to abound unto the edifying of the Church* (1 Cor. 14:12); and above: *not seeking that which is profitable to myself but to many: that they may be saved* (1 Cor. 10:33). Then when he says, *to one is given*, he presents the distinction of graces which, indeed, as has been said, are given for the common good." With this qualification in mind, it is helpful to note that Hugon's discussions of Mary's possession of these gifts follows suit—it is all in terms of how Mary used them for the common good of the early Church.

32. Translator's Note: Here, Hugon is following St. Thomas's threefold division of the gifts. See St. Thomas, *Commentary on 1 Corinthians*, ch. 12, lect. 2, n. 727: "Therefore, it is required to take the distinction in the sense that by one the salvation of others can be procured. Man, indeed, cannot do this by working within, for this belongs to God, but only by persuading outwardly. For this, three things are required: first, the faculty of persuading; second, the faculty of confirming the

in divine things. *Wisdom* is the eminent gift of explaining the mysteries of religion at its heights, that is to say, by its highest reasons. *Knowledge* engages with truths more easily and presents them with proofs better adapted to natural intelligence. Next is *faith*, not the theological virtue, but an excellence and a particular firmness of that virtue, or again that faith which works miracles and moves mountains. Furthermore, it is necessary to convince souls by irrefutable arguments which are like the voice or seal of the Almighty. To do that which God alone can do, there is the *gift of healing* and the *power of miracles*; to manifest that which God alone can know, there is *prophecy* and the *discernment of spirits*. Finally, there is need to communicate with souls that we want to lead to salvation, which requires the *gift of speaking in tongues* and that of *interpreting tongues*.

The economy of these graces in the Church

These gifts were more frequent in the first centuries, when it was necessary to spread the faith and confound unbelief, but they will never abandon the true Church. Just as the world will always have its share of unbelievers, Heaven will always raise up miracle-workers. Miracles will be the powerful thunder that drowns out rationalism and irreligion. These graces, while they do not sanctify someone in themselves, are nonetheless the mark and crown of sanctity, for they serve to make resplendent in the Church of Christ that aspect which distinguishes her from all other sects: *Credo sanctam Ecclesiam*.

Wisdom, knowledge, and faith in Mary

According to our principle that the favors accorded to the Church are to be found in Mary, we must conclude that the Mother of God received the gratuitous graces and that she even made use of all of them, which were not incompatible with her sex or condition in life. *Wisdom* and *knowledge* gave her a penetration something like an intuition of divine mysteries. United so closely to the soul of Christ in which are hidden all the treasures of supernatural knowledge, she read the secrets

---

persuasion; third, the faculty of proposing the persuasion intelligibly." The first division includes wisdom, knowledge, and faith; the second includes the gift of healing and the power of miracles; the third includes the gifts of speaking and interpreting tongues.

of eternity more clearly than the prophets, evangelists, and doctors. Hers was not a role of the public ministry of preaching, but of very efficacious teaching, even if private, which is not prohibited women and which the first faithful came to ask of Mary. With what pious eagerness the writers and evangelists must have received from her lips the precious details about the Incarnation, the infancy of Jesus, and the other events for which she was hero or witness![33] Even from this point of view, she is the queen of evangelists, apostles, and doctors.

Her faith was of such an excellence and firmness that it could never be equaled. As to faith, Mary, the mother of miracles, made use of it on more than one occasion, and especially in a particularly solemn circumstance, during the Wedding at Cana, by asking of Our Lord his first miracle and not being troubled by the response. Instead of interpreting it as a refusal, she immediately told the servants: "Observe and do all that he will command you."[34]

Did the Virgin perform miracles after the Ascension?

What about the power of healing and of working miracles? It does not seem that she used these graces before the Ascension. It was necessary that all eyes be fixed upon Christ, and this is why neither the Blessed Virgin nor John the Baptist should have been revealed to the world through miracles. We admit along with the Angelic Doctor that, even after the Ascension, Mary never had to work those solemn miracles destined to accompany the preaching of the Gospel.[35] These divine

---

33. Cajetan, *In IIIam ST* q. 27, a. 5: "Nevertheless, one could say that not by public teaching, but by private instruction—which, as it well known, is not prohibited women—the Blessed Virgin explained certain particular events to the Apostles" (Leon. 11.298; n. 4).

34. TRANSLATOR'S NOTE: See Chapter 10, p. 161.

35. See St. Thomas, *ST* III, q. 27, a. 5, ad 3: "There is no doubt that the Blessed Virgin received in a high degree both the gift of wisdom and the grace of miracles and even of prophecy, just as Christ had them. But she did not so receive them so as to put them and such like graces to every use, as did Christ, but accordingly as it befitted her condition of life. For she had the use of wisdom in contemplation, according to Luke 2:19: *But Mary kept all these words, pondering them in her heart.* But she had not the use of wisdom as to teaching: since this befitted not the female sex, according to 1 Timothy 2:12: *But I suffer not a woman to teach.* The use of miracles did not become her while she lived: because at that time the

deeds had to be as the lightning and thunder in the midst of those who were to promulgate the New Testament, that is, by the apostles, the official ministers of that law. This had to be done both by preaching by word and confirmation by supernatural signs.

But there are other miracles which, without having a public character, are nonetheless an act of praise to God and a service of charity to neighbor. They are not the exclusive prerogative of the apostles or doctors: they fill the annals of the Church, and we see such power granted to lay persons and simple women. No one will contest this regarding the Mother of God. This good was necessary for her to satisfy the yearnings of her goodness, her urge for mercy, to relieve dejected hopes, to soften bitterness, to dry the flowing tears she saw, to rescue so many unfortunate people who already called their mother and whom she carried in her heart. Finally, if a miracle is also a testimony of heroism, can it be lacking from a life full of heroic deeds? Venerable traditions report that miracles occurred after the death of the Blessed Virgin by merely touching her sacred body, or the sepulcher which sheltered it for a short time, or her clothes or other relics. Why could her living body not have done what even her corpse did before her glorious Assumption? We therefore believe, as did St. Antoninus, who himself follows St. Albert the Great, as well as Suárez and the greater part of the current works on Mariology, that the Mother of God made frequent use of the grace of healing and working miracles.[36]

If these events remain hidden in the shadows, God now wills as a dazzling compensation that great marvels be worked by Mary. It is remarkable indeed that historic miracles like the triumph of the Faith over the Albigensian heresy, the victory at Lepanto, and the celebrated cures of our century, are due to the intercession of the Virgin or are accomplished in her sanctuaries and in her name. Christ desires that his Mother be revealed again to the world in this way, as he was formerly made known

---

teaching of Christ was to be confirmed by miracles, and therefore it was befitting that Christ alone, and His disciples who were the bearers of His doctrine, should work miracles. Hence of John the Baptist it is written (John 10:41) that he *did no sign*; that is, in order that all might fix their attention on Christ. As to the use of prophecy, it is clear that she had it, from the canticle spoken by her: *My soul doth magnify the Lord* (Luke 1:46, etc.)."

36.   St. Antoninus, *Summa Theologica Moralis*, IVa, tit. 14; Suárez, *Opera Omnia*, t. 19, *De Mysteriis Vitae Christi*, d. 20, s. 3, 312–13.

in the Incarnation. He would visit suffering humanity once more, but he wills that Mary announce his presence through the voice of her miracles.

The gift of prophecy, the Magnificat

As to the gift of *prophecy*, the *Magnificat* is proof of the highest order. Prophecy is that gaze that reads with certitude what lies in the shadows of the present and above all those of the future, things which are known to God alone. The Blessed Virgin perceived the secrets of the present, those profound mysteries regarding the Incarnation and the divine Maternity which are still veiled from creaturely eyes and which she saw clearly realized in her: *Fecit mihi magna qui potens est.* The secrets of the future she understood, for she already heard that universal voice in remote ages to come which proclaimed her blessed: *Ecce enim ex hoc beatam me dicent omnes generationes.* Certain oracles of Scripture seem obscure and vague; this is a particularly clear and determinate one. This is not some chance effect. Behold a humble daughter without any fame, even in her own country, who confesses her lowliness and who, at the same instant in the clearest terms and with a most absolute certitude, affirms that all peoples of all tongues will glorify her in times to come. How can such an idea and such a conviction in someone unknown, especially one so modest, be explained?

The fulfillment of the prophecy is as obvious as the statement is accurate. There is in humanity a sacred need to praise and to love Mary. No, humanity is not mistaken as to the meaning of this oracle. Just ask the young girl, the mother, the old man, the child—the glories of Mary are dearer to us than our own. When the Council of Ephesus proclaimed the divine maternity, there was in that town an immense outburst of joy. They acclaimed and feted the bishops who had come to exalt Mary; women burned perfumes in the celebration.[37] The same cry of joy was renewed when Pope Pious IX defined the Immaculate Conception. Everyone rejoiced in heartfelt celebration. Always and everywhere one sees the crowds teeming to Mary's sanctuaries, as if to appease their

---

37. TRANSLATOR'S NOTE: See St. Alphonsus Ligouri, *The History of Heresies and Their Refutation*, trans. Mullock (Dublin: Duffy, 1857), p. 126, who describes this scene and mentions this practice of burning perfume.

need of loving her and exalting her. Thus has it been possible to defy the incredulity that presents serious argument against the fulfillment of this prophecy, so brief and so clear, or tries to escape the demonstrative value which emerges from such a manifest accomplishment.

Doubtlessly, this was not the only prophecy during the life of the Blessed Virgin. God cannot be stingy with her over a gift that he so liberally granted to so many others, and which is so often of such importance in the supernatural economy.

The Mother of God could not have lacked the grace of discernment of spirits

The *discernment of spirits* is a light from on high, a type of complement to prophecy, which permits one to distinguish with surety the workings of good and evil spirits or to sound out the secrets of the heart. Mary could not have lacked this grace. She habitually enjoyed familiar conversation with the angels. Thus, when Gabriel brings her that sublime message, she did not hesitate but recognizes with certainty the divine envoy. She questions him about the great mystery and he gives a complete account of the wonder to take place in her. The Holy Spirit owes to his spouse such assistance and illumination, to protect her against every illusion of the devil in those instances when she was externally tempted, just as Our Lord himself was.

Further, she had to instruct and direct the numerous faithful who would come from everywhere to seek her counsel, her lights, and her charity. No one would doubt that her words were ever opportune, being always adapted to the needs of souls. She penetrated the secrets of the heart, God opening to her gaze that most intimate of sanctuaries. We further note that such a favor is frequent enough in the lives of the saints. It suffices to recall St. Anthony, St. Martin, St. Monica, St. Vincent Ferrer, St. Catherine of Sienna, St. Catherine de Ricci, St. Magdalen de Pazzi, and Blessed Anne Marie Taigi. We can rightly conclude that the Mother of God excelled in such knowledge to a yet greater degree.

Mary had the gift of tongues and interpretation of tongues

St. Antoninus, who follows the opinion of St. Albert, as well as Gerson, Suárez, Cornelius a Lapide, and the majority of modern theologians are willing to grant that she possessed the *gift of tongues*.[38] The Holy Spirit, who manifested himself in the form of tongues of fire upon the day of Pentecost, rested first of all in Mary with a fullness of all the gifts which would later be imparted to the apostles and disciples. He had not waited for that day to communicate such graces to her. While she was not commissioned to carry the faith to the various peoples of the universe, she still had to travel to foreign countries, at least to Egypt and to Ephesus. Could one believe that God would refuse to his Mother what he did so frequently for his servants? St. Dominic, traveling a day with German pilgrims who had given him food as alms, obtained from Heaven the gift of speaking their language, so that in his turn he might nourish them with the divine word. Without exercising the official role of apostle, the Blessed Virgin had to instruct, console, and encourage the priests and faithful who had recourse to her from every country. It would have been no less necessary to know their languages than to read the thoughts of their hearts.

This gift is completed by another, that of the *interpretation of tongues*. These two graces are distinct, and sometimes even given separately in the simple faithful, but can one conceive that they were not united in the Blessed Virgin? The first favor would be of little use without the second, and God does not do things halfway where his Mother is concerned.

Such, in summary outline, are the various plenitudes of grace in Mary. Let us end with this thought, already noted several times: God gave to Mary without measure and, when one abyss was filled, he would make another, so as to always and everywhere be giving to her.[39]

---

38. St. Antoninus, *Summa Theologica Moralis*, IVa, ch. 19; Jean Gerson, *Serm. I de Spiritu Sancto*, *Opera Omnia*, t. 3, 1245–46; Suárez, *Opera Omnia*, t. 19, *De Mysteriis Vitae Christi*, d. 20, s. 2, 311.

39. We willingly recognize that some of our conclusions could be controversial and that they oblige no one where the Catholic faith is concerned. We have indicated the main authorities upon which we rest our teaching: St. Ambrose, St. Thomas Aquinas, St. Anthony, St. Thomas de Villeneuve, Cajetan, Medina, Suárez, Contenson, St. Alphonsus. We have advanced here deductions or inductions which do not always give rise to absolute certitude, but which deserve to be taken into consideration by the theologian.

* * *

PART II

THE ROLE OF MARY IN THE ACQUISITION
AND DISTRIBUTION OF GRACES

* * *

CHAPTER 7

The Manifold Role of Mary in the Matter of Salvation: Her Exemplar Causality

Christ Jesus, the only necessary mediator

Full of divine life herself, the Mother of the human race superabounds in grace for us: *Plena sibi, superplena nobis.* One must not forget that there is a unique mediator between God and men, Christ Jesus. He alone could make reparation equal to the offense, he alone could merit and satisfy all the demands of justice on behalf of the fallen race. Again, it is he who provides to us each day, of his own power, the effects of salvation. This celestial rain and dew are engendered in the humanity of Christ. Yet this principal role does not exclude the universal action of Mary.

Mary, inseparable from Christ

The Savior could assuredly do without any helper in the work of Redemption. It pleased him, and it was the eternal plan, that the Virgin would be associated with him in all things. After having received physical life through her, he willed that she give birth to him spiritually in souls. She was to be the mother of his mystical body as well as his physical one. She, therefore, must give birth to all the brothers and sisters of Jesus, and it is by her plenitude, after that of Our Lord's, that we must be enriched. Hence the famous proposition that all graces reach us through the Blessed Virgin.

She is, like him, an exemplar, meritorious, satisfactory, and intercessory cause

This teaching, in order to be completely plausible, must not be understood solely of present intercession, abstracting from the part Mary took formerly in the matter of Redemption. The role of our Mother in the distribution of graces is the consequence of the role which she had in their acquisition. A single eternal decree having determined together both the Incarnation and the divine maternity, Christ and the Blessed Virgin were inseparable in the work of salvation. Their wills are united in a single consent and concourse, their actions united to merit and make satisfaction, their prayers and their intercession still united today to obtain and distribute graces. Let us never lose sight of this relationship. Just as in every church we reserve a place for the Redeemer and for his Mother—for the Blessed Sacrament and the Blessed Virgin—so too must we, in each mystery, perceive the work of Jesus and of Mary. The forgetfulness of this truth inspired St. Louis-Marie Grignion de Montfort with an eloquent and pious complaint:

> Here I turn to you for a moment, dear Jesus, to complain lovingly to your divine Majesty that the majority of Christians, and even some of the most learned among them, do not recognize the necessary bond that unites you and your Blessed Mother.[1]

If one wishes to express this relation precisely, one must say that the Mother of grace is the secondary cause wherever Christ is the principal cause. We happily contemplate in Jesus first of all our immaculate ideal; after him, Mary is the model of predestination. Jesus is the meritorious cause who obtains grace for us by right; Mary is a meritorious cause by way of fittingness and by right of friendship. Jesus offered satisfaction equal to and even superior to all the crimes of humanity; Mary, without paying such adequate ransom, made satisfaction in her own way for our faults. Jesus, in glory, remains our recognized intercessor; his wounds, those marks he retains, still act to intercede for us, and every heavenly

---

1. St. Louis-Marie Grignion de Montfort, *Treatise on True Devotion to the Blessed Virgin*, n. 63.

gift reaches us through him, just as every prayer of the Church is made in his name. Mary is, after him, the all-powerful one who pleads our cause, the one through whom every prayer must rise and every grace descend. To understand the universal action of Mary, one must study her exemplary causality, her meritorious power, her role in satisfaction, and her power of intercession.

Jesus, the ideal and mold of the elect

First of all, let us consider in her the ideal of our eternal predestination. The Word of God is the exemplar of all others, the principal light, source of all splendor, and primal beauty and every beauty's ideal and cause. It is in this mold that all was contained in eternity and it is by him that all has been created in time. Broken by the malice and cunning of the devil, God restored us through his Word, as an artist uses the same mold to shape his work and to repair it.[2] Christ became in all things our exemplar. He was predestined principally for natural sonship, and it is by his model that we are called to become sons of God by adoption. Someone predestined is someone chosen and, since election is a preferential love, someone predestined is first and foremost beloved. Thus God, in separating his elect from the common masses, looked upon his first Beloved, Christ the Savior, and took him as a model. In second place, Jesus was predestined to glory and the supernatural goods which accompany it. By his steps we are pointed towards eternal beatitude and all which that implies. All the elect must reflect this supreme ideal, as a crystal reflects the heavens. The Eternal Father must be able to recognize in beloved souls the features of Jesus. He must be able to say, "This is my Christ." They must revive in themselves his image and his visage, and predestination consists in giving us such conformity: *Praedestinavit conformes fieri imaginis Filii sui.*[3]

---

2. See St. Thomas, *ST* III, q. 3, a. 8, c.: "For the craftsman by the intelligible form of his art, whereby he fashioned his handiwork, restores it when it has fallen into ruin."

3. See Romans 8:29: "For whom he foreknew, he also predestinated to be made conformable to the image of his Son."

Mary, mold of God and ideal of the predestined

Christ and Mary, we have explained many times, are so closely linked in the divine plan, and there is between them such a likeness, that we could call them each the mirror of the other. So too Mary, according to St. Augustine, is the mold of God,[4] and by the same token the model for all of Christ's brethren. To have a right to glory one must be a little Christ, and to be a little Christ one must pass through the virginal mold that is Mary. God has formed us also after this model, and predestined us to reproduce in ourselves the radiant and blessed features of our Mother. Such is the traditional teaching.

The primicerius of our redemption

A pious writer, George of Venice, called the Blessed Virgin the *primicerius* of our redemption.[5] One gave the title of *primicerius* to the royal notary whose duty it was to inscribe soldiers in the army's rolls and to place the seal upon the tablets of functionaries and royal decrees. The Blessed Virgin is, in the supernatural order, the first "notary" of the great King. Not only is she at the head of the eternal rolls, but she is charged with enrolling all the predestined and sealing their names in the book of the elect. One must be marked with her seal and show her features in order to have a place among the Lord's beloved. The blessed Hugh of Saint-Cher goes even further. He does not shrink from calling the Mother of Jesus *librum vitae*, the book of life.[6] It is in her and

---

4.   TRANSLATOR'S NOTE: This quote, employed also by St. Louis-Marie de Montfort, is actually from an unknown author. See Sermon 208, n. 5, *PL* 39:2131: "Si formam Dei appellem, digna existis."

5.   See *De Harmonia Mundi*, cant. 2.

     TRANSLATOR'S NOTE: This appears to be a reference to the Franciscan friar Francesco Giorgi's *De Harmonia Mundi*, from 1525. I have been unable to locate the precise reference. Fr. Hugon's word in French is "primicière," taken from the Latin, which literally means "the one listed first on the wax tablet."

6.   Hugh of Saint-Cher, *Opera Omnia in Universum Vetus et Novum Testamentum*, t. 3, *Commentaria in Ecclesiastici*, ch. 24, 219b: "'All these things are the book of life,' that is, of all these things which we are speaking, the Blessed Virgin, who is the book of life, the great book, she contains them in herself by likeness and nature [*similitudinem et rationem*]."

     TRANSLATOR'S NOTE: Hugh of Saint-Cher (1200–1263) was a Dominican friar, cardinal, and biblical commentator. He wrote a biblical concordance as well as

through her that God etched the names of his chosen, just as he willed to form Christ in her and through her, his first chosen one. This is to say that all the saints are formed in the likeness of Mary.

God brings souls to Mary for her to name them

We could adopt for our subject the pleasing story told by Anastasius of Sinai.[7] He depicts the Eternal Father bringing all peoples to Christ so as to see what name he would give them. God also had Mary in view when calling his elect; he would consult her, bring souls to her, wait for her to choose a name for them, the one she gave being that which suited each best. Some are called sheep or lambs, because they are to conform to the image of the Virgin: they are the beloved, the chosen, the ones standing on the right. The others, who will not achieve their ideal, are called goats, foxes, ravenous wolves: such are those scum on the left, the crowd of the rejected and the accursed.

Mary, mark of the predestined

Furthermore, those who write about Mary say that she is the mark of the predestined. The reprobate are marked with the sign of the beast; those whom God preserves from eternal death are indelibly imprinted by Christ and bear the mark of his Mother. Whoever has the mark of the Virgin will be included among the elect.

The heritage of Mary, St. Louis-Marie Grignion de Montfort

St. Louis-Marie Grignion de Montfort explains this doctrine in a few very theological and pious pages. He depicts God the Son saying to his Mother: *In Israel haereditare*—"Take Israel for your inheritance."[8]

---

a commentary on the entirety of the Scriptures. Hugon's citation is to Sirach, Chapter 25, but it appears that Chapter 24 of Ecclesiasticus or Sirach is meant, the chapter wherein Wisdom praises herself; Sirach 24:32a is the verse in question: "All these things are the book of life."

7.   St. Anastasius of Sinai, *Hexaemeron*, lib. 9, PG 89:997–98.
      TRANSLATOR'S NOTE: Anastasius' comparison is between Adam and Christ, and Adam naming the animals and his wife to Christ naming all the predestined in the Church.

8.   TRANSLATOR'S NOTE: Note how Hugon interprets these expressions of Mary's involvement in election, that is, as involving her exemplarity.

It is as if he said, God the Father has given me as heritage all
the nations of the earth, all men good and evil, predestinate and
reprobate. To the good I shall be father and advocate, to the
bad a just avenger, but to all I shall be a judge. But you, my
dear Mother, will have for your heritage and possession only the
predestinate represented by Israel. As their loving mother, you
will give them birth, feed them and rear them. As their queen,
you will lead, govern and defend them.[9]

All such expressions aim at making comprehensible how the Mother of
grace is the exemplar of our predestination. Just as the artist contemplates an ideal internally in order to execute his masterpiece physically,
God looks upon Mary to produce his elect. Just as the work is the
imitation of the model, the predestined are the imitation of the Blessed
Virgin. Our concern must therefore be to transform ourselves to our
model, to carve in ourselves each of her characteristics by the practice
of her virtues, so that we might always be able to recognize in ourselves
her beloved image. It is pleasing to think that our Mother aids us in this
work, since she has merited for us and distributes graces to us.

---

9.   St. Louis-Marie de Montfort, *True Devotion*, n. 31.

CHAPTER 8

Mary as Cause of Merit and Satisfaction

The threefold value of the works of the saints

One distinguishes in the acts of the just a threefold worth: that they are meritorious, satisfactory, and intercessory. Merit grants one the right to eternal glory in the fatherland and the increase of grace on earth. Satisfaction has as its end the reparation of affront caused by sin to God's infinite majesty, and it is in this way expiatory; that is, it makes us favorable again to God whom we offended, and it becomes in that case propitiatory. One can pass on to others one's satisfaction, as many martyrs have done. Merit is inalienable. Those who heroically abandon to other suffering souls all the expiatory value of their good works do not strip themselves of their merits. Intercession is the power which the saints possess to obtain through prayer the graces necessary for salvation. It can be understood in what follows as efficacious merit. Thus, final perseverance escapes from the sphere of merit, it falls under the domain of intercession, for it is promised to all those who pray in the name of Our Lord Jesus Christ, with the required conditions.

Condign merit and fitting merit

Let us recall the well-known distinction between merit properly speaking, or condign merit, and the merit of fittingness. There is perfect merit, worthy of its reward, *de condigno*, when the worth of some work is equal to the worth of the recompense, and this is conferred in the name of justice. Fitting merit is based upon the right of friendship; it calls for a recompense which is a matter of liberality rather than an absolute obligation.

The condign merit of Christ and the just

Condign merit in Christ possesses all the stricture of a right in justice, for it proceeds entirely from the Savior. Among us, there is no such requirement, for it is a sort of grace, itself already a divine beneficence, such that Our Lord by crowning our merits crowns his own gifts. But, in view of God's promise or pact, there is a true proportion between merit and glory. This is why eternal life is called a recompense,[1] the salary for a day's work,[2] a crown of justice,[3] a retribution that is owed according to one's works,[4] and the payment for labor which divine justice cannot forget.[5]

It is a matter of faith that the just can, by their good works done with the grace and merit of Jesus Christ, obtain by true merit the growth of grace, eternal life, the possession of that happiness (if they die in the divine friendship), and lastly the increase of glory.[6] But can we merit for others, by a condign right? Our sphere of merit cannot extend further than the divine mark we are given for our own sanctification. Merit is entirely exhausted in us. In order to apply it to others, one would have to be the supernatural head of humanity. This role belongs to none but Jesus Christ. The universal principle of salvation, he becomes our justice by attributing to us his merits, just as he is our life by giving us his grace.

---

1.   Matthew 5:12: "…your reward [*merces*, recompense] is very great in heaven."

2.   Matthew 20:2: "And having agreed with the laborers for a penny a day…"

3.   2 Timothy 4:8: "There is laid up for me a crown of justice, which the Lord the just judge will render to me in that day."

4.   Romans 2:6–7: "Who will render to every man according to his works. To them indeed, who according to patience in good work, seek glory and honor and incorruption, eternal life."

5.   Hebrews 6:10: "For God is not unjust, that he should forget your work."

Fitting merit in Mary—B. Virgo de congruo meruit quod Christus de condigno

The Blessed Virgin, being neither the head of humanity nor the first cause of the supernatural, having herself received grace in view of the merits of her Son, cannot obtain salvation for us by a strict claim in justice. However, there is still merit of fittingness to consider, that right of friendship which is sovereign and efficacious. It is in this way that she takes part in our redemption: *B. Virgo de congruo meruit quod Christus de condigno*—the Blessed Virgin merited by a claim of fittingness all that which Christ merited in strict justice. This is an axiom commonly admitted by theologians.[7] In short, it states that the Mother is indissolubly joined to the Son in the entire economy of reparation.

Proofs of this assertion

If God asks for her consent with such formality, this is proof that he has decreed to make her will contribute to our salvation. The consent of the Virgin, says St. Thomas, was made in the name of the entire human race.[8] Why so? The Word came to contract an immortal alliance with our nature, and needed acceptance to be given in the name of the fiancée. This duty and honor was given to Mary. Furthermore, the free will of the first woman had been the cause of our death; so as to reestablish order and give the good its complete revenge, it had to be that our salvation come about through the free choice of the new Eve.

Once she had pronounced that *fiat*, she began her mission and became God's auxiliary. Our destiny is, so to speak, at her mercy, for

---

6. Council of Trent, Session 6, Can. 23: "If anyone says that the good works of the justified man are the gifts of God in such a way that they are not also the good merits of the justified man himself; or that by the good works he performs through the grace of God and the merits of Jesus Christ (of whom he is a living member), the justified man does not truly merit an increase of grace, eternal life, and (provided he dies in the state of grace) the attainment of this eternal life, as well as an increase of glory, let him be anathema" (Denzinger, n.1582).

7. See, among others, Véga, *Theologia Mariana*, t. 2, n. 1792, 400ff.; Lépicier, *Tractatus de Beatissima Virgine Maria*, 5th ed.; and Pius X, *Ad Diem Illum Laetissimum*, n. 14, the encyclical on the jubilee of the Immaculate Conception. There, the Pope takes into account the theologians' axiom.

8. St. Thomas, *ST* III, q. 30, a. 1, c: "Wherefore in the Annunciation the Virgin's consent was besought in lieu of that of the entire human nature."

our deliverance depends upon her acceptance.[9] At that unique moment in the history of divine mercies, Heaven regarded the humble girl from Nazareth, waiting upon her word.

> He did not choose that she should be a merely passive channel of His grace. He made her, further, a voluntary instrument who should contribute to the great work by the use of her own will. Is not this clear from the manner in which the Incarnation was announced to Mary? When the moment for accomplishing that Mystery—which has kept all nature expectant throughout the ages—has arrived, the Eternal Father sends an angel to make it known to her; and the angel awaits the maiden's decision, so that the great act shall not be performed without her consent. The moment she has given this the heavens are opened, the Son of God is made man, and the world has a Savior. Hence, the love and longing of Mary were in a measure necessary for our salvation.[10]

Once the angels had understood her response, they all with one voice burst forth—says St. Lawrence Giustiniani—into a triumphant hymn of thanksgiving: *Blessed be the Lord, the God of Israel, who has visited his people to redeem them.*[11]

The will of Mary is united to that of Jesus in the entire economy of reparation

From that point on the will of the Mother and the Son could not be but one when offering to God their life, their common supplications, and the same holocaust. Christ and Mary form a restorative couple, the celestial Father always considers them together, whether in the scenes of the Joyful Mysteries or in those of the Sorrowful Mysteries of the Passion. It is consequently natural that they had a common effect for the salvation

---

9. St. Bernard, *Super Missus Est*, Homily IV, *PL* 183:83, n. 8: "Offertur tibi pretium nostrae salutis; statim liberabimur si consentis.—The price of our salvation is offered to you; we will be free the moment that you consent."

10. Bossuet, *Devotion to the Blessed Virgin*, "On the Grounds of Devotion to the Blessed Virgin and the Saints," 2.

11. St. Lawrence Giustiniani, *Sermo de Annuntiatione*, 341.

of the world: *Cum Christo communem in salute mundi effectum obtinuit.*[12]
Grace flows from both of them, although in different ways, for Mary
obtains by a merit of fittingness what Christ does by a claim of justice.

The worth of her consent; Mary is charged with giving us life, thus she had to merit for us

The Mother of Christians is charged with giving to souls that supernatural life which begins in eternity and which redounds to eternity.
She does not produce it by her own power, of course, since that life is a
participation and an overflow of the divine nature, and which will arise
by way of merit. She is our mother in all things, as Christ is the principle of all our goods. Her efficacy must reach all that is also affected by
the causality of her Son, and her universal maternity demands that her
secondary merit, that of fittingness, extend to all which falls under the
primary and principal merit of Jesus Christ.

The respect God shows her demands that all her desires be granted

Lastly, the respect that God gives her demands that all her desires
be fulfilled. The author of grace perceives in her a dignity which borders
on the frontiers of the divine. Prayers coming from someone who is so
close are like orders. She wills for us the graces of the Lord, and with a
very ardent desire. Her excellence and dignity merit that such goods be
granted to us. God has no motive to refuse her. In her there is no shadow of imperfection, all is pure, all is beautiful. She is the charm of God,
the sovereign delight of the primal Love. Joined to the life and passion
of Christ Jesus, a martyr with him, offering with him heroic sufferings
and works of such a degree, she is worthy of being looked upon by the
Trinity in the same gaze with Jesus, such that all belonging to the Son
in strict justice be given also to her in friendship. We would henceforth
take the principle as incontestable: *B. Virgo de congruo meruit quod*

---

12. Arnold of Chartres, *Libellus de Laudibus B. Mariae Virginis, PL* 189:1727.
   TRANSLATOR'S NOTE: This quotation is given by St. Alphonsus, *The Glories of Mary*, p. 379, as follows: "Ipsa in nostra salute communem cum Christo effectum obtinuit.—She herself effected our salvation in common with Christ."

Christus de condigno. In Mary, the merit of fittingness is as extensive as the condign merit of Jesus Christ. She attained to half of the celestial kingdom. She is queen of mercy there, where Christ is king of justice.

Mary, aide of Christ and helper of the Most High

It is in thus cooperating with the Lord that she has become his aide. Richard de Saint-Laurent comments:

> The Lord was with Mary and Mary with him in the same trial and the same work of our Redemption. The Mother of mercy aided the Father of mercies in the affair of our salvation. It had been said in the earth paradise: *It is not good that man be alone; let us make a helper who is like unto him.* The first Eve was not an aid to man, but rather a cause of ruin; Mary is the true aid of the new Adam.[13]

The blessed Hugh of Saint-Cher, regarding Psalm 91:1, "He that dwelleth in the aid of the most High," quite gracefully explains how this aid is the Blessed Virgin Mary.[14] Denis the Carthusian summarizes the tradition when he affirms that it is by the prayers and the merits of the Virgin that the power and fruits of the passion of Christ Jesus are applied to men, and that the Apostles were filled with the Holy Spirit.[15]

Such is the universality of her merit. Let us now examine her role in the order of satisfaction.

Satisfaction in Mary—B. Virgo satisfecit de congruo ubi Christus de condigno

Here again, we would recall that Christ Jesus alone can offer reparation equal to the offense of mortal sin. If at issue is a simple venial fault which leaves the life of the soul intact and does no injury to one's last end, the just soul can, with divine aid, pay that limited debt. But

---

13. Richard de Saint-Laurent, *De Laudibus B. Mariae Virginis*, lib. 1.
    TRANSLATOR'S NOTE: Hugon does not give a more precise citation.
14. Hugh of Saint-Cher, *Opera Omnia in Universum Vetus et Novum Testamentum*, t. 2, *Comm. in Psalm. 90*, 240b.
15. Denis the Carthusian, *Opera Omnia*, t. 36, *De Laudibus Virginis*, lib. 2, a. 24, 100, and lib. 4, a. 1, 150.

the malice of mortal sin it cannot bear, since it attacks one infinite in majesty. Such an injury cannot be healed except by way of an infinite satisfaction. Now, the worth of satisfaction, like that of merit, comes from the excellence of the person. It lays claim to an extent and proportion based upon that dignity and cannot be infinite except on those grounds. That is to say that it would require a person of infinite dignity to make amends for a mortal sin, insofar as this is demanded by divine justice. But, already supposing the plenary satisfactions of Christ, Mary was able to offer for all our faults a fitting satisfaction—*B. Virgo satisfecit de congruo ubi Christus de condigno.* This second axiom is the corollary of the first principle of merit.

Proof of this assertion—satisfaction is proportional to merit

Satisfaction is always proportional to merit and grace. The meritorious treasures of Mary, augmented without interruption after the moment of her Immaculate Conception up until the hour of her blessed death, are truly unfathomable. It is the same regarding the riches of her satisfaction. And, since she never had to atone for herself, all her goods became our inheritance. These fell under the domain of the Church, who applies them to us through indulgences.

Satisfaction depends as to its worth upon a person's excellence

We note that the excellence of the person of Mary elevates the value of her actions in a unique fashion. That ineffable maternity, which bore her so close to God, constitutes as we have said a dignity of an order set apart.[16] All that proceeds from the Mother of God—merits or satisfactions—has a perfection that could never be found in any of the saints.

The sacrifice of Mary offered at Calvary

Let us recall as well that she offers the Trinity an infinitely propitiatory sacrifice. The sublime act *par excellence* in a life whose fabric was woven out of heroism was the gift of her only Son for the salvation of the human race. More generous and difficult than that of Abraham, she constantly renewed that offering, from the hour when the infant was

---

16. See Part I, Chapter 5, p. 75.

born, and in a more solemn manner on the day of the Presentation in the Temple. The victim was already dedicated to be immolated, indeed, from that moment when ancient Simeon announced the Passion of the Son along with that of the Mother.

The true and definitive sacrifice was made upon Golgotha. One could say that Mary was a priest at the foot of the Cross. She completed the sacrifice that we have described as having cost her all the pains possible to nature and grace. She herself, says St. Bonaventure, offered for us the only Son who is incomparably more dear to her than her own life.[17] She is a victim with him. There, two altars were raised by a single love, two innocent victims mutually immolated. This is a thought familiar to the holy Doctors, who contemplate upon Calvary's hill two altars. Upon the one lies the body of Jesus, suspended on the cross, offered by his passion. Upon the other the soul the Virgin is transfixed by her compassion. A sword of pain runs from Son to Mother to make of the two a single burning wound. The piercing of the Heart of Jesus is mirrored in the Heart of Mary with a strength so great that it ignites anew that wound in their souls.

The compassion of Mary

To fully appreciate her power of satisfaction, one must understand what the "compassion" of the Blessed Virgin was. Recall what we have said about her love for her Son,[18] and consider her intense desire to procure the glory of God and to save souls, her inexpressible anguish at the sight of the world's sins, at the thought of so many ungratefully refusing to benefit from the Passion, and of so much pointless suffering. Who has ever explored the depth of the wound made by that mysterious sword at Golgotha? Such tribulation, according to the explanation

---

17. St. Bonaventure, *Serm. I de B. V.*

TRANSLATOR'S NOTE: This quotation is given by St. Alphonsus, *The Glories of Mary*, p. 56, as follows: "Nulla post eam creatura ita per amorem nostrum exardescet, quae filium suum unicum, quem multo plus se amavit, nobis dedit, et pro nobis obtulit.—This love of Mary greatly obliges us to love her, seeing that she has loved us more than any other created being loves us, since she has given for us her only Son, whom she loved more than herself."

18. See Part I, Chapter 3, p. 39.

of the Fathers, was signified by the phrase *the sword which pierced*, by the violence of pain in her maternal soul. What the nails and the lance did to Christ's flesh, adds St. Bernard, maternal love did in the soul of the Blessed Virgin.[19] St. Lawrence Giustiniani says quite rightly that the Heart of Mary was the perfect mirror of the Passion of Christ.[20] All the blows, the wounds, and the pains of the Son are represented, reproduced, and experienced anew in the heart of the Mother. Ancient authors explain, in their innocent and exquisite manner, that between Christ and the Virgin there is more sympathy than between the two eyes of the same body, or between two lyres that vibrate with mutual resonance. Thus, all the sufferings of the Crucified find a living response in the compassionate soul of the one who is transfixed along with him.

Mary, martyr with Christ; her sorrowful maternity

As Adam and Eve cooperated in the same fault, so Christ and Mary were joined in the very same passion and the very same reparation. The two are both martyrs. Now, it is incomparably greater and more beautiful to be a martyr with Christ than to be a martyr for him: *Plus est esse commartyrem Christi quam esse martyrem Christi.*[21] St. Anselm says:

> Whatever cruelty was exercised upon the bodies of the martyrs was light, or rather it was as nothing, compared to the cruelty of Mary's passion. St. Bernardine of Siena says that so great was the

---

19. See St. Bernard, *Sermo de Passione.*
    TRANSLATOR'S NOTE: This appears to be a reference to Pseudo-Bernard; see *PL* 184:769ff.
20. St. Lawrence Giustiniani, *De Triumphali Christi Agone*, ch. 21, P. 277.
    TRANSLATOR'S NOTE: Again, see St. Alphonsus, *The Glories of Mary*, p. 524, who cites ch. 11; ch. 21 is meant. The passage is as follows: "Clarissimum passionis Christi speculum, effectum erat cor Virginis, necnon et perfecta mortis imago. In illo agnoscebantur sputa, convitia, verbera, et redemptoris vulnera. —The heart of Mary was the clearest mirror of the passion of Christ. Indeed, it was a perfect image of His death. In it were to be seen the spitting, the insults, the scourgings, and the wounds of the Redeemer."
21. William Abbas, *In Canticum Cantorum*, III.
    TRANSLATOR'S NOTE: See William of Newburgh, *Explanatio sacri epithalamii in matrem sponsi: A Commentary on the Canticle of Canticles (12th-C.)*, ed. J. C. Gorman (Fribourg, Switzerland: The University Press, 1960), p. 164.

dolor of the Blessed Virgin that if it was subdivided and parceled out among all creatures capable of suffering, they would perish instantly. An Angel revealed to St. Bridget that if Our Lord had not miraculously supported His Mother, it would not have been possible for her to live through her Martyrdom. It would be easy to multiply similar passages, both from the revelations of the Saints and the writings of the doctors of the Church.[22]

Therefore, Mary endured for us upon Calvary the pains of childbirth from which she was preserved in giving birth to her divine Son. In so giving birth to us she paid a ransom with her tears and suffering. Indeed, if she was immolated with Christ, she made satisfaction with him. A martyr like him, she is his aide in the work of Redemption. Before the Eternal Father, both of them share together in the great work of redeeming the human race. They establish together the inviolable covenant of our salvation. Mary was immolated with Christ in spirit, and intercedes for the salvation of the world. The Son implores and obtains grace for us; the Father pardons.[23]

I understand that the Doctors of the Church call Mary the redeemer of captives, the salvation of men, the mother and reparatrix of the human race.[24] Such diverse considerations and expressions reach the same conclusion: she atoned for us, and she can assert for our salvation in the order of satisfaction the sovereign right of fittingness, wherever Christ invokes the right of justice: *Maria satisfecit de congruo ubi Christus de condigno.*

22. Frederick William Faber, *The Foot of the Cross: Or, The Sorrows of Mary* (London: T. Richardson and Son, 1858), p. 9.

23. Arnold of Chartres, *Libellus de Laudibus B. Mariae Virginis*, PL 189:1726–27: "Dividunt coram Patre inter se Mater et Filius pietatis officia, et miris allegationibus muniunt redemptionis humanae negotium, et condunt inter se reconciliationis nostrae inviolabile testamentum. Maria Christo se spiritu immolat et pro mundi salute obsecrat, Filius impetrat, Pater condonat."

24. St. Ephrem, *Orat. ad Virg.*, ed. Venice, t. III, p. 195: "Captivorum redemptio et omnium salus." St. Lawrence Giustiniani, *Sermo In Nativitate Gloriosissima Viginis Mariae*, 364: "Genetricem, reparatricem saeculi."
    TRANSLATOR'S NOTE: I have been unable to locate the edition of St. Ephrem the Syrian that Hugon cites; later on, he cites from an edition published in Rome. However, this passage is cited by others (for instance, St. Peter Canisius or Cornelius à Lapide).

* * *

CHAPTER 9

The Power of Intercession

– WHETHER ALL GRACES, WITHOUT EXCEPTION, COME TO US THROUGH MARY – THE OPINION OF THE DOCTORS AND THEOLOGIANS

Catholic doctrine regarding the intercession of the saints

The Council of Trent defined as Catholic doctrine that the saints, once admitted to reign with Christ in heaven, offer to God their prayers for men, such that it behooves us to invoke them and to have recourse to them in our needs.[1] Jesus Christ alone is the necessary and principal intercessor, but it is no insult to him when we present him with our request through Mary or her companions. Since all merit depends upon his merits and every expiation upon his infinite satisfactions, there is consequently no intercession that does not draw its worth from him. He is always implicitly invoked, even if our demand is only addressed to one saint. Likewise, the Church concludes her prayers and orations with that equally eloquent formula so often repeated, *through Christ Our Lord.*

Mary, united to Christ for the distribution of grace

The collaborator with Christ in the acquisition of graces, Mary must remain united with him in the distribution of those same benefits, for the latter role is a consequence of the former. To simplify the question, we could speak only of the time which follows her glorious Assumption. Is it true that all the graces granted since then, or which will be granted to humanity until the end of time, had to or will have to pass through the hands of our Mother?

She is always at least implicitly invoked in every prayer

One could think of several hypotheses. Either one prays explicitly to the Blessed Virgin, and in that case it is natural that the favor asked be granted us by her mediation. Or one addresses oneself to one of the saints, who becomes our intermediary before the Queen, and then again it is she who obtains the grace. She is always implicitly invoked in every prayer. Or, lastly, celestial aid is conferred upon us without any demand on our part, just like the first grace, or the illuminations or inspirations which so frequently arise in the course of our life and inform our intellect and will, or like those pious movements which are freely accepted but for which we have not asked. Even in the case of such favors we concede that Mary is mediator.

Nor is it in a general way that divine life is communicated to us through her. Each grace in particular, for each individual person, whether it is a favor begged by our own prayers or a gift considerate and unasked-for, is due to the constant intercession of the Blessed Virgin. This is the case even of sacramental grace, for it is the Mother of God who procures for us the ministers of the sacrament and the dispositions to be admitted to the sacred ritual with profit.[2] It is in the most absolute sense that we understand our thesis. Without exception, no grace descends from heaven upon earth without having passed through the hands of Mary, that is to say, by her present mediation.

Status quaestionis

The Fathers and theologians of old, without having posed the question in such terms, left in their writings the substance of this teaching.

---

1.   Council of Trent, Session 25.
     TRANSLATOR'S NOTE: See Denzinger, nn. 1821–1822.
2.   TRANSLATOR'S NOTE: See the discussion of Otto Semmelroth's argument in the respect in the Translator's Essay "*Ancilla Domini et Ancilla Theologiae*," p. 277.

In the seventeenth century, Théophile Raynaud examined this opinion *ex professo*, one which he called pious but did not himself adopt. Jansenism tries to sustain the view contrary to this belief. A scholar of the eighteenth century, Muratori, combated it in the name of "well adjusted" devotion; he was refuted by St. Alphonsus Ligouri. Trombelli, although he constructed a beautiful theological monument to the glory of Mary, does not dare to embrace this opinion; he seems rather to be swayed by the opposite argument.[3] In the nineteenth century, which was Mary's century, the belief of pious souls became the common doctrine of the theologians.

This concerns graces granted after the Assumption

Before proving our proposition, we must clarify a preliminary question. In order for Mary to intercede in each case and for every grace, it is necessary that she know the prayers, needs, and concerns of each and every person. Does she possess such knowledge? We think the answer is yes, if we are considering favors granted after the Assumption. It is a principle admitted by all theologians and which has no need of being proven at the moment that, in heaven, the blessed have the right to the knowledge of all that could interest them here below by reason of their office, or their role, or their relationship with us. All this is a part of their beatitude, and we would not call perfectly happy a state which did not satisfy such legitimate desires. The founder of an order sees the struggles and the triumphs of his spiritual family; a father and mother, the needs of their children.

Mary is mother of all men in that efficacious maternity which is achieved through grace. Thus, it is necessary that she know all that which bears upon that supernatural life with which she is charged to provide us and maintain in us: the good acts which we pursue, the faults which are thus diminished or erased, along with all our thoughts and our desires, the dangers which menace us and the aid which she must preserve, as well as all our needs, temptations, and the graces which are useful or necessary for us. This universal knowledge, so certain and

---

3. See Trombelli's *De Culto Publico ab Ecclesia B. Mariae Exhibito*, in J. J. Bourassé, ed., *Summa aurea de laudibus Beatissimae Virginis*, t. 4 (Paris: Migne, 1862), d. 2, 23ff.

precise, extending to each detail of our destiny, is a prerogative of the divine maternity. It enters into the very notion of the rights and duties which the Blessed Virgin has towards us. It is all her concern, because she is our mother.

Mary knows all the graces we need, because she is our mother; she asks for them, because she is all good; she obtains them, because she is all powerful

Now, if she sees our necessities, there is no doubt that she is able and willing to remedy them. It is enough for a mother to suspect that her child has some need for her to try to relieve it. And, since her prayers are always efficacious and her desires always granted, we are thereby able to conclude that all supernatural aid reaches us through her intercession. This entire teaching can be summarized and proven in three steps: Mary knows all the graces of which we stand in need, because she is mother to all; thus, she asks for them, because she is all good; thus, she obtains them, because she is all powerful.

Testimony of tradition

Such is the pious belief which we embrace without hesitation, while declaring that one is free to think otherwise on this point. Let us examine its theological worth. This proposition is not new. We will find the seed of this doctrine in Christian antiquity.

Writes St. Germain of Constantinople: "No one receives the gifts of God except through you, O most pure! No one is granted divine grace except through you, O most honored!"[4]

St. Peter Damian declares that the Blessed Virgin holds in her hands all the riches of the divine mercy: "In your hands are the treasures of the Lord's mercies."[5] To say that she is the universal treasury, is this not to proclaim that all graces must arrive by way of her mediation? This is not a matter of a restrained intercession as is the case with the other saints, for the illustrious doctor adds that this privilege is reserved

---

4.   St. Germain of Constantinople, *Homily In S. M. Zonam*, PG 98:380.
5.   St. Peter Damian, *Sermo I De Nativitate Beatissimae Viginis Mariae*, PL 144:740: "In manibus tuis sunt thesauri miserationum Domini."

to the Mother of God alone: "Only you were chosen to be granted such a grace."[6]

St. Anselm, to fully explain how Mary is implicitly invoked in every prayer and that no aid can reach us without her intercession, says to her: "O Virgin, if you keep silent, no other saint could either pray for or aid us; as soon as you pray, the rest can both pray for us and come to our aid."[7] Yet it is above all St. Bernard who sheds light on this doctrine.

God placed in Mary the plenitude of every good. All that we have of hope, of grace, or salvation comes from her. Take away the star that enlightens the world, and where then is the day? Take away Mary, the Star of the Sea, of that vast and spacious ocean upon which we are tossed, and what is left? We become enveloped in obscurity and the shadow of death, wrapped in the thickest darkness. Therefore, let us honor Mary from the depths of our hearts, with our most intimate affections, with our whole will, for such is the will of the One who willed that we receive everything from Mary.[8]

Furthermore, he says: "God has decreed that nothing reach us without having passed through the hands of Mary."[9] This is expressed in nearly the same terms by St. Albert: "The universal distributor of all goods."[10] We draw the same lesson from St. Thomas:

The Blessed Virgin is called full of grace, because she pours out this divine life upon all men—*quantum ad refusionem in omnes homines*. It is already a great thing to possess the grace sufficient

---

6. Ibid.: "Sola electa es, cui gratia tanta concedatur."
7. St. Anselm, *Oratio 46 ad Sanctam Virginem Mariam*, PL 158:944: "Te tacente nullus orabit, nullus juvabit; te orante omnes orabunt, omnes juvabunt."
8. St. Bernard of Clairvaux, *Sermo In Nativitate B. V. Mariae, De Aquaeductu*, PL 183:441, nn. 6–7.
    TRANSLATOR'S NOTE: This is a translation of Hugon's French.
9. Ibid., *Sermon 3 In Vigiliis Nativitatis Domini*, PL 183:100, n. 10: "Nihil nos Deus habere voluit, quod per Mariae manus non transiret."
10. Pseudo-Albert, *Mariale*, q. 29: "Omnium bonitatem universaliter distributiva."

for the salvation of a great number of souls; it is exceedingly great to have the grace that suffices for the salvation of the entire human race. Such is the privilege of Christ and of his Mother. In *every* peril you can obtain salvation from her; in *every* work of virtue you can have recourse to her. It is said of her in Scripture (Sirach 24:25): "In me is all hope of life and of virtue."[11]

Thus, according to the Angelic Doctor, Mary can obtain for us all aid to practice every virtue, to avoid every peril, to conquer every temptation, that is to say the whole array of supernatural goods. St. Thomas does not speak here of a sterile or indifferent power. He knows well that in the case of the Mother of mankind *to be able* is *to do*. If she can procure all graces for us, we can conclude that, in truth, she wills to obtain them and she does so.

Here is the clear testimony of St. Bernardine of Siena:

Such is the economy of graces which descends upon the human race. God is its universal source, Christ its universal mediator, Mary the universal distributor. The Virgin, indeed, is the mystical neck of our divine head, for it is through that organ that the celestial gifts are communicated to the rest of the body. This is why it is said of Mary (Song of Songs 7:4): "Thy neck is as a tower of ivory."[12]

---

11. St. Thomas Aquinas, *Commentary on the Angelic Salutation*.

    TRANSLATOR'S NOTE: The translation of J. B. Collins reads: "The plenitude of grace in Mary was such that its effects overflow upon all men. It is a great thing in a Saint when he has grace to bring about the salvation of many, but it is exceedingly wonderful when grace is of such abundance as to be sufficient for the salvation of all men in the world, and this is true of Christ and of the Blessed Virgin. Thus, "a thousand bucklers," that is, remedies against dangers, "hang therefrom" (Song of Songs 4:4). Likewise, in every work of virtue one can have her as one's helper. Of her it was spoken: "In me is all grace of the way and of the truth, in me is all hope of life and of virtue" (Sirach 24:25). Therefore, Mary is full of grace, exceeding the Angels in this fullness and very fittingly is she called "Mary" which means "in herself enlightened": "The Lord will fill your soul with brightness" (Isaiah 48:11). And she will illumine others throughout the world, for which reason she is compared to the sun and to the moon."

12. St. Bernardine of Siena, *Sermones*, t. 2, *In Quadragesimali*, Sermon 10, 54.

And furthermore:

> Mary possesses the beauty of the moon. She dispenses to her companions the light of divine wisdom, the celestial rose. So we can say with St. Bernard, "No grace descends from heaven upon the earth without passing through the hands of the glorious Virgin." Or with St. Jerome: "The plenitude of grace is in Christ as in the head from which all grace proceeds, while it is in Mary as the mystical neck which transmits the power of the head." This is why Solomon spoke of the Virgin in so speaking of Christ: "Thy neck is as a tower of ivory." Just as in the physical order the effects of the head are distributed to the other members by the organ which unites the head to the other members, so also is it through Mary that the powers of grace descend from the head, Christ, to the spiritual body, and in particular to the souls devoted to such an august Queen.[13]

Gerson is of the same mind:

> O you who are the Mother of grace, the illustrious Virgin through whose hands we receive, in the words of St. Bernard, all the goods that are granted to us, you who are rich for all those who invoke you; we implore you by so greeting you, and greet you by so imploring you.[14]

Suárez was himself a champion of this doctrine.[15] Vega expressly taught it and founded it upon numerous authorities.[16] Contenson explains it in language that is as pious as it is theological:

---

13. St. Bernardine of Siena, *Sermones*, t. 4, *De glorioso nomine Virginis Mariae*, Sermon 3, a. 3, ch. 2, 81.

14. Gerson, *Sermo in Coena Domini*.
    TRANSLATOR'S NOTE: The 1728 Hague edition of Gerson's works lists three sermons on the Lord's Supper. I have been unable to find this quote.

15. Suárez, *Opera Omnia*, t. 19, *Mysteria Vitae Christi*, d. 23, s. 3, n. 5, 336.

16. Véga, *Theologia Mariana*, t. 2, n. 1725ff., 402ff.

By pronouncing the words *Behold your mother*, Christ seems to say: Just as no one can be saved except by the merits of my Cross, no one can share in the benefits of my blood except by the intercession of my Mother. He alone will be regarded as the son of my sufferings who would have Mary for mother. My wounds are the eternal sources of grace, they remain ever open. But their streams cannot reach souls except by flowing through the conduit and channel that is Mary. You invoke me in vain as a father if you do not wish to honor Mary as mother.[17]

Therefore, seek grace, but through Mary, for such is the will of God. He has decreed that every gift reach us through Mary, and he placed in her the fullness of every good.[18]

The Virgin is called the complement of the Trinity for various reasons. One of these is that all the blessings which flow from the Trinity upon us must be applied to us through the prayers of the Mother of God. Thus the expression that the Fathers loved to use: Mary, artery of the Trinity, vein of salvation. Just as blood is the life of the body, circulating through the arteries and veins, so also grace, the life of the soul, descends and ascends through Mary. St. Bernard has admirably summarized this teaching: "The Virgin knew how to be all to all, to the wise or to the unlearned, supporting their weak wills by the abundance of her charity. To all she opened the breast of her mercy so that all might receive from her fullness: the captives, deliverance; the sick, healing; the afflicted, consolation; sinners, pardon; the just, grace; the angels, joy. To the entire Trinity she gives a new glory, to the person of the Son human flesh. In such a way, no one escapes from her sweet warmth." Since, therefore, this plenitude is poured out upon all things, the Virgin is rightly called the complement of the Trinity.[19]

---

17. Contenson, *Theologia Mentis et Cordis*, t. 3, lib. X, diss. 4, ch. 1, 211.
18. Ibid., lib. X, d. 6, ch. 1, 269.
19. Ibid., ch. 2, 287–88.

Let us now listen to St. Louis-Marie Grignion de Montfort:

God the Son imparted to his mother all that he gained by his life and death, namely, his infinite merits and his eminent virtues. He made her the treasurer of all his Father had given him as heritage. Through her he applies his merits to his members and through her he transmits his virtues and distributes his graces. She is his mystical channel, his aqueduct, through which he causes his mercies to flow gently and abundantly.

God the Holy Spirit entrusted his wondrous gifts to Mary, his faithful spouse, and chose her as the dispenser of all he possesses, so that she distributes *all his gifts and graces* to whom she wills, as much as she wills, how she wills and when she wills. *No heavenly gift is given to men which does not pass through her virginal hands.* Such indeed is the will of God, who has decreed that we should have all things through Mary.[20]

Bossuet will summarize for us, in his grand manner, this exalted theology:

God having one time willed to give us Christ Jesus through the Holy Virgin, the gifts of God being without repentance (Romans 11:29), this arrangement does not change. It is and always will be true that having received through his charity the universal principle of grace, *we still receive through his mediator the various applications in all the different states which constitute the Christian life.* Her maternal charity having thus contributed to our salvation in the mystery of the Incarnation, which is the universal principle of grace, *she thus eternally contributes in all other works, which are thereby but dependent.*[21]

---

20. St. Louis-Marie de Montfort, *True Devotion*, nn. 24–25.
21. Bossuet, *Oeuvres oratoires de Bossuet*, ed. J. Lebarq, et al., t. 5 (Paris: Libraire Hachette, 1922), "Sermon for the Conception of the Blessed Virgin," pp. 603–604.

St. Alphonsus has extensively considered this question, which is particularly dear to him, in *The Glories of Mary*.[22] He has answered the attacks aims at such a pious and solid doctrine.

In our own day this opinion has become the common one. It suffices to cite Petitalot, Suavé, De La Broise, Lépicier, and Terrien (who gives a complete list of the supporters of this pious belief).[23]

It remains to prove our thesis through the teachings of the Church and theological arguments.

---

22. See Part I, ch. 5, and Part II, Discourse 5.

23. John-Baptiste Petitalot, *La Vierge Mère d'après la Théologie*, 2nd ed. (Paris: Bray & Retuax, 1869), t. 2, ch. 16; Charles Suavé, *Jésus intime: Élevations dogmatiques*, (Paris: Vic & Amat, 1907), t. 3, pp. 385ff.; René-Marie de La Broise, "Sur cette proposition: Toutes les grâces nous viennent par la Sainte Vierge," *Études*, Vol. 68 (1896), pp. 30ff (this work was later published as a book); Lépicier, *Tractatus de Beatissima Virgine Maria*, pp. 404ff.; Terrien, *La Mère des hommes*, t. 3, lib. VII, chs. 3–4, pp. 561ff. See also Jean Bainvel, "Marie, Mère de grâce," *Etudes*, Vol. 94 (1903), pp. 577–603, on the same subject. This work was also published separately.

TRANSLATOR'S NOTE: Hugon refers to some works involved in the late nineteenth- and early twentieth-century movement supporting a dogmatic definition of Mary as the Mediatrix of all graces; concerning this movement, see Gloria Falcão Dodd, *The Virgin Mary, Mediatrix of All Graces*.

* * *

CHAPTER 10

Proof of the Power of Mary's Intercession

THE OPINION OF THE CHURCH AND THEOLOGICAL ARGUMENTS

The declarations of the Sovereign Pontiffs, Benedict XIV and Leo XIII

We have first of all the declarations of the Sovereign Pontiffs. Although it is not a dogmatic definition, this official and solemn teaching does not propose or recommend to the faithful a doctrine without a solid foundation in the tradition. What is more, it expresses a general Catholic belief. Thus it will be enough to mention two sources. Benedict XIV, at the beginning of his celebrated bull *Gloriosae Dominae*, proclaims that "Mary is as the celestial channel through which descend into the hearts of unfortunate mortals the waters *of all graces and of all gifts.*" Leo XIII is even more explicit. He explains the economy of the Rosary as follows:

> First, as is meet and right, comes the Lord's Prayer, addressed to Our Father in Heaven: and having, with the elect petitions dictated by Our Divine Master, called upon the Father, from the throne of His Majesty we turn our prayerful voices to Mary. Thus is confirmed that law of merciful meditation of which We have spoken, and which St. Bernardine of Siena thus expresses:

"Every grace granted to man has three degrees in order; for by God it is communicated to Christ, from Christ it passes to the Virgin, and from the Virgin it descends to us."[1]

Let us clearly understand what these degrees mean. If it concerns the physical production of graces, God puts them directly into the soul, using the Humanity of Christ as an efficacious instrument. Yet in the order of moral causality there is an order and way of proceeding truly harmonious. God sees and grants the prayers of Mary, and the Virgin, whether she had been called upon indirectly or directly, provides for our needs and makes sure than heavenly blessings reach us. Every divine gift reaches us through her intercession.[2]

The Liturgy implies that Mary is charged with presenting our prayers to Christ and assisting us in all our needs

In the second place we have the liturgy. It conveys in its actions the belief of the Church, and one could say, with Pope St. Celestin, that dogma and prayer have one and the same law: *Lex supplicandi statuit legem credendi.*[3] Now, the Liturgy of Hours frequently recall this universal intercession. It implies that Mary is charged with presenting our prayers to Christ—*Sumat per te preces.*[4] She also aids Christians in all of their necessities:

Holy Mary, succor the wretched, help the faint-hearted, comfort the sorrowful, pray for the people, intervene to aid the clergy,

---

1.   Pope Leo XIII, *Iucunda Semper Expectatione*, n. 5.

2.   TRANSLATOR'S NOTE: For more on this topic, and Hugon's argument that Mary is not merely a moral cause of grace, see the Appendix, "The Instrumental Causality of the Most Holy Virgin."

3.   TRANSLATOR'S NOTE: The law of praying establishes the law of believing. See *The Catechism of the Catholic Church*, n. 1124: "The Church's faith precedes the faith of the believer who is invited to adhere to it. When the Church celebrates the sacraments, she confesses the faith received from the apostles—whence the ancient saying: *lex orandi, lex credendi* (or: *legem credendi lex statuat supplicandi* according to Prosper of Aquitaine, fifth century). The law of prayer is the law of faith: The Church believes as she prays. Liturgy is a constitutive element of the holy and living Tradition."

4.   TRANSLATOR'S NOTE: "He accepts our prayers through you," from the *Ave Maris Stella*.

intercede for virgins, let all feel thy help who celebrate thy holy commemoration.[5]

An argument taken from the Our Father and the Hail Mary at the beginning and end of the Divine Office

To show clearly that her mediation is present for every grace, after that of Christ, the Church desires that at the beginning and the end of every hour, and even the beginning and end of every complete Office, the Hail Mary be recited after the Our Father. This practice furnishes us with the argument that De La Broise proposes as follows:

> The means which the Church uses to remind us that Our Lord is the universal mediator and that every grace comes through him is to present all our prayers to God through him. Indeed, in every liturgical prayer, the mediation of Our Lord is indicated at least by the Our Father, which we learned from him and which we recite with him, as also by the conclusions to prayers. Likewise the Church, in her daily Office, presents no prayer to God without having recourse secondarily to the intercession of Mary. Does this not imply that her intercession, although of a lower rank than that of Christ, is nonetheless also a universal and necessary intercession?[6]

The Rosary—its solemn recitation by all the faithful is an indicator that the Church looks to Mary for every help and aid

Another proof of this belief is the devotion of the Rosary. The Church, by her general and daily practice and by the repeated teaching of the Pontiffs recommends the Rosary to us insistently, that highest power of Marian invocation. When nations trembled and whole peoples seemed to stagger upon quaking ground, when political men were

---

5. Prayer of the Office, "O Beata Virgo," taken from St. Augustine, Sermon 18, *De Sanctis*.
6. De La Broise, "Sur cette proposition: Toutes les grâces nous viennent par la Sainte Vierge," 29.

anguished in their dealings with one another, Pope Leo XIII published every year a humble encyclical on the Rosary. He was sure of having found the true cure to the maladies of our age, he who was a great theologian and who had plumbed the depths of Christianity, the great man of State who had seen all the needs and aspirations of our modern times. Why this insistence on prayer to the august Virgin? Why the solemn month dedicated to her throughout Christendom, a practice maintained by all his successors?

Why is the Hail Mary repeated in the most critical situations and during the most pressing dangers? Is this not a sign that the Church has hope in Mary, even in the most difficult and desperate circumstances? And, if the Church recognizes that the most efficacious and extraordinary aid reaches her through the mediation of the Mother of mercy, does this not imply that it must be so, and all the more so, when it comes to other particular gifts and all common graces? Such spectacular supplication by the Universal Church through the Rosary provides for our thesis an argument of the first rank. This seems to fit well with what Leo XIII understands in the encyclical already cited. After having recalled that grace reaches us in three degrees, from God to Christ, from Christ to Mary, and from Mary to our souls, he adds:

> And we, by the very form of the Rosary, do linger longest, and, as it were, by preference upon the last and lowest of these steps, repeating by decades the Angelic Salutation, so that with greater confidence we may thence attain to the higher degrees—that is, may rise, by means of Christ, to the Divine Father. For if thus we again and again greet Mary, it is precisely that our failing and defective prayers may be strengthened with the necessary confidence; as though we pledged her to pray for us, and as it were in our name, to God.[7]

Let us now consider theological proofs.

---

7. Pope Leo XIII, *Iucunda Semper Expectatione*, n. 5.

In every solemn circumstance when Christ Jesus distributed grace during his earthly life, he willed that it would be through the intercession of Mary; it is by her that he grants the call to faith, justification, and perseverance

The first is drawn from the Gospel. In every solemn circumstance when Christ distributed grace during his earthly life, he willed that it would be through the intercession of Mary. It is through her that he sanctifies the Forerunner, through her and at her behest that he reaffirms the faith of the Apostles in the miracle of Cana, through her that he confirms in grace the Apostle John at Calvary, where from his lips came that marvelous phrase: *Woman, behold thy son; Behold thy mother.* These three scenes summarize the entire supernatural economy. The principal operations of salvation flow from three orders of grace: the call to faith (which is the first step), justification (which causes our progress), and perseverance (at the end of our journey).

Now, according to the traditional interpretation, so well explained by Bossuet, the grace of vocation is depicted in the sudden illumination that the Forerunner received in the womb of his mother. Justification is represented in the wedding feast of Cana in the person of the Apostles, who were then confirmed in faith and grace upon seeing that great miracle. St. John, the beloved disciple, who with Mary followed Christ even to the Cross, represents on Calvary both mercy and grace—both adoption and eternal predestination, the faithful companions of the Savior Jesus, who both persevered with him until the end.[8]

By depicting through Mary these three stages of salvation, Christ allows us to understand that any other aid must pass through her, since such aid is nothing but the consequence of, or dependent upon, or the application of these three fundamental graces. Thus we conclude, along with that profound theologian Bossuet, that Mary's charity is "a general instrument for the operation of grace," that is to say, a universal cause which contributes to each and every effect of salvation.

---

8.   Bossuet, *Oeuvres oratoires de Bossuet*, t. 5, pp. 604ff.

After the Ascension, Christ Jesus willed that the effusion of the Holy Spirit be effected by the intercession of the Blessed Virgin; this is the image of what is to take place in the Church until the end of time

After the Ascension, Our Lord wills that the effusion of the Holy Spirit take place through the intermediation of the august Virgin. He teaches us by this mystery what the economy of grace will be for all subsequent time. Pentecost was the image of all that God must work in souls until the end of time. Christ will maintain the order that he established for the distribution of his gifts from the beginning of his Church, for all other graces are the consequences and as it were the particular application of that great and holy event which sanctified and confirmed the nascent Church. Now, this first effusion of grace in the Upper Room was accomplished through Mary; therefore, until the end of time, the gifts of God will be transmitted through her.

> Nevertheless, for the fulfillment of the task of human redemption there remains still the coming of the Holy Ghost, promised by Christ. And behold, Mary is in the room, and there, praying with the Apostles and entreating for them with sobs and tears, she hastens for the Church the coming of the Spirit, the Comforter, the supreme gift of Christ, the treasure that will never fail.[9]

The power of intercession advances along with merit—Mary having merited all graces in union with Jesus, must also distribute all graces in union with him

Another decisive reason can be drawn from the doctrine we have previously explained regarding the merits and satisfactions of the Blessed Virgin. The power of intercession advances along with meritorious or expiatory worth, for it is due, just like them, to the state of grace and the dignity of the person. One's mediation in heaven depends upon the merits acquired here below. Since in Mary the power of merit and satisfaction attained to a secondary degree all that which Christ

---

9. Pope Leo XIII, *Iucunda Semper Expectatione*, n. 4.

Jesus obtained as the principle cause and in strict justice, it is fitting that the secondary intercession of the Mother of Christians extend just as far as the principal intercession of the Savior, that is to say to all graces without exception. Indeed, it seems just that the role of the Virgin in the distribution of graces correspond entirely to the role she previously had in their acquisition. She merited all for us, secondarily and in union with her Son; she must distribute all to us, albeit through a secondary mediation and in union with Jesus.

Response to a difficulty

One might object that Mary was able to merit without knowing us, whereas her role in distributing graces demands an intimate and detailed knowledge of all people and of all their needs.[10]

We reply, first of all, that in the Old Testament, graces were given as it were on credit, in virtue of the future merits of the Redeemer and his Mother. The efficacious merit of the Virgin is therefore extended by anticipation to the ancient saints, just as it must reach all those called under the New Law. As to her intercession, she was already all powerful during her mortal life. We believe that her prayers drew from heaven the gifts received by the Apostles and the first faithful. But was it necessary that she already know all human souls, their conditions, and their needs? Some venerable mystics have thought that she received this knowledge through private revelation. Yet could she not pray for men without knowing them in every detail?

Be that as it may, she had this plenary knowledge after her crowning in heaven, for such is a prerogative of her beatitude, as we have explained above. In the case of graces conferred after the Assumption, the thesis escapes from all difficulties. Just as in her life the Blessed Virgin shared with Christ in the acquisition of the treasures of salvation, so too is she in heaven charged with distributing them to us. Knowing all our needs, she is able and she wills to shower them upon all. Let us repeat once more: she knows all the graces of which we stand in need, because

---

10. TRANSLATOR'S NOTE: That is, since merit involves the rewards for one's own works, one need be aware only of what one is doing as oneself; but *voluntary* distribution to others implies a knowledge of other persons.

she is wholly a mother; she asks for them, because she is all good; she obtains them, because she is all powerful.

As Mary was united to Christ in the work of Redemption, she must yet remain so joined in the heavenly work of sanctification

Our Lord having decreed that his Mother would be united with him in the work of Redemption, it is natural that she remain associated with him still in heaven for the work of sanctification, which is indeed the complement of the former. The Incarnation could not have been accomplished without her formal and specific consent. What resulted, the prolongation of the Incarnation, supernatural gifts, salvation, must also depend upon her consent, constant and renewed without ceasing. This influence is thus continuous and applied to all effects: the graces of pure thoughts, generous desires, firm resolutions, holy deeds, sublime heroism, and divine enthusiasm all come from that universal intercession. The life of the body requires the presence of the atmosphere, and supernatural life cannot be maintained without the double efficacy of Christ and the Virgin. They both form the enveloping atmosphere in which our souls breathe.

The fundamental reason, her title as Mother of mankind

The fundamental reason is her title as Mother of mankind. The virginal fecundity of Mary works its effects upon the Mystical Body just as much as upon the physical body of Christ. This spiritual childbirth is but the complement of her divine maternity.

Supernatural maternity requires an action renewed without ceasing

The office of mother, in the supernatural order, is not only to give life but also to preserve it, to look after it, to strengthen it. Physical existence, once given, can be developed through the normal course of nature; the womb of the mother is not continually necessary. The life of salvation, in order to grow, requires an immediate and continuous influence from on high. For every meritorious or even salutary action, new power is required, a new movement, an actual grace. If Mary is truly and entirely our Mother, she must grant to us at each of those movements an increase of our supernatural strength, of those vital energies needed to bring the soul to its maturity—in a word: each of those graces that cultivate the spiritual life.

Mary is wholly mother; she gives and conserves in us all that we have in the spiritual life

Now, it is true that Mary is wholly a mother—all mother, *tota mater*—in her whole soul, with all her heart, in all her tenderness, in all her joys, in all her sorrows. She is all mother for all of us, for everyone, for everything that is relevant to our life. After having given birth to us at the price of so cruel a martyrdom, she does not abandon her children who are so many Christs she is charged with fashioning. Since this formation is not finished except at the last moment of our earthly pilgrimage, our Mother is continually occupied with giving, conserving, protecting, and developing all that we have in the supernatural life. Now, it is by procuring each and every grace for us that she will be all mother, wholly mother, in the order of salvation. Try to remove some one of these gifts from her intercession and merits, and you would have diminished her maternity. Yet that is in no way allowed. It is too pleasant to think of and speak of her as all mother.

Mary, heart of the Church, transmits life to all its members

Let us consider, lastly, the place that she occupies in the Church. The magnificent teaching of St. Paul on the subject of the Mystical Body of the Savior is well known. We could distinguish in it three organs which communicate life to the members. The head is Jesus Christ. From him descends all energy and movement, and without that immediate and continual influence the body would be left inert, paralyzed. The role of the head, clearly, belongs to Our Lord by reason of his visible humanity. The heart of the Church is the Holy Spirit. The function of the heart, in fact, is interior and hidden. It is very appropriate to the divine Paraclete, who exercises in the Church a secret and mysterious operation, but universal and all-powerful. It provides circulation to all the members, that blood and life which promotes youth and immortality, and it communicates this to us by its strong heartbeats so that the blood of our soul might well up to eternal life.

After the Holy Spirit, in a secondary manner, Mary too is called the heart of the Church, and we have previously said how this mystical organ had ever been awake,[11] how the Church could say: I sleep, my other members suspend at times the series of their merits; but my heart, Mary, is awake ceaselessly, continuing day and night her blessed work of sanctification. This heart, without a doubt, depends upon the head, Christ, and receives its motion from him, but it is thereupon charged with transmitting life and warmth to all members, even to the body's extremities. Not a single drop of divine blood, that is to say no grace, does not flow from the heart, from Mary.

Maria collum Ecclesiae—*the power of the head, Christ, flows through Mary, the neck, in order to reach us*

There is a third organ whose function is attributed to Mary: *Maria collum Ecclesiae*. All the influence of the head must, in order to reach the body's members, pass through that living column upon which the head rests. Mary is the mystical neck. She is in all things dependent upon Christ, and it is from him that she draws the plenitude of her perfections. But the Savior must make use of her to act upon our souls, having willed that she be the immortal and efficacious organ that would link him to the other members of his body.

This comparison colorfully expresses how, in the order of intercession, grace descends from Christ to Mary, and from Mary to our souls. It shows also how grace, thus transformed into merits and supplications, returns from our souls to the Mother of glory and then to Jesus, and through him, into that eternity of which she partakes.[12]

Maria aquaeductus—*Mary, the Channel*

Mary is therefore the conduit which carries to us the living waters of salvation, an *aquaeductus*, as St. Bernard says. The ocean of grace, as we have often repeated, is Our Lord Jesus Christ. But these inexhaustible

---

11. See Chapter 5, p. 81.
12. Regarding this comparison, see St. Bernard of Clairvaux, *Sermo In Nativitate B. V. Mariae, De Aquaeductu, PL* 183:437ff.; St. Bernardine of Siena, *Sermones*, t. 4, *De glorioso nomine Virginis Mariae*, Sermon 3, a. 1, ch. 4, 79; St. Robert Bellarmine, *Conciones*, Sermon 42, *De Nativitate B. V. M.*, 293ff.

waters, in order to come to us and return to their sources, must follow that channel, pure and deep, that is Mary. The Blessed Virgin is, therefore, the river that is always full, where the waves of time meet and are united to those of eternity.[13]

---

13. See the work of Bover, S.J., *De Universali Mediatione Beatae Mariae Virginis* (Barcelona, 1925).

TRANSLATOR'S NOTE: I have been unable to locate a record of this book.

$*\ *\ *$

CHAPTER I I

Final Doctrinal Precisions

This pious belief, combatted during the eighteenth century and again at the start of the nineteenth, has become little by little the common view of theologians, and has been confirmed finally by the Popes.

The teaching of Pope Leo XIII

Pope Leo XIII expresses it as follows in the document already cited.[1]

It may also be affirmed that *nothing* from the immense treasure of grace provided to us by Our Lord…*nothing—as God has willed—is granted to us except through Mary*, such that, as no man can go to the Father except through the Son, so no man is able to go to Christ except through His Mother.[2]

Now, if *nothing* reaches us except through Mary, it is clear that her mediation is universal and extends to *all graces* without exception.

Pope Pius X in the encyclical for the jubilee of the Immaculate Conception

Pope Pius X, in his encyclical written for the jubilee of the Immaculate Conception, explains his magnificent teaching which confirms our principal theses on the role of Mary in the acquisition and distribution of graces. The papal document notes the satisfactory worth of the actions of the Blessed Virgin, whose "was also the office of tending and nourishing that Victim, and at the appointed time presenting Him for the sacrifice. Hence that uninterrupted community of life and labors of the Son and the Mother."[3] Also, her role in merit: "[She] has been associated by Jesus Christ in the work of redemption, she merits for us *de congruo*, in the language of theologians, what Jesus Christ merits for us *de condigno*."[4] And, the power of intercession and universal mediation for the distribution of graces: "She is the supreme Minister of the distribution of graces."[5]

The encyclical validates the fundamental reasons upon which we have tried to shed light: Mary is at the same time mother of the natural and the mystical body of the Savior. She is indissolubly united to her Son to merit, satisfy, and intercede: "Mary, as St. Bernard justly remarks, is the channel…or, if you will, the connecting portion the function of which is to join the body to the head and to transmit to the body the influences and volitions of the head—We mean the neck."[6]

For this reason, in order to worthily celebrate the august Virgin, the Sovereign Pontiff thought it necessary to associate the two most glorious privileges of Mary: her Immaculate Conception and her two-fold maternity.

1.　TRANSLATOR'S NOTE: Hugon cites Pope Leo XIII's 1894 encyclical on the Rosary, *Iucunda Semper Expectatione*. However, the quote is from his 1891 encyclical on the Rosary, *Octobri Mense*.

2.　Pope Leo XIII, *Octobri Mense*, n. 4: "Affirmare licet, nihil prorsus de permagno illo omnis gratiae thesauro, quem attulit Dominus…*nihil nobis, nisi per Mariam, Deo sic volente, impertiri*: ut, quo modo ad summum Patrem, nisi per Filium, nemo potest accedere, ita fere, nisi per Matrem, accedere nemo possit ad Christum."

　　TRANSLATOR'S NOTE: Note that the standard English translation of this passage obscures by omission the passage which Hugon italicizes for emphasis; I have followed Hugon's rendering of the Latin.

3.　Pope Pius X, *Ad Diem Illum Laetissimum*, n. 12.

4.　Ibid., n. 14.

5.　Ibid.

6.　Ibid., n. 13.

Pope Benedict XV and the title of Mediatrix and Coredemptrix

Pope Benedict XV confirms all this by giving to the Blessed Virgin the two titles that express this doctrine effectively, that is to say, *Mediatrix* and *Coredemptrix*. Indeed, he approved in January 1921, for Belgium and other countries which would seek it, the feast of the Blessed Virgin Mary, mediatrix of all graces: *De Festo Beatae Mariae Virginis Mediatricis omnium gratiarum*. And in a letter addressed to the Confraternity of Our Lady of a Good Death, he wrote:

> The virgin suffered with her suffering Son, she underwent a sort of death with her dying Son, she abdicated her maternal rights for the salvation of men, and, to appease divine justice, insofar as it depended on her, she sacrificed her Son. One can therefore rightly say that she has, *in union with Christ, redeemed the human race.*[7]

In what way these two titles are warranted

The title of "coredemptrix" cannot shock those of our separated brethren who, desirous of entering into the bosom of the Holy Church in all sincerity, refuse at the same time all that would be a diminishment of the truth. Now, a fundamental truth is embodied by this title.

"Coredemptrix with Christ" is to indicate having collaborated with him in the entire ensemble that constitutes the work of salvation, and it is true that Mary collaborated marvelously in such a way. The redemption is a satisfaction and a sacrifice which reconciles us with God, merits for us all the goods of salvation, delivers us from captivity to sin and the Devil, and restores us to the privileges of our divine origin.[8]

The Blessed Virgin cooperates in these various acts. She merited and offered satisfaction with the Savior in the sense explained above; she offered the sacrifice by preparing the victim and presenting him upon the altar. She reconciles us with God by offering him such a host. She grants us supernatural goods, since she is the supreme minister of

---

7.   Pope Benedict XV, *AAS* 10:182.
8.   See our book, *Le Mystère de la Rédemption*.

the distribution of grace. She delivered us from evil and restored us in our lost rights, since she is, according to St. Ephrem, the ladder and the gate of heaven, the key that opens paradise.[9]

Pope Pius XI

Pope Pius XI, upon his accession as Sovereign Pontiff, showed how much this doctrine was dear to him and did not delay to institute three theological commissions to study the issue thoroughly, reserving for himself—if the opportunity arose—to solemnly proclaim it.[10]

If this pious belief could be defined

Without wishing to anticipate the judgment of the Holy See, we would like to indicate, in broad strokes, the reasons that could motivate such a definition.

In order for a truth to become an article of faith, it must be the case that it is contained in revelation and that the Church proposes it as revealed for our assent.[11] The pious belief we have been discussing is reduced to these main fundamentals: that the consent of the Blessed Virgin was required by God in the work of the Incarnation and in the offering of the sacrifice of the Cross; that Mary is always associated with Christ in the distribution of graces; and lastly, that she is our mother in the supernatural order. Now, these three points are affirmed clearly enough in revelation.

In what way the three points thus contained are affirmed in revelation

First, the Gospel testifies that the angel Gabriel was sent by God to Nazareth in order to seek the consent of the Virgin, and that this was given in her response: *Behold the handmaid of the Lord; be it done to me according to thy word.* And St. Elizabeth, under the inspiration of

---

9. St. Ephrem, *Orat. ad Virg.*, ed. Venice, t. I, p. 570: "Porta caelorum, et scala, portarum paradisi reseramentum."

10. TRANSLATOR'S NOTE: On these three commissions, see Dodd, *The Virgin Mary, Mediatrix of All Graces*, pp. 133ff.

11. See St. Thomas, *ST* II-II, q. 1, aa. 6–10, and Reginald Maria Schultes, O.P., *Introductio in Historiam Dogmatum* (Paris: Lethielleux, 1922).

the Holy Spirit, praises Mary for this consent: *Blessed art thou that hast believed, because those things shall be accomplished that were spoken to thee by the Lord.*[12]

Second, St. John writes clearly that Mary cooperated in the sacrifice at Calvary, when he says: "Now there stood by the cross of Jesus, his mother—*Stabant autem juxta crucem Jesu mater ejus*" (John 19:25). This admirable and heroic attitude is done justice in the commentary of St. Ambrose:

> She gazed with the eyes of her maternal piety on the wounds of the one by whom she knew that redemption was to come. She stood by without weakness, without fear of the executioner, and, while her Son hung upon the cross, she offered herself to his persecutors.[13]

Third, Scripture attests again that every time Our Lord caused the manifest distribution of grace, he willed that this take place through the intermediation of his Mother: to sanctify his Forerunner, to confirm the faith of the apostles in the miracle of Cana, to confirm St. John in grace upon Calvary, to accomplish the effusion of the Holy Spirit on the day of Pentecost. Thus, revelation teaches us that the general economy of salvation cannot be conceived without the Blessed Virgin.[14]

Fourth, that Mary is our mother is a truth that is known from the deposit of faith. Even though the words *Behold your mother* are commonly understood by the Fathers of the apostle St. John in a literal sense, they are interpreted mystically to apply to us all, since the time of Rupert.[15] Its reality is included in the entire Christian economy.

It is *de fide* that Mary is Mother of God. Furthermore, we know that her physical maternity of Christ is ordered to her spiritual maternity of Christians, just as the Incarnation is ordered to redemption. This is what St. Thomas expresses when saying that the end of the

---

12. See Luke 1:26–45.

13. St. Ambrose, *De Institutione Virginis, PL* 16:318 (ch. 7, n. 49).

14. We have explained this economy in the previous chapter, p. 161.

15. Joseph Knabenbauer, *Commentarius in Quatuor S. Evangelia domini n. Jesu Christi. IV, Evangelium secundum Ioannem* (Paris: P. Lethielleux, 1906), pp. 546–47.

Incarnation is that men become sons of God: "...the very end of the Incarnation of Christ, which was that men might be born again as sons of God."[16] We obtain complete certitude from this principle. Since the end of the Incarnation is to make us the children of God, the blessed mother by whom the Incarnation was accomplished is also the mother through whom our divine filiation is realized, or, in other words, Mary through her virginal and spiritual maternity conceives us in the life of grace, just as through her virginal yet bodily maternity she conceived Christ in the flesh.

This is why Tradition has declared, from the beginning, that Mary is our mother in the supernatural order. The most expressive form in which Tradition affirms this is in the well-known antithesis between Eve and Mary, the latter being the mother of life even as the former was the principle of death.

This antithesis, already present in St. Justin, is particularly highlighted by St. Irenaeus, as well as by St. Ephrem of Syria, upon whom in 1920 Benedict XV conferred the title of Doctor of the Universal Church.[17] The deacon of Edessa writes:

> The one became the cause of our death, the other, the cause of our life. It is clear that Mary is the cause of light, since by her are illumined the world and its inhabitants, who had been plunged into darkness by Eve, the cause of all our ills.[18]

Now, if the Blessed Virgin is the mother of our spiritual life, she must grant us all graces, having as her goal conserving, augmenting, and furthering that life.

We thus find contained clearly enough in revelation all the elements of Mary's universal mediation.

---

16. St. Thomas, *ST* III, q. 28, a. 1, c.: "Quarto, propter ipsum finem incarnationis Christi, qui ad hoc fuit ut homines renascerentur in filios Dei."
17. St. Irenaeus, *Adversus Haereses*, lib. III, c. 23, *PG* 7:964ff., n. 7. See also Bover, *Anuari de la Biblioteca Balmes*, vol. 1 (Barcelona, 1925).
18. St. Ephrem, Ed. Rom., pp. 327-329.

The Immaculate Conception and universal mediation

In order to arrive at an article of faith, it is necessary, finally, that the Church propose such a truth as divinely revealed. Now, what the Doctors have already set forth for our pious consideration, the supreme Magisterium could proclaim. We cite, on this point, the remarkable statement of a well-known theologian:

> This truth is not only a truth acquired by way of theological deduction: it is a truth that we could regard as belonging to the deposit of faith and contained in the Magisterium of the Church. When one compares it with the dogma of the Immaculate Conception, when we look at, on the one hand, the paucity of explicit and formal ancient testimonies in favor of the Immaculate Conception and the formidable difficulties that gave rise to that affirmation of Mary's privilege, and, on the other hand, if we look at the abundance and the precision of the testimonies which, from the first centuries to our days, have accumulated in favor of her cooperation in the work of redemption and regarding all graces which are thus spread throughout the world, in favor of the universal mediation and her maternity of grace, and without being able to oppose to this unanimous agreement any discordant voice that needs be taken into account, no other serious objection, one is nearly stunned that the Immaculate Conception could make it so far, while the maternity of grace has not been elevated to a dogma.[19]

Objection and reply

One could object that, if such a definition is possible and desirable in itself, it is ill-timed practically speaking, because to proclaim this belief and impose it under the pain of anathema would be to dismiss from the Church those whose minds are not yet prepared for such a dogma, and to compromise or delay numerous conversions.

---

19. Jean Bainvel, "Marie, Mère de grâce," (Paris, 1901), 98–99.
    TRANSLATOR'S NOTE: On these three commissions, see Dodd, *The Virgin Mary, Mediatrix of All Graces*, pp. 55ff.

An objection of this sort has been raised in every age. What did not go unsaid at the Vatican Council in order to halt as ill-timed the definition of papal infallibility? Yet the Church was not left shaken and the work of conversion did not let up.

Generous souls in search of an ideal and desirous for lasting union do not take long to understand that the Catholic truth is a whole which must be accepted in its entirety, just as true believers refuse to take as their method in the apostolate silence regarding our dogmas or the weakening of our doctrines.

Besides, if the Blessed Virgin is honored as she deserves, she will obtain even more abundant graces for the world, and new conversions would be one of the effects of her universal mediation, once it is rightly recognized.

That is why we join our voice with that of Cardinal Mercier, and those of so many other prelates, priests, and faithful throughout the whole world, to hasten this proclamation, one that is so glorious for Mary and of such benefit for Christians.[20]

---

20. TRANSLATOR'S NOTE: See Hugon's Preface, as well as the work of Dodd, previously cited.

* * *

CHAPTER 12

How Mary is Mother of Grace for the Angels

Up until now, we have spoken about the graces granted to humanity after the Fall, merited by the passion and death of Our Lord. It remains to inquire whether the causality of Mary extends also to the angels.

Whether the angels were sanctified in view of the merits of Jesus Christ and the merits of Mary—opinions

There are several views on this subject that are freely entertained. Faithful to their theory that admits the Incarnation of the Word independently of the Fall and Redemption, a number of theologians maintain that every grace comes from Christ, even those granted to the angels, or those that justified our first parents. The Virgin being indissolubly associated with her Son, helping acquire by a merit of fittingness all that which comes from Christ by a claim of justice, it must be said that the angels were sanctified in view of the merits of Jesus Christ principally and, secondarily, those merits of Mary. On this hypothesis, all divine grace comes from Christ, and the supernatural gifts imparted to the pure spirits would be Mary's benefits, since all the riches of the Redeemer belong also to his Mother. Other authors have thought that the divine maternity was the object of the angels' trial. In order to answer these opinions, we must treat of the subject with a bit broader scope.

The Fourth Lateran Council defined that God created spiritual and corporeal creatures at once, both the angels and the world, and then the human creature, who is in part both, composed as it is of a spirit and a body.[1] On this subject, St. Augustine sets forth a profound and magnificent doctrine.[2] God showed his generosity to his angels by creating their nature, infusing it with grace, and, while this was done outside the corporeal world, he still imprinted its image within the angelic minds so that through their powerful ideas the might be able to understand the totality of the universe.

Two questions can be raised here: (1) Were the angels elevated to the supernatural order *in statu viae*? (2) Did they receive grace from the first moment of their existence?

The angels were elevated to the supernatural order in statu viae; *proofs of this assertion*

The Council of Trent declared that Adam was created in justice and sanctity before the Fall.[3] It does not pronounce on the angels, but it is certain that all these spirits received grace before arriving at their end. Our Lord says of Satan: "He stood not in the truth" (John 8:44). In the language of Scripture, to stay in the truth is to persevere in justice and supernatural rectitude. This text proves, therefore, that the demons were established in a supernatural condition from which their malice caused them to fall. St. Jude also declares in the verse "the angels who kept not their principality" (Jude 6) that the rebels were unable to keep their original dignity. This clearly concerns the excellence of grace, since the goods of nature remained intact despite the fall.

---

1.   Fourth Lateran Council, Chapter 1, "Firmiter Credimus."
     TRANSLATOR'S NOTE: See Denzinger, n. 800: "[The Three Persons of the Trinity] are the one principle of the universe, the creator of all things, visible and invisible, spiritual and corporeal, who by his almighty power from the beginning of time made at once out of nothing both orders of creatures, the spiritual and the corporeal, that is, the angelic and the earthly, and then the human creature, who, as it were, shares in both orders, being composed of spirit and body."
2.   St. Augustine, *De Civitate Dei*, lib. 12, c. 9, *PL* 41:357; *De Genesi ad Litteram*, lib. 2, ch. 8, *PL* 34:355.
3.   Council of Trent, Session 5, Can. 1.

Did they receive grace at their first instant? Various opinions; testimony of the Fathers

The answer to the second question is less certain. Theologians of note, such as Hugh of St. Victor, the Master of the Sentences, St. Bonaventure, Victoria, and Molina have taught that the Creator first established the angels in the state of pure nature, as if in a state of waiting, and then elevated them to the supernatural order. St. Thomas, in his early writings, does not dare to oppose this opinion, but he does so later in the *Summa*.[4] Theologians have followed him, and the common opinion today is that God produced their nature and simultaneously infused it with grace. The well-known passage of Ezekiel is invoked, where the prophet cries out against the fallen angel under the figure of the King of Tyre: "Thou wast perfect in thy ways from the day of thy creation, until iniquity was found in thee" (Ezekiel 28:15).

Thus, Lucifer left God's hands having a beauty and perfection that iniquity took away from him. This excellence that sin annihilated could only have been grace and sanctity.

We have already mentioned the account of St. Augustine. St. Basil speaks in the same way: It was not into a state of infancy that the angels were born. When God created their substance, he infused it with sanctity.[5]

Argument from fittingness

Briefly, the argument from fittingness is as follows. God, in creating beings, must instill in them the seed of their effects and sufficient strength so as to arrive at their end. The angels, in truth, having but one end, which is the supernatural order, had to receive from the beginning the power allowing them to reach their last end, the seed of supernatural beatitude. This virtue, this seed, is grace, which is called the seed of eternal life. It is therefore fitting that the angels were created in a state of justice.[6]

---

4. See St. Thomas, *ST* I, q. 62, a. 3.
5. See St. Basil, *Homilia in Psalmum XXXII*, PG 29:333–34.
6. See St. Thomas, *ST* I, q. 62, a. 3, c.

Theories concerning the angelic trial

As to the angelic trial, the theories are numerous and contradictory. Some ecclesiastical writers of the first centuries—such as Clement of Alexandria or Tertullian—thought that the bad angels were seduced by carnal beauty. Others claimed that their lust was spiritual, an excessive delight in their own beauty, or an envy of man, or a desire for the hypostatic union, or the will to be adored by Christ and by humanity. It would be silly to refute in detail these far-fetched opinions, but there is a theory relevant to our subject about which we must speak at some length.

The thesis that the trial of the angels had as its object the Incarnation and the divine maternity

This is a well-known thesis. It is found many times even in our Christian pulpits, that the angelic trial had for its object the Incarnation and the divine maternity. God, revealing to the angels this twofold mystery, would have commanded them to believe in the abasement of the Word, to adore in anticipation the deified humanity of Jesus, and recognize as their Queen the Mother of this Man-God. Some, in their pride, refused, while others did so eagerly and lovingly, and these acts of faith and adoration or submission obtained their perseverance. Their salvation was thus assured in view of the graces of that God Incarnate whom they adored beforehand, and of the graces of that divine Mother, whom they already hailed as their princess and their Queen.

This theological view is at once both appealing and does not lack for grandeur. Since the Church respects it, we think that preachers can present it to the piety of the faithful. However, it does not receive our support.

Critique

We have previously explained why we do not embrace the optimistic theory that desires the Incarnation at any cost, independently even of the Fall. As to the claim that the mystery of the Word Incarnate and that of the divine maternity were the object of the angelic trial, it is a guess, and no proof. In the case of such profound questions, it is not permissible to have recourse to such divinatory methods without very serious arguments. Now, as Pétau says, such reasons do not exist: "Nor do I judge it right, without the gravest argument—which is wholly lacking here—to prophesy wildly about such things."[7]

The three moments in the angelic path

According to a very plausible opinion, grounded in the nature of spiritual substances itself, the chain of events for angels would have taken place in three moments.[8] In the first, they were created and all had a motion of love, which, furthermore, was not entirely free, since it was impressed in them by the very author of their being. In the second instant, a choice was necessary. Some turned towards God with all the plenitude of their liberty, others willed themselves as their final end. In the third moment, the good angels were crowned, the evil angels handed over to torment.[9]

The angels knew of the Incarnation at that point along the angelic path; testimony of St. Augustine and St. Thomas

Could they have known, in these stages of an angelic life, the mystery of the Incarnation? We think so. St. Augustine is also of this opinion: "The angels were not entirely ignorant of the secret of the kingdom of heaven which has been revealed in the fulness of time for our salvation."[10] St. Thomas repeats this teaching: "The mystery of the Kingdom of God was not entirely hidden from the angels, as Augustine observes."[11] Again:

> All the angels had some knowledge from the very beginning respecting the mystery of God's kingdom, which found its

7. Denis Pétau, S.J., *Dogmata Theologica*, 9th ed. (Paris: Vivès), lib. III, ch. 2, n. 10, 66–67: "Neque sine gravissimo argumento, quod nullum est omnino, vaticinari de re tanta fas esse arbitror."

8. Gonet, *Clypeus Theologiae Thomisticae*, v. 3, *De Angelis*, d. 12, 172–95; Billuart, *Cursus Theologiae*, t. 2, *De Angelis*, d. 4, a. 7, 196ff.

9. TRANSLATOR'S NOTE: The first "moment" of angelic time corresponds to the existence and ordination of natural desire or natural love in the angels; thus, it is not entirely free in the sense of its origin being the very angelic nature itself.

10. St. Augustine, *De Genesi ad litteram*, lib. 5, c. 19, *PL* 34:334.

11. St. Thomas, *ST* II-II, q. 2, a. 7, ad 1.

completion in Christ; and most of all from the moment when they were beatified by the vision of the Word, which vision the demons never had.[12]

And again: "From the beginning, all [the angels] knew the mystery of the Incarnation in a general fashion."[13] It was supremely fitting indeed that Christ, the future king and judge of the angels, be revealed to them at least in a general way.

This mystery was not the occasion of the fall of the rebellious angels

While supporting this proposal, we do not admit that the Incarnation was the occasion of the fall of the rebellious angels, nor that the first sin could have been an act of jealousy or envy towards the Man-God, or a refusal to adore and to submit to his Mother.

The two sins of which the angels are capable: pride and envy; the first sin could only have been pride

St. Thomas explains how all the faults of which the angels are capable are reduced to two species: pride and envy. An intellectual nature, entirely free from sensible concupiscence, cannot but turn itself towards spiritual realities. In this case, evil is to covet these perfections excessively, without regarding the rule of the superior. This is the disordered desire of one's own excellence, pride. But, in so fixating upon oneself in this exclusive manner, one regards the good of the other as an impediment to personal glory, from which comes jealousy and envy. This act is a recoiling movement, one of repulsion, since it is a displeasure at the good of another. Now, one does not recoil in the face of something regarded as an obstacle to one's own excellence except due to excessive self-love. Jealousy and envy always presuppose the love of self taken beyond its proper bounds. They could not be the first act of an intellectual creature. The first sin of the angels, then, which was their original act, could only have been one of pride.

---

12. Ibid., I, q. 64, a. 1, ad 4. See also q. 57, a. 5, ad 1.
13. St. Thomas, *Commentary on Ephesians*, ch. 3, lect. 3, n. 162.

The Sacred Scriptures and the Fathers of the Church frequently return to this idea that pride has been the origin of every evil, the beginning of all perdition. Pride is called the diabolic sin *par excellence, peccatum diabolicum.* St. Paul clearly implies this doctrine when he recommends that a neophyte not be ordained bishop, for fear that a weak soul be taken by pride, or fall into the fault that condemned the devil: "Not a neophyte: lest being puffed up with pride, he fall into the judgment of the devil" (1 Timothy 3:6).

This pride consisted in the perverse will of equality with God—to be their own natural end as God is His own, or, if they would accept supernatural beatitude, it would be on the condition that they reach it by their own power

This pride, according to revelation, consisted in the perverse will of equality with God: "I will be like the most High" (Isaiah 14:14). "Because thy heart is lifted up, and thou hast said: I am God" (Ezekiel 28:2). It is clear that the rebels did not aspire to equality of nature with God, knowing all too well that such a desire is absolutely unrealizable. They willed to be independent, like the Most High. Just as God is his own end and needs nothing but himself, so too did they purport to be their own natural end and need no other master, or, if they were to accept supernatural beatitude, it would be on the condition of achieving it through their own power.[14] Independence, that *Non serviam,* such was the motto of Satan, such is the motto of those angels and men who are members of his party. Such is what we learn from Scripture and Tradition. The other theories seem too hypothetical and a bit like raving prophecy—*vaticinari,*[15] as Pétau said above.

Consequently, they committed the sins of envy and hate, but these were a consequence of the first and not the initial fault

Consequently, the demons committed without a doubt the sins of envy and hatred against man, Our Lord, and his Mother, but all this

---

14. See St. Thomas, *ST* I, q. 63, aa. 2–3.
15. **TRANSLATOR'S NOTE:** The word means both "to prophesy" and "to rave, talk wildly."

was a consequence of their first act, not the original fault. We can well say that the condemned angels, from the moment of their damnation, refused to adore Christ and to recognize Mary as queen, and that the good angels, from the beginning, adored their God who would become man, and submitted in advance to their future sovereign. Yet we maintain that the occasion of ruin for the former and the cause of salvation for the latter was neither the Incarnation nor the divine maternity.

What the good angels received from Christ and from Mary was accidental and not essential grace

Can we go further and conclude that the faithful angels received nothing from Christ or from his Mother? Let us distinguish here between two sorts of grace. One is essential, which sanctifies, which gives on a permanent participation in the divine nature and confers a right to the eternal inheritance. The other is accidental, which consists in certain illuminations or revelations regarding the great work of the Word Incarnate, a new blessedness, more intense joys arising from the knowledge of these mysteries. The essential grace of the angels comes from Our Lord as the Second Person of the Trinity, but not as the Word made flesh. It is a grace from God, not a grace from Christ or from Mary. Such is the doctrine commonly taught by the Thomists (Lugo, Vásquez) against the Scotists (Suárez, Valentia, etc.).

Proofs taken from Scripture

Because the Incarnation was not the cause of salvation for the angels, the heavenly messenger declares to the shepherds "Fear not; for, behold, I bring *you* good tidings of great joy, that shall be to all the people: For, this day, is born *to you* a Saviour" (Luke 2:10–11). It is not to *us*, the angels, but to *you*, men. We possess him in his greatness, he did not diminish himself. It is for you that he was made small, that he who is the Savior reduced himself to your stature. St. Bernard exclaims: "Indeed, to us he is born, to us he is given, because he is necessary for us."[16] The

---

16. St. Bernard of Clairvaux, *Sermo Super Missus Est, PL* 183:78, n. 13: "*Nobis* ergo natus, *nobis* est datus, quia *nobis* necessarius."

pious Guerric has written the same thing: "It is for us human beings, not for them, not for the angels, that he is born."[17]

St. Paul will explain for us this high theology. All those who are sanctified by Christ have one life with him, they are his brothers, bone of his bone. He has taken their flesh and their blood. They communicate in the same nature: "For both he that sanctifieth, and they who are sanctified, are all of one" (Hebrews 2:11). Jesus does not belong to the family of the angels, he has not taken on their likeness, he has not shared in their nature. It is not, therefore, his Incarnation which sanctifies them.

If it is true, on the other hand, that all the grace of Christ presupposes the Fall and the redemption of men, it is not allowable to make the justification of the angels dependent upon such a hypothesis. The merits of the Savior not having been consummated except in the Passion, his grace is applied to those for whom he died: the elect whom he sanctifies and redeems, for those whom he offered the unique sacrifice whose power is eternal: "For by one oblation he hath perfected for ever them that are sanctified" (Hebrews 10:14). Now, it is not the angels who benefit from the oblation of Calvary. His sacrifice was useful only for those who were dead because of sin: "If one died for all, then all were dead" (2 Corinthians 5:14). The faithful angels, who had never known death, consequently did not receive from his merits their justification and perseverance.

Proofs taken from St. Thomas

St. Thomas summarizes this teaching in so many words:

> Now angels are not wayfarers with reference to the essential reward, and so Christ did not merit for them in this respect. But they are in some sense wayfarers with reference to the accidental reward in so far as they minister to us. In this respect, then, Christ's merit is of value to them as well.[18]

---

17. Guerric, *Sermon 3 De Nativitate Domini*, PL 185:35: "*Nobis* prorsus, *non* enim *sibi*, non angelis."

18. St. Thomas, *De Veritate*, q. 29, a. 7, ad 5.

And: "Our good works must be based upon the merits of the
Redemption, thus not upon the works of the angels.—*Operatio hominis
fundatur in merito Christi, non vero operatio angeli.*"[19]

However, Our Lord, even insofar as he is man, is king of the angels,
head over every principality and power: "Who is the head of all principality and power" (Colossians 2:10). He exercises over them a manifold
role as head. He has primacy over them, he surpasses them in perfection, and he communicates to them a truly vital effect. He has granted
them, indeed, numerous accidental graces: a growth in knowledge regarding the mysteries of salvation; a growth in joy at the restoration of
the ruin and void which the angelic rebellion had left in the ranks of
the celestial hierarchies; a growth of glory and honor as a result of the
triumphs of Christ and the Church. It will only be in the full light of
eternity that we will comprehend all that the angels owe of their blessedness and glory to the Incarnation and Redemption.

In what sense Mary is called mother of the angels

According to the principles already established, all that comes from
Jesus passes also through Mary. The blessed spirits are therefore indebt-
ed to her for those graces and accidental glories which complete their
perfection and complement their happiness. To them also is she the
mother of grace.

It is in this sense that one must understand the passages where the
holy Doctors laud Mary as the Mother of the Angels, that is to say, that
she has given birth to their growth in knowledge, dignity, delight, and
accidental glory. In this same way the text of St. Antoninus is explained:
"Mary, being the mother of the divine Redeemer, is *in a certain way* the
principle and the source of the glory of the angels, and could rightly be
called their mother."[20]

---

19. **Translator's Note:** This passage does not occur in the works of Thomas;
Hugon claims that the text is from St. Thomas, *In II Sent.*, d. 9, q. 1a, a. 8, ad 2.
However, this quote is merely attributed to St. Thomas by Gonet, in his *Clypeus
Theologiae Thomisticae*, v. 5, d. 14, 674. This passage in Gonet also mentions the
previously cited text in the *De Veritate*, which is a genuine quotation.

20. St. Antoninus, *Summa Theologica Moralis*, IVa, tit. 15, c. 14.

She is already their queen in many ways: because she has more grace and glory than all creatures taken together, because she is elevated above all the angelic choirs and all the greatest creatures, and above all because she inherits all the goods of her Son, she is above every creature, above every principality, above the most perfect of the seraphim, a true power over all dominations. Sovereign of the angels, she is also their mother because she communicates to them a certain supernatural life, that is to say those secondary graces and glories we have explained.

Mary means more to us than to the angels

Thus we reach a conclusion fitting for gentle piety. Mary means more to us than to the angels. She belongs to us more. We have cost her more; she has given more to us than to them. For them, she is but their mother in accidental graces and glories. For us, she is mother of all grace, of all glory, of every good. *Tota mater*—she is all mother. We are the children of her sorrows, the angels the heirs of her triumphs. For them, her maternity is only a joy; for us it is a true childbirth with all its sufferings and all its loves. Because we have cost her so much, we belong to her, and she to us under a unique title. Because we owe her more in grace, we are held to a higher order of gratitude, and we must be entirely hers and she is entirely ours.

* * *

CHAPTER 13

The Action of the Mother of Grace on the Separated Souls in Heaven and in Purgatory

The dispensatrix of supernatural goods in this present life, Mary is also the mother of the saints who triumph with her in the heavenly homeland—*in patria*. Glory being the crown of grace, and every grace having passed through her mediation, one can say that glory comes from the Blessed Virgin. It has been obtained, in a secondary way, through her merits and intercession and, what's more, all the glory of the saints is a participation in and an imitation of the glory of Mary.

The accidental glory that Mary procures for the elect

The Queen of Heaven procures for the elect an increase of happiness. While their essential beatitude is immutable, the saints are capable of receiving accidental glories, new joys or revelations, which complement their happiness. They enjoy knowing Mary's goodness, power, and glory, and learning that through her the just walk the path of perseverance, reach the heights of heroism, that the demon is brought low, that the Church continues to flourish throughout the centuries with Christ, never knowing death.

It is thanks to Mary that the blessed find in heaven their friends and their parents who were so dear to them upon earth. This joy, although accidental and secondary, surpasses all earthly happiness. One often hears descriptions of the joy of a mother upon all of a sudden finding her child whom she had thought dead. However, this mother does not rejoice completely. She realizes there is a limit, a separation. Amidst all her smiles and tears of happiness there flits about flashes of sadness and fear, because her child could be lost again. In heaven, parents and children, friends, or spouses cannot be separated, for they will never more be separated from God. They are bound for all time by chains of happiness.

The delight of seeing Mary

The joy that surpasses all other accidental felicities is that of seeing Mary as she is. There are two facets to that object of rest, satisfaction, and delight: her beauty and goodness. One knows the delight that exists even in this life at the very presence of a beautiful person. There are some who would leave all behind for the sake of such a person's charm. Mary is beauty and goodness, and of the most exquisite in all creation, since she is the ornament and charm of God. If the angels—according to the poet's account—are in ecstasy before the Virgin, mute and enraptured just by looking in her eyes, what must it be like to see her whole person with all her graces and glory![1]

Next to the essential beatitude of seeing the adored Trinity—primal Beauty and primal Love, face to face—after the accidental felicity of contemplating the humanity of Jesus—the ideal of all that is pure and beautiful—there could be no greater joy than seeing and loving the divine Mary.

She is, then, the mother of glory for the elect, just as she is in the present life the mother of grace for all men. We now wish to inquire how she is the mother of mercy for her children in Purgatory.

Purgatory is the realm of suffering, resignation, and hope

One could call Purgatory the realm of suffering, resignation, and hope. On earth suffering is often accompanied by complaints and is vented with grumbling, while hope is subject to illusions. In Purgatory three great realities are ever united: indescribable suffering, unalterable patience, and infallible hope. There is unspeakable suffering that grips

---

1.   TRANSLATOR'S NOTE: As in Chapter 1, it seems that Dante is meant; see p. 11, n. 6.

the poor captives there, taking hold of all their powers, as if their entire being were soaked in pain. Patience unalterable: even if these souls have been there for centuries, their resignation would only have grown. They would with joy adore always the judgment of the Lord. According to the original proposal of Msgr. Gay, if they could have a particular devotion, it would be to the hands of divine justice which keep them there in that place of torment. Lastly and above all, infallible hope: they sustain themselves upon the promises and satisfactions of Christ Jesus, but also upon the generosity of Mary. Just like exiles upon earth, the suffering souls of Purgatory can say to their Mother: *Spes nostra, salve*—Hail, our hope!

The queen of Purgatory, according to revelation

St. Bridget affirms on several occasions that the Virgin is the mother of all those who suffer in that place of expiation and that her prayers soften their torments.[2] Other revelations depict for us Mary descending into Purgatory amid shafts of light and dew to enlighten its darkness and cool its heat. In a vision of the venerable Paula of St. Thérèse, a Dominican religious of the monastery of St. Catherine in Naples, it is especially on Saturdays that the Queen of Purgatory visits her imprisoned subjects. St. Peter Damian, a doctor of the Church, assures us that each year, on the day of the Assumption, Mary delivers many thousands of these captives.[3] St. Alphonsus Ligouri adds, citing Denis the Carthusian, that such deliverance takes place particularly on the feasts of the birth of the Lord and his Resurrection.[4]

These accounts, although very respectable, do not entirely command our belief. We must, therefore, place them upon more solid and exclusively theological ground.

What can be asserted theologically

First, it is certain that the Mother of Mercy knows all the needs of all the souls of Purgatory. This universal and detailed knowledge is

---

2. St. Bridget of Sweden, *Revelationes S. Brigittae*, lib. 1, c. 16, and lib. 6, c. 10.
3. St. Peter Damian, *Letters*, lib. III, *Epist.* 10, *PL* 144:296, which is printed as Opusc. 34, *De Variis Apparitionibus et Miraculis*, c. 3, *PL* 145:586–87.
4. See St. Alphonsus Ligouri, *The Glories of Mary*, p. 271.

a prerogative of her maternity. Her beatific state must ensure her the complete revelation of all that could interest her regarding those who are her children, whether in heaven, on earth, or in Purgatory. Have her prayers, by themselves alone and as her simple prayers, the power to deliver these souls?

Theologians are not in agreement on this point. However, while it is fitting that she not suppress the work of divine justice, she can support their prayers with her previous satisfactions. We have already explained how this treasure of merits and satisfactions surpasses those of all creatures taken together, attaining an extent and depth of proportions that our mind could never measure. Since she was exempt from even the slightest blemish, since the shadow of evil never even touched her, she never had a need to use her satisfactions and left them to the Church, who distributes them to souls through indulgences. Thus understood, an indulgence is the celestial coin by which one settles the debts contracted against God's justice. Since, then, the satisfactions of Mary are applied to the poor debtors in Purgatory, she has a certain right to their deliverance, since she pays their debts with her own wealth.

Mary's satisfaction applied to souls—the work of the Mother of Mercy to relieve her children

Although her satisfactions have an inestimable worth, they are not infinite. Yet she is not lacking in other ways of coming to the aid of her servants. Her prayers, relying upon her old satisfactions, can incline Our Lord himself to apply to souls the infinite merits of the Passion. She obtains through her maternal diligence that her children on earth pray for the inhabitants of Purgatory, offering for this intention their good works, their alms, their penances, and by celebrating that august sacrifice of deliverance. How many times, unbeknownst to themselves and heeding secret but efficacious influences, have pious persons been the instruments of Mary. They have allowed her, through these works, prayers, and Masses, to extinguish the expiatory flames with the blood of her Son! It is she who inspires and directs these intentions. She can also arrange that the suffrages destined for souls who have no more need of them or who are incapable of receiving them benefit other children of her preference.

The Scapular and the Rosary

Her mercy has found a twofold and permanent way of applying the satisfactions of Christ Jesus to the departed: the Scapular and the Rosary. We will not discuss here the famous privileges of the Sabbatine Bull, but we would recall that the Holy Office (on February 15, 1615) and the Congregation of Indulgences (December 1, 1886), have permitted preaching "that the people can piously believe in a special protection of Mary after death, particularly on Saturday, for the brothers and fellows of Mount Carmel who have died in charity."

As to the Rosary, it is the permanent institution of mercy in favor of the poor souls in Purgatory. The indulgences applicable to the departed are so numerous that Pope Pious IX could say one day, showing his rosary beads to the pilgrims attending the audience: "Behold the most valued treasure in the Vatican!"

Finally, it is very probable that, from time to time, she gladdens that kingdom of suffering with the visit of angels. If she so often charges these celestial envoys to go and strengthen her servants upon earth in their hour of trial, or anguish, or agony, why should she not entrust them with her joyful messages to her children, mourning and weeping in Purgatory? We can, therefore, in piety legitimately consider the angels coming to encourage the captive souls, speaking to them of the divine Mother and telling them of her part in their future deliverance. Theologically, however, we cannot be certain of this.

Our Lady of the Keys

A village in France celebrates every year the feast of Our Lady of the Keys. By a miracle of the most touching sort, the keys of that place, which a traitor had handed over to the enemy, were found all of a sudden in the hands of a statue of the Virgin. We can believe that the suffering souls lovingly call their Queen "Our Lady of the Keys," since she is the one who opens their terrible dungeon. Indeed, since all grace upon earth is transmitted to us through her intercession, we can think that every consolation, every solace, every deliverance reaches the souls in Purgatory through her mercy.

Pious persons desire to aid Mary in her work of charity and, by their works, their prayers, and their sacrifices, would help her in breaking the chains of suffering. They will thus obtain that Mary be for them Our Lady of the Keys, since she possesses the key of their heart, just as she holds the key of Purgatory and of Heaven.

Mary is, therefore, Mother of grace both in this world and the next. The echoes of eternity answer what echoes through all time: *Maria, Mater Gratiae.*

* * *

CHAPTER 14

Conclusion

It is therefore established that the influence of Mary, more universal than that of the sun, extends as far as the supernatural realm: *Nec est qui se abscondat a calore eius.*[1] No soul can entirely avoid her light and her warmth.

The privileges of Mary

Yet, if she is a cause of salvation for all, she still has her privileges. She is a mother with more tenderness towards those whom Christ cherishes more. Why are certain souls inundated with so many graces? The first and last reason is the merciful will of God, who freely loves and chooses them. But, rather than trying to probe this mystery of eternal predestination which can trouble minds to no advantage, let us content ourselves with this very practical and consoling thought. If we want Mary to love us more tenderly, to be ever so much more a mother of grace for us, let us love her the more. She tells us: "*Ego diligentes me diligo*—I love them that love me" (Proverbs 8:17). My blessings are poured out with more abundance when my considerate love knows to answer the grateful and faithful love of my children.

Devotion to the Blessed Virgin as a sign of predestination

Devotion to Mary is therefore a sign of predestination. Insofar as one remains attached to the dispensatrix of graces, one is with the Lord. The more one is united to her, the more one receives divine influences, just as one participates in a greater abundance of water when one is closer to the source. St. Germain of Constantinople says:

> Continuous breathing is the sign and the cause of life; Mary is a sign that we are alive, she is the cause that maintains that life, the one who obtains for us from the Lord all holy joy and all heavenly aid.[2]

Mary and the Ark

St. Bernard compares the Virgin with Noah's Ark:

> The ark saved from the flood, Mary saves from the shipwreck that is sin. The first was made by Noah to shelter him against the flood of destruction, the new ark was prepared by Christ to preserve the human race from death; the first saved but eight persons, our own ark saves the entire human race.[3]

To honor Mary, adds St. Bonaventure, is to find life. If we know to invoke her with piety when it is suitable, we have a pledge of perseverance, a sign that Our Lord has given us salvation.[4]

---

1. TRANSLATOR'S NOTE: It helps to read the context, Psalm 18:6–7, to which Fr. Hugon alludes, especially in view of Our Lady as the tabernacle of the Incarnation: "He hath set his tabernacle in the sun: and he, as a bridegroom coming out of his bride chamber, Hath rejoiced as a giant to run the way: His going out is from the end of heaven, And his circuit even to the end thereof: and there is no one that can hide himself from his heat."
2. St. Germain of Constantinople, *Homily In S. M. Zonam*, PG 98:379.
3. St. Bernard of Clairvaux, *Opera Omnia* (1839), t. 2, pt. 1, "Sermo de Beata Maria Virgine," 1364–65.
4. St. Bonaventure, *Psalter of the Blessed Virgin Mary*, Psalm 48: "Ipsa pie invocata est signum nobis ad salutem a Domino datam."
    TRANSLATOR'S NOTE: These lines are not part of Psalm 48 of St. Bonaventure's *Psalter*, but they are quoted as such in Christiano Stamm, *Mariologia: Potiores de S. Deipara Quaestiones* (Junfermann: Paderbornae, 1881), p. 537.

Salvation by Mary

It is superfluous to multiply testimonies, Christian sense suffices. It is manifest, for that matter, that one cannot fall into the abyss while one is united to the two principles of salvation: to Christ, the universal, primary cause, and to Mary, the universal yet secondary cause. The mother of grace during life, she is above all the mother of perseverance during the hour of our passing. We have explained elsewhere her role as patron of a good death.[5]

True devotion to the Blessed Virgin is a practice of imitation and a way to union

But, in order that this devotion be a guarantee against Hell, it cannot consist only in a few prayers and certain external, hollow practices, which are also compatible with vanity and leave free reign to the passions. It is a practice of imitation, a veritable way of union with our Mother.

The Rosary

The Rosary rightly understood is the true form of this devotion. This is because, with its vocal prayer, it gives us in its mysteries striking examples of all the virtues, and it can confer on us sufficiently efficacious wherewithal such that we might enter more profoundly into union with Jesus—Heart, Soul, and Divinity—to live the life of Mary, and to reach the summit of perfect and even heroic sanctity.[6]

All our action in union with Mary

It does not enter into our purpose here, which is purely doctrinal, to outline on this subject a method of spirituality. Our theological principles would suffice, nonetheless, to orient a Christian life towards the Blessed Virgin. For details, one ought consult the very pious work of Giraud, missionary of La Salette: *The Way of Union with Mary*.[7] There

---

5. See *The Rosary and Sanctity* [*Le Rosaire et la Sainteté*].
6. Ibid.
7. Sylvain M. Giraud, *De la vie d'union avec Marie, mère de Dieu*, 6th ed. (Paris: Delhomme, 1885).

one will see how our actions, prayers, communion, study, and work can be done with Mary and through Mary. Souls have diverse opportunities to practice this intimacy, and each can legitimately follow the method of his choosing.

The exhortations of the Sovereign Pontiff, Pope Pius X

We wish to close this work by citing some of the pious exhortations from the Sovereign Pontiff Pius X, in his encyclical on the Immaculate Conception:

> Let them each one fully convince himself of this, that if his piety towards the Blessed Virgin does not hinder him from sinning, or does not move his will to amend an evil life, it is a piety deceptive and lying, wanting as it is in proper effect and its natural fruit .... Whoever moreover wishes, and no one ought not so to wish, that his devotion should be worthy of her and perfect, should go further and strive might and main to imitate her example.[8]
>
> It is a divine law that those only attain everlasting happiness who have by such faithful following reproduced in themselves the form of the patience and sanctity of Jesus Christ .... But such generally is our infirmity that we are easily discouraged by the greatness of such an example: by the providence of God, however, another example is proposed to us, which is both as near to Christ as human nature allows, and more nearly accords with the weakness of our nature. And this is no other than the Mother of God. "Such was Mary," very pertinently points out St. Ambrose, "that her life is an example for all." And, therefore, he rightly concludes: "Have then before your eyes, as an image, the virginity and life of Mary from whom as from a mirror shines forth the brightness of chastity and the form of virtue."[9]

The important thing is that this way of union be well understood, that we remain attached to the Virgin as to a principle of our salvation, in

---

8.   Pope Pius X, *Ad Diem Illum Laetissimum*, n. 17, n. 20.
9.   Ibid., n. 20; see also St. Ambrose, *De Virginibus*, lib. 2, c. 2, *PL* 16:208ff.

such a way that Mary would be for us the mother of grace during our terrestrial pilgrimage, the mother of perseverance at the hour of death, and the mother of glory forever and ever.

* * *

APPENDIX

PART I
TEXTS BY AND ABOUT HUGON

* * *

THE INSTRUMENTAL CAUSALITY OF THE MOST HOLY VIRGIN[1]

by Édouard Hugon, O.P.

Once it has been established that the angels and saints are often the physical, secondary causes of miracles, it seems entirely natural that we would claim that the Mother of God possess this power to a higher degree.

Mary's causality in relation to miracles

A moral cause by her intercession, Mary would be the physical instrument of all those effects that pious Catholics call the miracles of the Blessed Virgin. If the arguments of St. Gregory and St. Thomas, and the other arguments developed in the preceding chapter, have some value, they must be applied above all to the Mother of God, Queen of the angels and saints.

Yet can we go further? Is it permissible to believe that Mary is the physical instrument of the graces that she dispenses?

Is the Mother of God the physical instrument of the graces she dispenses?

Here, the question becomes rather delicate. We do not approach it without some reserve and timidity, not as regards the goal of resolving it ourselves, but rather to draw the attention of theologians to a subject which has not yet been explored. We will not venture any categorical affirmation, but rather we would only discuss a hypothesis that other authors are free to reject.

The question of possibility is easy to resolve

Let us first take up the question of possibility. Recall the conditions of being an instrument.[2] There is first of all transitory virtue, the efficacious motion which can pass through a material subject in order to attain a spiritual effect. This could without any doubt be sustained by the nature and exquisite faculties of the Blessed Virgin.

The question of distance can be taken as resolved. God, who is simultaneously present in Mary and in our souls, can clearly transmit to us the loving action of our mother.

Lastly, the prerequisite disposition is not lacking. Mary exercises a ceaseless causality in our regard, since every grace must pass through her actual mediation. Her acts of intellect and will in this case are constantly renewed, her prayers by which descend every heavenly gift. These are the preparatory operations which God can elevate, transform, and associate with his infinite activity and make them contribute to the production of grace.

Are there arguments from fittingness? Every prerogative that belongs to the role, office, and dignity of the Mother of God must be found in Mary

Once its possibility is admitted, is the theory probable? It will be

---

1. A translation of Chapter 6 of Fr. Hugon's book *La causalité instrumentale dans l'ordre surnaturel*, 2nd ed. (Paris: Pierre Téqui, 1924).

2. See Chapters 1 and 3.

    TRANSLATOR'S NOTE: Fr. Hugon refers to the chapters of the book from which this appendix is taken. As can be gathered from context, however, a physical instrument must possess some transitory virtue, be immediate to the cause using the instrument, and possess a proper disposition in order to be so used. For example, consider a pair of scissors used to cut a shape from paper. The scissors of themselves do not possess the power to cut the shape; thus, the form realized through this action flows through the scissors, as it were, from the one using them. This is because the scissors are immediately related to the principal cause moving them. The scissors are able to undergo this because they have the proper dispositions (hard metal composition, aligned lever motion about a fixed point, sharp wedge-shaped cutting edges) that make them a fit tool.

asked if there are reasons to assign this perfection to Mary. We would appeal to a principle that theologians call the rule of fittingness, which we have explained in our study *Mary, Full of Grace*.[3] Every prerogative, every privilege that is possible and fitting to the role, office, and dignity of the Mother of God must be found in the Blessed Virgin. Now, physical concourse in the production of grace is a high perfection that we have claimed belongs to the humanity of the Savior. Is it befitting to the role of a Mother of God? We have also shown there how the Blessed Virgin is inseparable from her Son in the divine plan, how she receives to a secondary degree all that which Christ possesses plenarily and principally. Her merits, her satisfactions, and her intercession obtain for us by a right of fittingness all that Jesus acquired by a right of justice. *Maria de congruo ubi Christus de condigno.*[4]

Does this include physical concurrence?

Thus, in the order of moral causality the action of Mary, albeit inferior and subordinated, is as universal as that of the Savior. Why should this relationship cease in the order of physical causality? Does it not rather seem, on the contrary, that this supernatural parallelism must be found throughout, and that the Mother must be the secondary instrument everywhere that the Son is the primary and conjoined instrument?

All graces reach us through the intercession of Mary; if God requires the moral cooperation of the Blessed Virgin, then why would He not also use her physical cooperation?

According to the pious belief set forth in *Mary, Full of Grace*, all goods reach us through the intercession of Mary. Her occurrent knowledge, her prayer, and her present consent are required for the distribution of the divine largesse. Now, if God condescends to associate the moral worth of the actions of the Mother to the moral dignity of the actions of the Son, why not associate physical causality, why not make

---

3. **Translator's note:** Fr. Hugon refers to the book by its earlier title, *The Mother of Grace*. See above, Part I, Chapter 6.

4. See *Mary, Full of Grace*, Part II, and Pope Pius X, *Ad Diem Illum Laetissimum*.

this concourse, like that of Christ, part of the production of the very grace that derives from this double mediation? It seems natural enough that the acts which God wills be used in every instant in the order of intercession be elevated, transformed by an infinite fecundity, and charged with instrumentally communicating heavenly life to souls.

In this way is better understood how Mary is all mother for Christians

One can also better comprehend how Mary is all mother, *tota mater*, if she physically cooperates in giving us supernatural existence. Without doubt, her moral role in the acquisition and distribution of graces is already enough to account for her maternity, and Catholic teaching requires nothing further. Yet how this maternity would be that much more full, more intense, and more akin to the paternity of Christ in our regard, if grace, the blood of our souls, were formed by the instrumental activity of Mary! As the Incarnation extends itself and is indefinitely renewed by the instrumental cooperation of Our Lord, this too would the virginal maternity achieve through the physical cooperation of Our Lady.

Maternity in the full sense, indeed, requires the constant action of the mother towards her children. The presence of the Blessed Virgin among us would be more real, more efficacious, if, instead of being limited to the power of intercession, it implied a physical and constant influence in the souls of Christians. Once again, her maternity can be understood without this instrumental cooperation, but with it, it seems more fruitful, more universal, and more divine.

The priest is a physical, instrumental cause of grace; why would Mary not posses this to a superior degree?

Yet, perhaps *too* divine, one might reply. Such cooperation is the exclusive prerogative of Jesus Christ, and it seems incommunicable.

Yet, is this true? Thomists typically teach that instrumental efficacy, while it is above all else the privilege of Christ's humanity, is nonetheless transmitted to the priests of the New Law. The minister of the altar is the physical instrument of Christ, just as human nature in Jesus is the physical instrument of the Word. Now, it is a theological principle, which we explain elsewhere, that every favor imparted to a creature must be found eminently in the Mother of God.[5] While she has not received the character of orders, the Queen of the clergy, who exercised in an eminent way the role of priests in giving Jesus to the world, possesses in a way and in a more elevated degree the graces of the priesthood. Is it therefore absurd to think that she is the instrument of Christ in a way that is even more real than the priest? The priests are cooperators of God through their ordination; she would be minister of the supernatural through a higher causality, closer to that of Christ, *princeps ministra*, as Pope Pious X says.[6] If it does not seem arbitrary to recognize in her, in a superior degree and in a non-sacramental manner, the attributes of priests, is it so unbelievable that she be a physical instrument of graces more efficacious than they?

Such are the principal reasons from fittingness that one could propose. They are not fully convincing, they do not immediately demand the mind's assent. We can appreciate that someone might contest their demonstrative force. However, a mere smile of disdain does not suffice to overthrow them.

Is this theory new?

A formidable objection could be made based on the novelty of this view. We reply first of all: Doctrinal development can pose *new* questions and consequently formulate *new* conclusions. When the Apostle enjoins us to avoid "the profane novelties of words" (1 Timothy 6:20), he does not mean to speak of those *new expressions* which are in no way profane and which are the natural outgrowth of theological sense. Those who understand that such is the way of dogma and development in theology cannot contest this assertion.

We would suggest a second answer. The holy Doctors have affirmed that all graces are transmitted to us through the hands of Mary, since she is the treasury of Christ Jesus, the channel of all celestial gifts, the mystical neck through which the power of our head, Jesus, reaches us.[7] They did not enter into philosophical distinctions between physical or moral causality. It is up to us to analyze their expressions and determine

---

5. See *Mary, Full of Grace*, Part I, Chapter 6.
6. **TRANSLATOR'S NOTE:** See Pope Pius X, *Ad Diem Illum Laetissimum*, n. 14.
7. See *Mary, Full of Grace*, Part II.

their meaning.[8] Often, such analysis and examination of ancient formulas is what causes theology to advance. While such terms could be understood of the power of intercession, they comport quite well with physical causality. Many of these same comparisons, such as Mary as *aquaeductus* or as mystical neck, etc., as a venerable priest once told us, do not have their full and rigorous signification except in a theory of instrumental causality. The causality of the Head is physical, therefore the causality of the virginal neck that unites the head to the members is physical also. Some eminent professors, of both the secular and religious clergy, have told us that they are favorable to this thesis.

Support from St. Louis-Marie Grignion de Montfort

It is also in this sense, so it seems, that a well-known passage of St. Louis-Marie Grignion de Montfort must be understood. It is the passage where he says that:

> God the Holy Spirit, who does not produce any divine person, became fruitful through Mary whom he espoused. It was with her, in her and of her that he produced his masterpiece, God-made-man, and that he produces every day until the end of the world the members of the body of this adorable Head. For this reason the more he finds Mary his dear and inseparable spouse in a soul the more powerful and effective he becomes in producing Jesus Christ in that soul and that soul in Jesus Christ.
>
> This does not mean that the Blessed Virgin confers on the Holy Spirit a fruitfulness which he does not already possess. Being God, he has the ability to produce just like the Father and the Son, although he does not use this power and so does not produce another divine person. But it does mean that the Holy Spirit chose to make use of our Blessed Lady, although he had no absolute need of her, in order to become actively fruitful in

---

8. The Sovereign Pontiff Pius X, in his encyclical on the Immaculate Conception (*Ad Diem Illum Laetissimum*), indeed declares that Mary does not physically produce grace, but it is clear that he is speaking of principal physical causality, for he adds that this power belongs to none but God alone. The Pope, however, would clearly not wish to deny the instrumental causality of Our Lord.

producing Jesus Christ and his members in her and by her. This is a mystery of grace unknown even to many of the most learned and spiritual of Christians.[9]

The external fecundity of the divine Paraclete is the production of grace, not in the order of moral causality (for the Holy Spirit is not a cause through merit or intercession), but in the order of physical causality. To reduce this fruitfulness to act is to physically produce grace and the works of sanctity which belong to the Third Person. If it is true that the Holy Spirit brings about this fecundity through the intermediation of Mary, if he exercises his power and works through her, if it is through her that he physical produces grace in souls, then Mary is therefore the physical, secondary instrument of the Holy Spirit.

Such seems to be the meaning of this strong expression of St. Louis-Marie. This would indeed be a high doctrine which he calls "a mystery of grace unknown even to many of the most learned and spiritual of Christians."

We stop short of an absolute affirmation

For our part, we would hold back from concluding fully and be content to have explained the arguments from fittingness which seem attractive, worthy of God, worthy of Mary, and capable of producing probable certainty. However, we would not wish to attribute to them more importance than is appropriate, nor to join it to that theory of the doctrine of universal mediation.[10] It is in this sense that we understand the thesis of Commer: *De munere Matris Dei in Ecclesia gerendo*. If this thesis is not studied further, this would not be a reason to exclude it indefinitely from theology. It is already glorious for the Mother of Christians that such a question can be raised on this subject, even if it is not yet possible to answer it.[11]

---

9. St. Louis-Marie Grignion de Montfort, *True Devotion to Mary*, nn. 20–21.

10. See the decree of the Sacred Congregation of the Liturgy, January 1921, approving the Office and the Mass *Beatae Mariae Virginis Mediatricis omnium gratiarum*.

11. TRANSLATOR'S NOTE: For more concerning this question, besides the thesis of Commer just cited (which is difficult to find), see Garrigou-Lagrange, *The Mother of the Saviour and Our Interior Life*, pp. 194ff.

In any case, we would that we belong entirely to Mary, as she is entirely ours, and we would find an immense delight in this sole thought that Mary is all Mother for us, *tota Mater*!

* * *

THE ROLE OF MEEKNESS IN THE SPIRITUAL LIFE[1]

by Édouard Hugon, O.P.

The truly spiritual man is the one who manages to pacify his home, to establish harmony among the diverse parts of his being, assuring the dominion of the superior part against the inferior appetites that are always inclined to revolt against it.[2] In order to permanently constitute this equilibrium, so as to never descend to the level of passion or to the level of trivialities, but to rest always at God's level, one needs that peace which St. Augustine calls the tranquility of order, *tranquillitas ordinis*.[3]

This tranquility ought to reign in our mind, so that it can in all serenity and without bias judge the truth; it ought to reign interiorly, so that all stirrings therein might be measured by and in accord with sound reason; it ought to reign exteriorly, so that all words, actions, attitude, and deportment might be as a hymn of praise and a song of love for the Lord.

It is one of those little virtues decried as passive which assures a man this complete mastery of himself and permits one to look after his soul, to fully possess it, to keep it well for himself: meekness. "*Fili, in mansuetudine serva animam tuam*—My son, keep thy soul in meekness" (Sirach 10:31). We shall try to explain how meekness contributes to establish the tranquility of order in our entire being and makes it such that God can dwell in us, which is true spirituality.

I. Tranquility of Order in the Mind

Created for the truth, our mind does not rest except in it. It must therefore make an effort so as to arrive there. It goes there by multiple acts and as it were by successive leaps and bounds. First, a movement so as to seize the first notions, bring together ideas, concepts, the elements of our knowledge; then, it must unite them by judgments; finally, it must associate many judgments, coordinate them, and by analyzing and synthesizing, construct the edifice of science. God and the angel see the truth in a single glance; as for ourselves, we must scurry from one object to the other, a *discourse*. The best definitions that we give of realities are the result of long investigation, and, so to speak, of a laborious hunt—*venari definitiones*, to hunt definitions, according to the expression of Aristotle and St. Thomas. Intellectual peace requires that all these motions of human understanding be harmonious, that concepts, judgments, and arguments are produced and maintained in order. Mental tranquility is obtained only in the light. A serenity so complete supposes in the mind a complete freedom to judge soundly of the truth and of the good and the truly noble so as to not contradict the truth once it is known and understood.

---

1.   A translation of a short essay by Fr. Hugon, published in Abbé Henri Hugon, *Le Père Hugon*, 3rd ed. (Paris: Pierre Téqui, 1930).

2.   See St. John of the Cross, *The Dark Night of the Soul*, 1st strophe: "En una noche oscura / con ansias, en amores inflamada, / ¡Oh dichosa ventura! / salí sin ser notada, / estando ya mi casa sosegada."

3.   St. Augustine, *The City of God*, XIX.13 (*PL* 41:640): "The peace of the body then consists in the duly proportioned arrangement of its parts. The peace of the irrational soul is the harmonious repose of the appetites, and that of the rational soul the harmony of knowledge and action. The peace of body and soul is the well-ordered and harmonious life and health of the living creature. Peace between man and God is the well-ordered obedience of faith to eternal law. Peace between man and man is well-ordered concord. Domestic peace is the well-ordered concord between those of the family who rule and those who obey. Civil peace is a similar concord among the citizens. The peace of the celestial city is the perfectly ordered and harmonious enjoyment of God, and of one another in God. *The peace of all things is the tranquility of order*. Order is the distribution which allots things equal and unequal, each to its own place. And hence, though the miserable, in so far as they are such, do certainly not enjoy peace, but are severed from that tranquility of order in which there is no disturbance, nevertheless, inasmuch as they are deservedly and justly miserable, they are by their very misery connected with order. They are not, indeed, conjoined with the blessed, but they are disjoined from them by the law of order."

This is the twofold service that meekness renders to our intellect. It prepares for the contemplation of God by dispelling obstacles. First of all, meekness assures a man in self-possession because it curbs precipitation and fits of anger. It is, indeed, the impetuosity of this passion which takes that freedom of mind away from us, that sovereignty over ourselves, without which our judgments are exposed to a lack of impartiality. Second, meekness keeps us in the truth, causes us to love it, prevents us from contradicting it, because what ordinarily enables men to contradict the words of truth are the agitation and disturbance that anger arouses in them.[4]

Meekness will produce, therefore, little by little, that composure of soul, equanimity, which is necessary to contemplate the truth.

This is why Blessed Jordan of Saxony says of St. Dominic: "Nothing would disturb his equanimity unless it was compassion and mercy. And, because a content heart gladdens the face of a man, one could easily divine his interior serenity from the goodness and joy of his features, which the least movement of anger would never obscure."

Thus, the superior excellence of the virtue of meekness lies in causing calm and serenity in the mind and putting the entire soul in the best disposition. At the same time, it leads to the charm and attractiveness of the truth, which it renders victorious by taking on the face of amiability. "Reason clothed in meekness," says St. Francis de Sales, "has more force and brilliance; clothed in anger, it loses its brilliance and its force. The truth is never established without charity; but impiety does the opposite."[5]

Furthermore, a man who has the tranquility of order established in his mind will bear souls infallibly, so to speak, towards God. Hence the well known *cri du coeur* of St. Vincent de Paul: "Oh, my God! If my Lord of Geneva is so good, then so must you be yourself!"[6]

---

4. See St. Thomas, *ST* II-II, q. 157, a. 4, ad 1: "Meekness disposes man to the knowledge of God, by removing an obstacle; and this in two ways. First, because it makes man self-possessed by mitigating his anger, as stated above; second, because it pertains to meekness that a man does not contradict the words of truth, which many do through being disturbed by anger."

5. See André Jean Marie Hamon, *Vie de Saint François de Sales, Éveque et Prince de Genève*, ed. M. Gontheir and M. Letourneau, rev. ed., 2 vols. (Paris: Victor Lecoffre, 1917), vol. 2, p. 509. Hereafter, *The Life of St. Francis de Sales*.

6. Ibid.

But the dominion of meekness must be exercised over all our faculties, and in so doing make them supple and docile instruments of the supernatural.

II. Interior Tranquility of Order

The harmonious equilibrium of virtue can be broken by the impetuous or violent attacks of impatience and anger. What sustains anger is the desire for retaliation, and this desire itself is accompanied by a certain bitterness which accompanies grudges and antipathies. There are people who, on the outside, will avoid making a scene, but on the inside they keep an accumulation of gall. It awaits an occasion. Self-love, ever prolific in its schemes, will find fresh industry so as to take its revenge. It will nourish these feelings for years and one day, all of a sudden, as if coming out of an ambush, it takes revenge and savors the triumph so long awaited. They are unspeakably miserable, these joys of great or petty vengeances! The property of meekness is that is suppresses these secret resentments and goes even to the point of forgetting injuries. It does not know the malicious phrase: "I forgive, but I do not forget," for it knows that to forgive is to forget, or that the forgiving is complete in the measure that the forgetting is complete. Such is the true way of "taking anger by the collar," in the words of St. Francis de Sales, "to rebuke it, to trample it underfoot."

All that demands a prolonged effort, in order to collect meekness drop by drop, according to the expression of the same saint, as a rose in the vase of our poor heart, and to prevent anger from seething in the brain, like water in a boiling pot.

Christian meekness has other refinements which cause it to carefully remove anything that could hurt one's neighbor. Indeed, to hurt someone, says St. Thomas, that would provoke horror in the truly meek soul: "This moderation of soul comes from a certain sweetness of disposition, whereby a man recoils from anything that may be painful to another."[7] It is thus possible for some people to not only have no horror of hurting others, but to feel an intense satisfaction, a bitter pleasure, upon seeing their neighbor humiliated, who feel an unhealthy joy at

---

7.	St. Thomas, *ST* II-II, q. 57, a. 3, ad 1.

another's pain, savoring in secret the triumph of seeing another's down-fall, defeat, or hurt?

The saints take these refinements to such a level that they refuse to disturb even a servant: "I assure you," said St. Francis de Sales to his servant, "that I called you several times, I even went to your bed, and I found you sleeping so soundly and peaceably that I did not want to wake you."[8] Traits no less exquisite are recounted of St. Dominic: "When Dominic had spent a long space of time in vigils, prayers, and tears, and had offered his soul and body as a sacrifice, if the matin bell had not rung, he would go and visit his children, as if longing to see them again. He would enter their cells very quietly, making the sign of the cross on each of the inmates, and re-covering those whose clothing had become disarranged in sleep. After this he returned to the choir."[9]

The virtue of meekness does even more. It suppresses the root of all feelings of bitterness, at the same time it also banishes grudges and antipathies. Just as it is madness to take delight in the pains and sufferings of one's fellows, because it shows that one is no longer a man or that one is deprived of that human heart from which clemency is born, so also it is a contradiction for Christians to keep this animosity after having met at the same table of communion and having recited the same prayer: *Our Father, who art in heaven.*[10] To nourish antipathies would be to keep a viper in one's chest. The meek crush its head before it can bite them or hurt them.

Lastly, true meekness takes pity on its own wretchedness, it does not get angry at itself in spite of self-love, it encourages one to correct oneself with calm and energy, as it is said of St. Francis de Sales: "Bearing with his faults in meekness, he never would get upset at himself, and his displeasure at his faults was peaceful, steadfast, and firm, believing that we chastise ourselves better by tranquil and constant repentance

---

8.   Hamon, *The Life of St. Francis de Sales*, vol. 2, p. 523.

9.   Lacordaire, *The Life of St. Dominic*, trans. E. Hazeland (London: Burns and Oates, 1883), p. 188.

10. See St. Thomas, *ST* II-II, q. 157, a. 3, ad 3: "But that a man who takes pleasure in the punishment of others is said to be of unsound mind, is because he seems on this account to be devoid of the humane feeling which gives rise to clemency."

than by sour and angry repentance."[11] "One must," St. Francis would say, "suffer our own imperfection in order to have perfection, having patience with our imperfections and working to correct them, beginning again every day and never thinking that we have done enough."[12]

If the tranquility of order is thus established in all our interior life, our soul will be a peaceful kingdom in which the Lord will truly be able to dwell as in his own abode. He will find himself at home in coming to us, and thus the beautiful words of the Doctor of the Church, St. Hilary of Poitiers, will come true: "Because of our interior meekness Christ dwells in us."[13]

This influence will shine forth through our whole person, so as to submit even our exterior itself to the blessed reign of the Lord Jesus.

III. Exterior Tranquility of Order

Christian meekness must rule all that which manifests virtue externally, as far as speech as well as manners and actions.

There is no need to repeat here the warnings of Sacred Scripture against malicious speech, an inferno which devours, a sharpened razor whose wounds do not heal, an unruly power that wreaks much havoc. It suffices to quote the words of St. James: "And if any man think himself to be religious, not bridling his tongue, but deceiving his own heart, this man's religion is vain" (James 1:26).

One could also say that sometimes it becomes like a tiger's claw, drawing blood, or like the painful grip of an ape. For there are some people who make it a profession, a consummate art of lashing out—suddenly, unexpectedly, without one being able to foresee anything—with the treacherous stroke of the malignant allusion, the hurtful or cutting remark, the remembrance that saddens and sorrows.

Meekness, habituated to possessing its soul in peace, acts as did the holy cardinal who prayed for a quarter-hour before his audience with the Sovereign Pontiff so that nothing in his speech might be harmful to

---

11. Jean Goulu (Dom Jean de Saint-François), *La vie bienheureuse de Monsieur François de Sales*, 2nd ed. (Paris: Jean de Heuqueville, 1625), p. 468.
12. Hamon, *The Life of St. Francis de Sales*, vol. 2, p. 529.
13. St. Hilary of Poitiers, *In Matt.*, IV.3; *PL* 9:932.

his neighbor; it acts as St. Francis de Sales, of whom a witness reports: "It seems to me that all meekness which could exist in a man was assembled in him. I could never get enough of seeing him and hearing him, he was so meek and agreeable, never doing anything or even saying anything which was not caused by the meekness of Our Lord."[14]

The tranquility of order will be reflected in the body and in one's entire countenance. It is said of St. Dominic that a certain radiant light would shine from his forehead and from between his eyelashes, which called forth respect and love, and that he was always agreeable, except when he was moved with compassion by some affliction of his neighbor. Baron de Cusy also said of St. Francis de Sales: "One never saw the Lord of Geneva but with a visage so meek and so sweet that he spread devotion into hearts."[15]

There are persons, by contrast, whose actions impugn them of a poorly contained anger, whose mere presence is enough to injure, whose countenances are feared, who cause harm even before speaking or before arriving, whose eyes seem full of venom and their mouths full of bitterness. To them one must propose the example of St. Theresa of the Child Jesus: "I ought to anticipate the wish, and show myself glad to be of service."[16]

To establish the tranquility of order in its full development, meekness must rule one's attitude, comportment, gestures, composure. To lack calm, restraint, or dignity in all this is sometimes to compromise the efficaciousness of the most generous zeal. There are some of whose noisy passage it is said: "It's a hurricane that's coming!"

The meek are never a hurricane, because they know that the Lord is not to be found in noise or in agitation. One shows one's self-possession of soul in the way that one conducts and comports oneself, in the opening and closing of doors, as has been well said by Lacordaire in the description of one of the monasteries in the time of St. Dominic: "Along these spacious and lofty corridors, whose sole luxury consisted in their

14. Hamon, *The Life of St. Francis de Sales*, vol. 2, p. 509–509.

15. Ibid.

16. St. Thérèse of Lisieux, *The Story of a Soul*, trans. T. N. Taylor (London: Burns Oates & Washbourne, 1912), p. 150.

cleanliness, the charmed eye discerned a symmetrical line of doors on the right hand and on the left .... At the sound of a clock every door gently opened. Hoary and serene-looking old men, men of precocious maturity, young men in whom penance and youth had formed a type of beauty unknown to the world, every age of life here appeared wearing the same garb."[17]

This quick overview allows us to see that the role of meekness is vast and universal in the domain of the spiritual life. This virtue puts into play the multi-part organism of nature and of grace. It forms and tempers true character, since the saint who was both the master and the model of meekness and the hero of strength could say: All meekness is strength, as all anger is weakness.

Thus Moses by his great meekness merited that God appear to him.[18] The meek who imitate him become in appearance like Christ Jesus, as the revelation of His beauty: "But when the goodness and kindness of God our Savior appeared" (Titus 3:4). They are, so to speak, the beauty of grace which passes through the world; somehow, they are the charm and attractiveness of the Savior himself.

This is why Jesus said: "Blessed are the meek: for they shall possess the land" (Matthew 5:4). But these meek, the conquerors of the world, these heroes to whom are reserved the true victory, are also the humble, as an upcoming article will attempt to demonstrate.

---

17. Lacordaire, *The Life of St. Dominic*, 118.
18. See Dionysius the Areopagite, *Letter VIII to Demophilius, Therapeutes* (PG 3:1083): "Holy, distinguished Moses was deemed worthy of the Divine manifestation on account of his great meekness."

* * *

PANEGYRIC ON FR. ÉDOUARD HUGON, O.P.[1]

by Réginald Garrigou-Lagrange, O.P.

To them that love God, all things work together unto good.

— ROMANS 8:28

The ancients would say that in order to praise a man, to pronounce definitively upon his life, one must wait until he is dead. Indeed, the true praise of those who now rest is to those who showed to all a good life crowned by grace and final perseverance: "He that shall persevere unto the end, he shall be saved" (Matthew 10:22). When, after having assisted the last moments of one of our brothers, we hold for certain that he made a good death, that he received the grace of grace, that reserved to the elect, then we can apply to him the consoling words of St. Paul: *"Diligentibus Deum omnia cooperantur in bonum, iis qui secundum propositum vocati sunt sancti.*—To them that love God, all things work together unto good, to such as, according to his purpose, are called to be saints" (Romans 8:28).

In the life of the servants of God who persevere until the end, everything, absolutely everything, remark St. Augustine and St. Thomas, is ordered to salvation and to the degree of glory to which they have been predestined. All prior graces, from those received in the first days of infancy, all merits retained or recovered and revived, all absolutions, all communions, all these supernatural gifts work together unto good. This includes even natural gifts, both one's qualities of temperament

219

and difficulties, trials, illnesses, conflicts, and failures. St. Augustine and St. Thomas even go so far as to say that, in the life of the elect, sin itself is not permitted except to allow them to reach a truer humility, a greater degree of despising themselves, and a more perfect trust in God. In this sense, even those sins permitted in the life of the elect are an effect of their predestination, as seems clear enough in the life of St. Peter, when the Lord willed to permit his three denials so as to lead the apostle to a deeper humility and true contempt of self.

> Hence, God is said to exercise a special care over the just...he takes care of them in such a way as to permit no evil to affect them without converting it to their good .... To the extent that if they deviate and stray from the path, he even makes this contribute to their good .... Furthermore, because he has fallen, he rises more cautious and more humble.[2]

In light of this deep and universal principle, after the holy death of a brother with whom one has lived many long years, we can make out the divine traces in his existence and in his spiritual features, drawn from all eternity such that he was inscribed for all time in the book of life.

We also see, at the same time, the profound void caused by his departure, for his charity was inexhaustible, and there are many to whom he secretly did some good who come now to ask for the continuation of this spiritual assistance. This is what anyone can see after the death of our dear and universally missed Fr. Hugon.

Since I am addressing mostly students in philosophy and theology, I would say a few words about his intellectual life, and then about his interior and apostolic life.

---

1. TRANSLATOR'S NOTE: A translation of a homily given by Réginald Garrigou-Lagrange, O.P., at the memorial service for Fr. Hugon, on 9 May 1929, at the office for the dead *"Quarantième,"* or the fortieth day after death, and published in *In memoriam: un théologien-apôtre, le père maître Édouard Hugon, professeur de dogme à l'Angelico, à Rome, consulteur de la S. Congrégation pour l'Eglise orientale* (Rome: Angelicum, 1929).
2. St. Thomas, *Commentary on Romans*, ch. 8, lect. 6, nn. 697, 698.

* * *

It is said that a beautiful life is a thought had in one's youth that flowers in maturity, and if this thought was not only true but supernatural or divine, its flourishing has a superior beauty which escapes beyond our natural intelligence and which is seen only by God, the angels, and the saints. Such a life had our dearly departed Father.

I am told by his brother, an apostolic missionary of the diocese of Lyon and who has come to attend this service, that from his earliest years, the dearly departed showed manifest signs of a priestly vocation. The eldest of a family of thirteen children, he learned the catechism very early, so as to teach it to others, and according to his parish priest, he knew the little catechism even before he knew how to read and write. People would say: "The boy will be a priest." It was proposed that he enter into an apostolic school, and was even given a choice between three, belonging to different religious orders. When he heard the Dominicans spoken of for the first time, he felt drawn to enter with them. In the apostolic school of the Dominican province of Lyon, he dreamt of making God, the author of grace, known to souls, as well as Our Lord Jesus Christ and his holy Mother, and the life of the Church as it began to be revealed to him and which he never ceased to see despite human infirmity. We can really say that our dear Father has truly realized that thought and holy desire of his youth.

He did not discover any documents from the origins of Christianity, nor even from the history of medieval theology, and neither did he greatly advance the most important philosophical, theological, or sociological questions. But he knew, as only a few theologians do, the entire doctrinal corpus, the various dogmatic positions, both from a positive and scholastic point of view, as well as those issues of speculative and practical morals and their relationship with the law, not to mention with asceticism and mysticism. He had, then, in these different matters a generally sound judgment.

After forty years of teaching the doctrine of St. Thomas, he became a particularly complete theologian, such a one that is rarely found. His mind had a deep grasp of the principles that clarify the great questions. He would hardly insist on difficulties, with his pleasant nature he was never troubled by them. But when they were presented to him, they would not catch him off guard. He would always return to traditional principles to resolve them, which he knew how to express in a typically very exact terminology, the fruit of sometimes long study, which he would accomplish without great effort, his mind having the benefit of an exceptional memory.

One could cite many debated questions of our day where he would provide a truly luminous formula. For example, take the problem of the grace of the first man considered by some as *caput solum physicum generis humani*, and by others as *caput morale*.[3] He resolved this in a few words that seem to express the truth well: "Adam was constituted the *head of elevated nature* [*caput naturae elevatae*], such that he would have had to transmit all that goes along with the species...thus the Council of Trent defines in Session V, Canon 2, that Adam lost for us also holiness and justice."[4]

Having taught all parts of philosophy, dogma, and morals, Fr. Hugon never forgot anything of what he had learned. He could, without preparation, clearly explain and thoroughly defend this or that particular thesis without having had reviewed it in twenty years. Constantly consulted as a living encyclopedia, he could give at once a solid answer to the majority of questions posed to him from speculative theology or casuistry or even canon law. He achieved what St. Thomas describes: "Although among the philosophical sciences one is speculative and another practical, nevertheless sacred doctrine includes both."[5]

How many times in twenty years, almost every week, did I not put his knowledge to work, whether regarding practical matters or to see if such or such an interpretation of a passage from St. Thomas seemed to him to be in keeping with the rest of his doctrine! How many times did I answer visitors, come in haste to pose some case that troubled their consciences: "Go look for Fr. Hugon." And, attentive as if without effort to the complexities of the matter, no less to the principles of the solution, he would not delay in clarifying the issue. Often, he

---

3. **TRANSLATOR'S NOTE:** The contrast is between "only the physical head of the human race," and "as also the moral head of the human race."
4. Hugon, *Tractatus dogmatici*, 5th ed., t. 1, 811.
5. St. Thomas, *ST* I, q. 1, a. 4, c.

was presented with not only philosophical and theological works for review and approval, but also exegetical ones, it being known that he was always judicious and benevolent in his examinations, no less firm regarding principles as he was obliging in practice in a spirit of charity.

How many dossiers from the Congregations were addressed to him? His desk would be covered with them at the beginning of the school year, and at the end they would be like strata upon that poor desk, the remains of consultations sent in the course of the preceding months. When the Pope instituted a commission for a new edition of the catechism, he was called away and every Sunday for a long time he took part in it.

Is all this speculative and practical knowledge lost to us? No. Students of philosophy and theology will make use of, for a long time yet, those great Latin or French works, approved by the three last Popes, who each honored our dear departed brother with a particular benevolence, and would often consult him and consider him the *theologus communis*, a faithful echo of the *Doctor communis Ecclesiae*.

In his *Cursus philosophicus* he presented with clarity the substance of the philosophical doctrine of Aristotle and St. Thomas such as the great Thomists have understood it, in particular John of St. Thomas. An extraordinary fact is that this *Cursus* was translated in large part into Arabic, for the use of several seminaries of the Church in the East, all because of the the clarity with which he set forth difficult questions of natural philosophy and metaphysics.

Of great use also will be his *Tractatus Dogmatici*, which quickly reached a fifth edition. For many years, Fr. Hugon would teach it in Rome and he was able to give it definitive form two years before his death. It was a complete treatment of dogma, and distinctly Thomistic, considering the one and triune God, angels, men, grace, the Incarnate Word and Redeemer, the Sacraments in general and individually, and the Last Things. It was always set forth in very clear terms, in both its positive and speculative aspects, its solutions and arguments generally expressed in the very words of St. Thomas.

That guide gave to our theologian a profound clarity, which would show up most of all in his treatises, where at the beginning of important questions he would insist on the principal difficulty to be resolved. By

drawing such attention to the knot of the difficulty, after the manner of
Aristotle and St. Thomas, one would then see better the great intellectual worth of the principles to which he had recourse. For instance, he
condenses in an excellent fashion the Thomistic solution to the problem of the efficacy of grace in this argument:

> That which is greatest in every created or supernatural order
> cannot escape from the divine causality. And that which is great-
> est in every created or supernatural order is the good use of grace,
> or the transition from potency to a free supernatural act. Of
> course, this is what effects merit and confers the right to eternal
> life…. In this is contained the entire difference between the evil
> and the elect…. Two things are above all to be remembered in
> the business of salvation: every good is to be assigned to God,
> and every defect is to be attributed to human liberty.[6]

On occasion, he would propose arguments at the Angelicum that
would bring a halt to all debate. For instance, there was this one which
he presented for consideration: "That which is not its own being, is pri-
or to the mind's consideration (that is, really) distinct from its being,
as every created essence. And the created person, or more correctly its
personality, is not its own being, and thus the person of Peter or Michael
the archangel differs from the person of the Word. Therefore the created
person, or rather its personality, is really distinct from its being or from
its existence."[7] The argument is demonstrative, and the difficulty was
solved. Gradually, our theologian would move on and forget the debates
that he had settled, but he always retained the light of the solution.

What we have said of the value of his *Tractatus dogmatici* must
also be said of his French works—on the mystery of the Holy Trinity,
on the Incarnation, the Redemption, the Holy Eucharist, about Mary,
the Mother of Divine Grace, on the doctrine that outside the Church
there is no salvation, on instrumental causality in theology, on the 24

---

6. Hugon, *Tractatus dogmatici*, t. II, *De Gratia*, 202–203.
7. TRANSLATOR'S NOTE: Garrigou-Lagrange gives no citation to a published work,
   but rather the Latin of a reported conversation of Hugon's.

Thomistic Theses, and on the vows of religion—works often read not only by students of theology but in many religious communities.

* * *

What we will insist upon, finally, is how he turned his knowledge to the good of souls just as in God the Word breathes love—*Verbum spirans amorem*. In his letter of May 5, 1916, his Holiness Benedict XV wrote: "The special merit of these books is, on the one hand, to clarify and defend the dogmas of salvation and, on the other hand, to arouse in the souls of their readers the love of true piety."[8]

In effect, he knew how to order his speculative and practical knowledge to the good of souls, and that is why he was so beloved by his students, and even by those more advanced whom he had helped. He truly was doing good through his teaching.

Here are clearly realized the words of St. Paul we quoted at the beginning: "*Diligentibus Deum omnia cooperantur in bonum*." To this good concurred his great faith in Our Lord, the influence of the Holy Spirit in the life of the Church, his love of neighbor, his mind (ever attentive even to the least details of a question posed to him), and about all his benevolence, his good-heartedness that never left him, even in regard to his adversaries—but these numbered very little, for he would never have offended anyone.

These natural and supernatural qualities of mind and heart made of him an apostle and a dear guide. He was not only consulted by Congregations of the Vatican, but by bishops as well, many of whom were friends. Religious superiors would often consult him. One superior recently wrote: "For all twenty years of Fr. Hugon living in Rome, there was never a single difficulty of mine that I did not refer to him." How many superiors of religious houses have written similar things after his death! One cannot recount all such services that he rendered; the testimonies on this are unanimous.

Along with all this, how many priestly and religious retreats did he preach! Each one of his vacations was occupied with this ministry. He

---

8. TRANSLATOR'S NOTE: This letter was printed as a prefatory note to certain of Fr. Hugon's French works of theology.

would habitually dedicate June and July to this, right after the tiring time of final exams.

If he thus turned his knowledge to the good of souls, this is because it did not arise only from a natural need for knowledge or a natural activity of the mind, but from a supernatural search for God and love of neighbor. The order of agency answers to the order of ends, St. Thomas often says. That knowledge that makes known a supernatural good, attains to a supernatural end because it comes from a supernatural source, from a faith vivified by true charity and enlightened by the gifts of the Holy Spirit, which facilitate the natural work of the mind and memory.

The soul of his apostolate was his interior life, very simple, but sustained and nourished by the practice of regular devotions.

If one keeps in mind the doctrine according to which supernatural contemplation of the mysteries of the faith is the normal way to sanctity, one can see that the gifts of understanding and wisdom, joined to charity, grow all together. And those who lived with him saw this principle realized, in a way as simple as it was practical. The light of the gifts of wisdom, understanding, and counsel made themselves manifest in this way, that he never deviated from the truth in difficult questions, and would stop discussions of things that seemed to have become useless. This light appeared in his constant benevolence, in his good counsel as well as in his preaching when he spoke from the fullness of his heart—for instance, when preaching on holy obedience, he said with deep conviction: "The authority of God is found in the least superior just as the sacred body of Our Lord is really present in the smallest bit of a consecrated host." In such a spirit he himself would obey, always accepting the most modest tasks.

Thus, he lived the motto of the Orders Preachers: *contemplari et contemplata aliis tradere.*[9]

St. Augustine says that the beatitude of peacemakers corresponds to the gift of wisdom, which lets us see in what way all things relate to God, even the most unexpected and difficult events. This peace our dear Father possessed and gave to others.

---

9. TRANSLATOR'S NOTE: To contemplate and to hand on to others what has been contemplated.

Truly, he has left us with a life full of merit, for he lived for God and for souls, and never rested, as the saying goes. He would say his Mass every morning at five o'clock, and after his thanksgiving and the recitation of the minor offices, he would write or teach until midday. Right after recreation—and he was its very soul, due to his amiability and the news he would share—he would every day pray a "Way of the Cross" and would go to hear confessions or preach until five o'clock in the evening, and then return to work until it was time for evening prayers.[10]

You would meet him sometimes, on the less noisy streets of Rome, reading his breviary or his journal. He would be praying or preparing a sermon that he was going to give, as he would preach every week or every month in several communities. Despite the coming and going of passers-by, he would remain at ease, pensive in that way of his, and attentive to the last detail of what he was reading. He truly would pray with simplicity and trust; moreover, numerous souls to whom he had done good would be secretly praying so much for him, for his teaching apostolate and his ministry.

Such was that inexhaustible source of charity to which so many had recourse. It was as if he had taken a vow to never refuse to help anyone, and one and all, inside the convent or without, they would come ask him for aid from morning to evening. How many persons from so many communities asked that he be their confessor! And I never knew him to refuse anyone. What is astonishing is that, although so very busy, he would find time for everyone. Often this meant sacrificing his best hours, and he never was impatient. His good nature helped him in

---

10. You can read in his notes these pious resolutions from a retreat given in 1927: "To give myself to God more and more and aspire to the way of union.—For Mass and office, more in union with the Humanity of Our Lord and the Holy Trinity.—Matins: the Holy Trinity.—Minor hours: the Holy Humanity.—Vespers and Compline: the Blessed Virgin and the angels.—To remain faithful to the practice of celebrating the votive Mass of the Holy Trinity, of Christ the King, of the Sacred Heart, and to the Rosary.—Every day, to take a mystery of the Rosary to shelter and protect the journey. To show tenderness to the divine Master, to not take the initiative or accept it unless there is a good reason.—Always to exert myself in the apostolate of charity...to hasten to render service for love of Our Lord.—To devote myself more and more to the Church, to aid better the Sovereign Pontiff and to strive with him for the glory of the only Master."

this, doubtlessly, but it was also certainly great self-denial on his part, and truly admirable!

In addition, at the age of nearly 62 years, despite his erudition, his experience of people and times, and having had experienced evil and injustice, he had kept the soul of a child, with a simplicity that constituted the charm of his goodness. There was no troubled religious who, having recourse to him, did not experience his goodness of heart.

He loved to recognize the good qualities of everyone, and was jealous of no one. He would especially appreciate those whom he called balanced minds. He had no interest in conundrums and could not comprehend why someone with a brilliant mind would waste time and effort to defend them. He would hardly admit in such cases that exceptional mental faculties could make up for a lack of likelihood, and yet he would stay benevolent to all.

His simplicity and his goodness did not prevent him from seeing his neighbor's defects, as are sometimes appropriate to point out. He would do so very gently such that you could not be cross at him. To the speculative mind who lived in the enchantment of eternal principles, but who would too easily abstract from actually existing persons, he would often say: "You are a poet, I am a man." And against those who claimed they could not see certain principles, he would reply: "And yet we do not live without them."

He easily avoided the erroneous extremes of these opposites, but not because of a spirit of opportunistic utility, but by a character and love of the rightly proportioned subordination to superior ends. In this his honesty clearly bore him up, as others are by what is useful. He had a sense for the subordination of things to principles and causes, yet he never confused this with mere mental organization.

He would grant the superiority of the mind to the faculties which it directs, but he did not diminish the role of the will or of the senses. He was not content with vague generalities about sentimentalism, and he knew how to see in the superior sentiments of the spiritual order the highest aspirations of nature and grace.

One would have thought that with his phlegmatic-sanguine temperament, which led him to see the good side of everything, he would have never suffered. He was certainly not one to fret, and he never

seemed to have endured long, purifying sufferings or hidden difficulties. But people would notice such things sometimes. He would show
for a moment a sharp pain, something flashed in his eyes, yet immediately the suffering was accepted and offered to God. The appearance of
sadness passed quickly, and he kept towards all the same benevolence
and amiability.

The deepest and most prolonged sufferings that he felt were those
that affected him, not personally, but due to his love of the Church and
his Order. Every deep love here below is made to suffer when the object
of our love is hurt. Now, our dear Father Hugon loved the Church and
his religious family very much. Despite his happy nature, he experienced certain interior sufferings in his apostolate to the same degree
that he had a love of the truth and a love for souls.

When something would affect him personally, or when things did
not go as he would have hoped, he would quickly console himself, and
remember with a smile while putting into practice the words of St.
Thomas: "Moral virtue fixes the mean in the passions, not according to
mathematical quantity, but according to quantity of proportion, so that
the passion shall not go beyond the rule of reason."[11]

Those who have lived with him for many long years and with
whom he would joke willingly are profoundly afflicted by his death,
which certainly leaves a great void. Everyone, even and perhaps especially those who are not like he was in temperament, character, or wit,
perceive how difficult it was for him to continue to accomplish all the
good he did, seemingly without effort. All recognize that his main characteristic was that great goodness of his, always simple and radiant for
whoever encountered it.

* * *

He truly exemplified in this life the words of St. Paul: "To them
that love God, all things work together unto good." One saw this especially at the moment of his death, while he felt the worst, after his bout
of double pneumonia. He himself asked, after confession, for viaticum

---

11. TRANSLATOR'S NOTE: Fr. Garrigou paraphrases, in Latin, this passage, from St.
Thomas, ST III, q. 46, a. 6, ad 2.

and extreme unction. He followed the liturgical prayers with such a
calm that one could believe him cured. But some hours later the signs
of death's approach were clear in his painful moans. However, when
the brothers, according to the Dominican rite, gathered around his bed
and chanted the *Salve Regina*, the moans stopped and he listened with
a great peace, as if the Virgin Mary, whose plenitude of grace he had
so frequently preached, had come to look for him. The *Salve* finished,
his painful groans began again, and when he was exhorted to unite the
sacrifice of his life to the Masses being celebrated—thinking about the
four purposes of sacrifice—he replied, "But of course," as if it were
entirely natural. He was repeatedly given the crucifix to kiss: "There is
only Him, there is only Him," he said: "Nothing so sweet as the Heart
of the Savior." Soon after, he died in the simplicity of great faith and the
love of Our Lord, as he had lived.

Truly his death shows us, at the end of his earthly existence, that for
those who love the Lord until the end, all works for the good: natural
and supernatural qualities, difficulties, trials, and sufferings of all sorts.
The honored founder of the Angelicum, the holy Fr. Hyacinthe-Marie
Cormier,[12] would say: "When, in the course of life, you are working
for the good Lord, you do more and less than what you had dreamed."
We do less, because there are still gaps that we had hoped to fill; we do
more, because the Lord in his mercy makes our efforts fruitful beyond
what we had imagined: "God, who is rich in mercy...is able to do all
things more abundantly than we desire or understand, according to the
power that worketh in us" (Ephesians 2:4; 3:20).

Such is what was realized in the life of our dear Father Hugon. We
see in the numerous testimonies and memorials arriving after his death
that he did, in a sense, more than he had dreamed, for the divine mercy
which makes the work of the apostle bear fruit is greater, more attentive, and more generous than we had imagined.

It is true that God's infinite justice surpasses in an absolute manner
our way of understanding, and, the saints say, a painful purification is
often necessary when all seems pure to us. Along the voyage to eternity,

---

12. TRANSLATOR'S NOTE: Blessed Hyacinthe-Marie was beatified by Pope John Paul
II on November 20, 1994. His feast is May 21.

for most of the elect, a time in Purgatory is needed, which had for all eternity been included in their predestination, so as to fully complete God's work. Let us not cease, therefore, to pray for our dearly departed brother, particularly at Holy Mass, to hasten his deliverance if he does not yet enjoy the vision of God, where he might find all theology, infinitely transfigured.

The spiritual features of dear Father Hugon recall us, in closing, to a point of doctrine well emphasized by a great Thomist who often inspired him, John of St. Thomas. This commentator, who was in his own time a man of prayer, a true contemplative, would say that theologians who devote themselves to theology upon earth, not because of natural curiosity but due to love of God and of souls, would also see theology in heaven, not *extra verbum* in the created light of the vision called evening knowledge, but *in Verbo*, in the uncreated light of morning knowledge, the Eternal Morning. This high and beautiful reward our dear Father Hugon has received or soon will receive, because he did not study and teach theology through curiosity or for earthly erudition, but truly because of love of God and of souls.

Let us not forget the great example that he has left us: the example of living faith, trust, love of God, of Our Lord, of the Holy Church, of unwavering devotion to the Vicar of Christ, of true fraternal and apostolic charity. May our dear Father Hugon deign to send from on high to the Church and the Order, which he so loved and served, new laborers to work in the vineyard of the Lord, as he worked himself before entering into eternity.

* * *

APPENDIX

PART II
TRANSLATOR'S ESSAYS

ANCILLA DOMINI ET ANCILLA THEOLOGIAE:
MARY AND PHILOSOPHY

for Carlos Taja

Mary kept all these words, pondering them in her heart.

— LUKE 2:19

INTRODUCTION

To conclude the encyclical *Fides et Ratio* on the great harmony between faith and reason, Pope St. John Paul II ponders the relationship between Mary and philosophy.

I turn in the end to the woman whom the prayer of the Church invokes as *Seat of Wisdom*, and whose life itself is a true parable illuminating the reflection contained in these pages. For between the vocation of the Blessed Virgin and the vocation of true philosophy there is a deep harmony. Just as the Virgin was called to offer herself entirely as human being and as woman that God's Word might take flesh and come among us, so too philosophy is called to offer its rational and critical resources that theology, as the understanding of faith, may be fruitful and creative. And just as in giving her assent to Gabriel's word, Mary lost nothing of her true humanity and freedom, so too when philosophy heeds the summons of the Gospel's truth its autonomy is in no way impaired. Indeed, it is then that philosophy sees all its enquiries rise to their highest expression. This was a truth which the holy monks of Christian antiquity understood well when they called Mary "the table at which faith sits in thought." In her they saw a lucid image of true philosophy and they were convinced of the need to *philosophari in Maria.*[1]

In what follows, I consider each part of this passage, particularly in conjunction with Mariology as a part of theology. Indeed, the "deep harmony" to which the Pope draws our attention is the idea that just as Mary is *ancilla Domini*, the handmaiden of the Lord, so is philosophy *ancilla theologiae*, the handmaiden of theology.

Note at the outset to what a great extent Mary is, in her very person, both object and cause of our contemplation, in a secondary way, yet still in likeness to Christ. Jacques Maritain, in a letter, comments on this twofold aspect. We ought both to contemplate Mary in her contemplation and realize to what degree she is exemplar and aid of our own contemplation.

Let us think of young Mary brought up in the Temple, of this immaculate daughter of the Hebrews, and of her total, absolute eagerness for divine truth—for that divine Truth which was to take flesh in her. Let us think of her during the Passion of Christ, and later on, after Pentecost. The entire life of the Blessed Virgin was steeped in contemplative wisdom. She also had, in an infused and superior way, and through connaturality with her Son, theological wisdom and philosophical wisdom. It is impossible to imagine to what degree the Mother of the Incarnate Word cherishes the integrity of truth and abhors any stain on intelligence. In the tympanum of a portal of the cathedral of Chartres, she is represented surrounded by the seven liberal arts. She is interested in our work, poor philosophers that we are. She looks at, and loves, the least spark of truth in any effort of ours. She hates lying and sophistry .... In any case a lasting war is going on between the Woman and the Serpent. In the face of intellectual delusions

---

1.   Pope St. John Paul II, *Fides et Ratio*, n. 108.

and betrayals, I believe that in our times, when the main struggles of the mind are taking place at the level of philosophy, Mary has especially at heart the fate of Christian philosophy.[2]

Indeed, the concrete way of life that is Christian philosophy, and its vitality, finds an exemplar in Our Lady, and indeed the supreme heroine to follow into the intellectual battles of our times. For these, of their nature, are intimately spiritual actions.

This is contained in what the Pope says in *Fides et Ratio* above, that the person and life of Mary are a "true parable" about faith and reason. To explain this assertion, he introduces three key ideas in sequence. So, we can arrange our considerations as follows. First, how should we understand the first analogy that Pope St. John Paul II provides us? What follows from the likeness between the person of Mary and the activity of philosophizing in the service of sacred theology? Second, how are we to understand the second analogy that the Pope gives? What manner of freedom is it that philosophy retains when its serves theology in its ancillary mode? Third, what should be made of the emphatic conclusion drawn after the second of these analogies? That is, not only is there an analogy between the two handmaidens, and not only are both, precisely as *ancillae*, servants in perfect freedom, it is also in this service that they find their excellence: *Indeed, it is then that philosophy sees all its enquiries rise to their highest expression.* We will consider, then, (1) Mary's own faith and reason; (2) Mary as exemplar of philosophy's freedom in theology; and (3) how philosophy sees its inquiries reach their height when called to theological service in Mariology.

MARY'S FAITH AND REASON

Let us reread Pope St. John Paul II's first analogy:

Between the vocation of the Blessed Virgin and the vocation of true philosophy there is a deep harmony. Just as the Virgin was

---

2. Jacques Maritain, "Letter to Fr. Lynch," October 31, 1954, The Jacques Maritain Center at the Unviersity of Notre Dame, https://maritain.nd.edu/jmc/jm0216.htm (accessed September 1, 2019).

called to offer herself entirely as human being and as woman
that God's Word might take flesh and come among us, so too
philosophy is called to offer its rational and critical resources
that theology, as the understanding of faith, may be fruitful and
creative.[3]

Our first task, of course, is to understand the analogy itself. The first
part of the analogy concerns the relationship between Mary and the
Incarnation; the second part concerns the relationship between philosophy and theology. It is the relationship between the two elements
of the first part of the analogy that is supposed to illuminate the relationship between the two elements of the second part of the analogy.
The properly theological character of the analogy should therefore be
clear. We are supposed to learn something about philosophy in its relationship to theology based upon the relation between Mary and the
Incarnate Word.

The first part of the first analogy is this: "The Virgin was called to
offer herself entirely as human being and as woman that God's Word
might take flesh and [become one of us]."[4] Note that he highlights
how Mary offered herself both in her *human* and *feminine nature*.[5] He
also notes a twofold effect: that God's Word might both *take flesh* and
also *become one of us*—"The Word was made flesh, and dwelt among
us" (John 1:14). The second part of the analogy is this: "Philosophy is
called to offer its rational and critical resources that theology, as the understanding of faith, may be fruitful and creative." If we carefully align
the elements of the two parts, we obtain: Mary is likened to philosophy,
her human and feminine nature is likened to the resources of philosophy, God's Word is likened to theology, and Christ's incarnation and

---

3. Pope St. John Paul II, *Fides et Ratio*, n. 108. The Latin text reads: "Etenim inter
    vocationem Beatae Virginis et verae philosophiae strictam consonantiam prospi-
    cere licet. Quemadmodum namque ad suam humanitatem et femininam natu-
    ram tradendam ipsa vocata est, unde Dei Verbum carnem sumere posset fieretque
    unus ex nobis, sic ad operam sustinendam, rationalem videlicet et criticam, voca-
    tur philosophia, ut theologia, veluti fidei intellectio, fecunda sit et efficax."
4. Translation slightly modified.
5. See the Latin text, quoted above, n. 3.

dwelling among us is likened to the understanding of the faith being fruitful and creative—or perhaps, "fruitful and efficacious [*fecunda... et efficax*]."

Note that the Pope does not draw our attention to the *graces* which Mary required so that she might become the Mother of God. Rather, what belongs to her *naturally* is the key to the analogy: her humanity and femininity. That is, her natural "resources" are elevated to serve the Word who was to become incarnate. So too, philosophy is a natural mode of knowledge, elevated to serve the understanding of faith. Mary is human by nature, and feminine in her person; philosophy of its nature is rational, and in its character *critical*. How to understand this? Indeed, if the comparison is meant to align Mary's human nature with the rational nature of philosophy, then how is Mary's femininity helpfully paired with a "critical" philosophy?

We must not understand the "critical" character of philosophy in the sense modernity imbues both the word "critique" and the spirit of the philosopher who carries it out. By contrast, the better meaning of this "critical" character of a true philosophic spirit is explained by Giussani:

> The word *crisis* (from the Greek *krino*, "to test or sift") is ordinarily and unfortunately interpreted, in today's mindset, as being doubtful and negative, as though crisis and critique necessarily implied denial. Thus, in practice, critique is raised only for the purpose of scandalizing, always on the lookout for something to impugn, something to object to. This is clearly a short-sighted (or petty!) concept of crisis and critique. On the contrary, critique is, first of all, the expression of the human genius that is in all of us—a genius that strains to discover being, to discover values.... All of us used not to exist. Therefore, each of us is formulated from antecedents, from a package of things that constitute us, that shape us. The word *problem* refers to this phenomenon, which is crucial for true novelty in an individual life and in the life of the human cosmos. Tradition, the endowment with which life enriches us at birth and during our early development, must be lifted before our eyes so that the individual, to the extent that

he or she is alive, intelligent, may sift and test (*krinei*). Tradition must "become crisis." Tradition must become a problem. Thus, crisis means becoming aware of the reality from which we feel we were made.[6]

That is, the true *problematizing* of a tradition is our becoming aware of the meaning of our being placed and made *here* in the world, at *this* time, and for a purpose. It is our own being *critically received*. That is, "critique" is a discerning and judgment based fundamentally upon philosophical receptivity of the truth. Now, as Alice von Hildebrand points out:

> Clearly passivity is inferior to activity, for one is only being "acted upon." But this is not true of receptivity which involves an alert, awakened, joyful readiness to be fecundated by another person or by a beautiful object. All created persons are essentially receptive because "there is nothing that we have not received." Women feel at home in this receptivity and move in it with ease and grace.[7]

Indeed, as John Paul II himself noted: "A woman's dignity is closely connected with the love which she receives by the very reason of her femininity."[8] In this, then, the pairing of Mary's femininity with the critical spirit of philosophy is seen to be more apt, and indeed, a very close analogy. A true philosophical critique of reality is not opposed to but is rather characterized by the full receptivity to the truth about being. This notion of critique corresponds more closely to the ancient understanding of *theory* as it arises from an *eros* for the truth. Modern theory is, by contrast, *thumetic*, arising from a desire for the conquest and mastery of nature: "Mary exemplifies philosophy's initial task to receive reality and not manipulate it. Unlike some Baconian mastery

---

6.   Luigi Giussani, *The Risk of Education*, trans. M. Sullivan (Montreal: McGill-Queen's University Press, 2019), pp. 69–70.

7.   Alice von Hildebrand, *The Privilege of Being a Woman* (Ann Arbor: Sapientia Press, 2002), p. 63.

8.   Pope St. John Paul II, *Mulieris Dignitatem*, Apostolic Letter of August 15, 1988, n. 30.

or Cartesian orchestration of the world, Mary symbolizes the awe of standing before a reality wholly independent of the human mind."[9]

To more deeply understand this first analogy in *Fides et Ratio*, let us develop an analogy from St. Thomas and St. Augustine. I have highlighted how Mary was called to offer herself in service to God's Word, and philosophy is called to offer itself to theology. Note, however, that the analogy considers the Word *to be incarnated*, and qualifies theology with the phrase, "as the understanding of faith." That is, theology is understood here as "disembodied," as it were, or as it is contained in the intellect, that is, "*veluti fidei intellectio.*" So too, the Word in the Godhead, prior to the Incarnation, had not yet taken flesh.

In his first lecture in his *Commentary on The Letter to the Hebrews*, St. Thomas is explaining the following verses:

> God, who, in many ways and in diverse manners, speaking in times past to the fathers in the prophets, last of all, in these days hath spoken to us by his Son, whom he hath appointed heir of all things, by whom also he made the world. (Hebrews 1:1–2)

What does St. Thomas make of the idea that "God...hath spoken to us by his Son"? To interpret this text, the Angelic Doctor notes three aspects of human speech: the *conception* of a thought, its *expression* in the spoken word, and the *manifestation* of the thing spoken about. That is, there is the word of the human heart, of the human voice, and what is understood through what is heard. Based upon this comparison, and in relation to Hebrews 1:1–2, St. Thomas first explains that God's conception is an eternal conception, and "this eternal conception is the engendering of the Son of God."[10] Next, the expression of God's Word is considered as follows:

9. David Vincent Meconi, S.J., "*Philosophari in Maria,*" in D. R. Foster and J. W. Koterski, S.J., eds., *The Two Wings of Catholic Thought: Essays on Fides et Ratio* (Washington DC: Catholic University of America Press, 2003), pp. 69–90, here p. 71; cited by Prudence Allen, "Mary and the Vocation of Philosophers," *New Blackfriars*, Vol. 90, No. 1025 (January 2009), p. 54.

10. St. Thomas, *Commentary on Hebrews*, ch. 1, lect. 1, n. 15, trans. Fr. Fabian Larcher, O.P. and The Aquinas Institute (Steubenville, OH: Emmaus Academic Press, 2018), https://aquinas.cc/la/en/~Heb (accessed September 1, 2019).

[God] expressed his concept in three ways: first, in the production of creatures, namely, when the conceived Word, existing as the likeness of the Father, is also the likeness according to which all creatures were made: *God said: be light made. And light was made* (Genesis 1:3). Second, through certain notions; for example, in the minds of the angels, in whom the forms of all things, which were concealed in the Word, were infused, and in the minds of holy men: and this by sensible or intellectual or imaginary revelations. Hence, every such manifestation proceeding from the eternal Word is called a speaking: *the word of the Lord which came to him* (Jeremiah 1:2). Third, by assuming flesh, concerning which it says: *and the Word was made flesh* (John 1:14). Hence, Augustine says that the incarnated Word is related to the uncreated Word as the voice's word is related to the heart's word.[11]

---

11. Ibid. The last sentence reads: "Et ideo dicit Augustinus, quod hoc modo se habet Verbum incarnatum ad Verbum increatum, sicut verbum vocis ad verbum cordis." There is no reference to St. Augustine in the text, but the closest point of comparison seems to be *De Trinitate*, Book XV, where St. Thomas is succinctly summarizing what St. Augustine explains at greater length; first, see ch. 11, n. 20: "Accordingly, the word that sounds outwardly is the sign of the word that gives light inwardly; which latter has the greater claim to be called a word. For that which is uttered with the mouth of the flesh, is the articulate sound of a word; and is itself also called a word, on account of that to make which outwardly apparent it is itself assumed. For our word is so made in some way into an articulate sound of the body, by assuming that articulate sound by which it may be manifested to men's senses, as the Word of God was made flesh, by assuming that flesh in which itself also might be manifested to men's senses. And as our word becomes an articulate sound, yet is not changed into one; so the Word of God became flesh, but far be it from us to say He was changed into flesh. For both that word of ours became an articulate sound, and that other Word became flesh, by assuming it, not by consuming itself so as to be changed into it. And therefore whoever desires to arrive at any likeness, be it of what sort it may, of the Word of God, however in many respects unlike, must not regard the word of ours that sounds in the ears, either when it is uttered in an articulate sound or when it is silently thought. For the words of all tongues that are uttered in sound are also silently thought, and the mind runs over verses while the bodily mouth is silent." Second, see Chapter 14, n. 24: "And that word, then, of ours which has neither sound nor thought of sound, but is of that thing in seeing which we speak inwardly, and which therefore belongs to no tongue; and hence is in some sort like, in this enigma, to that Word of God which is also God; since this too is born of our knowledge, in such manner as that also is born of the knowledge of the Father: such a word, I say, of ours, which we find to be in some way like that Word, let us not be slow to consider how unlike also it is, as it may be in our power to utter it."

It is the final, third mode of expression which concerns us here. Just as the word of the human heart is to the word in human speech, so too is the uncreated Word proceeding within the Godhead to the Word Incarnate. Indeed, this analogy of St. Augustine and St. Thomas can help us understand where Mary falls in God's "expression" of his eternal Word. This will help us to deepen our appreciation of the analogy between the *ancilla Domini* and the *ancilla theologiae*.

However, we need one further element of St. Thomas's doctrine about the nature of human speech.[12] Following the Aristotelian analysis of the human soul, St. Thomas notes that we can properly use the noun "word" (*verbum*) in three ways when it comes to human speech. The first is to name the elements of human speech itself, that is, physically spoken words. In another way, what we conceive in our minds, or *that in which we think* and judge reality, can be called a word; this is the interior word or *verbum cordis*, the word of the heart. Finally, however, there is the word in our imagination. This middle *locus* of the human word is necessary because the word of the heart *is without language*. It cannot but be the case that this word is without language because such "words of the heart" are those in which we contemplate the truth of things, which power is common to all human beings regardless of language.[13] This interior word is also a *spiritual* word, for the mind is a spiritual power. Therefore, some *medium* or *mediating cause* is necessary between the fully spiritual human word in thought and the fully physical human word in speech. This cause is the power of the imagination, which, although seated in a physical organ, possesses an operation that exceeds *purely* physical activity, even as its activity emerges hylomorphically from a physical organ. Thus, Aquinas summarizes:

> Therefore it follows that, first and chiefly, the interior concept of the mind is called a word; secondarily, the vocal sound itself,

---

12. We note in passing that the most extensive and beautiful consideration of human speech as a philosophical basis to illuminate, as a basis of comparison and contrast, the nature of the Divine Word is found in St. Thomas's lecture on John 1:1–2.

13. See Aristotle, *On Interpretation*, I.1. Did this interior "word" or "affection of the soul" (in Aristotle's terms) not exist, translation between human languages would be impossible in the strict sense.

signifying the interior concept, is so called; and third, the imagination of the vocal sound is called a word.[14]

What is important for us to realize is this: The power of the imagination, in conjunction with our faculty and habits of speaking a language, particularizes the *verbum cordis* into a certain human tongue, with all its attendant habits of expression. Those universal ideas of truths conceived, dimly seen, or fully grasped in the innermost recesses of the heart are contracted to more earthly terms so that they might be spoken and manifested at a given place and time to human hearers.

Let us now apply this threefold meaning of "word" to the case of Our Lady. To do so, we must recall what St. Augustine teaches about Mary's conception of Christ. St. Thomas recalls his words when considering the reasonability of the Annunciation:

> It was reasonable that it should be announced to the Blessed Virgin that she was to conceive Christ. First, in order to maintain a becoming order in the union of the Son of God with the Virgin—namely, that she should be informed in mind concerning Him, before conceiving Him in the flesh. Thus Augustine says (*De Sancta Virgin.* III): *Mary is more blessed in receiving the faith of Christ, than in conceiving the flesh of Christ*; and further on he adds: *Her nearness as a Mother would have been of no profit to Mary, had she not borne Christ in her heart after a more blessed manner than in her flesh.*[15]

That is, Mary gives true consent to the Lord's incarnation because of the knowledge she receives from the angel. Fr. Hugon also comments on this theme: "Mary was happier to conceive God by faith that in the flesh, and to carry him in her heart by grace than in her womb by motherhood."[16] St. Augustine also says that, upon hearing the words of the

---

14. St. Thomas, *ST* I, q. 34, a. 1, c.: "Sic igitur primo et principaliter interior mentis conceptus verbum dicitur, secundario vero, ipsa vox interioris conceptus significativa, tertio vero, ipsa imaginatio vocis verbum dicitur."

15. St. Thomas, *ST* III, q. 30, a. 1, c.

16. Chapter 4, p. 64.

angel, Mary, full of faith, responded with her *Fiat*, conceiving Christ "first in her mind and then in her womb."[17]

This being the case, we might expand upon the analogy that St. Augustine makes between our mental word and our spoken word, on the one hand, and between God's eternal, uncreated Word and the Incarnate Word, on the other hand. That is, as the human word of the heart (*verbum cordis*) is to the word of the imagination (*verbum imaginationis*) and thence to the spoken word (*verbum vocis*), so too the uncreated Word is to the Word conceived in Mary's faithful soul to the Word Incarnate conceived in her womb. Mary is, as it were, the imagination of God in which the Word first comes to be Incarnately; she is like the organ, or instrument, in virtue of whose operation the eternal Word is brought into time and space, contracted to a scandalous particularity so that He might *dwell among us*—for indeed, *in these days God hath spoken to us by his Son*. Of course, the human imagination is a *necessary* mediating cause given the specific form of human nature. Of course, strictly speaking, God was not limited in the means available to him to bring about our salvation, but is only limited via the *hypothetical* necessity of the means chosen for that end. Nonetheless, to follow the Augustinian analogy with the help of St. Thomas, as the imagination mediates the human spiritual *logos* so that it might be manifested in physical words, so Mary is the mediating cause of God's *Logos* that the Son might become incarnate.

Note that this analogy focuses upon Mary's whole person. She did believe what the angel told her. Full of faith, she conceived Christ first in her mind and then in her womb. She is, as it were, God's imagination in which He forms by a particular intention the Word Incarnate. That is, Mary accomplishes this role by the grace of divine maternity; she cannot be the Mother of God solely in virtue of her human nature. Yet Mary must offer her humanity and femininity to be elevated by the grace of the divine maternity so that the Word might become flesh. Without this natural basis, she cannot truly be the mother of a

---

17. St. Augustine, Sermon 215, n. 4, *PL* 38:1074: "Quae cum dixisset Angelus, illa fide plena, et Christum prius mente quam ventre concipiens, *Ecce*, inquit, *ancilla Domini, fiat mihi secundum verbum tuum*."

God-Man.[18] So, in the extended Augustinian analogy, Mary is considered under the aspects of both nature and grace.

However, in that first analogy quoted from *Fides et Ratio*, Mary was considered only as to *nature* (she is named as "Virgin"), and thus compared to *philosophy*. Thus, we might be justified in proposing the following comparison in order to grasp the deeper implications of Pope St. John Paul II's teaching: Mary in her nature (her humanity and femininity) is perfected by the grace of the divine maternity as the basis for her being the "imagination of God," so as to conceive the Word, which she does first in her mind and then in her womb, that He might be made flesh and dwell among us; so also, one employing the resources of philosophy (with its rational and critical character) is perfected by the grace of faith as the basis for being a believer, indeed, a theologian, so as to fully conceive theology, the understanding of the faith, in order that it may be fruitful and efficacious. The theologian imitates Mary's contemplation; in this, philosophy or natural reason is handmaiden of theology as Mary in her virginal, human nature is the Lord's. Mary's humanity is required to mediate the conception of the Word, enclosing the eternal Truth within matter, space, and time; philosophy is required to mediate the conceptions of theology, aiding our minds to grasp reality in the participated light of the science of God and the blessed.[19] The Word both takes flesh of Mary and through her is able to become one of us; without a basis of natural reason, theology is unable to bear efficacious fruit. Theology needs philosophy, as the Word needed the humanity of his mother.

THE USE OF PHILOSOPHY IN THEOLOGY

From the above, then, we can gather the fittingness of the first analogy made by Pope St. John Paul II, likening Mary as Virgin to the role of philosophy, comparing one handmaiden to the other. However, there is an objection to such a comparison, namely, that by yoking philosophy to theology, one enslaves reason to something irrational, insofar

---

18. This notwithstanding, Mary is "Mother of God" in virtue of her person, implying both her human nature and the grace of divine maternity.

19. This "participated light" was discussed in the Translator's Introduction.

as faith is by definition beyond demonstrative, rational proof, for the believer accepts in faith a proposition without evidence commensurate to reason's natural capacities. This is the sort of objection that the Pope has in mind, for he answers it in his second analogy without bothering to make the objection explicit.[20] Here it is again:

> And just as in giving her assent to Gabriel's word, Mary lost nothing of her true humanity and freedom, so too when philosophy heeds the summons of the Gospel's truth its autonomy is in no way impaired.[21]

This analogy clearly builds upon the first. It continues the meditation upon the event of the Annunciation and Mary's being called "to offer herself entirely as human being and as woman" by highlighting the event's key moment, that is, her hearing Gabriel's words and consenting to the divine proposal. So too are philosophy's nature and character—its rational and critical resources—called by the truth of the Gospel. This second analogy is, as it were, contained within the intelligibility of the first while adding to it the notion of retaining one's freedom or autonomy despite choosing to submit to a higher authority.

We should unfold the meaning of this analogy by beginning with its first part, the Annunciation scene. Above we cited St. Thomas's first argument for the need for the Annunciation, that is was reasonable that Mary be told of what God willed for her. The third reason is that, in this way, "she might offer to God the free gift of her obedience: which she proved herself right ready to do, saying: *Behold the handmaid of the Lord* [*ecce ancilla Domini*]."[22] Fr. Hugon comments "If God asks for her consent with such formality, this is proof that he has decreed to make her will contribute to our salvation. The consent of the Virgin, says St.

---

20. Compare *Fides et Ratio*, nn. 49 and 67.
21. Ibid., n. 108. The Latin text reads: "Atque sicut Maria, Gabrielis nuntio assentiendo, nihil suae verae humanitatis ac libertatis amisit, sic philosophica disciplina, in his accipiendis quae Evangelii veritas suppeditat, nihil suae autonomiae amittit, sed omnes suas inquisitiones ad summam perfectionem propelli experitur." The last clause is translated as an independent sentence in the English.
22. St. Thomas, *ST* III, q. 30, a. 1, c.

Thomas, was made in the name of the entire human race."[23] In his apostolic letter *Mulieris Dignitatem*, Pope St. John Paul II writes:

> Through her response of faith Mary exercises her free will and thus fully shares with her personal and feminine "I" in the event of the Incarnation. With her "*fiat*," *Mary becomes the authentic subject* of that union with God which was realized in the mystery of the Incarnation of the Word, who is of one substance with the Father. All of God's action in human history at all times respects the free will of the human "I." And such was the case with the Annunciation at Nazareth.[24]

This "respect" of human free will by God's historical action is not, of course, in conflict with the predestination of Mary as the Mother of God.[25] Thus, the Annunciation scene shows us Mary not only offering the free gift of her obedience, but also through this consent contributing to the salvation of the human race, which is not only her own personal and glorious act, but a prophesied and divinely predestined event. This is the height of divinely caused human freedom.

What freedom belongs to philosophy, on this analogy? Gabriel's message to Mary is compared to philosophy being summoned by the truth of the Gospel, that is, by the truths revealed by and in Christ and his Church. Mary's consent to the Incarnation is as the philosopher's consent to serve theology in the ancillary mode of *ancilla theologiae*. We should bear in mind here the analogous "conceptions" of Mary and of philosophy that are implied by the first analogy, discussed above. Philosophy's pursuit of the truth is not hindered by its subordination to theology.

The teaching of St. Thomas on this point is well known.[26] The harmony between faith and reason avoids both the extreme of fideism

---

23. See Chapter 8, p. 139. Hugon paraphrases St. Thomas's fourth argument for the necessity of the Annunciation.

24. Pope St. John Paul II, *Mulieris Dignitatem*, n. 4.

25. The Pope mentions this in the sentence prior to the quote above. This topic is discussed in brief below, and a bit more in the next appendix.

26. See in particular *Super Boetium de Trinitate*, q. 2, a. 3, and *Summa Contra Gentiles* (hereafter, *SCG*) I, cc. 1–8.

and the extreme of rationalism. In our age, the role of philosophy in the explanation and defense of the faith is also crucial to defuse the threats that excessive scientism poses to many minds.[27] Instead of rehearsing the exposition of various well-known texts, we can better appreciate this role of philosophy and the consequent freedom granted to it by commenting on the following passage from Ralph McInerny's book *Praeambula Fidei*:

> Because of the cause of assent in the act of faith, it is not the case that here cogitation or inquiry reaches its term and the mind is moved by its proper object to embrace one side of a contradiction, but rather that cogitation remains even after assent has been given. In faith assent and cogitation are equally balanced, for the assent is not caused by cogitation but by will. This is not the proper way for intellect to be determined to one, which is through understanding, and that is why the movement of inquiry does not cease. Thinking and inquiry about what is believed goes on even though the assent is most firm. The mind, being moved by something extrinsic to its object, is, in St. Paul's words, rendered captive (2 Cor. 10:5). "Hence it is that the believer can feel an impulse to the opposite of what he most firmly holds, something that does not happen when one knows or understands." This persistence of cogitation is the source of theology.[28]

McInerny is contemplating a source of theology, or why "*fides quaerens intellectum*" exists, which source he finds in St. Thomas's description of

27. Scientism can be defined as taking the natural sciences, especially mathematical physics, as the standards for truth, whether as to method or as to substantial claims about reality. For instance, if someone does not take seriously claims about the spiritual human soul because such a thing cannot be effectively investigated by neuroscience, then he is affected by scientism. Or, if someone is troubled in their faith in the Real Presence due to claims of modern chemistry or quantum mechanics, this might be due to scientism and a poorly received (or instructed) philosophy.

28. Ralph M. McInerny, *Praeambula Fidei: Thomism and the God of the Philosophers* (Washington, DC: Catholic University of America Press, 2006), p. 19. The source of McInerny's quote of St. Thomas in the penultimate sentence is *De Veritate*, q. 14, a. 1, c.

"an impulse to the opposite of what [the believer] most firmly holds," that is, believes by the theological virtue of faith. From whence arises such an impulse? McInerny, following Aquinas, locates it in the "balance" between assent and cogitation arising in the soul due to the innate character of faith. The one with faith believes God without evidence proportionate to the truth of the claim. For instance, we cannot *demonstrate* the truth of the Trinity or the Incarnation as we can the various truths of Euclidean geometry. The mind in the latter case does not feel an "impulse" to disbelieve a mathematical theorem, because in that case "one knows or understands." The mind *assents to* the truth of the conclusion due to the proportionate evidentiary cogitation provided in the proof. We think through the proof, understand it, and then *rest in* the conclusion, or *assent to* it.

By contrast, *assent to* the truth of the Trinity requires an act of will; it cannot arise from the intellect's cogitation or 'reasoning it out.' McInerny notes that "this is not the proper way for intellect to be determined to one, which is through understanding." That is, "it is not the case that here [in the case of something believed by faith] cogitation or inquiry reaches its term and the mind is moved by its proper object to embrace one side of a contradiction." Now, the doctrine of the Trinity is presented to our minds as is every other subject taught to us—we hear certain words, for instance, that the One God is Triune, a Trinity of Persons. We might understand the various analogies proposed and comprehend the descriptions of how this Trinity is "at work" in its various missions in salvation history. Yet accepting such proposals as verities rooted in a supernatural reality, the hidden life of God himself, is not an intellectual accomplishment but an act of faith, a graced movement of the will *to believe what God has revealed*. Thus, we believe and call true the proposition "God is a Trinity," while we disbelieve and call false the claim that "God is not a Trinity." Our minds are "determined to one" or "embrace one side of a contradiction," that is, *our minds are made up*. However, they are made up or determined by an act of will, which act is extrinsic to the immanent spiritual activity of the mind properly speaking, even if it is intimately conjoined to it. Hence, the intellect is, on its own terms or of its own power and operation, still restless. It can continue its searching or cogitation in regard to the object it itself judges true.[29] We can both accept such a truth in our mind (thanks to the grace of faith and its act, *to believe*), yet still circulate about it in transfixed wonder. This is the dynamic yet stable heart of *fides quaerens intellectum*.

How does philosophy figure into this faith seeking understanding? Quite naturally. Because the intellect determined by the assent of faith is still capable of operating according to its natural capacities, and because the assent of faith does not determine the intellect by an intrinsically intellectual mode of determination (as just discussed), the mind remains free, in a negative sense, to investigate the truths that it holds by an act of faith. That is, the mind is not bound by evidence as would be the case of someone who has demonstrated a mathematical theorem. This freedom is "negative" because the mind can inquire after alternative conclusions without the penalty of irrationality (for it does not possess proportionate evidence for what it believes). However, it cannot rest in positions to the contrary without the penalty of infidelity or apostasy. We perform such "inquiring" according to the capacities of natural reasoning when we ask questions about the possibility and intelligibility of various Catholic teachings or dogmas, and St. Thomas's scholastic style of disputation, with its detailed objections and responses, is an exemplar of such a method. Philosophy is required in this endeavor insofar as the natural capacities of the mind are only proportionately raised to their perfection in philosophy, and this perfection is a necessary but not sufficient condition of well-grounded theological inquiry.[30]

Is this what Pope St. John Paul II means by philosophy's "autonomy"? That the believing mind is intellectually "free to" ask questions and propose philosophical objections against the truths of the faith for the sake of theological disputation and, consequently, greater theological insight? We think not. Just as Mary's "*fiat*" was a personal act central to the economy of salvation, so too is philosophy's response to

---

29. This is not violence of the will upon the mind, for the intellect without sufficient evidence believes things *at the natural level* in such a fashion. The assent to truths of revelation elevate this operation into the order of grace.

30. This clearly requires that "philosophy" be taken in a broad sense, but with special reference to metaphysical or ontological inquiries (as mentioned in the Translator's Introduction).

theology still a positive achievement, a positive freedom, with some role in salvation history.[31] That is, the assent of faith enables philosophical inquiry by determining the intellect to certain truths, while leaving out the evidence to support them. The believer's mind is transfixed by a conclusion that he does not yet fully understand. He knows distinctly by faith what he does not yet grasp determinately by reason. To be sure, this does not make philosophy Christian, although it may make a Christian a philosopher. That is, by calling the philosopher to the philosophical heights of which reason is naturally capable (the *praeambula fidei*), the Christian who philosophizes achieves a natural end naturally, even though in the concrete case this was extrinsically conditioned or motivated by the light of faith.

Consider this example. A Catholic philosophy student first studying Immanuel Kant's *Critique of Pure Reason* is deeply troubled by the sage of Königsberg's powerful arguments against the possibility of any philosophical demonstration of the existence of God. The student cannot see a way out of these arguments. However, he knows *by faith* that it is possible for reason to demonstrate the existence of God.[32] Thus, he knows that Kant must be wrong. His intellect is therefore in a way free and in a way bound. He can know by faith that the Kantian critique of natural theology must be unsound, but, philosophically speaking, his mind does not yet see the rational arguments for why this is so. Yet it is *in his mind* that he attains to both standpoints, albeit under different modalities. Given time, study, and persistent thought, the student's later philosophical accomplishment of seeing why Kant is wrong, or even later, seeing the truth of arguments for God's existence, is therefore motivated by his faith but achieved on philosophy's own terms. That is, the student's intellect is "determined to one," to recall McInerny's phrase, by reasons grasped through themselves, with no extrinsic reliance upon a supernatural grace. In this way, he freely achieves a positive philosophical insight.

31. For instance, see St. Clement of Alexandra, *Stromata*, Book I, Chapter 5.
32. See First Vatican Council, *Dei Filius*, Canon 2, n. 1: "If anyone says that the one, true God, our creator and lord, cannot be known with certainty from the things that have been made, by the natural light of human reason: let him be anathema."

Let us expand upon this example. Let us say that the student persists, and reaches the philosophical insight that God is one. In a passage shortly after the one quoted above, McInerny asks this question: "What, then, of a believer who is a philosopher and who fashions a cogent proof of God's existence? Does he stop believing that God exists?"[33] The following is his answer:

> This follows on the truth that it is impossible to know and to believe the same truth at the same time. For all that, such a believer, say, Thomas Aquinas, continues to recite the creed, "I believe in God." In the Latin, it is *Credo in unum Deum*, which makes clear that the God in whom one continues to believe is not God as he is known. But doesn't the proof establish that God is one? It does, but to believe that God is one *and* a trinity of persons can only be believed.[34]

Consider this laconic conclusion in light of the foregoing example of the student. The student, upon achieving the natural insight that God exists and is one, would, according to McInerny, still have to *believe* that God is "one *and* a trinity of persons." His emphasis is upon how the mind grasps the truth of a *compound* proposition "God is one and God is a trinity of persons." Or, this could be rephrased as a simple statement with a complex subject term: "The one God is a trinity of persons." The student's mind, in its act of judgment according to either way of construing the statements, cannot resolve the truth of the predication to something knowable by reason's natural lights (e.g., by reasoning from created effects to their transcendent cause). In this judgment about God being one *and* triune, the grace of faith must make a positive contribution, as McInerny describes.

More precisely, the intellect confirms by faith the truth of the compound statement (or complexified simple statement), thus enfolding through grace a naturally known, simpler judgment of God's unity within a broader theological context. Stated the other way round,

---

33. McInerny, *Praeambula Fidei*, p. 30.
34. Ibid., emphasis in original.

the truth of the student's judgment about God being one can be seen without the supernatural causality of faith, but that same statement can be elevated and joined by a further act of judgment to the truth about the Trinity only by faith. Thus, McInerny's implicit logical distinction—which can be taken as referring to a compound statement or to a simple statement with a more complex subject term—indicates how the "lights" of faith and reason overlap without any "destructive interference," for one resolves the truth of one's judgments according to different formalities and so honors the principle of non-contradiction, for the believing philosopher does not both know and believe the same truth at the same time and in the same respect.

Thus, philosophy not only has its "freedom of indifference" in the light of the Gospel's truth, but it can reach a "freedom of perfection," since it retains its integrity by seeing the truth of its judgments for itself.[35] Philosophy's response to theology can result in its own positive achievements, even if these are also employed in the service of theology. Indeed, and keeping in mind the great debates about the nature of "Christian philosophy" in the twentieth century, the Pope seems to be referring here to the undeniable historical fact that theology has and continues to motivate deeper philosophical inquiry.[36] In this way, "it is then that philosophy sees all its enquiries rise to their highest expression."

If Christ reveals man to himself, this is not without transforming and elevating the various human modes of being and acting in the world through man's encounter with Christ. The chief of these intellectual modes, naturally speaking, is philosophizing. This, too, is relevant to the crucial role that philosophy has played and continues to play in salvation history, and manifests the danger of "the lack of metaphysical interest among many theologians, who do not take the trouble to instruct the *ancilla* in that truth which is within its domain, and who

---

35. Servais Pinckaers, O.P., *The Sources of Christian Ethics*, trans. Sr. Mary Thomas Noble, O.P. (Washington, DC: Catholic University of America Press, 1995), Chapters 14–15.

36. See McInerny, *Praeambula Fidei*, Chapter 4, and pp. 106–107, and see *Reason Fulfilled by Revelation: The 1930s Christian Philosophy Debates in France*, ed. and trans. Gregory B. Sadler (Washington, DC: Catholic University of America Press, 2011).

make use of any philosophy or ideosophy which happens to be in style at the moment."[37] We can see this importance by reviewing some of the points where philosophy comes to the aid of Mariology.

PHILOSOPHY AND OUR LADY

From the second analogy, then (and consequently with implicit dependence upon the first), Pope St. John Paul II draws out the following conclusion:

> Indeed, it is then that philosophy sees all its enquiries rise to their highest expression. This was a truth which the holy monks of Christian antiquity understood well when they called Mary "the table at which faith sits in thought." In her they saw a lucid image of true philosophy and they were convinced of the need to *philosophari in Maria*.[38]

The first sentence is the emphatic consequence of the second analogy. Not only does philosophy as *ancilla theologiae* retain its "freedom" as a discipline, its inquiries "rise to their highest expression," whether that is because of the aid it provides the believer seeking understanding in the face of mysteries of the faith or merely its preambles. How ought we to understand, then, that Mary is a "table" (or "altar") at which faith sits in thought, the altar which "furnished the bread of life to the world"?[39] The meaning of this phrase is captured by St. Luke in the epigraph to this essay. Mary's own contemplation is what furnishes substance and exemplar for our own contemplation.

Sister Prudence Allen turns to John Henry Cardinal Newman to develop this theme:

---

37. Jacques Maritain, "Towards a Thomist Idea of Evolution," in *Untrammeled Approaches*, ed. R. M. McInerny, F. Crosson, and B. Doering, trans. B. Doering, 20:85–131, *The Collected Works of Jacques Maritain* (Notre Dame, IN: University of Notre Dame Press, 1997), p. 96.

38. Pope St. John Paul II, *Fides et Ratio*, n. 108. The footnote provided here for the holy monks of Christian antiquity refers us to Pseudo-Epiphanius, "Homily in Praise of Holy Mary Mother of God," *PG* 43:493B: "*He noerâ tés písteos trápeza.*"

39. Allen, "Mary and the Vocation of Philosophers," p. 53, n. 13.

How Mary was well-prepared for this mission by her Son, was beautifully described Cardinal Newman: "Mary for thirty continuous years saw and heard him, being all through that time face to face with him, and being able to ask him any question which she wished explained, and know that the answers she received were from the Eternal God, who neither deceives nor can be deceived." Newman further amplifies Mary's active engagement in her intellectual formation in relation to the Truth: "She does not think it enough to accept, she dwells upon it; not enough to possess, she uses it; not enough to assent, she develops it; not enough to submit the reason, she reasons upon it...to investigate, and weigh, and define, as well as to profess the Gospel; to draw the line between truth and heresy; to anticipate or remedy the various aberrations of wrong reason; to combat price and recklessness with their own arms; and thus to triumph over the sophist and the innovator."[40]

St. Lawrence Giustiniani, reflecting upon the verse "Mary kept all these words, pondering them in her heart" (Luke 2:19), says the following:

While Mary contemplated all she had come to know through reading, listening and observing, she grew in faith, increased in merits, and was more illuminated by wisdom and more consumed by the fire of charity. The heavenly mysteries were opened to her, and she was filled with joy; she became fruitful by the Spirit, was being directed toward God, and watched over protectively while on earth. So remarkable are the divine graces that they elevate one from the lowest depths to the highest summit, and transform one to a greater holiness. How entirely blessed was the mind of the Virgin which, through the indwelling and guidance

---

40. Ibid., p. 67. Allen cites, respectively, John Henry Newman, *The Mystical Rose: Thoughts on the Blessed Virgin from the Writings of John Henry Cardinal Newman* (Princeton: Scepter Publishers, 1996), p. 95; and *Mary: The Virgin Mary in the Life and Writings of John Henry Newman*, ed. Philip Boyce (Grand Rapids, Michigan: Eerdmans, 2001), pp. 188–89.

of the Spirit, was always and in every way open to the power of the Word of God. She was not led by her own senses, nor by her own will; thus she accomplished outwardly through her body what wisdom from within gave to her faith. It was fitting for divine Wisdom, which created itself a home in the Church, to use the intervention of the most blessed Mary in guarding the law, purifying the mind, giving an example of humility and providing a spiritual sacrifice.[41]

Here, we find an echo of both the conception of the Word in Mary's mind before conceiving him in her womb: *Thus she accomplished outwardly through her body what wisdom from within gave to her faith.* Here also, we find that Mary is an "intervening" cause, and instrumental mediator not just as to giving Christ to the Church physically, but of providing her example of contemplation, *guarding the law* and *purifying the mind.* Mary is the exemplar of the natural activities of human knowledge being harmoniously elevated by *divine graces,* that *elevate one from the lowest depths to the highest summit.*

What is this interior life of Mary like? What can we know of her, straining the limits of ontological insight or phenomenological introspection? It is well known that St. Thomas has extended discussions about the knowledge of the Person of Christ in both its divine and human modes. Could a similar analysis be pursued with regard to Our Lady? Are we able to speculate fruitfully upon what contemplative treasures and preparations she must have possessed, given who she is in the plan of salvation history, and what we learn of her from her actions in the Gospels?

We can offer the following brief sketch with the help of Fr. Hugon, who draws our attention to the aspects of the contemplative and active life of Our Lady. In Chapter 5 of his treatise, Hugon spends some time to consider the four periods in the life of Mary. The first corresponds to the days she spends in her childhood, hidden in the Lord, as it were,

---

41. St. Lawrence Giustiniani, Office of Readings for the Feast of the Immaculate Heart of Mary, 2nd Reading (Sermo 8, *In festo Purificationis B.M.V.*: Opera, 2 [Venetiis 1751], pp. 38–39).

in the temple of Jerusalem, entirely consecrated to prayer and
the study of both the divine law and the Scriptures. It is like
a prolonged and continuous act of contemplation, the way of
union, the life of the perfect.[42]

The next three periods of her life correspond to the three divisions of
the mysteries of the Rosary (Joyful, Sorrowful, and Glorious). In each
period, Hugon proposes that there are aspects of her life that are contemplative, while others are active as a fruit of that contemplation. For
instance:

In the fourth period, which begins with the first of the glorious
mysteries, she becomes the transfigured ideal of contemplation.
She follows her Son to heaven in her mind and heart, and she
still enjoys him here below thanks to the union and the embraces
of the Eucharist. She is, as it were, caught between heaven and
earth, imitating the life of the blessed, thinking of God and
loving him. Her face shines already with the first rays of glory.
She lives in its splendor and she could say, with the Psalmist, that
night itself becomes her light in the bosom of her delight. At
the same time, she practices the perfect works of the active life,
for she instructs the apostles, encourages the faithful, directing
the newborn Church. In such a way she ends her days, in the
exercise of the heights of activity and contemplation, up until
the moment when a last moment of ecstasy delivers her from the
earth and leads to her definitive union with God—as one flame
is joined to flame, as love is joined to love.[43]

Perhaps, while writing these lines, our Dominican author has in his
mind the following words from St. Thomas, where the Angelic Doctor
is answering the objection that Christ ought to have led a solely contemplative life, since this is the most perfect mode of human life:

---

42. Above, p. 89.
43. Ibid., p. 91.

The contemplative life is, absolutely speaking, more perfect than the active life, because the latter is taken up with bodily actions: yet that form of active life in which a man, by preaching and teaching, delivers to others the fruits of his contemplation, is more perfect than the life that stops at contemplation, because such a life is built on an abundance of contemplation, and consequently such was the life chosen by Christ.[44]

In this too would Our Lady imitate Christ. Fr. Hugon might be forgiven for emphasizing the Dominican charism of Our Lady, but he does help to focus our attention upon how hers was a style of life in imitation of her Son. Hugon captures the universal totality of her contemplative life when he says that "contemplation became for the Mother of God the food by which she was nourished, the sphere in which she moved."[45]

Hugon also highlights that Mary's contemplation bearing fruit in action is central to her role in her *compassion* of Christ on Calvary. This bears important consequences for the role of Our Lady as Co-Redemptrix:

Knowing from its origins the eternal plan of redemption, she had long since made that sacrifice which cost her all the sufferings of nature and grace, and, as she was without ceasing concerned to obey the divine will and save poor souls, she frequently renewed this offering of sorrow and love. She accompanied the God-Man in all his agony and martyrdom, and her mystical immolation upon Calvary is the utmost of sorrow here below.[46]

That is, Our Lady knew "from its origins the eternal plan of redemption" due to her contemplative formation; this is wisdom indeed, for it belongs to contemplative wisdom to know the origins of things. This knowledge shaped both her life before the Passion—for "she had long

---

44. St. Thomas, *ST* III, q. 40, a. 1, ad 2. Consider also *ST* II-II, q. 181, a. 3, and q. 182, a. 1, ad 3.
45. Above, pp. 89–90.
46. Ibid., p. 90.

since made that sacrifice," and "she frequently renewed this offering"—
as well as her presence at Calvary, where "she accompanied the God-
Man." She must have known of Calvary in the depths of her faithful
contemplation because of her understanding of Christ's saying to her at
Cana that "My hour is not yet come" (John 2:4). It is this contemplative faith that allows her to stand firm by the foot of the Cross, as St.
Alphonsus emphasizes:

> Mary stood supported by her faith, which she retained firm
> in the divinity of Christ. And it is for this reason, says [St.
> Antoninus], that in the Office of Tenebræ, only one candle is
> left lighted. St. Leo, when treating of this subject, applies to the
> Virgin this passage of Proverbs: "Her lamp shall not be put out
> in the night."[47]

In this, the Mother is unlike her Son, for Christ did not have faith.[48]
Indeed, this was impossible for him to whom St. Peter said "Thou
knowest all things" (John 21:17). Yet in this also is Mary singular, for
her faith was—subordinate to God—a proximate, first principle of the
faith of the infant Church on the first Good Friday and Holy Saturday,
insofar as in her alone resided faith in Christ after the Crucifixion and
before the Resurrection. The depths of her contemplation were necessary for her, as Mother, to bring forth the Church.

Of course, "to philosophize in Mary" has another sense beyond that
of taking Mary as the exemplar of faith seeking understanding. Mary is
also an object of theological contemplation. This means, of course, that
the handmaiden of theology will be there, assisting one's understanding
of the handmaiden of the Lord. In what follows—without entering
into a full examination of the theological and philosophical topics attending those aspects, for which we have not the space—I briefly indicate various ways in which philosophy plays a role in Mariology.

---

47. St. Alphonsus Liguori, *The Glories of Mary* (New York: P. J. Kenedy & Sons,
    1888), p. 617.
48. See St. Thomas, *ST* III, q. 7, a. 3.

(1) *Mary's predestination as the Mother of God and her fruitful Immaculate Conception*

First, there is the topic of Mary's predestination—she was predestined to be the Mother of God. The very reason for her being is united to that of Christ; her predestination is essentially bound to His.[49] All her other privileges flow from this.[50] The role for philosophy in understanding the predestination of Mary is the same one which it plays in shedding what light we can have on the doctrine of predestination in general. Natural theology is capable of demonstrating the existence of God's eternal providence, and defusing objections against the coexistence of God's foreknowledge, universal causality and goodness, and human free choice. Mary is but the "first" among human persons in the regard. Mary is the eldest of creation, and uniquely preeminent "part" of the created universe, as we explore in the essay following this one.

If Mary's predestination is principally to be the Mother of God, then her other graces are related to this as to their defining focal point. This is particularly true of the grace of Mary's Immaculate Conception. Since grace requires the immaterial powers of the soul as its subject, this dogma places certain demands upon the philosophical analysis of the coming-into-being of the human person. (For instance, materialism is ruled out of bounds immediately, leaving only dualistic or hylomorphic accounts of the human being.) A related issue, which may strike the modern reader as odd, is Hugon's account of human generation in

---

49. See Garrigou-Lagrange, *The Mother of the Savior*, pp. 6–7: "Pius IX affirmed it in effect in the Bull *Ineffabilis Deus*, by which he defined the dogma of the Immaculate Conception, when he said that God the Father predestined Jesus to natural divine sonship---so superior to adoptive sonship---and Mary to be Mother of God, in one and the same divine decree. The eternal predestination of Jesus included not only the Incarnation itself as object but also all the circumstances of time and place in which it would be realized, and especially the one expressed by the Nicene Creed in the words: '*Et incarnatus est de Spiritu Sancto ex Maria Virgine.*'"

50. Ibid., pp. 23, 24: "Since Mary pertains by the term of her maternity to the hypostatic order, it follows that she is higher than the angels; higher also than the priesthood, which participates in that of Christ.... The divine maternity is therefore, as is commonly taught, the foundation, source, and root of all Mary's graces and privileges, both those that preceded it as preparation, and those that accompanied it or followed from it as its consequence."

the case of Mary. He follows St. Francis de Sales, among others, who teaches that Mary had the use of free will from the first moment of her conception. This implies that she had use of her reason also. Now, the metaphysics of "hominization" is still a heatedly debated point in Thomistic philosophy; however, in order to defend our theological understanding of such teachings (admittedly one that do not have the weight of dogma), a commensurate philosophical understanding of the human person is required.

This assertion of Hugon's, first brought forward in Chapter 2, that Mary had the full use of her reason from conception, appears *prima facie* to be an anthropological impossibility. Note, however, that Hugon's principal claim is theological: that based upon a fitting analogy to Christ's own condition, and by an argument *a fortiori* based upon the sanctification in the womb of John the Baptist, that Our Lady would have been granted by God a measure of infused knowledge sufficient for the effective spiritual operations of intellect and will.[51] However, note that he employs a distinctively Aristotelian philosophical argument to support these two arguments from theological fittingness.

> Given the condition and the excellence of the initial grace, the use of reason would seem natural, for it is necessary such that all the gifts are preserved from sterility and avoid a fatal inertia that is repugnant to their tendencies and their powers.[52]

That is, at work here are the truths that natures act for specific ends, and that powers in a living organism or in the human person are goal-directed tendencies which are perfected through their activity. It would be a frustration of the graces present from her first moment of existence in Mary's soul that they remain fruitless or inoperative. The Immaculate Conception and her first sanctification naturally demand—that is, according to the essence of those graces as spiritual

---

51. See Chapter 5, p. 33: "In order to understand the possibility of knowledge from the first instant, one must note that infused ideas are able to be caused without the exercise of the senses or the cooperation of the imagination."

52. Ibid.

powers—fructifying operation. Given this end, and given the state of natural development of Mary in the womb making natural acts of intellect and will of a sufficient kind impossible, the only alternative means to the end of permitting her graces to flower is infused knowledge.

(2) *Mary, the Mother of God, and her person*

Mary was chosen by God from all eternity as His mother; this presupposes a certain hypothetical necessity within God's providential design for the salvation history of the universe, namely, the extensive supposition that Christ would become Incarnate and undergo his passion to redeem a fallen humanity. To contemplate Mary as Mother theologically, one must have as a philosophical basis a grasp of what motherhood is. This entails a grasp of both causality and the relations possible between persons.

To assert that Mary is truly the mother of a divine Person, insofar as this Person is incarnate, we require a substantial understanding of the causal role of a mother in generation.[53] This nature of being a *"genetrix"* is not limited to the purely biological. Mary is not merely the created principle of Christ's human nature, for the relation of mother and son obtains between persons (hypostases) and not between natures. Of course, Mary's humanity is a cause by which she is Christ's mother, but such a cause is clearly insufficient to be the Mother of God Incarnate. A proportionate cause is required for this; consequently, the grace by

---

53. Charles De Koninck, *Ego Sapientia: The Wisdom That Is Mary*, in *The Writings of Charles De Koninck: Volume Two*, ed. and trans. R. McInerny (Notre Dame, IN: University of Notre Dame Press, 2009), pp. 7–8: "Generation means vital origin and assimilation. It is the procession of a living thing from within a living thing conjoined as a principle of life which assimilates the product of generation to its proper nature by virtue of this very procession. Generation consists therefore in expressing a likeness propagative of the nature of the generator. The generator draws that which is generated from its own substance while forming it. If the Blessed Virgin is truly a generator, this definition of generation must fully apply to her…. Birth regards primarily and principally the being of the hypostasis and person. Hence, since the Blessed Virgin is the mother of Christ according to the hypostasis, she is truly the mother of God and of the man, of the God-man. In relation to that in Him who is born, the Blessed Virgin is properly cause and origin of God, *causa Dei et origo Dei*."

which Mary attains to divine maternity has been termed "of the hypostatic order," that is, she is related in her person to each of the Persons of the Trinity. In the celebrated words of Cardinal Cajetan, Our Lady thus attains to the very "confines of the Deity" through *her own* operation.[54] That this operation is *personal*—and not, say, merely passing through her, as when a higher agent uses a mere instrument—tells us something of the character of how grace had to elevate her human nature so as to be able of such an operation.[55] Mary has Christ's person as the *unifying terminus* of her action of generation.

This precision redounds to affect our understanding of Mary's own personal being and the grace she must possess. Consequently, as Charles De Koninck argues, the personal grace of Mary precisely as the Mother of God is ordered to her *esse personale*—her personal being—in an analogous way as the grace of union is ordered to Christ's *esse personale*.[56] Hugon also discusses this personal grace of Mary at length, arguing that the grace of divine maternity is analogous to the substantial grace of Christ, namely, that this grace was a sanctifying "form" Our Lady possessed.[57] Such conclusions make clear that an adequate theological grasp of Mary as *Theotokos* cannot come

---

54. See the treatment of Hugon, in Chapter 4, p. 56.

55. On this point, Nichols nicely summarizes the development of St. Thomas's thought between his commentary on the *Sentences* and the *Summa Theologiae*. See Nichols, *There Is No Rose*, pp. 40–42.

56. See Charles De Koninck, "The Immaculate Conception and the Divine Motherhood, Assumption and Coredemption," in *The Dogma of the Immaculate Conception: Its History and Significance*, ed. E. D. O'Connor, (South Bend, IN: University of Notre Dame Press, 1958), pp. 363–412, at p. 393: "In Christ we distinguish the grace of union—ordained as it is to His *esse personale*—from his habitual grace, which is both personal and ordained to others. Likewise, in Mary, we distinguish the grace of Divine Motherhood from her habitual grace which may, nevertheless, also be called grace of motherhood inasmuch as it is ordained to her Maternity. But the grace of Motherhood in the first sense, is something of the physical order, of the *esse personale* of Mary herself inasmuch as in and by her nature of Mother she is the principal agent and the generating cause of her Son according to His humanity, to Whom she is referred by a real relation. And this is what St. Thomas calls the 'affinitas quam habet ad Deum,' which is the basis of the cult of hyperdulia. 'This affinity belongs to the Blessed Virgin alone,' Cajetan adds in his commentary, 'for she alone attains to the confines of the Deity by her own operation.'"

57. See Chapter 4, p. 54.

about in the absence of a thorough philosophical grasp of causality and personhood.

De Koninck also proposes a helpful aid to understanding how Mary's lowliness made her capable, so to speak, of fittingly receiving this grace of divine maternity. In the second part of his Mariological treatise *Ego Sapientia*, De Koninck provides an extensive commentary on Mary's humility, in both an ontological and moral sense, by way of a meditation on the verse "I am black, but beautiful—*Nigra sum sed formosa*" (Song of Songs 1:4a). I quote his argument at length with a few words of commentary:

> The assumption of human nature can itself be accomplished in two ways, either immediately, without prior condition, as would be the case if God formed immediately the nature assumed, or by assuming human nature by way of birth, God thus putting Himself in dependence on man and proceeding because of that into the universe itself by way of origination. And the nature itself from which He is born becomes in that way properly the origin of God.[58]

Here, De Koninck is proposing a dichotomy of means. On the assumption that God wills to save a fallen humanity by way of becoming man, this can come about either immediately or mediately. However, the natural means for bringing a human nature into existence is within the act of human generation.

> Let us quickly note that this most radical communication would in no wise be possible in assuming an angelic nature. God could not proceed from an angelic nature, for this nature is, on the one hand, too perfect to engender in the manner of natural beings, and, on the other, too imperfect to engender as God does. *Perfecta imperfecte, imperfecta perfecte.*[59]

---

58. De Koninck, *Ego Sapientia*, p. 27.
59. Ibid.

The angel, *imperfectly perfect* in comparison to God and yet *perfectly imperfect* when compared to material beings, cannot be the sort of nature to which God unites himself hypostatically by way of generation. Angels do not generate another of their kind, because they are so individually perfect as to exhaust the possibilities of their essential kind. That is, they are their own essences—each angel being unique in its species—and thus exist as created, necessary beings, having no need of perpetuating their species by generating other hypostases like unto themselves. Besides having no biological need to reproduce to avoid the extinction of their species, De Koninck's implicit reasoning also seems to be that angels cannot engender as God does because angels are not their own existence.

> It is then thanks to the potentiality of matter, indeed of matter as deprived of form, and thus to the privation that is the weakest, that the Son of God can proceed from within His creation, thus imitating in the most profound way His generation from the eternal Father. *Infixus sum in limo profundi: et non est substantia*—I am plunged into the mire of the deep, and there is nowhere to set my foot. [Psalm 68:3] Happy imperfection of matter that permits such a formation! This same Son arises from two extremes of the universe, reuniting our baseness with His supreme grandeur—*ima summis*.[60]

That is, making full use of the Aristotelian-Thomistic understanding of the hylomorphic composition of the human being, De Koninck argues that human nature's "ontological humility," as it were, permits it to be that by which God enters into time and space. This is possible to human and not to angelic nature because human beings are not identical with their natures or essences—more than one human being is possible, and each one only exists contingently. Unlike angels, we are able to die. This numerical multiplicity and contingency is rooted in the material element of our being. For this reason, in order that the human species not cease to be entirely, we have by nature faculties

---

60. Ibid.

which make or generate another like ourselves, in another matter. This passivity and imperfection is the "lowness of being" needed by God.

> Here in the substantial order the *nigra sum, sed formosa* can already be applied. Mary is beautiful because of the divine maternity, but, on the side of the creature herself, this maternity is possible only thanks to the darkness of potentiality and privation. Therefore, it is thanks to that darkness that God can Himself proceed from a created principle....[61]

Consequently, not only must theology call upon philosophy to provide it with proportionately intelligible accounts of causality and personhood, but, if we follow De Koninck's lead, the hylomorphic account of the human person is able to provide insight into the lowliness of Mary's humanity that was raised to the confines of the Deity through the grace of divine maternity.

(3) *Mary's perfection in body and soul*

Hugon devotes a good deal of space to considering Mary's human perfections, whether by nature or grace.[62] Here, his approach is typified by the Thomistic standpoint. For instance, Chapter 6 is devoted to the universality of Mary's graces, and discusses the privileges of body, intellect, will, and all her interior psychological faculties. Hugon argues that physically she suffered neither deformity nor illness. Furthermore, her "lower faculties were obedient without resistance to the will's orders."[63] Her intellect was graced with a multitude of natural, supernatural, and mystical insights; she was also free from error, Hugon argues. Her will was adorned with the virtues and exempt from all sin; she was also *impeccable*, Hugon argues, that is, not just someone who never sinned (although capable of it)—which would be *impeccant*—but one without the "power" to sin. Furthermore, Hugon says, her nature

----

61. Ibid., pp. 27–28.
62. See Chapter 1 and Chapter 6, respectively.
63. See Chapter 6, p. 107.

was "integrated," that is, her lower powers and concupiscence were in perfect harmony with her higher faculties of reason and will. In this, she was like Christ, who never experienced a disordered psychological movement, for in him the *fomes peccati* (the "spark" to sin) never existed.[64] Lastly, her soul was adorned with the various gratuitous graces, the fruits of the Holy Spirit.

Why such an extensive emphasis? Is it not, perhaps, excessive, an overdone pietism? Perhaps not. Mary enjoyed by nature certain human perfections, but these were elevated by grace. Her physical, psychological-emotional, and intellectual-volitional capacities were not walled off from the graces she received to be the Mother of God, but all of these aspects of her personal being were holistically caught up with this elevation to the hypostatic order of reality. If the Incarnation is a "scandal of particularity"—that the eternal God is born as man at a certain place and time, as an individual of a certain people and nationality—so too might Our Lady be a "scandal" to a materialistic or Manichean or dualistic understanding of fallen human nature. In her, rather—even if thanks to grace—we see human nature one and unified and brought to its height. There is here no Sartrean existential shame at the reality of being harmoniously both spirit and flesh. In her God is able to manifest the possible harmony of the spiritual and material elements of our created natures and how he intended to redeem us whole and entire—our souls, but our bodies also. Her perfection of body, sense faculties, interior emotional life, intellectual habits and activity, disposition and exercise of will, and an interior peace such as Stoic philosophers had never dreamed, all manifest an ideal of human nature—and an ideal modeled after Christ's perfect humanity—in which we hope one day to share. In such discussions, philosophical anthropology is an absolute prerequisite. Just as modern day Thomists, following St. Thomas's lead in the *tertia pars* of the *Summa Theologiae*, employ in the service of contemplating Christ's humanity the best of Aristotelian rational psychology and contemporary insights into the

---

64. Hugon does not go as far as to say that Mary enjoyed antecedent command over her emotions, or the "passions of the soul," as did Christ by nature of the hypostatic union; however, he seems to imply this as a grace.

human soul, so too can and ought this be done when turning to a theology of Mary's interior life.[65]

(4) *Mary's knowledge*

Hugon's is especially a reflection on the glory of what the height of graced humanity is like. With regard to knowledge, his discourse avoids a lazy reductionism regarding "knowledge" and "certainty" to portray Mary's mind in its full glory and yet in its limitations. That is, he defends the idea that Our Lady was wise according to both natural and infused capacities, in her constant relationship with her divine Son and her ceaseless contemplation of God. Yet at the same time, her knowledge is not infinite; the gaps in her knowledge were limitations, albeit not lacunae. That is, there were places where her mind had not yet gone, but not failed or erred. Hugon also argues that Mary exemplified epistemic modesty. Thus, her "esteeming" or "regarding," "guessing" that Christ was among their relatives (Luke 2:44) is not a case of her being wrong, but of her supposing something plausible:

> Mary was in every circumstance preserved from error, but as to the particulars of a given case she did not have all the aspects of certitude, and thus had to employ conjectures or opinions, which, however, always enjoyed a real and solid probability.[66]

All such distinctions are useless, however, without various philosophical prerequisites in logic or epistemology.

Understanding Mary's knowledge is essential, in the Thomistic perspective, as a prerequisite for understanding her free choice. That is, according to the elevation of her informed intellect, her voluntary capacities shaped by that intellectual form are proportionately free. In her case, this elevation in grace is a necessary condition for her impeccability. Here, in a passage that echoes the consideration necessary to

---

65. See Nicholas E. Lombardo, *The Logic of Desire: Aquinas on Emotion* (Washington, DC: Catholic University of America Press, 2011); also, Paul Gondreau, *The Passions of Christ's Soul in the Theology of St. Thomas Aquinas* (Providence, RI: Cluny Media, 2018).

66. See Chapter 6, p. 111.

understand how Christ in his human mode of experiential cognition was able to grow in wisdom and knowledge, Hugon asserts that

> Mary knew how to read easily from the book of the world, the Scriptures, from the entire breadth of revelation, into the mysteries which surrounded her, all to which the course of her thoughts and reflections ceaselessly returned: *conferens in corde suo*. Guided by infused light, her natural knowledge had a penetration which genius itself is not granted, and from the two resulted a treasure of knowledge which would baffle our timid and meager ideas. Next to the beatific vision, there is no knowledge as clear, as profound, and as sure as that which Mary enjoyed during her mortal life, just as, next to glory, there is nothing which could compare with the grace of the Mother of God.[67]

That is, her intellectual operations, thanks to natural and infused knowledge, are proportionate to her being in both the orders of nature and grace. While Mary as to her nature is less than even the least angel, the graces attending her divine maternity exalt her above the entire heavenly host.[68] Yet, here too, there is order and distinction in what God has done for Mary: "The regular exercise of her faculties was not harmed in the least, just as in Jesus Christ the beatific vision and infused knowledge did not at all impede the normal course of human life."[69]

(5) *Mary's impeccability*

The consequence of her height of divine contemplation is Our Lady's impeccability. On this topic too, the philosophical prerequisites are manifest: freedom and determinism, the relationship of intellect and will, and of the higher powers of the soul to the lower. According to Hugon, the impeccability of Mary can be understood by comparing it to the impeccability of Christ; both are rooted in the spiritual

---

67. See Chapter 6, p. 113.

68. See De Koninck, *Ego Sapientia*, pp. 23–26.

69. Hugon, Chapter 5, p. 80. See also Hugon, *Tractatus Dogmatici*, t. 2, *Tractatus De B. Virgine Deipara*, q. 2, a. 3, n. 8, 764.

heights of knowledge granted by God. Thus, hers was the impeccability of perfected freedom. She had no power to sin because her power of choice was fully confirmed in the universal good. Our minds and wills are fickle, able to be turned away from what is always and everywhere good in virtue of our rebellious sense appetites, distracted by what may appear good here and now. However, as Hugon argues, this weakness was not present in Mary:

> Thus, two conditions must be met by absolute impeccability: first, a continuous, right contemplation of divine things, such that God is the rule of end of every action; second, an interior grace so powerful that it maintains all the impulses of the inferior powers under the empire of reason. Our Lord Jesus Christ, elevated from his first instant to the Beatific Vision, ever enjoyed this perfect state; it was his by right. No mortal could have met these two conditions without a gratuitous and absolutely extraordinary privilege. Yet such were according to Mary from the beginning.[70]

Now, the theological components of Hugon's argument are left for the reader's consideration. However, his proposal would be philosophically unintelligible if one did not properly understand the nature of the will as a power, and consequently the nature of freedom. While the power of free choice requires the possibility of the contrary outcome, this is a condition in the order of the person to surrounding causes (that is, this condition denies fatalism and compatibilism). However, to conflate this condition with the perfection of free choice as the defining note of virtuous moral agency would be an error. That is, what has been called the "freedom of indifference" is free choice taken in its capacity to choose *this* or *not-this* (as permitted by the ontology of real possibility). However, this is not what makes the power of free choice a human perfection. Instead, free choice is perfect when it unfailingly chooses the good; this has been called the "freedom of perfection."[71] This is how

---

70. See Chapter 6, p. 117.
71. See Pinckaers, *The Sources of Christian Ethics*, Chapters 14–15.

God or the good angels are both free and unable to do evil; the good angels knowingly choose to do what is good.

Thus, "impeccability" names a certain escaping from a privation. Mary's interior psychology, the disposition of her personal moral agency, lacked the disorder that we possess which is a condition for actual sin. Thus, "impeccability" does not name Mary's lack of a positive power that we possess, but is the correlative, negative name for her possession of perfect freedom. A particularly moving example of this impeccability can be found by reflecting on what Hugon says about the "legend of the spasm" of Mary.[72] This is the view that Mary swooned or fainted from grief on the road to Calvary. On the contrary, Hugon avers,

> at that unique moment in the history of the world and the supernatural, an abundance of graces, the power of her virtues, and sublime gifts all joined together resulted in heroism. Our piety cannot imagine otherwise for the Mother of God, and the Gospel does not tell us otherwise. Her body, soul, mind, courage, will, were standing: *Stabat*.[73]

That is, Mary's impeccability is manifested here in her heroism. Where the apostles abandoned Jesus or betrayed him, she *stood by* steadfastly— *stabat Mater dolorosa*. Her sorrows, like Christ's sorrows in the Garden of Gethsemane or at the death of Lazarus, are not those of faintheartedness or a dark despair. Our Lady at Golgotha shows us the perfection of the heroically courageous soul. Hers is the soul that does not fail Christ, and never could, due to her love for her Son. This is what impeccability means.

(6) *Mary's Assumption*

The privilege of Mary being assumed body and soul into heaven might appear to be so unique and above the ordinary course of things that the philosopher would have nothing to contribute. Charles De

---

72. See Chapter 6, p. 107.
73. Ibid.

Koninck would say otherwise. Here we can only mention his lengthy considerations of the "moment" of Mary's glorious death.[74]

De Koninck argues that Mary's death is gloriously unique in that *in the same moment of time* she died and was assumed into Heaven. Death enjoyed no victory, not even for an instant, over Our Lady. To defend this idea, he draws upon the Aristotelian ontology of change and the nature of the continuum of time. The key idea here is that when something changes—in this case, undergoes death—being alive and being dead are separated by a moment. In this moment, then, is one dead or alive? Aristotle answers that the nature of change demands that the character of the *terminus ad quem*, or the state being assumed, also characterize that moment joining the temporal span of the two states.

To illustrate this, suppose that for a span of time a lightbulb is off, and then it is turned on. Because of the infinite divisibility of the time leading up to the light's being on, there is no "last" instant of the light being off, but there is a first instant of the light being on. This first instant is the diving point between the prior state and the posterior one. To make this image serve as an analogy for death, we need only take the case of switching the bulb off. There is no "last" instant of it being illuminated, but only the first instant of it being darkened.

How does this apply in the case of Mary's death and Assumption? De Koninck notes:

> Now, considering things absolutely, there is no reason why the last instant of one's earthly life, the one in which body and soul are separated, could not be the same instant in which the glorified soul is already reunited to the body now immortal. The only difficulty of this doctrine arises from the fact that we imagine the last instant of earthly life as still occupied, as it were, by the person who in reality has already ceased to be; yet, if this were so, nothing could cease to be, nor could anything new become.[75]

---

74. See "The Immaculate Conception and the Divine Motherhood, Assumption and Coredemption," pp. 404ff.

75. Ibid., p. 405.

Here, De Koninck takes the Aristotelian ontology of change and its alignment with the continuum of time (discussed above) and applies it to the soul in death. The "last moment" of one's earthly life is not the same as the first moment of being in the next life. If the prior stage still occupied that "moment" that divided the prior from the posterior, then nothing could ever change, for the prior state would always exist wherever the posterior stage "attempted" to arise! Thus, there is an ontological openness because of the change that is death. What follows?

> But, you might say, if such were the case…a person might die and be resurrected *in ipso temporis puncto* [in the same temporal instant], he would not have died really; for the same instant in which he ceased to exist, would be exactly the one in which he already exists anew. True enough, there would be not a single instant in which he did not exist; there would be neither a time nor even an instant in which the man, the very person, did not live. But there would have been—and this is the crux of the matter—a last instant of his life according to the union of corruptible body and soul, viz. the first instant of the *primum non esse* [first non-being] of earthly life, which is death *proprie et essentialiter* [properly speaking and essentially]; and there would have been a first instant, the same as the latter in which glorified soul and body were already reunited, viz. the instant of the *primum esse* [first being] of the glorified life of the person, which is resurrection essentially.[76]

That is, the ontological "open end" of the moment of death grants the logical space for one's being *in the same moment* resurrected. The moment joining earthly and resurrected life would itself be the moment the natural philosopher would typically call the point of death, yet not because that cut in one's temporal history is made by the posterior state of bodily non-being. Rather, that moment of death is made such by the ontologically discontinuous status of resurrected glory. One might, nonetheless, sense a problem

---

76. Ibid., pp. 405–406.

But would this not imply that, in the same instant, a person would be both dead and alive? be and not be? Does not the principle of contradiction object to that sort of thing? Indeed it does preclude the possibility of being simultaneously dead and alive according to the same kind of life; of being and not being in the same respect. But that is all.[77]

That is, there is no contradiction because, in that moment where the life of glory takes over, one is not dead and alive according to the same sense of the word "life." There is, then, no logical opportunity for the contradiction to obtain.

It is this philosophical reflection upon the logical, temporal, and ontological structure of death that De Koninck brings to bear in the case of what he terms the glorious death of Mary and her immediate Assumption into Heaven, that is, the glorified state of her body and the beatific vision of God. While his argument at this juncture is properly theological, our purpose here is merely to point out the philosophical tools—and no meager ones at that—which the Laval Thomist brings to bear in the service of further understanding the dogma of the Assumption.

(7) *Mary's intercession*

This is a topic which Hugon takes up in the appendix translated above, "The Instrumental Causality of the Most Holy Virgin." There, he asks whether the Mother of God is the *physical* instrument of the graces she dispenses. This is as opposed to a *moral* cause, that is, that these graces are granted by Christ due to her intercession and because of the dignity of her person. He argues, tentatively, for Mary's physical causality. His case for her universal mediation—that she is the mediatrix of all graces—is made much more strongly.[78] Indeed, this theme is the focal point of the second part of Hugon's book.

That second part corresponds to the second half of St. Bernard's phrase *plena sibi, superplena nobis.* De Koninck observes: "Now Mary's singular plenitude of grace, bestowed upon her in virtue of the merits

---

77. Ibid., p. 406.
78. See Chapters 9–11.

of her Son, sanctifies her own person, but in such a preeminent way that, essentially the same, her grace overflows to others."[79] Whatever the precise nature and scope of Mary's causal role in the distribution of graces, its complete unfolding rests upon the Mariological first principle discussed above in the Translator's Preface, namely, that Mary is that human person uniquely related as Mother to Christ and also to His Church. Hugon finds this expressed scripturally in the connection between Cana and Calvary.[80] De Koninck also comments on this connection:

> Whatever the implication of the epithet *Woman* at the Marriage Feast of Cana, the sole assertion of Christ, "*My hour has not yet come*" (John 2:4), is sufficient to warrant St. Augustine's teaching on this point, which St. Thomas makes his own. The power to work miracles belongs to Christ's Godhead, not to the nature he received from the Mother. St. Augustine explains that Christ will acknowledge Mary publicly as His Mother when the weakness of the nature which He owes to her shall be exhibited upon the Cross, where, at the same time, her spiritual motherhood shall be made known to all. *Behold thy Mother* (John 19:27). We may understand, therefore, that the Son of Man and new Adam designed this solemn manifestation to express at once the unity between her natural motherhood with regard to Him and—owing to her fullness of grace and union with the Savior in His sacrifice—the new Eve's spiritual fecundity with regard to us.[81]

If we follow De Koninck's defense of Mary's universal mediation, it is always one articulated in connection to Christ's universal headship of the Church. (De Koninck also cites the image of St. Bernard used by Hugon, where Mary is compared to the "neck" of the Mystical Body.)[82]

---

79. De Koninck, "The Immaculate Conception and the Divine Motherhood, Assumption, and Corredemption," p. 388.

80. See Chapter 10, p. 161.

81. De Koninck, "The Immaculate Conception and the Divine Motherhood, Assumption, and Corredemption," p. 395.

82. See ibid., p. 388.

Here, too, the principle of Mary as archetype of the Church is shown to full advantage, as Nichols indicates:

> Otto Semmelroth...proves conclusively, I believe, that ecclesio-typicalism does not necessarily lead to a low Mariology. How does it prove that? In the last chapter, on Mary as mediatrix of graces, we saw how scholastically trained theologians working in a Christo-typical idiom in the French Catholicism of this period drew back from the assertion that sacramental graces—as distinct from "providential arrangements" and "actual" graces—are given through the mediation of Mary. By contrast, Semmelroth has absolutely no difficulty at all with the claim that grace in every mode, including the sacramental, is communicated through our Lady. This is because he understands Mary to be, as the primal church, the total recipient, in a single all-encompassing act of acceptance, of all the spiritual good the Savior has to give to the world. As Semmelroth writes, "the Mother of the Lord is 'the depository for the plenitude of all graces for the Church.'...Christ stands before the Father living on 'ever to make intercession on our behalf' (Hebrews 7:25), or to use the idiom of piety, showing his wounds to the Father. Mary stands as the perpetual Orante [the praying person] in the eternally changeless attitude of the Church's receptivity before Christ, and she receives what the Church needs." Since she receives whatever the church needs she can be called, in Semmelroth's formula, the "receptive co-redeemer."[83]

What philosophy can propose in regard to this super-plenitude of grace that overflows to us, Mary's children, is the basis of an understanding of causality so as to analogously apply it to the existence, nature, and operation of grace. For instance, St. Thomas utilizes the philosophical notion of instrumental causality when considering the causality of the sacraments.[84] Just as to fail to understand the nature

---

83. Nichols, *There Is No Rose*, pp. 145–46.
84. See St. Thomas, *ST* III, q. q. 65, a. 3, c.; q. 66, a. 1, c.; q. 72, a. 3, ad 3; q. 78, a. 4, c.; Suppl., q. 82, a. 3, c.

of the sacraments as *causes* of grace, that is, to fail to understand their real efficacy, would be to empty the sacraments of their meaning in the order of the Christian life, so too to fail to understand the nature of Mary's causality in the acquisition and distribution of graces is to fail to understand her in the order of the Mystical Body.[85] Of course, Christ is not limited to choosing his Mother as a means to distribute graces to His Church. However, De Koninck observes, "that God might have governed all without subordinate universal causes, does not imply that we can behave as if He actually does."[86] Instilling *within* the universe of grace an ordered series of causes, as it were, grants more dignity and unity to creation as redeemed by the grace of Christ.

Conclusion

In so many ways, therefore, the handmaiden of theology assists us in contemplating the mystery of the person of Mary, the Mother of God and handmaiden of the Lord. Indeed, a brief review of the "philosophical prerequisites" listed above will show that not a single area of philosophy is omitted. Our Lady truly is, in the words of *Fides et Ratio*, the table at which faith sits in thought. As we have seen through the two analogies proposed by John Paul II, Mary's role in salvation history is as philosophy's role in the theological work of proclaiming the Gospel; both thereby achieve freedom in the fullest sense. Mary's life offers a "true parable" of the harmony between faith and reason to the believing philosopher. The next essay aims to illustrate more fully a particular instance of philosophy at the service of theology, by considering Mary as Queen of Heaven and Earth, that as, Mary as Queen of the Universe.

---

85. See Romanus Cessario, O.P., "*Ego Sapientia*: The Mariology of Laval Thomism," p. 235.

86. De Koninck, "The Immaculate Conception and the Divine Motherhood, Assumption, and Corredemption," p. 389.

* * *

MARY, QUEEN OF THE UNIVERSE

in memory of Genevieve Turner
requiescat in pace

The queen stood on thy right hand, in gilded clothing;
surrounded with variety.
— PSALM 44:10

Who is she that cometh forth as the morning rising, fair as the
moon, bright as the sun, terrible as an army set in array?
— SONG OF SONGS 6:9[10]

And a great sign appeared in heaven: A woman clothed with
the sun, and the moon under her feet, and on her head a
crown of twelve stars.
— APOCALYPSE 12:1

Behold, I offer you the first place as the Queen of the universe.
— ST. GERMANUS[1]

INTRODUCTION

St. Thomas interprets Psalm 44:10 to describe qualities of the bride
of Christ, the Church. However, he also notes that the verse and the
qualities of the Church

can be explained as referring to the Blessed Virgin, who is Queen and Mother of the King, who stands above all the choirs of angels, arrayed in gold, that is the gilded array of divinity, not because she is God, but because she is the Mother of God.[2]

As we have seen previously, this connection between Mary and the Church is the second component of the first principle of Mariology.[3] Likewise, both Song of Songs 6:9 and Apocalypse 12:1 can be interpreted as referring to both Mary and the Church.[4] In this essay, I will focus on the title of Our Lady noted by the Angelic Doctor, that Mary is Queen. What is more, she is Queen of the Universe, or as this title is more commonly known and meditated upon during the fifth glorious mystery of the Rosary, the final mystery, she is Queen of Heaven and Earth.

To approach this subject and gain some understanding of it, I propose the following route. We must begin with a basis in philosophical reflection in order to strengthen our theological contemplation. Therefore, first, we will consider what a universe or the universe is, from both a philosophical and a theological point of view. We will then ask about Mary's status as queen. Is Mary queen of the universe? Why is this the case? What can we say about the nature and role of her queenship? What effect does this have upon our devotion to her? The Blessed Virgin Mary is Queen of the Universe because she is the unique created person who holds "the first place" in the universe in its truest and fullest

1. Cited in George F. Kirwin, OMI, "Queenship of Mary: Queen-Mother," *Marian Library Studies*, Vol. 28, No. 1 (2007), p. 73 (at *PG* 98:303). Hereafter, "Queenship of Mary."

2. St. Thomas, *In psalmos Davidis expositio*, Psalm 44, n. 7. See also *Super III Sent.*, d. 22, q. 3, a. 3, qc. 3, ad 3: "Although the Blessed Virgin is exalted above the angels, she is nonetheless not exalted to the level of equality with God or personal union. Therefore, she is not said 'to be seated at the right hand' [*sedere ad dexteram*] but 'to stand at the right hand' [*astare dextris*] insofar as the honor of the Son in some measure participatively but not plenarily overflows to her, in as much as she is the Mother of God but not God."

3. See above, "Translator's Introduction," p. xxxiv.

4. Regarding the first, see Paul J. Griffiths, *Song of Songs*, Brazos Theological Commentary on the Bible (Grand Rapids, MI: Brazos Press, 2011), p. 141. Regarding the second, see the work of Edward Sri, cited below.

sense; she, the great sign to appear in her glory at the end of the age, standing at Christ's right hand as the Mother of God, leads the whole heavenly host, that is, all the angels and saints, herself clothed in the sun-like gold of divine beatitude, the saints surrounding her in all their variety. To advance this thesis, we consider (1) the universe from a philosophical point of view; (2) the universe of the Incarnation and how Mary is a part of that order; (3) the fact that Mary is Queen; (4) why Mary is Queen; and (5) how these truths impact our relationship with the Queen of the Universe.

THE UNIVERSE FROM THE PHILOSOPHICAL POINT OF VIEW

"Heaven and earth" and "the universe" can name the same reality under different notions.[5] "Heaven and earth" divide the created order into a vertical hierarchy; "heaven" could name the stars or the celestial, angelic realm, while "earth" or "the world" names the lowest regions of creation that we inhabit, or this era or age.[6] "Universe" attempts to signify the entirety of the created order, all of being that proceeds *ad extra* from God by his ordered power, that is, his omnipotence in creating joined to his providential wisdom in ordering that creation.[7] While "the universe" is usually taken to mean the physical order of creation, as we shall see, it is important to keep in mind the entire breadth of what the created order includes, even if its highest reaches are only visible to theological eyes. So, in what follows, the name "universe" signifies the entirety of the created order, or all creatures in their unified, ordered totality. "Cosmos" or "physical universe" will be used to indicate the material order of reality, that is, our world.

---

5. In what follows, while I follow the teaching of St. Thomas on the nature of "the universe," I only have the space to cite sparingly from his texts. An academic essay in preparation is devoted to the task of a more rigorous Thomistic exposition of this philosophical topic.

6. See St. Thomas, *Commentary on the Gospel of St. John*, Ch. 1, l. 5, nn. 128, 133.

7. This is also called the "ordinary" power of God, that is, his power considered together with his wisdom. See St. Thomas, *De Potentia*, q. 1, a. 5, ad 5: "The absolute and the regulated are not attributed to the divine power except based upon our consideration. To the power of God considered in itself, which is called *absolute*, something is attributed which is not attributed to it insofar as when it is compared to his wisdom, which is called *ordered*."

It is clear that we cannot understand Mary as Queen of the Universe if we restrict ourselves to the physical universe insofar as it is captured by the natural sciences. The mathematical models of the expanding "Big Bang" cosmos can only indicate the good of all things by indirectly supporting arguments about the fine-tuning of certain physical constants or fundamental interactions for biological life in general. These grounds are as insufficient as they are broad, and lack all notions of nobility that are potentially parts of a salvific order. Clearly, a grasp of the universe is needed that can understand the order and goodness of all things in such a way as to assist the Catholic theological understanding of redeeming a fallen creation. We require, therefore, a philosophical understanding of the universe as a basis for our inquiries. Such an ambit alone can escape the loss of cosmic beauty that a scientist view of things foists upon us. Theology needs philosophy to rejuvenate the now archaic-sounding talk of "heaven and earth," which conjures up the old Aristotelian specter of a geocentric universe filled with concentric, ethereal spheres.

What is this philosophical viewpoint? The essence of the universe is the unity of order of all created beings: "The form of the universe consists in the distinction and order of its parts,"[8] where this order is the condition of its unity. That is, the *to be* or the *quiddity* of "universe" is to be the very order between things which makes of them all a single reality; *unus–verto*, it is the form that turns all things "into one." The universe is not a monadic singularity of things without distinction, nor a collection of all things in a great heap without order, nor the mere "sum total" of all things, for there is more to the universe than its being everything that is the case. When St. Thomas speaks of this "unity of order" in other places he is speaking about how people are united in a single city, or how many men are ordered in a single army.[9] We must ask, therefore: why it is that the universe is this unity of many-in-one order?

8.   St. Thomas Aquinas, *SCG* II, c. 39 "Forma autem universi consistit in distinctio-
      ne et ordine partium eius."
9.   See St. Thomas, *De Potentia*, q. 3, a. 16, ad 2: "The creature is likened to God in
      unity insofar as each is one in itself, and insofar as all are one by a unity of order."
      Also, *ST* III, q. 4, a. 1, ad 4: "The perfection of the universe is not a perfection
      of a single person or supposit, but of something that is one by position or order."
      See also A. Krempel, *La doctrine de la relation chez saint Thomas: exposé historique
      et systématique* (Paris: J. Vrin, 1952), pp. 610–12.

St. Thomas treats of this when he discusses the final cause of the universe, that is, God's purpose in creation. Because God is perfect, he does not need the universe to make up for some lack in himself; furthermore, no created being can be as perfect as he, for only God can be his own subsisting, existent perfection, which is to say that created goodness cannot but derive from and imitate him. Any created being must therefore be referred to God as its good; the end of creation is, therefore, to communicate and manifest God's goodness to creatures by their very participation in it. Furthermore, since every agent makes something like itself, creatures are bound to imitate God, their agent cause. For instance, it is for this reason, among others, that Aquinas argues that the universe would not be complete or perfect—it would remain "unfinished"—were intellectual creatures not a part of the universe.[10]

Generally, then, any creature imitates God by being, in its own mode, a limited participation in the divine perfection. Created essences are more or less like unto God. However, since God's perfection is infinite, he is imitable in an infinite variety of ways. There must be, furthermore, a minimal number of kinds of things that a universe possesses, for merely one kind would not suffice to achieve the end of fully manifesting God's goodness by way of imitating his essence. Yet there is also no maximal number of kinds that a universe could possibly have; that is, God being infinitely imitable could have made a different and better universe with even more species, even if the universe that God has from eternity freely chosen to create must of necessity have a finite number of species of created beings.[11] Of course, philosophy knows all this about the universe "after the fact," that is, after it has traversed the ordered universe of kinds in thought to proof of God's existence and nature; only then does it turn around and look upon creation—insofar as this is possible—from a "top-down" perspective as sketched just now.[12]

---

10. See St. Thomas, *SCG* II, c. 48.
11. Concerning whether or not God could have made a better universe, see St. Thomas, *In I Sent.*, d. 44, q. 1, a. 2; and *ST* I, q. 25 a. 6 ad 3; q. 56, a. 2, ad 4.
12. See, for example, St. Thomas's consideration in *SCG* III, c. 97.

It follows from all this that, in order for the object of God's creative act to sufficiently correspond to the final cause of creation (to manifest and communicate God's goodness), what is created must be many in kind, and yet all ordered to God as to the ultimate good. What is created, in this sense, cannot but be a universe, a multiplicity of beings diverse in kind that are ordered to each other by their mutually comparable, gradated imitation of the divine goodness. This formal unity amongst things by which they, as many-yet-one, imitate the divine essence is what Beatrice points out to the sojourning Dante:

> So she made matters plain: "All things possess
> order amongst themselves: this order is
> the form that makes the world resemble God."[13]

Now, this unification of kinds by interrelating them insofar as they imitate God is a mode of formal unity, for it is the unity of order among species that approach the divine essence by a greater or lesser similitude, that is, a likeness in kind or form. This unity is of the sort that numbers have in comparison to each other, for they are all members of a single type of enumerated order. Thus, the unity of order which characterizes the essence of the universe is the purest sort of unity of order, a form of forms, as opposed to the unity of order that is characterized by material composition (e.g., the parts of a house).[14] The universe cannot concretely exist without its individuating or material causes, but what *typifies* the universe is such a form, which also reveals its characteristic of being the realization of a plan or idea of God's mind.

Now, the "parts" of the universe are, first and foremost, kinds or species, and only secondly are they individuals. This is because a multitude of individuals are all of the same kind, whereas a variety of species is what is commensurate to the purpose of God's act of creating (to manifest his goodness by way of participated imitation of his essence). Individuals are, in this perspective, more of the same, whereas a universe requires ontological diversity. St. Thomas argues, incidentally, that

---

13. Dante Alighieri, *The Divine Comedy: Paradise*, Canto 1, 103–105.
14. See Krempel, *La doctrine de la relation chez saint Thomas*, p. 611.

the multitude of kinds is incredibly great, and the closer the creature is to God, the more numerous do species become. The multifariousness of the kinds of higher angels increases in its multitude the closer they approach the divine essence in ontological imitation—increasing, as it were, according to an ever-denser logarithmic spiral of being.[15] This means that we are on the ontological "tail end" of that spiral, for the dust of which we are made is the most distant created being from the divine essence.

There are, however, other modes of unity that the universe possesses besides its formal unity. The warp and woof of the universe is especially found in the interaction of agent causes, whether free or natural, according to their various interrelated natural ends, symphonically orchestrated towards an overarching final end of the universe. This is important, for it corresponds to the notion that God's *ratio* or plan for the universe as a whole is not a static structure or form (like the series of numbers) but is a *logos* according to which the universe *achieves* some final end through the operation of all of its members, as an army achieves victory or as a city rests in the attainment of peace. What is this final end of the universe itself?[16]

St. Thomas, following Aristotle, says that the good or end of the universe is twofold, and in both cases it is a common good.[17] That is, there exists an intrinsic and an extrinsic common good of the universe. Aristotle compares this to the common good of an army; St. Thomas expands on this image as follows:

> Now a twofold order is found in things. One kind is that of parts of a totality, that is, a group, among themselves, as the parts of a house are mutually ordered to each other. The second order is that of things to an end. This order is of greater importance than

---

15. See De Koninck's "Thomism and Scientific Indeterminism," *Proceedings of the American Catholic Philosophical Association*, Vol. 12 (1936), pp. 59-64; "The Problem of Indeterminism," in *Writings*, vol. 1, pp. 377, 380–82, 390–96; and "Reflections on the Problem of Indeterminism," ibid., pp. 404–411; also, *Ego Sapientia*, pp. 23-26.

16. Note that this is a different question than asking about the final cause of God's act of creation.

the first. For, as the Philosopher says in the *Metaphysics*, the order
of the parts of an army among themselves exists because of the
order of the whole army to the commander.[18]

We have again, then, a distinction in types of order. The first is
merely the order of parts in a whole; it has more the character of a material ordering of parts. The army possesses this insofar as its various units
are deployed in places and times by the various commands of the army's
leaders, ultimately, by the general. The second type of order is the order
of things to a goal, that is, their order to a final cause. The final cause
of the army is victory, of course, and this second type of order is what
explains the first type of order. That is, the general deploys the army's
battalions in a certain order so that victory can be realized; the demands
of victory shape the army's arrangement. Thus St. Thomas says, "The
order of an army exists for the purpose of achieving the good of its commander, namely, his will to attain victory."[19] In this way, the army possesses two common goods. The first is its intrinsic good of order, which
is for the sake of the extrinsic common good, namely the general's will
(which is victory). In the case of the universe, by analogy, the intrinsic
common good is the ordering of things by which they exist and operate,
all parts cooperating towards the common work of existence in imitation
of God.[20] The extrinsic common good is God, who, unlike the general,
is identical to the good that He wills for the universe, namely, himself.

This twofold common good permits us to understand in what ways
in which the universe is perfect; St. Thomas himself distinguishes three
senses according to which we can speak of the perfection of the universe.[21]
We can consider these three by analogy to the three sorts of perfection

17. That is, a numerically single good which is shared in by many without diminish-
ing, and which good thereby serves to unify them.
18. St. Thomas, *In Ethic.*, lib. 1, lect. 1, n. 1. See also *In Meta.*, lib. 12, lect. 12, nn.
2629–2631.
19. Ibid.
20. For instance, see *ST* I, q. 49, a. 2, c.: "However, it is clear that the form which
God principally intends in created things is the good of order of the universe."
21. For instance, *ST* I, q. 6, a. 3, c. See also Oliva Blanchette, *The Perfection of the
Universe According to Aquinas: A Teleological Cosmology* (University Park, PA:
Pennsylvania State University, 1992), p. 70.

Aquinas speaks of elsewhere in regard to a single substance. The first perfection of a thing is its substantial existence, or merely existing as that kind of thing. The second perfection of a thing is insofar as it achieves the operations proper to its kind. So, for instance, a human being as existing is perfect in the first (minimal) sense; a virtuous, adult human being living a good life is perfect in the second (more maximal, operational) sense. However, the third sense of perfection is insofar as a thing attains and rests in its final end. For a human being this is nothing short of the beatific vision, which can be desired naturally through an elicited desire.[22]

Analogously, therefore, the first perfection of the universe consists in its being established in being according to its kind; that is, having existence according to the multitude of kinds of beings requisite for the what-it-was-to-be of "universe." Its second perfection, which it possesses "according to the present state of mutability"[23] is the perfection it has in the operation and activity of those various kinds. Its final perfection is "according to the state of the future restoration,"[24] that is, the final rest of creation in God (see Hebrews 4:9–11).

This eschatological perfection, inscrutable to the philosopher apart from guesses in various Platonic myths, will be attained when the saints and angels enjoy forever the beatific vision and life in God himself. Those not called to the wedding feast of the Lamb (Apocalypse 19:7) are still part of the universe, but exist outside it, as it were, and joined to its order only by their sentence of exile from the celestial city, into that lost and doomed land: "Bind his hands and feet, and cast him into the exterior darkness: there shall be weeping and gnashing of teeth" (Matthew 22:13). The universe in God's luminous presence will then be the City of God, the heavenly Jerusalem, truest of cities with its own intrinsic good of order, whose members are united by the victory and peace which is God himself. In this place and time alone will the intrinsic and extrinsic common goods of the created universe be the most united. At present, they are not fully one, and so "we know that every

---

22. Lawrence Feingold, *The Natural Desire to See God According to St. Thomas and His Interpreters*, 2nd ed. (Ave Maria, FL: Sapientia Press, 2010).

23. St. Thomas, *Super Sent.*, lib. 4, d. 48, q. 2, a. 5, ad 3.

24. Ibid.

creature groaneth and travaileth in pain, even till now" (Romans 8:22). Yet we are now ahead of ourselves; we must continue according to the strictly philosophical point of view.

The universe is, therefore, the unity of order through all the many kinds of created beings, where this unity obtains amongst them not only formally (in virtue of how their essences are comparatively more or less akin to the divine essence), but also between them in the lines of agent and final causality. However, the universe possesses a still greater mode of unity that, as it were, is born from within this causal texture. In order that the universe, in some part of it, may imitate the intellectual power and activity of God, and thus be complete or perfect in its kind, some intellectual creatures must exist. Furthermore, the universe of kinds imitating God requires not just the perfection of things according to their kind, but the further perfection that some things are able to share the very perfections of other things by knowing them. Yet further, Aquinas also argues:

> Nothing else moves God towards producing creatures except His own goodness, which He willed to communicate with other things after the manner of likeness to Himself, as is clear from what was said. However, the likeness of one thing is found in another in a twofold way. In one way, as to the existence of a nature, just as the likeness of the heat of fire is in something heated by fire. In another way, according to knowledge, just as the likeness of fire is in the sense of sight or touch. To this end, therefore, that the similitude of God might exist completely in things by these possible ways, it was necessary that the divine goodness be communicated to things not only through likeness in being, but also in knowing. However, only an intellect is able to know the divine goodness. Therefore it was necessary that intellectual creatures exist.[25]

This cognitive order is, of course, the prerequisite for the moral order, insofar as intellectual knowledge is the necessary condition for the free

---

25. St. Thomas, *SCG* II, c. 46, n. 6 (translation my own).

choice of one person to love and enter into communion with another. For one cannot love what one does not, in some way, know.

Charles De Koninck discusses the difference between these two modes of order between things in the following passage:

> We said that the perfection of the universe consists in the coordination of parts. But it is important to distinguish two species of coordination: the objective coordination which is essentially perfection, and subjective coordination which is essentially imperfect. The former is a unity founded on the distinction of things, the latter is founded on their confusion. Subjective coordination keeps things linked to one another in a more or less common subject by imposing on them their limitation. Thus natural things have a common matrix, the matter which makes them subjectively dependent on one another, and which is an obstacle to knowledge, that is, to objective presence. In this coordination things are prisoners of their subjectivity: *intus existens prohibet extraneum*. Knowers are perfect in the measure that their form emerges from matter. To know is to be the other as other. In the measure that natural things are subjectively coordinated, they are hidden from one another as objects: they communicate in the obscurity of matter, and not in form .... Subjective coordination is only truly vanquished by intelligence which alone can attain true objectivity.[26]

De Koninck begins by noting that the universe's essence, its first perfection, is "the coordination of parts," that is, a unity of order. He then distinguishes, within the material cosmos, between two modes of the unity of order: subjective and objective coordination. Things are subjectively coordinated insofar as different kinds of things exist in different subjects; like so many material atoms, such things exist and move and have a kind of being, and even can physically interact with

---

26. Charles De Koninck, *The Cosmos*, in *The Writings of Charles De Koninck: Volume One*, ed. and trans. R. McInerny (Notre Dame, IN: University of Notre Dame Press, 2008), pp. 318–19.

each other, but have no knowledge of this. A kind of being which is a knower, however, emerges from this material subjectivity. This perfection is the perfection of knowledge, which includes sense knowledge, but its highest instance is intellectual knowledge. According to knowledge, one thing can "be the other as other"—the known is an object of knowledge to the knower, and they are thus coordinated as objects. This is especially true when the two are both knowers. Therefore, apart from the "subjective" coordination of one being to another, each existing through its own specific form or kind, there exists within this subjective order an "objective" coordination among beings, insofar as the universe interpenetrates itself, as it were, in virtue of the activities of knowledge and love rooted in certain of its members.

Immanuel Kant bifurcated the universe into the kingdom of nature and the kingdom of ends, into a material and a moral universe.[27] Insofar as laws of necessity ruled the former while the law of freedom governed the latter, these universes were hopelessly disjoint from each other. This was a dualism of transcendental proportions in Kant's system, a dualism which remains necessarily unresolved. By contrast, the human person is, in the universe of St. Thomas, on the horizon between matter and spirit, a metaphysical amphibian that unites the two:

> The human soul...exists on the border of corporeal and incorporeal substances—on the horizon, as it were, of eternity and time. Receding from the depths, it draws near to the heights.[28]

This is not the place to discuss the resolution of the mind-body problem that faced Descartes and, subsequently, Kant. It is the great claim of the Aristotelian hylomorphism that Aquinas employs, however, that the human person is no longer split in two, one side subjected to the blind necessity of mechanical laws of material nature, while the other side is free in view of a moral law man writes out of his pure

---

27. Thus, Kant's own tombstone is engraved with this passage from one of his works: "*Two things* fill the mind with ever new and increasing admiration and awe, the more often and steadily we reflect upon them: the starry heavens above me and the moral law within me." My emphasis.

28. St. Thomas, *SCG* II, c. 80, n. 13.

autonomy. Rather, there is a gradated order and hierarchy within the cosmos as it approaches the intellectual and volitional being of man, the *raison d'être* of the material universe.

Furthermore, if we accept Aquinas' view that—regardless of how things stand with the burgeoning tree of life in the material order—the angels constitute by sheer multitude of kinds the vast majority of creation,[29] then the universe, on the whole, is in truth a communion of persons. That is, the universe's deepest unifying feature is its intersubjectivity, or rather, its being the complete or perfect objective coordination of its spiritual inhabitants. That is, the universe is more perfect as a unity of order in its objective coordination; the moral universe is the better face of the universe, and indeed the material and subjectively coordinated elements exist for the sake of the objectively coordinated ones. However, such coordination or mutual relationship occurs most of all between persons (for any sort of cognition results in objective coordination).

We should note two nuances about the essence of the universe that we have defined in the above. The first is that the universe is not merely a static, structural schematic, that is, its essence is not merely a blueprint for the hierarchy of being. The second is that the universe does not merely have existence but goodness; it is good, particularly insofar as the objective coordination amongst persons flowers in their moral goodness.

That is, first, the natural sciences, especially by way of natural history in biology and astronomy, have reformed our understanding of the physical cosmos. We now possess a basis for giving due emphasis to the history of the cosmos as one of its necessary features, not just something that accrues to it via the passage of time. Its motion and change is not merely repetitive, as it was in Aristotle's cosmos of concentric spheres, turning forever about the same axis, but it can be characterized organically, as the unfolding of certain stages according to various principles and causes, themselves not subject to evolutionary change, that contribute to

---

29. St. Thomas, *ST* I, q. 50, a. 3, c: "Hence it must be said that the angels, even inasmuch as they are immaterial substances, exist in exceeding great number, far beyond all material multitude." Also, consider his interpretation of the Parable of the Lost Sheep; see *Super Matt.*, ch. 18, lect. 2.

its development. "The universe" is something much more goal-directed in its very history, at least if we take the larger philosophical view of what the specific natural sciences are providing for our reflection.

Second, if the cosmos possesses a history essentially, and it is most of all characterized, in its highest perfection, as a community of persons, then it is not inconceivable to the philosopher that the universe's members have a destiny according to their good and evil, or state of justice and injustice. The material preparation of the cosmos for the sake of man's existence would then subserve man's preparation for his own end. Plato proposes likely accounts, his myths, about divine justice rendered to human souls in the afterlife; Aristotle notes that, despite our soul's natural order to being perfected by virtue, perfect virtue is rare; Aquinas proposes a probable philosophical argument for the existence of original sin.[30] The aboriginal fall and its eschatological consequences surmised by these arguments speak to the deeper insight that the final perfection of an ordered universe must include not just goodness in being but justice before the universe's creator, the goodness of souls, and purity of heart. This is the accounting of a universe, to the philosopher's mind, which can be taken up into a theological discussion of a creation in need of salvation.

THE INCARNATION AND THE UNIVERSE

The universe seen in the light of theological contemplation is itself a multifaceted jewel. However, given our goal of understanding Our Lady's queenship, we must approach the existence of the universe insofar as it is bound up with the Incarnation. To do so, I will take for granted Aquinas' well-known view that the Incarnation would not have occurred but for the Fall of mankind in the original sin of Adam and Eve.[31] While many universes are possible, considering the omnipotence of God in the

---

30. See Plato, *Phaedo*, 107c–115a; Aristotle, *Nicomachean Ethics*, VII.1; St. Thomas Aquinas, *SCG* IV, c. 52, n. 4: "Although defects of this kind may seem natural to man in an absolute consideration of human nature on its inferior side, nonetheless, taking into consideration divine providence and the dignity of human nature on its superior side, it can be proved with enough probability that defects of this kind are penalties. And one can gather thus that the human race was originally infected with sin."

31. See St. Thomas, *ST* III, q. 1, a. 3.

abstract, the universe in which we live was chosen from eternity in God's wisdom as an incarnational universe, that is, one in which God becomes Man. What does this mean as regards Our Lady?

Returning to the purpose of God's act of creation, the selection of an incarnational universe from among the infinitely many possible ways of imitating God's goodness exhibits clear and superior perfections over non-incarnational universes. In such inferior universes, for instance, there would never exist the perfection of a hypostatic union, where created human nature so closely imitates God's perfections through it being hypostatically united to the divine nature in a divine Person. These are not our universe, however. This idea forms the basis of Aquinas' argument for the fittingness of the Incarnation of Christ.

> To each thing, that is befitting which belongs to it by reason of its very nature; thus, to reason befits man, since this belongs to him because he is of a rational nature. But the very nature of God is goodness, as is clear from Dionysius (*Divine Names*, I). Hence, what belongs to the essence of goodness befits God. But it belongs to the essence of goodness to communicate itself to others, as is plain from Dionysius (*Divine Names*, IV). Hence it belongs to the essence of the highest good to communicate itself in the highest manner to the creature, and this is brought about chiefly by His so joining created nature to Himself that one Person is made up of these three—the Word, a soul and flesh, as Augustine says (*On the Trinity*, XIII). Hence it is manifest that it was fitting that God should become incarnate.[32]

Of course, this also requires that God's election of our incarnational universe was one which included his permissive will of the Fall of man and all this entails. Here we encounter, philosophically speaking, the problem of evil and the burden of theodicy, justifying the ways of God to man; theologically, this involves nothing less than the mystery of predestination, for the human nature—*this* particular nature—of Christ was predestined to be hypostatically united to the Second Person of

---

32. Ibid., a. 1, c.

the Trinity. As we saw above, from De Koninck's discussion of Mary's ontological lowliness as a prerequisite for being a mother of God, this predestined incarnation was also effected through human generation and birth, not via some miraculous occurrence outside the course of nature.[33] An angel could not generate God; a human woman was needed to be God's mother. "Christ and Mary have this privilege, that their stories begin before their birth and never end."[34] Thus, God's election of an incarnational universe in which God becomes man by way of human generation and birth is a universe in which a Mother of God must be eternally predestined to be joined to the God-Man.

De Koninck comments on the merciful brilliance of such an order as follows:

> Now that we know, most explicitly, with divine certitude, that in the very first instant of her conception, Mary was already freed from every subjection to the Serpent, we see that the Order of Redemption is, universally, both more divine and human, comprising at its very root a mere human person raised to the dignity of *a help like unto* the Savior. How radically different this order would have been if, for no matter how brief a time, Mary had been subject to the hereditary fault, as St. Thomas believed, and thus under the dominion of the one whose name is *Enemy*. Though by her Motherhood she would have attained, nevertheless, to the hypostatic union, her habitual grace would not have been of the hypostatic order; the Virgin would not have been conceived a second Eve as *a help like unto* the new Adam. No human person would have been that close to Him in sanctity, at the very foundation and principle of the Order of Redemption; nor would the Woman have been so one with her seed in complete enmity against the *father of all liars*. A more merciful design towards mankind is inconceivable.[35]

---

33. See above, p. 294.
34. Above, Chapter 2, p. 17.
35. Charles De Koninck, "The Immaculate Conception and the Divine Motherhood, Assumption and Coredemption," p. 399.

Mary is chosen to exist as that unique person predestined to be Christ's mother; this elevates her in the following two ways. She is, in the eternal now of God's election of that created order which imitates His goodness *ad extra*, unique among all the members of the moral universe, that is, the universe elected to be created and redeemed. This implies that the moral universe is elevated *through* her, in some way, and now exists through the modality of a universe according to the order of grace and not mere nature.[36] How are we to understand this?

Her uniqueness is due to her alone, of all created persons, belonging to the hypostatic order. She, a mere member of humanity, the lowliest intellectual kind within the order of creation, she is elevated by the grace of divine maternity to a real relationship to each Person of the Blessed Trinity: "What sets the measure of the graces allotted to a creature is the dignity or the function to which God has destined them."[37] In the universe of grace she is herself a new type, a new essential "part" in the universe to be redeemed—"For the Lord hath created a new thing upon the earth" (Jeremiah 31:22); "He hath regarded the humility of his handmaid…he that is mighty, hath done great things to me; and holy is his name" (Luke 1:48, 49).

> This God, whose mother she is, is God the Redeemer who as Redeemer is the final and consequently absolutely first cause of the entire universe, for Christ was never efficaciously willed as the end of all things except as the Redeemer. As Mother of the Redeemer, Mary is inseparably united to this final cause as co-principle. *The Lord possessed me in the beginning of his ways, before he made any thing from the beginning. I was set up from eternity, and of old before the earth was made.* [Proverbs 8:22–23] Mother of Emmanuel, that is to say, of "the Mighty with us," she is the first one predestined among all pure creatures. "She came from God in the beginning," says St. Albert, "because from all

---

36. Recall Hugon, Chapter 4, p. 69.
37. Hugon, Chapter 4.

eternity she was predestined to become the mother of the Son of God."[38]

What sort of "part of the universe" is she, in this role of Mother of God?—"Who is she that cometh forth as the morning rising?" (Song of Songs 6:9a) We will address these questions in the reverse order, since the answer to the latter makes clear the answer to the former. That is, first, we consider Mary's place in the universe; second, we consider why this universe of which she is the first created part must be a universe elevated by grace.

We can specify Mary's place in the universe by considering what it means that she is the predestined Mother of the God-Man and Redeemer. In answer to our first question, we should consider the arguments of De Koninck's *Ego Sapientia*. The overarching theme of De Koninck's essay is to show that Mary is wisdom, that is, she is a principle of order in creation and thus can herself be identified with that quality of knowledge whose office it is to know order—*sapientis est ordinare*. That Mary is joined with Christ in his predestination is foundational to this line of thinking. Mary is conceived from the beginning as a principle, a cause, but a principle that is the origin of the Principle originating her.

> The mother is inconceivable without the Son, nor is the Son and the Redeemer Son conceivable without the mother. She proceeds from Him who made her in order that He might proceed from her. It is as principle that she proceeds from the Principle: her procession from the Principle is ordained in the procession of this same Principle, and she envelops the Principle in her procession from Him, she is held by Him in His procession from her.[39]

---

38.   Charles De Koninck, *Ego Sapientia: The Wisdom That Is Mary*, in *The Writings of Charles De Koninck: Volume Two*, ed. and trans. R. McInerny (Notre Dame, IN: University of Notre Dame Press, 2009), p. 10. The reference to St. Albert is to pseudo-Albert's *Mariale*.

39.   De Koninck, *Ego Sapientia*, p. 10.

Thus, the relationship between Mary and her Son is "a kind of circular motion wherein the principle is the term, and the term, principle."[40] This "symbol of Wisdom" makes Mary contain in her own person the entire grand order of the *exitus* of things from God and their *redditus* to him, albeit "writ-small." What exactly follows from Mary's unique status as such a principle?

De Koninck begins to propose an answer to this in the following dense passage.

> Order is implied by wisdom. Wisdom is at once one and mani-
> fold, steadfast and mobile. Wisdom may be predicated of the
> principle of the sapiential order insofar as this principle is the
> root, and pre-contains the order, of which it is the principle.
> Together with her Son at the very origin of the universe, she is
> in a way the root of the universal order: *Ego sum radix*—I am the
> root. [Mass of Mary the Mediatrix] That which God principally
> desires in the universe is the good of order. This order is better
> in proportion as its principle, which is interior to the universe,
> is the more profoundly rooted in God. But Mary is the purely
> created principle of this order, the purely created principle which
> is nearest to God and the most perfect that can be conceived. As
> a principle of the sapiential order, she participates in the unity
> and the unicity of this principle, she is at once an *emanation* and
> an *indwelling*, her power extends to all things which take from
> her their constant renewal.... Daughter of the eternal Father,
> mother of the Son, spouse of the Holy Spirit, she is rooted in the
> order of the Trinity, and she links up the order of the universe in
> a radically new way to the order which is in God according to
> the processions.[41]

The proposed answer as to how Mary is a principle is that she somehow pre-contains the order of the universe. De Koninck expands on
this thought by claiming that Mary is this "principle...interior to the

---

40. Ibid.
41. Ibid., pp. 14–15.

universe" that is "profoundly rooted in God." This universal extension of Our Lady's causality seems impossible—surely this role belongs to God alone. To be sure, Mary's belonging to the hypostatic order gives makes her "rooted in the order of the Trinity," but how does this, in turn, so profoundly affect "the order of the universe" itself "in a radically new way"?

To answer this difficulty, we need clarity regarding exactly how Mary is both part and cause of the universe.

> Being the mother of God does not make Mary the principle of all things unless He makes Himself principle of all things according to His humanity—in and through it, as the God-Man. Yet He would not be the principle of all things as Man unless He were God. And again, because He is God, He could not become Man without thereby being as man the intrinsic final cause of creation. If God becomes Man, that Man, being God, cannot but be the apex, and the final cause of creation: the end, and hence the first cause of the whole created order. And since Mary could not become the Mother of God unless He became Man, to call her the Mother of God is already to imply that God has chosen to establish the order of all things to Himself as Man.[42]

Thus, Mary is a principle of all things insofar as God has elected to create an incarnational universe. Such a universe must have God for its final cause in a way that exceeds all other possible universes, precisely because in the case of the incarnational universe God himself is contained within the order to be made. Consequently, Mary is not the agent principle of all things, or the universe. Rather, as the mother predestined along with Christ, she is a key part of the planned final cause of the universe. She is a cause of all things insofar as God's election of our universe includes her role as Mother of God as an essential part of the very *logos* of the universe, its plan in the divine mind.

---

42. Katherine M. Gardner, "The Lord Possessed Me in the Beginning of His Ways: Mary and the Trinitarian Order of the Universe (A Commentary on Charles De Koninck's *Ego Sapientia: The Wisdom That Is Mary*)." Ave Maria University, Ph.D. Thesis, 2013, pp. 57–58. Hereafter, "A Commentary on *Ego Sapientia*."

The final cause is the first cause (the cause of causes) because it is that for the sake of which the agent acts, his reason for acting at all. It is particularly in the order of final causality that Mary's character as principle comes to light, together with the aspect of formal causality, to which it is closely allied. Mary could not have been a principle of creation in the order of efficiency .... Nevertheless, Mary is an inseparable principle and a cause in an efficient mode (that of generation) of the final cause of all things. Since the order of nature is ordained to the order of grace, Mary is found at the beginning of all things, in the mind of God, as principle in all that comes forth from Him.[43]

That is, Mary is, as final cause, prior to the being of the universe; however, within the order of the existing universe, the universe that has been created, she is still an efficient cause of the final cause of all things. This is true because of her unique relationship to the Trinity, her being "daughter of the eternal Father, mother of the Son, spouse of the Holy Spirit," as De Koninck avers, and through this elevation in grace she becomes the cause by which the source of all grace enters the world. She therefore "links up the order of the universe in a radically new way to the order which is in God according to the processions."[44] Gardner comments: "This is why Proverbs 8:22–23 is truly applied to Mary: 'The Lord possessed me in the beginning of his ways, before making anything that was made, from the beginning. I was established from all eternity, and from ancient times, before the earth was created.'"[45]

De Koninck further specifies, however, that Mary as a cause of the universe as its good is in a way exterior to or separated from the universe and in another way interior to the universe.

As the principle whence comes the good of the universe, as *Regina et Domina* of all things, she is a good separated from the universal order, a good which is properly universal, a good

43. Ibid., pp. 61, 62.
44. De Koninck, *Ego Sapientia*, pp. 14–15.
45. Gardner, "A Commentary on *Ego Sapientia*," p. 62.

which in its indivisible and superabundant unity is the good of all things. This good is better than the good which exists as a form in the order of the parts of the universe, it is anterior to it and is its principle, as the leader is the principle of the order in an army. Her good does not even imply a material dependency upon the things which are ordained or upon the form that is their order.[46]

We note with some anticipation that Mary's status as a "separated good" is a ground for her being the Queen of the Universe. I return to this below. For now, I paraphrase De Koninck's dense theological argumentation. Mary is in a way "separate" from the universe precisely insofar as she belongs to the hypostatic order, which sets her apart from every other creature. As the Mother of God she stands to all else that has been created as its superior, both in God's conceiving of her existence and in her actual existence. In her is found the *better good* of the intrinsic common good of the created order; she is not, in this respect, a merely subservient part or member of the universe, but it finds the reason for its order and goodness in *her*, just as, following Aristotle's analogizing an army to the universe, the army finds its good of order in the will of its commander.

Yet Mary is, of course, also a part within the universe.

When from another point of view, we consider the Blessed Virgin as interior to the universe, we can compare her to the intrinsic good of the universe, a good which consists in the form which is none other than the order of its parts. This form is comparable to the visage and the face. In this form consists the highest dignity of pure creation, that is to say, that which by God's will is the most desired for itself and most perfectly ordered to Him. Considered as a separate good of the universe, the Blessed Virgin is more worthy than the order of the universe whose transcendental principle she is.[47]

---

46. De Koninck, *Ego Sapientia*, p. 15.
47. Ibid., p. 16.

That is, Mary as a part of the universe is one of its principal parts; as the Mother of the God-Man, that final cause of the entire universe, she is therefore the most proximate member of the universe to the entire purpose of creation. As such, the reason for the being of the universe is to be found in her or by reference through her to Christ.[48] This is how she contains the "form" of the entire universe. While she is more worthy under the aspect of her being an exterior principle, as an interior principle, she is "the form and the purely created principal cause of the dignity which ordains them most proximately and most perfectly to the dignity of the whole. As the prior and principal part, she draws all the other parts after her toward the dignity of the whole."[49] Thus, while as a separate principle she is prior (in the order of final causality) to herself viewed purely as a part within or a principal member of the universe, "her position as a part is ordained to her position as a separate principle. She is born within to be a separated principle, she is born in the universe to become the mother of all things."[50] In her we find the circular motion that images the wisdom behind the entirety of creation, wherein all things proceed from God and return to him.

Fr. Hugon echoes the considerations that we have been developing, and this passage from Chapter 4 can serve as a helpful recapitulation. What De Koninck has described in the language of Mary being a "universal principle," Hugon describes in terms of Mary being "the eldest of creatures":

> In what sense, then, is Mary, after Jesus, the eldest of creatures? Although God has decreed the Incarnation as a means of saving man, He has willed that all things be directed towards Christ as towards their center and directed towards him as to their end and their ideal. In the order of intention and of final causality, Christ was the first in sight, then creation, glory, justification,

---

48. See Chapter 1, p. 9: "'For whatever expression the clay took upon it, the thought was of Christ who was to become man.' Have we not more than enough reason to say with Bossuet that God, in forming the body of Mary, had Jesus Christ in mind and was laboring for him?"

49. Ibid., pp. 16–17.

50. Ibid., p. 17.

and the permission of sin, even though it is the opposite in the order of execution and material causality. Thus, without the Fall of man, Jesus would not have been. But, in decreeing the Incarnation to right this Fall, God saw further; he regarded his Christ before all things and ordained that all things which would exist be for his sake and that he would be the end of all. In this way, Jesus was the first in the eternal thought, the first in the sight of the Almighty, the foremost of the divine works. It is in an analogous sense that Mary, inseparable from Christ in the plan of mercy, is the eldest of creation, the first in the thought and the works of God. The Eternal One decreed at one and the same time the existence of Mary and the fact of the Incarnation, and he contemplated in advance, in the same scene, the radiant figure of his Christ and the immaculate figure of Mary.[51]

Indeed, says De Koninck, "It would be impossible for a pure creature to be raised any higher. By the grace of her maternity, she exhausts, so to speak, the very possibility of a higher elevation."[52] Hugon says: "She is the unique, the favored, the one more beloved than all worlds, real or possible."[53] This helps us to make sense of the apparently excessive proclamations of some saints that the universe was created out of God's love for Our Lady, or that she was the model of all the predestined.[54] In her is found the entire order of creation:

Just as all the worlds of nature, both the corporeal and the angelic world, are united in man who thus becomes a sort of résumé of creation, *microcosmus naturae*, so also all the marvels of the supernatural are condensed in Mary, who is the masterpiece and the résumé of grace, *microcosmus Ecclesiae*.[55]

---

51. Chapter 4, p. 58.
52. De Koninck, *Ego Sapientia*, p. 11.
53. Chapter 6, p. 69.
54. See Chapter 7, p. 135: "God also had Mary in view when calling his elect; he would consult her, bring souls to her, wait for her to choose a name for them, the one she gave being that which suited each best."
55. Chapter 4, p. 58.

The Virgin Mary is, therefore, the first purely created part of the universe that God conceived to be redeemed. This is true simple speaking in the order of final causality, and it is qualifiedly true in the order of efficient causality, since she is the Mother of God. This makes it clear why the deeper perfection that is the objective coordination of the universe among intellectual beings, between persons, is a moral order of things to be elevated by *her* presence, through by the birth, death, and resurrection of her Son.

Commenting upon the *final* perfection of all things, which we mentioned above, Fr. George F. Kirwin observes that "Church and Kingdom are identified in eschatological fulfillment; likewise cosmos and Church."[56] That is, at the consummation of the age, the universe of beings will be principally the Church itself. The physical cosmos is for the sake of the realization of the higher ends of the happiness and beatitude of persons.[57] That is, the "moral" universe that subsists through the objective coordination among created persons is ultimately and eschatologically more important. Thus, to answer our first question, raised previously, regarding how we are to understand the elevation of the universe in Our Lady, we can see clearly that it is her role as Mother of God and Mother of the Church that makes this order of the universe possible. As both the extrinsic as well as the intrinsic first, created principle of the universe's very purpose, she contains as the good and noble form the very "that for the sake of which" God has called all things into being. Thus apply to her the words of Psalm 44:12, "The king shall greatly desire thy beauty."

One may say, in view of what has been discussed so far, that it is all well and good, but why does Mary's place in the universal order of redemption demand that she deserves the title of Queen? Why is this not a mere pious metaphor, a poetic, if definitive, image in our faith held

---

56. Kirwin, "Queenship of Mary," p. 230.

57. See St. Thomas, *ST* I, q. 23, a. 7, c.; also, see *De Potentia*, q. 3, a. 10, ad 3 and ad 4. While Aquinas employs the cosmological model specific to his time when discussing the ordination of the physical cosmos to the existence of persons, his general argument is transferrable. That is, our understanding of the cosmological mechanisms undergirding the "moral universe" has changed, but we can still say that the heavens move for the sake of the saints.

up for our assent and belief? Why does not "Mother of God" do just as well? What is there to the reality of queenship that ought to attract our theological contemplation and draw our hearts in love and reverence?

Is Mary Queen of the Universe?

Thus far, I have argued, first, that a Thomistic philosophical approach is capable to providing theology with a conception of the existing universe sufficiently ample and potent as to be of ancillary aid when attempting to understand Mary's status as Queen of Heaven and Earth. The universe is the unity of order that is the form and good of all things precisely as many-yet-one created order. Second, I argued that, when this conception of the universe is theologically contemplated in view of the Incarnation of Christ, and that consequently it can be asserted that Mary is the *first part* of the universe in the order of final causality and its overall *ratio* or plan in the divine mind, at least when created persons are concerned. I must now establish the specific grounds that and why Mary's primacy means she is queen of all things, for such primacy of place is itself only a general conception that is compatible with the human conception of queens, but not a sufficient reason. We will consider in this section the *fact* of her queenship, and the specific reasons *why* she is queen in the next section.

While Mary's queenship has not received a dogmatic definition as has her Divine Maternity, Immaculate Conception, or Assumption, the magisterial teaching of Pope Pius XII in *Ad Caeli Reginam* nonetheless places the issue beyond doubt.[58] He teaches that:

> In this matter We do not wish to propose a new truth to be believed by Christians, since the title and the arguments on which Mary's queenly dignity is based have already been clearly set forth, and are to be found in ancient documents of the Church and in the books of the sacred liturgy.[59]

---

58. See Pope Pius XII, *Ad Caeli Reginam*, Encyclical of October 11, 1954. This encyclical also established the feast of Mary's queenship (in the old calendar, which was retained). The first epigraph (above) is the introit to the Mass of Our Lady as Queen.

59. Ibid., n. 6.

That is, the theological tradition of the Church is also clear regarding the fact of Mary's queenship. He refers to St. Ephrem, St. Gregory Nazianzen, Origen, St. Jerome, Epiphanius, St. Andrew of Crete, St. Germanus, St. John Damascene, St. Ildephonsus of Toledo, as well as other doctors and previous popes. The testimony, therefore, from tradition is also beyond question. Thus, Kirwin notes, Catholics are not free to dispute the truth that Mary is queen, "although many questions remain open for discussion."[60]

Given this testament of magisterial authority and theological tradition, one wonders what objections or calls for clarification could be raised against the foundation of the claim that Our Lady is Queen of Heaven and Earth. The central difficulty, however, is how this truth is revealed in the Sacred Scriptures and not just propounded by theological argumentation. Indeed, the scriptural basis for this teaching is, as some have noted, rather sparse.[61]

Furthermore, various other points of opposition exist. As noted above in the Translator's Preface, the *ressourcement* theology of the twentieth century sought a renewed understanding of the scriptural roots of Catholic doctrine. Thus, the "maximalizing" Mariologies with more currency among neo-scholastic writers were seen as too conceptually hasty and enthusiastic in the exploration and demarcation of Mary's various titles and privileges. Kirwin argues that such approaches to understanding the fact of and reasons for Mary's queenship were excessively conceptual, and biased on by an aprioristic notion of what queenship means.[62] These approaches are also excessively Christ-centric, and thus emphasize the first half of the primary Mariological principle (Mary as Mother of Christ) to the exclusion or underdevelopment of

---

60. Kirwin, "Queenship of Mary," p. 116.

61. Ibid., p. 115. See also Sri, *Queen Mother*, Kindle loc. 513: "The encyclical does not offer an argument from Scripture in a strict sense. Rather, Pius XII includes the biblical foundations within the argument from Tradition, showing how the Church Fathers and popular piety deduced Mary's queenship from certain biblical texts: 'This already leaves a glimpse that the biblical proof is not explicit, but that tradition and the piety of the faithful have deduced certain logical consequences from some biblical facts read and understood in a comprehensive manner and in their full sense.'"

62. See Kirwin, "Queenship of Mary," p. 216.

Mary as exemplar and Mother of the Church.[63] Edward Sri notes also that the very notion of queenship is more difficult to understand in a democratic age; the political category does not analogously transfer well to theological realities.[64] Thus, a deeper understanding of Mary's queenship rooted in proper Scriptural interpretation is necessary, a reading which will place Mary's queenship within its true context, salvation history, within the truest and most adequate theological conception of the universe as the order of creation to-be-redeemed in Christ.

These scriptural foundations for Mary's queenship has been well defended in the work of various theologians; we summarize here the findings of the work of Kirwin and Sri.[65] Their common contention is that Mary is revealed to us as queen when looking to the historical custom in the ancient Near East of the *Gebirah* or Queen-Mother, who, as mother of the new king, had a defined place and role in her son's kingdom. This approach clearly fits more appropriately with the twofold Mariological principle enunciated previously.

---

63. Ibid., p. 45: "In the past, the study of Mary's queenship was founded upon the fact and nature of Jesus' kingship. While it is true that Mary herself can only be understood in light of her Son, Jesus, nonetheless a proper understanding of her relationship to him must be sought within the total context of God's revealing word rather than as an abstract schema drawn up to parallel his person and mission. The analogies used to explicate the nature of her queenship have fallen short of the goal because they were the result of a reasoning process which was simply deductive."

64. See Sri, *Queen Mother*, loc. 182: "Finally, in the summary conclusions, we will offer some suggestions on how the biblical approach taken in this study can deepen our understanding of the Christological and ecclesial dimensions of Mary's queenship in ways that contribute to our understanding of the meaning of her royal office. In an era when most societies have moved away from the monarchical political structures of the past, referring to Mary as queen can appear anachronistic or triumphalistic to some, or as a symbol void of any real meaning to others. However, the biblical methodology this study employs can help underscore that her queenship must be understood in the context of Christ's kingdom—which is very different from the kingdoms of this world (cf. Jn. 18:36; Lk. 22:25–26)."

65. Sri himself, who wrote later, himself closely follows Kirwin's arguments when it comes to the Old Testament prefigurations of Mary's queenship. What Sri adds is the requisite New Testament interpretation which completes the "intra-biblical" typology and salvation-historical account required to say that Mary is queen as a truth revealed by the Scriptures. Consequently, the following summary presentation will follow Sri. On Sri's methodology, see *Queen Mother*, loc. 478, 642, 673, 708, and 776.

The mother of a ruling monarch held a powerful position in many ancient Near Eastern kingdoms. She often influenced political, military, economic, and cultic affairs in the royal court and played a key part in the process of dynastic succession. In fact, the mother of the king often was more important than the king's wife! Indeed, it was generally the king's mother who ruled as queen, not his wife.[66]

The reason the king's mother was superior even to the king's wife was that in many such kingdoms the king practiced polygamy. Thus, the concubine-mother of the future king often solidified her status insofar as she had a role in the new king's accession to power. The queen-mother was also a custom in Israel. Sri notes:

> Most of all, Bathsheba's seat at the king's right hand has the greatest significance. In the Bible, to sit at the right is to be given the place of ultimate honor. "She was seated at his right, the place offered to the king by God (Psalm 110:1), i.e., she took precedence above all others." Thus, the queen mother sitting at the king's right hand symbolizes her sharing in the king's royal authority and illustrates how she holds the most important position in the kingdom, second only to the king.[67]

The queen-mother also had various offices, e.g., as a royal authority with sway over the king, as advocate to other before the king, and as counselor to the king.[68] It is therefore to be noted that the historical context to the queen-mother, present even in non-Jewish customs, are so many places, people, and events that are used by God to *signify*

---

66. Ibid., loc. 829.
67. Ibid., loc. 928.
68. Ibid., loc. 962: "In sum, we have seen how the queen mother held an important office in the kingdom due to her unique relationship with the king and her role in dynastic succession. This position seems to have been second only to the king himself in the royal court. In her office, the queen mother served as an intercessor for the people and a counselor to her royal son. All this serves as background for understanding two key Old Testament texts that took on messianic significance, and that involve a royal mother figure and her son."

through things the reality of Mary as queen.[69] The human historical and political reality is then taken up typologically within the Old and New Testaments to tell us of Mary's status and role.

Sri focuses, in the Old Testament, upon Isaiah 7:14 ("Therefore the Lord himself shall give you a sign. Behold a virgin shall conceive, and bear a son, and his name shall be called Emmanuel") and Genesis 3:15 ("I will put enmities between thee and the woman, and thy seed and her seed: she shall crush thy head, and thou shalt lie in wait for her heel"). Sri notes that in the former, the passage highlights the Queen Mother instead of the king; she is more important to the sense of the prophecy given her role. He argues in regard to the latter that

> For our purposes, after having highlighted the many royal overtones in Genesis 1–3 and in 3:15 itself, and after having established the woman's association with her royal offspring's triumph, we conclude that Genesis 3:15 presents a mother figure placed within a dynastic context and associated with her kingly offspring in bringing about some type of royal victory over the enemy. Such a mother sounds somewhat like the queen mother in the Davidic kingdom. In fact, it is also significant that the woman takes center stage in relation to the royal offspring—the man is left out. We found a similar scenario in the queen-mother-and-son prophecy of Isaiah 7:14. With all this in mind, a number of scholars have suggested the possibility of seeing the woman in Genesis 3:15 as a prototypical queen-mother figure.[70]

Thus, hope for the royal Savior of Israel becomes bound up with the hope for his Mother also.

Sri finds this Old Testament presaging fulfilled within the New Testament on the basis of various passages. The genealogy of Matthew

---

69. See St. Thomas, *ST* I, q. 1, a. 10, c.: "The author of Holy Writ is God, in whose power it is to signify His meaning, not by words only (as man also can do), but also by things themselves. So, whereas in every other science things are signified by words, this science has the property, that the things signified by the words have themselves also a signification."

70. Sri, *Queen Mother*, loc. 1136.

places Mary within the Davidic lineage as another queen-mother.[71] The Annunciation scene of Luke 1:26–38 shows the angel Gabriel addressing Mary as the future mother of a king, a king not only of the line of David but of divine origin. Sri concludes:

> Luke's Annunciation scene clearly presents Jesus as the Davidic Messiah-King. This is seen especially in the allusions to two key Davidic texts from the Old Testament. Verse 31 seems to tie Jesus with the Immanuel prophecy of Isaiah 7:14, which became associated with hopes for the future Davidic King who would restore the kingdom. Luke 1:32–35 associates the child of Mary with the foundation of the Davidic covenant, when God promised that one of David's sons would receive a great name, sit on a throne in an everlasting kingdom, and be called God's son (2 Samuel 7:9–16).[72]

Finally, the Visitation scene in Luke 1:39–45 reveals to us, in Elizabeth's words, that Mary is the "mother of my Lord." That is, "this unique title for Mary seems to draw attention to her role not just as mother of Jesus in general, but as mother of Jesus specifically in His role as messianic Lord. In other words, Elizabeth greeting Mary as 'the mother of my Lord' refers to her as mother of the Messiah-King."[73] Taking these passages, then, as the Scriptural basis for the fact of Mary's queenship, we can say that she is queen insofar as this coheres, in biblical typology, with her being the mother of a king. Thus, we should turn to more closely examine this central reason why Mary is queen.

---

71. See Sri's Chapter 3, §§3.1.1–2.

72. Ibid., loc. 1449. He continues: "In conclusion, the presentation of Mary as the mother of the Messiah in this passage may offer some biblical support for the Church's doctrine regarding Mary's royal office. Understanding Mary in light of the Davidic kingdom tradition, which Luke clearly evokes throughout this scene, would suggest that as mother of the messianic King in the Davidic kingdom, she could be seen as a queen mother. Thus, while the angel's words speak of Jesus as the Messiah-King, they also provide a basis for Mary's royal maternity.... Similarly, Montague concludes, 'Though it is only implied in the text, any Jew hearing this would understand that Mary is here being given the vocation of queen-mother.'"

73. Ibid., loc. 1482.

WHY IS MARY QUEEN OF THE UNIVERSE?

"*Propter hanc totus mundus factus est.* Because of her, the whole world was made."—These words of St. Bernard (or pseudo-Bernard[74]) draw our attention to the profoundly cosmological dimensions of Our Lady's being, and thus at the same time and in the same way to her status and role as queen of the universe. That is, as we just argued, the fact that Mary is Queen derives from her being Mother of Christ, the King. Yet this fact is inextricably joined with her role as the Mother of God, for which reason, as argued in a prior section, she holds the first place in the universe redeemed by Christ. We can now say, based upon the Scriptural exegesis just summarized, that for Mary to be Mother of God means, at one and the same time, that she holds the first place among all creatures (she is the eldest of creation, the first part of the universe) and that she is Queen of the Universe. She was not chosen by us, but by God for us, and consented for us, at the Annunciation and at Calvary, to the redemption of the world.[75] That is, God chose her before the foundation of the world, knowing He could redeem a fallen world through her as mother of the Savior. "The king shall greatly desire thy beauty" (Psalm 44:12). Because of her, the whole world was made and remade.

To return to our philosophical analysis of the universe's form (which is a unity of order possessing its own common good that imitates God), we should now add that God conceived of this form of the universe such as to destine certain of its members to glory; the universe was made so as to become the Heavenly Kingdom, the City of God and the Church Triumphant. Such hierarchy of order necessarily has a first part; such an order as redeemed by a God-Man necessary has a Queen Mother. This is the conception of Mary that drew God's love towards the very idea of such a universe and moved him, as it were, to bring it into being. *Propter hanc totus mundus factus est.*

---

74. See Henri De Lubac, *The Splendor of the Church*, trans. M. Mason (San Francisco: Ignatius Press, 1999), p. 338, who notes it is Pseudo-Bernard, and comments: "If it is true that the Church, through the extension and the sufferings of temporal existence, reconstitutes bit by bit the first paradise, then our Lady is the first cell of the organism of that restored paradise, which is more glorious than the original one. If it is true that the world was made for the Church, then the world was no less made for our Lady."

75. See Kirwin, "Queenship of Mary," p. 205.

It is typically asserted that Our Lady's queenship must be understood according to the character of Christ's kingship. This assertion I do not intend to put into any doubt. That is, past treatments of Mary's queenship would compare her office and its roles to those belonging to Christ as King. However, the scriptural foundations in the work of Kirwin and Sri provide the commensurate, holistic ambit for our "deductive" reasoning about Mary, as well as the proper context for understanding the nature of her queenship properly, as something transcendent and even the very form of queenship or the prime analogate. That is, as Sri suggests, just as Christ's kingdom is not of this world, neither is Our Lady's. The very nature of her queenship is truer and more profound than political regimes led by kings or queens: "For lo, the kingdom of God is within you" (Luke 17:21c).

The reasoning supporting *why* Mary is queen can be summarized by employing a division developed by Suárez. Our Lady, he reasons, had three principal dignities, and the first two lead naturally to the third: "The first dignity of the Virgin was to be the Mother of God…and with this title there is joined another, namely to cooperate in the redemption…. From these there follows a third, namely that in a singular way she is the Lady of all things and the Queen of the angels."[76] The close connection between the first two dignities, her being the Mother of God and her being Co-Redemptrix, must be emphasized. Kirwin notes:

> We cannot speak of the divine maternity alone or in the abstract as being the foundation for Mary's proper queenship. It is her divine maternity as it was concretely realized in the order of events as they evolved under divine Providence. It is her consent to the incarnation and redemption (not two separate acts but one consent continued from Nazareth to Calvary) which fundamentally establishes her as queen. Any title she has to queenly power originates in this consent and the reality it brought into being, the grace-filled hypostatic order of redemption.[77]

76. Cited in Kirwin, "Queenship of Mary," p. 81.
77. Ibid., p. 118.

Still, the fundamental reason why Mary is Queen of the Universe flows from her fundamental nature in the order of redemption: she is the Mother of God: "It seems to me that we can best express the nuance proper to this approach in contrast with others by saying: 'Queen because Mother' or not merely 'Mother of the king,' but 'Queen-Mother.'"[78] As Hugon himself argues, "The divine maternity confers an inalienable right to the eternal inheritance, and even to the dominion over all things."[79] This fundamental reason is merely the remote grounds for her queenship; the proximate grounds are in her mediation of graces, a role tied closely to her compassion with Christ.[80] Thus, Hugon argues:

> this maternity conferred certain rights to the eternal heritage. If the adopted child is called to enjoy the goods of strangers, cannot the natural mother lay claim to the prerogative of her son? Now, eternal beatitude is due to Christ as a natural good which accrues to him by right, by reason of the hypostatic union. It is also necessary that Mary, his necessary and principal heiress, possess that kingdom which she had so deservedly merited by her heroic correspondence with all grace. Pious authors go further, and pushing the argument into its utmost consequences, maintain that the Holy Virgin is, by her motherhood, queen of the whole universe. For, if she is a mother, she is naturally heiress of the entire patrimony of the Son: *si mater, et haeres*. The Son of Mary received dominion over all things, both by right of birth in virtue of the Hypostatic Union and also by right of conquest in virtue of his works and their merits. Mary will be by right queen with him. This is why we call our Sovereign by the antonomasia *Our Lady*.[81]

---

78. Ibid., pp. 253–54.
79. Chapter 4, p. 62.
80. See Kirwin, "Queenship of Mary," pp. 55–56: "Mary's motherhood is the ultimate reason why she is a queen, just as it is the ultimate foundation for all her prerogatives, but it is to her mediation that we must look for the proximate foundation of her queenship. It is in understanding her mediation that we shall understand her queenly powers."
81. Chapter 4, p. 62.

In light of this, we can more fully grasp the fittingness of Mary's being Queen of the Universe through her other roles in salvation history, which are also other of her privileges or titles. These are her roles as Co-Redemptrix, Mediatrix, and as first creature in glory, as the Woman Clothed with the Sun. Here we draw from indications by Kirwin, at the conclusion of his study:

> In tracing Mary's role in the history of salvation we have seen that God has chosen this Woman from among all others for a twofold task. As an individual she has actively united her will to that of God so that salvation might come into the world in the Person of her Son, the King of kings and the Lord of lords. At the same time she has acted as the representative, the Archetype of redeemed humanity in responding in its name to the presence of salvation, Emmanuel, in its midst. In her, the first and most excellent member of the Church, the whole Church is present and active.[82]

That is, her being Mother of Christ who suffered (so, as Co-Redemptrix) is joined to her being Mother of the Church (and so—as indicated in the previous essay—Mediatrix: "Mary [is], as the primal church, the total recipient, in a single all-encompassing act of acceptance, of all the spiritual good the Savior has to give to the world."[83]). In this, then, we can see the due harmony contained within the twofold primary Mariological principle. I add that her being the first and most excellent member of the Church—that is, the final configuration of the universe redeemed by Christ—provides us with an eschatological cause of her Queenship. In each of the following three arguments, we can see how fittingly the scriptural basis of Mary's queenship as signified by the role of the queen-mother or *gebirah* helps us to grasp her queenship.

First, Mary is Queen because she is Co-Redemptrix with Christ. As Hugon writes:

---

82. Kirwin, "Queenship of Mary," p. 284.

83. Nichols, *There Is No Rose*, p. 146.

This is a thought familiar to the holy Doctors, who contemplate upon Calvary's hill two altars. Upon the one lies the body of Jesus, suspended on the cross, offered by his passion. Upon the other the soul the Virgin is transfixed by her compassion. A sword of pain runs from Son to Mother to make of the two a single burning wound.[84]

Sri points out that she is the woman in anguish standing by Christ on the Cross, and thus the Woman spoken of in Apocalypse 12:1, who cries aloud in anguish, giving birth to the Savior, the man of sorrows.[85] She, the "Weeping Mother of God" is the one who suffers with Christ, and her tears are "the way to 'resolve the cosmic grief.'"[86] As Co-Redemptrix, then, Mary shares in what Christ earns by right of conquest due to His passion and death, that is, His kingdom. Furthermore, both Christ and Mary are those whose office it is, precisely as Redeemer and Co-Redemptrix, to care for the true common good of the universe, as son and mother. Yet this concern is a kingly and a queenly concern, and this exhibits their claim to kingship and queenship of all things.

Second, Mary is Queen because she is Mediatrix of all graces.[87] The universality of her intercession corresponds, just as her authority with Christ, to the ancient role that queen-mothers had as advocates before the king. Mary does this precisely insofar as she is Mother of the Church.[88] If she is such a Mediatrix, however, then she is truly a universal principle in the universe of grace; she holds the first place in this universe as a created person. In this, she again must be compared to Christ, who is the substantial cause of all the Church's grace, and to whom Mary is subordinate in this role.[89] It follows again that she is fittingly called a queen.

---

84. See Chapter 8, p. 144.

85. See Sri, *Queen Mother*, loc. 1655.

86. Nichols, *There Is No Rose*, p. 78.

87. See also Pope John Paul II, *Redemptoris Mater*, n. 41.

88. See Chapter 5, where he discusses Mary's motherhood of the faithful. See also the discussion of Semmelroth's insights about Mary and Church in the previous essay, p. 277.

89. See Chapter 5, p. 162.

Third, Mary is Queen because she is the Woman Clothed with the Sun. Says Hugon: "The Blessed Virgin is clothed with the sun, that is to say with the dignity of her Son. All the stars of created greatness crown her and her last adornment is made from the infinite."[90] This is less of a proof from a fact known prior in salvation history and theological reflection and more of a proof from an eschatological mystery that we know now only dimly. This image of the Woman from Apocalypse 12:1 unites in its literal sense the roles of Mary as Mother of Christ and of Mary as Mother of the Church:

> The woman of Chapter 12 is adorned with the symbols of royalty; at the very moment she gives birth to the Messiah she is depicted as a queen crowned with the twelve tribes of the ancient and the new Israel. The activity of the devil recalls the scene in Genesis 3:15. The woman will receive special protection from God typified by God's concern for His chosen people in Exodus 19:4 there is no doubt, [Garcia del Moral] says, that the Son of the woman is Jesus Christ. He thinks that two different opinions concerning the woman of the Apocalypse (one considering her as the personification of God's people, the other as the individual woman, namely, Mary) can be harmonized. Luke's infancy narrative and the fourth gospel seem to present Mary as adorned with a dignity representative of the whole people of God. At the same time, this people finds in Mary its most perfect expression.[91]

Our Lady of the Apocalypse is a commanding figure, a woman who stands at the head of the army of heaven (Song of Songs 6:9), who like the dawn heralds the rising of the sun, and we ought to heed her: "Whereunto you do well to attend, as to a light that shineth in a dark place, until the day dawn, and the day star arise in your hearts" (2 Peter 1:19). Mary in this mystical image is therefore the very form, the face or visage, of both the Savior and the saved, his Church. In her is contained the whole order of things. In this her very person is, as it were,

---

90. Chapter 4, p. 70.
91. Kirwin, "Queenship of Mary," p. 68.

the counselor to the king, his wise mother and principle of wisdom, for she shows forth the plan God has for his people. This counseling role through her exemplarity is likewise a role belonging to a queen-mother.

A further reason that gives us confidence in these arguments as to why Mary is queen is that they manifest in what way her being "Queen of the Universe" is a *final* title, something that she has achieved as part of the consummation of her role in salvation history, and one which will perdure for all eternity. We could also see this from the way in which Mary's place aids us in understanding the hierarchy of good (or, obversely, the problem of evil) in the created universe. God having chosen a universe that would be afflicted by evil draws an ever-greater good from such circumstances, namely the Mother of God. Her Queenship is harmoniously at one with her being endowed by God with such graces, for it signifies and fully realizes her place at the head of the hierarchical order of creation renewed by the grace of Christ, the King of the Universe.

MARY, QUEEN MOTHER

In the foregoing, we have considered, first, the character of the universe from a philosophical vantage-point, which is required to ground theology's considerations; second, the place of Mary in the order of the universe to-be-redeemed; third, the fact that Mary is queen of the universe; and, fourth, the reasons why Mary is queen of the universe. These preparations will make it easier to see a bit more completely the nature of Mary's queenly status and office by way of recapitulation.[92]

While her status as Queen is above all a numinous truth contained in revelation, we can, humbly and slowly, approach and understand Our Lady's sovereign throne through certain philosophical aids, elaborated previously, concerning the nature of the universe itself. Here is a happy and marvelous discovery: her place in the universe redeemed contains within itself the entire plan and notion of the redeemed universe. The ancient philosophers proclaimed that *man is a microcosmos*, a

---

92. See, ibid., p. 127: "What does the [*Ad Caeli Reginam*] teach regarding the nature of Mary's queenship? How are we to conceive the regal power of the Virgin? The first point to make clear is this: The encyclical does not explicitly treat the nature of her queenship. There are at most indications of a solution to this question."

universe "writ-little." Of all the modes of human knowledge, Catholic theology alone can see that Mary is the true *microcosmos*, for the entire meaning of the universe and its hope are written into her unique place in that very universe.

We can exhibit this more clearly by indicating the harmonious correspondence between the three perfections of the universe, discussed above (its perfections of being, operation, and final rest), and the modes in which Mary is Queen. Thus: Mary is Queen of the Universe owing to her excellence; Mary is Queen of Mercy, she who perfects the universe in its activity of yearning towards God; Mary is Queen of Peace, she who perfects the universe in its ultimate configuration within the divine peace, wherein creation achieves its final, enduring rest in the sight and life of God.

First, Mary is Queen by excellence. In this she contains within herself the first perfection of the universe by her humility, both in being (her ontological humility as a creature) and action (moral humility). While this seems counter-intuitive, it follows the inner logic of the nature of Christ's own kingship.[93] That is, Mary as the first disciple and principal member of Christ's kingdom embodies its true characteristic, humility. This is how she is queen by dignity, as Pope St. John Paul II writes.

> Connected with this exaltation of the noble "Daughter of Sion" through her Assumption into heaven is the mystery of her eternal glory. For the Mother of Christ is glorified as "Queen of the Universe." She who at the Annunciation called herself the "handmaid of the Lord" remained throughout her earthly life faithful to what this name expresses. In this she confirmed that she was a true "disciple" of Christ, who strongly emphasized that his mission was one of service: "the Son of Man came not to be served but to serve, and to give his life as a ransom for many" (Matthew 20:28). In this way Mary became the first of those who, "serving Christ also in others, with humility and patience lead their brothers and sisters to that King whom to serve is

---

93. See Sri, *Queen Mother*, loc. 338, 1887.

to reign," and she fully obtained that "state of royal freedom" proper to Christ's disciples: to serve means to reign![94]

Thus, the dominion of Christ and Our Lady, albeit won through their conquest of sin and death, is not to be confused with an earthly dominion over conquered lands.[95] Nonetheless, hers is true dominion.[96] In this place or role as Queen through the dignity of her humility, she is "hailed as a 'preeminent and altogether singular member of the Church' and as 'the Church's model and excellent exemplar in faith and charity.'"[97] Mary, in helping to establish her Son's reign, becomes at the same time the first member of the Church thus constituted, and its very archetype or exemplar form. Thus, her status as queen leads us, again, to the universe, that is, the Church,[98] as pre-contained within her. As Queen Mother she provides the universe with the deepest *logos* of its fundamental perfection, to be the created, Mystical Body of Christ.

Second, Mary is Queen of Mercy. In this she contains within herself the second perfection of the universe by her service—the mark of her queenship noted by Pope St. John Paul II above. This service is her universal intercession on behalf of the Church militant and suffering. Kirwin argues:

> In this present stage of her salvific role Mary has rightly been called "the Eschatological Icon of the Church." The sense of this expression is that the Church sees in Mary the perfect fulfillment of all that she (the Church) is called to be. As [one scholar] indicates, she is not *the* sign of sure hope—that sign is the Resurrected Christ—but *a* sign of sure hope. In a subordinate way she serves as a source of attraction and encouragement for

---

94. John Paul II, *Redemptoris Mater*, n. 41.

95. See Kirwin's critique of this "dominion model" approach in "Queenship of Mary," pp. 141ff.

96. Compare the discussion in ibid., pp. 142–51, as to how this understanding of Mary's dominion is superior to former proposals.

97. Ibid., 181, citing *Lumen Gentium*, n. 53.

98. One must recall here that the Church is that for the sake of which the physical universe was made; our perspective here is ultimately eschatological.

the rest of mankind still on its pilgrimage toward final union with Christ. In her by God's grace has been realized the most perfect possible union with the heavenly Spouse.[99]

As eschatological icon and exemplar of the Church in her intercessory role, we can see that Mary's queenship—prefigured by the Old Testament *gebirah's* or queen-mothers—contains and exceeds the merely "intercessory model" of queenship sometimes proposed, which is modeled more closely upon the political model of a queen who is wife of the king.[100] While this model does indeed show that "Mary's association with Christ the King must be such that it is directed towards the common good of the entire universe,"[101] it ought to be connected with the typological prefigurement of the *gebirah's* influence over her son's reign as his mother, not as his wife.[102] If we join this line of thinking with Hugon's arguments in Chapters 8–9 regarding Mary's intercession, and the even *physical* and not merely *moral* instrumental causality of her acquisition and distribution of graces, then we see that in Mary is not only contained the exemplar of the form of the universe redeemed, i.e., the Church, but also its nutritive root of God's grace, subordinated to the causality of Christ. Her queenly title as Queen of Mercy is her most proper title while the Church "groaneth and travaileth in pain" and stands in need of the grace of Christ.[103]

Third, Mary is Queen of Peace. In this she contains within herself the final perfection of the universe by her supereminence among the blessed in the communion of saints:

> Through her mediation, subordinate to that of the Redeemer, Mary contributes in a special way to the union of the pilgrim Church on earth with the eschatological and heavenly reality of the Communion of Saints, since she has already been "assumed into heaven."[104]

99. Kirwin, "Queenship of Mary," pp. 212–13.
100. See ibid., p. 156, and generally the approach discussed at pp. 153–63.
101. Ibid., p. 158.
102. See ibid., pp. 257ff.
103. See De Koninck, *Ego Sapientia*, p. 39.
104. John Paul II, *Redemptoris Mater*, n. 41.

320 ÉDOUARD HUGON

That is, Mary, the "Eschatological Icon of the Church" has, like Christ, gone ahead of the faithful of the Mystical Body and assists Christ in preparing a place for the predestined in the heavenly Jerusalem. Thus, in her is exemplified and through her is prepared the final rest of creation in God, how the universe achieves its final perfection or end, just as the army achieves victory or the city exults in the common good of peace, that is, the tranquility of the final order of things.[105]

Thus, Mary is not only the principal created part of the universe that has been redeemed—along with the uncreated Person of her Incarnate Son—she is also the principal created part and person of the universe glorified, that is, the Church ultimately triumphant.

> At the moment of final consummation the salvific function of Mary and the Church will come to an end. Yet Mary's love will continue to be absorbed in Christ and through Him in mankind. She shall occupy the principal place among creatures, in the heavenly kingdom because of her preeminence in God's plan of salvation. Yet she shall be joined in love by all those who have kept God's commandments and remained faithful to His Word. All separation between her and the Church which she personifies will come to an end.[106]

In this way, Mary as Queen of Mercy is indeed her most fitting queenly title in this age. But in the age to come, this title will only be held in the memory of the blessed, just as faith and hope, in that land, pass away. At the end of the age, Mary will be the preeminent created person in the heavenly Jerusalem, for the saints "shall be brought with gladness and rejoicing: they shall be brought into the temple of the king"[107] and His Queen. Mary, Queen of Peace, that is, Queen of the Eternal Peace of Heaven, is the primary *created* being in whom we now hope to find realized a twofold victory: first, the complete, manifest triumph of Christ and his Mother over the ancient Enemy, the Devil,

---

105. See Hugon's "The Role of Meekness in the Spiritual Life," above, p. 211.
106. Kirwin, "Queenship of Mary," p. 213.
107. Psalm 44:16.

and second, the complete, manifest renovation of the created order by God.[108]

Mary is therefore fittingly compared to an army arrayed for battle, and fittingly taken in the Apocalypse of St. John to signify the people of the City of God. In the eschaton alone is the final and full realization of all generations calling Mary blessed. This will include, in imitation of her Son, the reverence "of those that are in heaven…and under the earth" (Phillipians 2:10). In this final triumph alone will the complete order of the universe be realized, as it was conceived and created for the sake of Christ and his Mother. As Hugon writes: "Mary would be for us the mother of grace during our terrestrial pilgrimage, the mother of perseverance at the hour of death, and the mother of glory forever and ever."[109]

* * *

A summary recapitulation is now in order. God so loved the world that He sent into it His only begotten Son to redeem it from the evil permitted in that universe, conceived from all eternity in the divine mind. In His wisdom, this required that God's Son be born of a woman, a virgin named Mary. God thus so loved the world to-be-redeemed that He made Mary a part of it. And yet, more than that. He so conceived of a universe-to-be-redeemed that it had this woman as its eternal heart, for it was created in a way *for her*, as she was needed to bring Christ into the world, the true final cause of creation. An entire history of a nation was written for her, such that she was anticipated as "Daughter of Sion." The prophecies of the end of time include her, for she is the "Woman Clothed with the Sun." Even more, she was not only the principal created person and part of the universe, but she contained that universal order of redemption, the Church of Christ, within herself by being its archetype and exemplar. She is thus the final cause of all creation, next to her Son, as its very form. Predestined as the truest of queens, exceeding every lower or misshapen type of queenship, she claims her title through her divine maternity, her co-redemption

---

108. See De Koninck, *Ego Sapientia*, pp. 41, 44.
109. Chapter 14, p. 199.

of mankind, and her universal mediation, all bearing reference to her Divine Son, Redeemer and Mediator of mankind. As such, and for such reasons, she is the Queen of the Universe. Lastly, in her queenship itself is found imaged or exemplified the very perfections of the universe of which she is principal part, for in her humility she contains the true excellence of all things, by her intercession she sustains the mercy needed for the working of all things unto salvation, and in her sovereignty over the peace of heaven she soothes God's children with the final tranquility of order of the universe.

DEVOTION TO THE QUEEN OF HEAVEN

There is no created person nobler or more powerful or more consequential in God's providential ordering of creation than she, for within her is contained to a more expansive and intensive degree the entire *raison d'être* of the entire universe, and through her has been effected what God so designed, such that by a fitting right she has merited her appointed place as Queen of the Universe. In view of this fact, what ought we do? What do we owe the Queen of Heaven?

What indeed but that which is proper to a queen, and yet more? This goes by a traditional name: "hyperdulia." Her nobility as queen demands an exceedingly high love from us:

> Because she carries with her the notion of the properly universal common good, because she is for us the principle of every spiritual good, it is not enough to love the Blessed Virgin as one loves oneself, nor to love her as much as oneself. Just as it is necessary to love Christ more than oneself, so too it is necessary to love the Blessed Virgin more than oneself.[110]

That is, Mary is Queen of Mercy is our universal intercessor; Mary is Queen Mother and as such the final cause of the universe, created as its preeminent part, and as Mother of God exceeding it by her relation to the Trinity. She alone of all created persons deserves an honor second only to God. We must seek to belong to her kingdom, which is one

---

110. De Koninck, *Ego Sapientia*, p. 15.

and the same as the kingdom of Christ.[111] To seek first the kingdom of Jesus Christ is nothing other than to seek out Our Lady's kingdom. This kingdom is our inheritance, the kingdom not of this world, the kingdom now hidden in the charity within the hearts of the faithful, and to be manifest only at the end of time, when God will be all in all.

CONCLUSION

In his short Mariology, Aidan Nichols draws our attention to the icon "In You All Creation Rejoices," which depicts the entire redeemed cosmos of creatures rejoicing around the figures of Mary and Christ. In Mary all creation rejoices, for she is "more honorable than the cherubim, more glorious than the seraphim, who without spot didst bear the Eternal Word."[112] All creation rejoices in her as queen; for the Blessed Virgin Mary is Queen of the Universe because she is the unique created person who holds "the first place" in the universe in its truest and fullest sense, the created order of things redeemed by her Son.

Her queenly place in this order is spoken of everywhere, and yet under a certain veil, it would seem. An alternative translation of Song of Songs 6:9[10] says "Who is this that appears like the dawn, fair as the moon, bright as the sun, majestic as the stars in procession?" (NIV) or again "Who is this that comes forth like the dawn, beautiful as the white moon, pure as the blazing sun, fearsome as celestial visions?" (NABRE)[113] It is perhaps a providential coincidence that the philosopher Aristotle's central analogy of the universe as ordered to God was as an army ordered to its commander. The march of an army arrayed for battle, or the procession of the universe's celestial crown of stars are distant, human images of what God had prepared for all time to be realized in His Mother: "The queen stood on thy right hand, in gilded

---

111. For this, one cannot but help recommend the practice of true devotion to Our Lady, taught by St. Louis-Marie Grignion de Montfort in his treatise *True Devotion to Mary*.

112. Nichols, *There Is No Rose*, p. 172, quoting a Byzantine liturgical hymn.

113. A note to the latter translation adds: "Celestial visions: the meaning is uncertain. Military images may be implied here, i.e., the "heavenly hosts" who fight along with God on Israel's behalf (cf. Judges 5:20), or perhaps a reference to the awesome goddesses of the region who combined aspects of both fertility and war."

clothing; surrounded with variety" (Psalm 44:10). We rest our hope through the Queen Mother in Christ the King of the Universe, and so apply to Mary also, as of someone who is implied by association, the meaning of these words of St. Bernard. They describe the desire of the Bride, the Church, for Christ:

> What is written elsewhere, "The memorial of thine abundant kindness shall be showed" (Psalm 145:7), refers doubtless to those of whom the Psalmist had said just before: "One generation shall praise Thy works unto another and declare Thy power" (Psalm 145:4). Among us on the earth there is His memory; but in the Kingdom of heaven His very Presence. That Presence is the joy of those who have already attained to beatitude; the memory is the comfort of us who are still wayfarers, journeying towards the Fatherland.[114]

---

114. St. Bernard, *The Art of Loving God*, ch. 3, https://www.ccel.org/ccel/bernard/loving_god.txt (accessed September 1, 2019).

* * *

REFERENCES

SCRIPTURE

All Scripture quotations are take from the Douay-Rheims Bible, available online at www.drbo.org.

Most of the following texts, long out of print, rare, and in the public domain, were accessed through online databases.

FATHERS, DOCTORS, AND SAINTS

Whenever the *Patrologiae Graeca* or *Patrologia Latina* are cited, they appear as *PG* or *PL*, followed by [volume number]:[page number], e.g., *PG* 2:848. The massive Migne edition is available freely online, as of this writing, at http://patristica.net/graeca or http://patristica.net/latina. Translations of these works can be found in various places, including the edition of the *Nicene and Post-Nicene Fathers*, revised and edited for New Advent by Kevin Knight, http://www.newadvent.org/fathers/index.html.

St. Alphonsus Ligouri. *The Glories of Mary*. New York: P. J. Kenedy & Sons, 1888.

———. *The History of Heresies and Their Refutation*. Translated by Rev. Dr. Mullock. Dublin: Duffy, 1857.

St. Bonaventure. *Opera Omnia*, t. 3, *In Tertium Librum Sententiarum*; t. 9, *Sermones*. Rome: Claras Aquas, 1887, 1901.

St. Bernard of Clairvaux. *Cantica Canticorum: Eighty-Six Sermons on the Song of Solomon*. Translated by Samuel J. Eales. London: E. Stock, 1895.

———. *Libelli de diligendo Deo et de Gratia et Libero Arbitrio*. Landishuti: Io. Nep. Attenkoferi, 1852.

———. *Opera Omnia*, 4th ed., t. 2, pt. 1. Paris: Gaume, 1839.

St. Bernardine of Siena. *Sancti Bernardini Senensis Ordinis Seraphici Minorum Sermones*, 5 vols. Venice: Andreae Poletti, 1745.

St. Francis de Sales. *Treatise on the Love of God*, 3rd ed., vol. 2. Translated by Henry Benedict Mackey. 7 vols. Library of St. Francis de Sales. London/New York: Burns & Oates, Benziger, 1910.

St. Francis De Sales. *Sermons of St. Francis de Sales On Our Lady*. Rockford, IL: TAN Books, 2015.

St. John Damascence. *An Exposition of the Orthodox Faith*. Translated by E.W. Watson and L. Pullan. From *Nicene and Post-Nicene Fathers*, 2nd Series, Vol. 9. Edited by Philip Schaff and Henry Wace. Buffalo, NY: Christian Literature Publishing Co., 1899.

St. Lawrence Giustiniani. *Divi Laurentii Justiniani Opera omnia*. Paris: Hermolaus Albritius, 1720.

St. Louis-Marie Grignion de Montfort. *God Alone: The Collected Writings of St. Louis Marie De Montfort*. Bay Shore, NY: Montfort Publications, 1995.

St. Louis-Marie Grignion de Montfort. *God Alone: The Collected Writings of St. Louis Marie De Montfort.* Bay Shore, NY: Montfort Publications, 1995.

St. Peter Canisius. *De Maria Virgine Incomparabili, Et Dei Genitrice Sacrosancta.* Ingolstadt: Sartorius, 1572.

St. Robert Bellarmine. *Opera Omnia,* t. 5, pt. 1, *Conciones.* Naples: Giuliano, 1861.

St. Thomas de Villanova. *Conciones.* 2 vols. Mediolani: Josephum Marellum, 1760.

SCHOLASTIC THEOLOGIANS ET AL.

Alexander of Hales. *Summa Universae Theologiae.* 4 vols. Cologne: John Gymnicus, 1622.

Bañez, O.P., Domingo. *Scholastica Commentaria in Secundam Secundae Partem Angelici Doctoris S. Thomae.* 3 vols. Douai: Borremans, 1615.

Bartolomé de Medina. *Expositio in Tertiam Divi Thomae Partem.* Salamanca: Renaut, 1596.

Billuart, Charles René, O.P. *Sermons,* t. 2. Paris: Jacques LeCoffre & C., 1846.

———. *Cursus Theologiae juxta Menti Divi Thomae.* 10 vols. Paris: Victor LeCoffre, 1904.

Bossuet, Jacques-Bénigne. *Devotion to the Blessed Virgin: Being the Substance of All the Sermons for Mary's Feasts throughout the Year.* Translated by F. M. Capes. New York: Longmans, Green, and Co., 1899.

———. *Oeuvres de messire Jacques-Bénigne Bossuet: Nouvelle édition revue sur les manuscrits originaux et les éditions les plus correctes, enrichie d'un grand nombre d'ouvrages de l'illustre auteur non encore imprimés.* t. 4 and t. 7. Paris: Boudet, 1872, 1873.

———. *Oeuvres oratoires de Bossuet*, t. 5. Edited by Joseph Lebarq, Charles Urbain, and Eugéne Levesque. Paris: Libraire Hachette, 1922.

Conrad of Saxony. *Speculum Beatae Mariae Virginis.* Florence: Claras Aquas, 1904.

Contenson, O.P., Vincent. *Theologia Mentis et Cordis*, t. 3. Paris: Vivès, 1875.

Cornelius à Lapide. *Comentaria in Scripturam Sacram.* 26 vols. Paris: Vivès, 1891.

Denis the Carthusian. *Doctoris ecstatici D. Dionysii Cartusiani Opera omnia*, t. 36. Tornaci: Carthusiae, 1908.

Faber, Frederick William. *The Foot of the Cross: Or, The Sorrows of Mary.* London: T. Richardson and Son, 1858.

Gerson, Jean. *Joannis Gersonii Doctoris Theologi et Cancellarii Parisiensis Opera Omnia*, t. 3. Hagae Comitum: Petrum de Hondt, 1728.

Gonet, O.P., Jean-Baptiste. *Clypeus Theologiae Thomisticae Contra Novos Ejus Impugnatores*, vol. 5. 6 vols. Paris: Vivès, 1876.

Hugh of Saint-Cher. *Opera Omnia in Universum Vetus et Novum Testamentum*, t. 3. 8 vols. Venice: Sefsas, 1600.

Hugon, O.P., Édouard. *Tractatus Dogmatici*, t. 2, *De Verbo Incarnato et de B. Virgine M. Deipara*, 5th ed. Paris: P. Lethielleux, 1927. (All told, there are three volumes of the *Tractatus Dogmatici*, which reached its 11th edition in 1935.)

Lépicier, Cardinal Alexis Henri Marie. *Tractatus de Beatissima Virgine Maria, Matre Dei.* 5th ed. Romae: Ex Officina Typographica, 1926.

Maldonado, Juan de. *Commentarii in Quatuor Evangelistas, t. 3: Qui complectitur evangelium Marci integrum, et Lucae capita priora XII.* Paris/Louvain: Moguntiae, 1842.

Miéchow, O.P., Justin. *Conférences sur les litanies de la Très Sainte Vierge,* 3rd ed., vol. 2. Paris: Walzer, 1870.

Monsabré, O.P., Jacques-Marie-Louis. *Exposition du dogme Catholique: préparation de l'Incarnation, Carême 1877.* Paris: Lethielleux, 1905.

Olier, Jean-Jacques. *Oeuvres completes de M. Olier: réunies pour la première fois en collection, classées selon l'ordre logique.* Paris: Migne, 1856.

Petitalot, John-Baptiste. *La Vierge Mère d'après la Théologie,* 2nd ed. 2 vols. Paris: Bray & Retuax, 1869.

Ripaldi, S.J., Juan Martínez. *De Ente Supernaturali,* t. 2. Paris: Victor Palmis, 1870.

Signoriello, Nunzio. *Lexicon Peripateticum Philosophico-Theologicum in Quo Distinctiones et Effata Praecipua Explicantur.* Naples: Bibliothecae Catholicae Scriptorum, 1872.

Stamm, Christiano. *Mariologia: Potiores de S. Deipara Quaestiones.* Junfermann: Paderbornae, 1881.

Suavé, Charles. *Jésus intime: Élevations dogmatiques,* 2nd ed. 3 vols. Paris: Vic & Amat, 1907.

Tanquerey, Adolphe. *Synopsis Theologiae Dogmaticae,* 12th ed. Rome/Turin/Paris: Desclée, 1921.

Terrien, S.J., Jean-Baptiste. *La Mère de Dieu et la mère des hommes, d'après les Pères et la théologie*, 3rd ed. 4 vols. Paris: P. Lethielleux, 1900.

Toledo, S.J., Francisco de. *Commentarii in Sacrosanctum Iesu Christi D.N. Evangelium secundum Lucam.* Cologne: Antonius Boëtzerius, 1611.

Richard de Saint-Laurent. *De Laudibus B. Mariae Virginis.* Antwerp: Martin Nutius, 1625.

Suárez, S.J., Francisco. *Opera Omnia*, t. 19. Paris: Vivès, 1860.

Véga, S.J., Cristóbal de. *Theologia Mariana.* 2 vols. Neapoli: Bibliotecae Catholicae, 1866.

OTHER RESOURCES

Denzinger, Heinrich. *Enchiridion Symbolorum: A Compendium of Creeds, Definitions, and Declarations of the Catholic Church.* Edited by Peter Hunermann, Robert Fastiggi, and Anne Englund Nash. 43rd ed. San Francisco: Ignatius Press, 2012.

CLUNY MEDIA

Designed by Fiona Cecile Clarke, the CLUNY MEDIA *logo depicts a monk at work in the scriptorium, with a cat sitting at his feet.*

The monk represents our mission to emulate the invaluable contributions of the monks of Cluny in preserving the libraries of the West, our strivings to know and love the truth.

The cat at the monk's feet is Pangur Bán, from the eponymous Irish poem of the 9th century. The anonymous poet compares his scholarly pursuit of truth with the cat's happy hunting of mice. The depiction of Pangur Bán is an homage to the work of the monks of Irish monasteries and a sign of the joy we at Cluny take in our trade.

"Messe ocus Pangur Bán,
cechtar nathar fria saindan:
bíth a menmasam fri seilgg,
mu memna céin im saincheirdd."